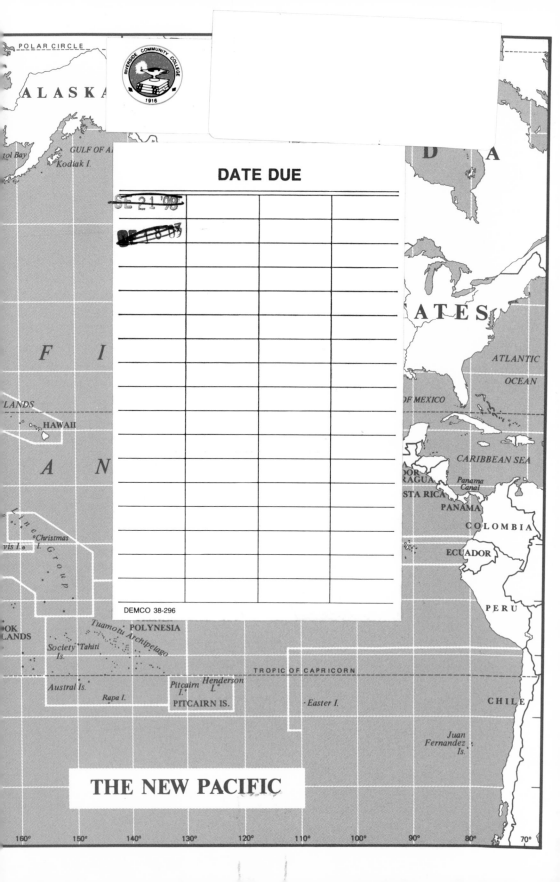

DATE DUE

THE NEW PACIFIC

THE AMERICAN PACIFIC

*Thus this mysterious, divine Pacific zones
the world's whole bulk about;
makes all coasts one bay to it;
seems the tide-beating heart of earth.*

HERMAN MELVILLE, Moby Dick

The

AMERICAN

PACIFIC

*From the
Old China Trade
to the Present*

Arthur Power Dudden

OXFORD UNIVERSITY PRESS

New York · Oxford · 1992

Oxford University Press

Oxford   New York   Toronto
Delhi   Bombay   Calcutta   Madras   Karachi
Petaling Jaya   Singapore   Hong Kong   Tokyo
Nairobi   Dar es Salaam   Cape Town
Melbourne   Auckland

and associated companies in
Berlin   Ibadan

Copyright © 1992 Arthur Power Dudden

Published by Oxford University Press, Inc.,
200 Madison Avenue, New York, New York 10016

Oxford is a registered trademark of Oxford University Press

Library of Congress Cataloging-in-Publication Data
Dudden, Arthur Power, 1921-
The American Pacific : from the old China trade
to the present / Arthur Power Dudden.
p. cm.   Includes bibliographical references and index.
ISBN 0–19–505821–6
1. Pacific Area—Relations—United States. 2. United States—
Relations—Pacific Area. 3. Pacific Area—History. I. Title.
DU30.D83 1992   973—dc20   91-17372

2 4 6 8 9 7 5 3 1

Printed in the United States of America
on acid-free paper

For Adrianne, Kathleen, Candace, and Alexis

Preface

In the pages to follow, the history of the United States of America in the Pacific Ocean and East Asia comes together in unitary form for the first time. The westernmost setting of the nation's history comprises a record of American activities among the cultures and peoples of the islands and mainlands in the Pacific basin since the opening of the China trade in 1784.

American history is a history of multiple origins, diverse beginnings, internal developments, and external relations. Flanked by the Atlantic and the Pacific, the earth's mightiest oceans, the United States faces outward in two directions, both east and west. The purpose of *The American Pacific* is to direct attention away from the almost exclusively European, Atlantic, and hemispheric context of traditional histories and toward, in addition, Asia and the Pacific. It serves to recall that the last three wars for the United States began as Asian wars, and that currently Asian immigrants significantly outnumber both European and Latin American.

Europe's colonizers superimposed their systems of belief, technology, and social structure on the indigenous Indian or native American cultures of the New World. The American Indians were themselves, of course, Asian in origin. Similarly, in the Hawaiian Islands and elsewhere, the native Polynesians were subdued by Westerners. In time, the European colonists, their descendents, and later immigrants spread westward across the continent toward the setting sun, where from Oregon and California they faced Asia beyond the vast Pacific Ocean.

From the harbors of New York City, Philadelphia, and Boston, American sailing ships began to reach China. Merchants, sailors, and missionaries discovered the Pacific's exotic peoples. They also encountered European adventurers motivated like themselves to promote trade and redemption. Would-be empire builders projected a manifest destiny without limits. In the nineteenth and twentieth centuries, Russian Alaska, the Kingdom of Hawaii, Japan, Korea, Samoa, and Spain's Philippine Islands acquired a strategic significance in American minds to outweigh commerce or conversion. The American Pacific, properly labeled, became the American Empire.

Two mentalities determined the nation's postures for East Asia and the Pacific. First, the obsession with China's apparent opportunities led to the acquisitions of Alaska, Hawaii, and the Philippines, a big navy, the Open Door policy, the construction of the Panama Canal, and a dangerous antagonism to Japan's own imperial dreams. Second, the militant, post-1945 fear and hatred of communism led directly to the Korean War and the Vietnam War.

The defeat of the United States in Indochina, augmented by the ending of the Cold War itself, has revived one of the older priorities, commercial exchange and a favorable balance of trade. Economic prowess has replaced military power in shaping international relations. Japan's modern economic miracle has, as a result, unsettled many Americans by introducing a new, competitive set of circumstances. China's inner turmoil and the mounting impact of Asian immigration combine to compound Americans' disquietude.

At the end of the Second World War, the United States bestrode the Pacific Ocean like a colossus. Today the outlook is unclear. The overriding question is whether or not the United States government and individual Americans can once again fashion their own destiny, with the fortitude, imagination, and daring of bygone generations, westward across the Pacific toward East Asia. If so, they will once again shape the future.

Acknowledgments

The American Pacific is the first book-length synthesis of its enormous subject. Ample room remains for other works and differing points of view.

The interest tendered by a number of distinguished scholars greatly fueled my undertaking. Foremost, I thank Professor Emeritus Caroline Robbins of Bryn Mawr College, my longtime colleague and friend, for critically reading the entire text and assisting me to write in a style more closely approximating good English writing than unaided I contrived to do. Sincere appreciation belongs as well to University of Pennsylvania Benjamin Franklin Professor Emeritus Thomas C. Cochran, my close friend, for his many helpful comments. Among other supporters were my Bryn Mawr College colleagues Professors Charles Brand, Jane Caplan, Michael Nylan, J. H. M. Salmon, Alain Silvera, William A. Crawford and William W. Vosburgh as well as Professors Ainslee Embree and Carol Gluck of Columbia University, and Betty Peh T'i Wei Liu, Ph.D., of Hong Kong.

The American Pacific is not a monograph rooted in primary sources such as personal manuscript collections or memoirs or even government documents. Most of its published sources are obtainable in good libraries and bookstores, though not in archives public or private.

From chapter to chapter, the resources available and the sources utilized vary widely in nature, quantity, and quality, with an unavoidable, though regrettable, unevenness the result. My principle has been to rely on the best books and articles, the most thoroughly informed persons, and personal on-the-spot investigations wherever possible. My obligation to librarians and historians is great. At Bryn Mawr College Library, I am most indebted to Charles A. Burke, Anne Denlinger, Florence Goff, Mary Leahy, M. Winslow Lundy, Andrew Patterson, Gertrude Reed, Judith Reguerio, and Penelope Schwind. I am grateful also to the library desk staffs at Haverford College, the University of Hawaii at Manoa, and the University of Pennsylvania, as well as Richard Boardman of the Map Collection, the Free Library of Philadelphia.

For the history of Alaska, I am deeply grateful to two superb historians: Robert N. DeArmond of Juneau and Professor Claus-M. Naske of the University of Alaska at Fairbanks. Also I am grateful to Suellen Liljeblad, senior curator of collections, City of Ketchikan; Janet B. Porter, museum director, Isabel Miller Museum, Sitka Historical Society; and Kathryn H. Shelton, historical librarian, Division of State Libraries, Juneau.

For the Hawaiian Islands and the Pacific region, I am indebted most of all to Professor Emeritus Donald D. Johnson of the University of Hawaii at Manoa, who generously shared with me a preliminary version of his forthcoming book, *The United States in the Pacific*. Similarly, I appreciate the opportunity to try out my ideas afforded me by Professors Pauline King and James McCutcheon at the University of Hawaii.

For the Philippine Islands, my gratitude for assistance belongs to David R. Whitesell, supervisor, Department of Rare Books and Collections (Dean Conant Worcester Collection), University of Michigan Library at Ann Arbor; Morton J. Netzorg, The Cellar Book Shop, Detroit; and, most profusely, to Stanley Karnow for copies of the galley sheets of *In Our Image* before his Pulitzer Prize winner was published. In Manila for my research, I was bountifully helped by Helen N. Mendoza, Ph.D., and Florencio M. Pineda, M.D.; at the University of the Philippines (Diliman, Quezon City) by Dean Leslie E. Bauzon, Professors Romeo V. Cruz, Zeus A. Salazar, and Bonifacio S. Salamanca; and at the American embassy by Librarian Arcadia C. Sabalones.

In Japan my tasks and insights were facilitated by many kind, helpful, and generous individuals. Among them were Ambassador of Japan (Ret.) Toshiro H. Shimanouchi, Dr. Caroline A. Mantano Yang, executive director of the Japan–U.S. Educational Commission, Mr. Hideo Kawabuchi of Osaka, and Professors Akira Mayama of Konan University at Kobe and Ittoku Monma of Osaka. A personal note of grateful appreciation and friendship goes to Mr. and Mrs. Katsuhiko Murai of Kyoto.

Other forms of support proved to be just as essential, if not even more so. For funding my travel and onsite research expenses, I once again thank President Mary P. McPherson, Provost Judith R. Shapiro, and the pertinent faculty research grant committee members of Bryn Mawr College; also the

Yoshida International Education Fund, Tokyo, and its late Executive Director Masuru Ogawa and Manager Takeo Kohnö. To my patient and hard-working typists, most especially Allyn McKay Bensing, Cara Sue Hendricks, and Deanne Bell, also Lorraine Kirschner, Bonnie B. Griffith, and Anna Canavan, go my heartfelt thanks. To my editors at Oxford University Press, Sheldon Meyer, Karen Wolny, Joellyn Ausanka, Leona Capeless, and India Cooper, my appreciation follows for their encouragement and skillful assistance. Adrianne Onderdonk Dudden, my wife, has again, as she invariably does, wrought a beautiful book design. I am once again admiringly grateful.

Finally, for the late Kay Sugahara of New York City and the world, a wishful hope that somewhere he could realize what unknown strengths he revealed in me.

Contents

List of Maps

Prologue

Imagine, if you will, two hardworking Americans who, in spite of the stupendous distances between them, are linked together through citizenship in common allegiance. One might be a lobsterman harvesting the Atlantic waters "down east" off Maine's coast in the Bay of Fundy virtually surrounded by Canada's maritime provinces. The other, an Aleut seal hunter, lives and works far to the westward in the North Pacific along the Bering Sea approaches to Russian Siberia. Their differences notwithstanding—remoteness from each other, distinctive ethnic origins, and disparate natures—the common denominator of United States nationality drives home for all of us the enormous size and diversity of the American republic.

The United States of America spans one-third of the Northern Hemisphere, crossing eight time zones from the northeasternmost promontory of the state of Maine, bordered by Canada and the Atlantic Ocean, then westward across North America to California, Oregon, and Washington, and continuing northwestward over the Pacific Ocean to the International Date Line, where just two watery miles separate Alaska's Little Diomede Island from the Soviet Union's Big Diomede Island. The fiftieth state of Hawaii lies some twenty-four hundred miles at sea southwest from Los Angeles, its volcanic chain of island peaks and atolls ranging into United States Navy jurisdiction another sixteen hundred miles northwestward across the world's biggest ocean toward Japan. The two noncontiguous states are divided from each other at their extremities by more than three thousand miles of land and water from Point Barrow, Alaska, at 71°17' N. to Ka Lae almost directly south on Hawaii's Big Island at 18°55' N. However, the extremes of United States sovereignty lie in the Virgin Islands in the Caribbean Sea and on Guam in the western Pacific. Both points, believe it or not, are named "Udall" for the Arizona brothers, Morris ("Mo"), former congressman, and Stewart, former congressman and ex–secretary of interior. From north to south, the continental forty-eight states range down some fifteen hundred miles of wonderfully assorted landscape from Canada to the Gulf of Mexico and Mexico itself. Approximately one-quarter of a billion American men, women, and children populate this vast domain.

The United States faces left and right, like the Roman god Janus, outward across *both* the Atlantic and Pacific oceans, confronting *both* East and West from opposite directions and asserting its influence simultaneously, though unevenly, over the Occident *and* the Orient. For over two centuries, the nation's Pacific and East Asian connections have comprised a geopolitical actuality, which will certainly continue into the foreseeable future. The American Pacific demands close attention to balance our grasp on national reality.

Histories, more often than not, are constructed along linear and chronological sequences from east to west, from early colonial times along the Atlantic seaboard through the winning of independence to transcontinental hegemony and global power at the dawn of the space age. The nation's western history suffers accordingly. The United States of America spread itself across the North American mainland rapidly to the Pacific Ocean's shores and territories in Alaska, Hawaii, Samoa, and the Philippines, establishing an imperial sway before the end of the nineteenth century over extensive areas of the Pacific Ocean. Parts of Japan, Korea, China, and Southeast Asia succumbed in due course, at least temporarily, to American influence and control. Unaware of their nation's role in those faraway regions, Americans hesitate even to admit the existence of an American empire. They were vengefully exhorted to remember Japan's attack on Pearl Harbor, but never expected to understand it.

Racing westward, the United States gained its Pacific shores before 1850. In 1783, the Mississippi River's midstream had marked the western boundary delineated by the treaty of peace following the long struggle for American independence. The Louisiana Purchase of 1803 and the annexation of Texas in 1845 flung the Stars and Stripes across the Great Plains to the Rocky Mountains. The Oregon Treaty of 1846 signaled the transcontinental triumph of manifest destiny to end years of bitter controversy (and joint occupation with Britain since 1818) by designating the forty-ninth parallel of north latitude as the boundary to Puget Sound between Britain's North

American possessions and the United States. The line proceeded to the middle of the channel separating the mainland from Vancouver Island and thence on a southerly heading through the middle of that channel and Juan de Fuca's Strait to the Pacific Ocean.

The American Pacific empire commenced at the moment of the Oregon Treaty's ratification. By 1848, the outcome of the Mexican War had forced Mexico to surrender her extensive lands and claims from New Mexico, Texas, and Alta California to Utah, Idaho, and Oregon. California entered the Union in 1850 as the thirty-first state. Oregon was admitted as the thirty-third state in 1859. Before the Civil War, the American republic had engrossed the richest slice of the North American continent. No longer would Europe, with its African and Atlantic satrapies, define American lives and outlooks. The Pacific Ocean and the ancient civilizations of Asia were beckoning enticingly. America's regular passage to the Orient was assured. Given the energy behind manifest destiny, an American Pacific empire was becoming, if not a certainty, a probability.

Long before, the American colonists had anticipated these developments. England's East India Company traffic with Asia in the seventeenth and eighteenth centuries introduced Oriental wares to the colonists as well as to the English people at home, though the company increasingly directed commerce to India because of the Dutch monopoly of the spice trade. Shipbuilding, fishing, and seafaring flourished after 1650. Holland's loss of the New Netherlands to England in 1664 included New York's superb harbor, Long Island Sound, and the Hudson and Delaware river routes into the interior. For the first time, England's mainland colonies in North America were linked together from Maine and Massachusetts Bay southward to the Carolinas. With the royal colony of New York and the New Jersey and Pennsylvania proprietorships, England consolidated most of the Atlantic seaboard into an imperial continuum. American adventuring onto the Atlantic was a natural outcome.

With the accession of William III and Mary II in 1689, hostilities broke out between England and France over the balance of power in Europe and their burgeoning empires in America and Asia. Their wars repeatedly involved the colonial populations of both nations and their Indian allies. In King William's War, as the colonists dubbed the first conflict, Yankee seamen sailed aboard English privateers to seek French ships and cargoes and sometimes buccaneered beyond their license into the Pacific Ocean by way of Panama and the Isthmus of Darien. Oriental gold, pearls, gemstones, and wonderously woven fabrics began to show up in America's seaports from Africa's Cape of Good Hope or the eastern Mediterranean.

In 1699, John Higginson of Salem wrote about East Asia's prospects to his brother Nathaniel, an East India Company official in Madras:

> What you propose of living in Boston and managing a wholesale trade of East India goods, I approve of, as best for you. . . . All sorts of calicoes, aligers, remwalls, muslin, silks for clothing and linings, all sorts of drugs prosper for the apothecaries, and all sorts of spice, are vendible with us. . . . Some of the China ware, toys and lacquerware will sell well, but no great quantity. . . . For musk, bezoar, pearl, and diamond, I believe some of them may sell well, but I understand not their value.

Tea, significantly, was not included in Higginson's listing. Tea first reached the American colonies about 1700, while Chinese porcelain bowls and lacquerware appeared shortly thereafter. By the middle of the eighteenth century, goods from the Far East, with their possibilities for profit, were pouring into the thirteen colonies. But the struggle for independence forestalled Asian adventures by American enterprisers until 1783.

THE AMERICAN PACIFIC

When we look at the possessions in the east of our great maritime rival England and of the constant and rapid increase of their fortified ports, we should be admonished of the necessity of prompt measures on our part. . . . Fortunately the Japanese and many other islands in the Pacific are still left untouched by this gigantic power; and as some of them lay in a route of commerce which is destined to become of great importance to the United States, no time should be lost in adopting active measures to secure a sufficient number of ports of refuge.

Matthew Calbraith Perry[1]

1

UNFURLING THE FLAG

By 1800, United States merchantmen were converging on China from both sides of the Pacific, and Yankee whalers were rounding Cape Horn to hunt their prey along the "onshore" fishery up South America's western coast. The first ship to show the Stars and Stripes in the Far East was the *Empress of China*, financed largely by Robert Morris of Philadelphia. She sailed from New York on February 22, 1784, by way of the Cape of Good Hope, the Indian Ocean, and Sunda Strait between Sumatra and Java to reach the Portuguese trading factory at Macao on August 23, departed from Whampoa, the anchorage for Canton (now Guangzhou), on December 28, and returned home on May 11, 1785. A regular commerce ensued along this route to China, Southeast Asia, and the ports of the Indian Ocean. Before long Indian textiles and Sumatran pepper would rival the goods exchanged with China.[2]

Meanwhile, from 1782 to his death in 1788, John Ledyard of Connecticut, who had sailed with James Cook on the peerless navigator's third and final voyage of exploration in the Pacific Ocean, endeavored to persuade American merchants to obtain sea otter and beaver pelts from the Indians of the Northwest Coast for trading with China. Ledyard and the other members of Captain Cook's company were astounded by the enormous profits realized from selling fifteen hundred skins. They grew further convinced of the lucrative potential of fur trading after encountering Russian hunters on the island of Unalaska. To merchants in New York, Philadelphia, and New

England, Ledyard proposed establishing trading posts on the northwestern coast to which cheap metal products and cloths could be sent for bartering with the Indians. Although no substantive evidence exists, Jared Sparks, Ledyard's first biographer, claims that Thomas Jefferson endorsed Ledyard's romantic ideas as supporting his ambitious design beyond the Louisiana Territory for the Oregon country. Ledyard's zealous effort to find patrons was, however, fruitless. Only after the publication of Captain Cook's journals confirmed his pleadings were two ships, the *Columbia* and the *Lady Washington*, dispatched from Boston around Cape Horn in 1787 to pursue the route urged earlier by Ledyard.[3] Not until midsummer of 1789, having bestowed her name and American claims on the mighty Columbia River, did *Columbia*, now commanded by Captain Robert Gray, make her way after tiresome delays to Canton with a cargo of furs, only to discover the Chinese markets glutted by British competitors. *Columbia* thereupon sailed homeward around the Cape of Good Hope to complete the first American circumnavigation of the globe. By 1790, twenty-eight United States vessels had cleared from Canton, and by 1800 more than one hundred. American trade at Canton by this time ranked second among Western nations only to that of the British.[4]

The first American whaling interests in the Pacific Ocean brought daring mariners from New England, New York, Philadelphia, and Baltimore into strange and exotic contacts with Hispanics and Indians from Rio de la Plata and Tierra del Fuego around Cape Horn to Chile, Bolivia, and Peru, as well as with Polynesians and Melanesians on the South Pacific islands, though seldom with Chinese directly, while a few ships followed the East Indiamen's track around South Africa through the Indian Ocean.[5] These private ventures proclaimed bold new initiatives. Their importance must not be exaggerated, however; in 1800, they added up to no more than one-tenth of the nation's maritime enterprises. Enough Americans grasped the Orient's opportunities, even so. "There is no better advice to be given to the merchants of the United States," John Adams wrote to John Jay in 1785, "than to push their commerce to the East Indies as fast and as far as it will go."[6]

The first Americans to involve themselves in the trade at Canton were entering into an ancient traffic between China and the world of the barbarians outside the Celestial Empire. Neighboring or distant countries were treated as inferiors or tributary states. No concept of foreign relations between equal sovereignties existed. Confucian ethics, which deprecated commerce, reinforced the presumption of the Chinese that they need not travel abroad to acquire material goods, for these would flow inward to them as the necessary particulars of tribute. The old China trade, in short, was singularly one-sided. No bulk shipment of Western goods could be found to incorporate equivalent value for the precious fabrics and objects prized in the West. Since Roman times and the opening of overland caravan routes between West and East, specie in the form of silver and gold coins had to make up the balances due. In 1557, the seaborne Portuguese managed to establish a trading post at Macao on the estuary of the Pearl River sixty-five miles below Canton, where all Westerners until the end of the seventeenth century, when the English broke the Portuguese monopoly, had to conduct the exchanges conceded them by the Chinese. The solitary exception, barring the caravan routes across central Asia, was Russia's overland trade with China at their agreed-upon frontier entry point.

Into this system, Americans intruded themselves after 1784. The fact that they spoke the same English language as British traders helped to win this foothold; confused, the Chinese admitted them as new entrepreneurs. That they arrived as private individuals, without any governmental representation to complicate their presence, assured the Chinese further that the newly independent Americans would not disrupt prevailing patterns.

Canton continued to serve as the only official port of entry for the maritime trade with China until 1842. Foreigners maintained their trading factories crowded together on the riverbank, while residences and opportunities for travel were closely circumscribed. The eventual opening of illicit trade, principally in opium, only intensified official Chinese determination to oppose any relaxation of restrictions. Fees and bribes to mandarin officials and innumerable intermediaries lubricated the trading process. But Americans and Europeans alike were only permitted to negotiate actual transactions through a designated "hong merchant," a member of the authorized Cantonese merchants guild or co-hong. The co-hong was a monopoly empowered to enforce imperial trading regulations and collect fees and duties. Its members acted privately as individual commission agents to undertake the trade itself. Complaints by Americans against the co-hong ordinarily were directed toward the high commissions charged by hong merchants for their services or the unequal constraints imposed on outsiders' relationships with the system. No United States government protests arrived, however. American traders in China suffered at times, but generally they profited. Toward China itself, American policy consisted of the sum of the policies of individual Americans trading there.

Unfortunately a vessel's cargo of American grain, cheese, rum, ironware, and assorted manufactures could not be exchanged for even a half cargo of Chinese teas, cottons, silks, lacquerware, and porcelains. Boxes and kegs of coins, Spanish dollars mostly, the surplus profits of trade with the West Indies and Europe, had to be shipped out to supplement any commodities that might find a market in Canton. In 1835, Timothy Pitkins calculated that in excess of $62 million in specie had been transferred to Canton from the United States between 1805 and 1825. After 1815, merchants began to avoid this costly outlay of hard cash by following various "chain trade" routes, selling and buying goods along the way to enhance the Canton value of their cargo. Eventually the abundance of inexpensive machine-made textiles and porcelains in the West and the spectacular rise in the opium trade lowered the specie drain toward China and left tea as the only Chinese commodity in great demand.[7]

By 1830, the opium traffic was generating spectacular rewards and unanticipated results, before long including the Opium Wars and the end of the old China trade. To import opium into China was illegal save under limited license for medicinal purposes. Opium incorporated a high value in condensed bulk and sold readily upon arrival at steadily rising prices and demand. The British attempted to control the export of Indian opium, and they succeeded so well that opium overtook raw cotton as their leading export to China, being one-third to one-half of all such exports. American merchants, notably from Philadelphia and Boston, hauled Turkish opium from Smyrna to Canton, though many others, like Nathan Dunn, steadfastly refused on moral grounds to engage in this trade. Although reliable statistics do not exist, the American opium trade was never economically significant. The traffic from Turkey to China was smaller than that from India; the quality and value of the product to the Chinese were lower, and the voyage was much longer. Yet the opium trade was unquestionably lucrative for certain Americans. For example, Philadelphia's Stephen Girard, already a large-scale China trader, commenced in 1805 to convey Turkish opium to Canton. "I am very much in favor of investing heavily in opium," Girard wrote. "While the War [Napoleonic conflicts] lasts, opium will support a good price in China." Girard halted his opium carrying after 1821 in favor of banking and financial ventures. He left at his death the largest fortune accumulated by anyone in the Republic until that time— some significant portion, at least, arising from opium's rewards.[8]

Problems from the opium traffic soon engulfed the China trade. Throughout the 1830s, China's resistance to illegal opium trading stiffened markedly, and official transactions with the "insufferable" foreigners became more and more arbitrary. Petitions to redress grievances submitted by Americans and Europeans alike through the co-hong, or in person humiliatingly through a public display of obsequious deference at Canton's city gate, the *kow-tow*, proved almost invariably unavailing. Endeavors by Westerners, especially Britons, failed to induce the Chinese to equalize the established patterns of trade and accept the forms and principles of international relations.

Encouraged by American and other Christian missionaries, the Chinese were highly aroused against the social evils opium was spreading, and alarmed also over the outlays of specie to pay for it. China's governing officials, outraged by the sharp increase in opium imports, posted an imperial commissioner to Canton in March 1839 to enforce the long-standing prohibitions and penalties against the narcotic drug. Commissioner Lin Tse-hsu immediately confiscated all of the foreign merchants' opium and demanded they sign a bond that their ships would never again import opium, under penalty of death. Severe punishment also threatened the Chinese hong agents. Trading of all kinds halted briefly in the uproar that ensued. American merchants, with individual exceptions, acceded to China's abrupt suppression of the opium business more readily than the British, probably because their share of its imports amounted to less than 10 percent, while British embargo pressures against the Chinese were frustrated by increased American trading activity. The first Opium War (1839–1842) broke out at this point, when the British attacked several coastal cities and quickly defeated the hapless Chinese, whose forces were unable to withstand Great Britain's modern navy and weapons.[9]

The resulting Treaty of Nanking (1842) between China and Great Britain opened the ports of Canton, Amoy, Foochow, Ningpo, and Shanghai to British trade and residence and ceded Hong Kong to the victor. News of the treaty's provisions, hurriedly sent home by Commodore Lawrence Kearney, USN, commanding the East India squadron, touched off an intense debate in the United States over the government's China policy, or rather its lack of one. Kearney also opened representations to the imperial commissioner at Canton, though lacking authorization he stopped short of attempting any negotiated agreement. With the British having established official relations, the traditional ways of trading were rendered obsolete. Americans had to reassert their basis of equality commercially with the British and other countries in China. Accordingly, Congressman Caleb Cushing of Massachusetts arrived in Macao on February 24, 1844, sent there by President John Tyler as the first United States commissioner. On July 3, at Wangshia close by, assisted by American missionaries Dr. Peter Parker, Elijah C. Bridgman, and Samuel Wells Williams, Cushing signed a treaty of amity and commerce to open diplomatic relations with China.

The treaty's provisions laid out official policy:

1. Americans sought freedom to trade with the Chinese and agreed to abide with China's regulation of that trade.

2. If other countries won specified commercial and political privileges from China, Americans expected equal treatment for themselves.

3. The United States sought no territorial gains, nor, though a powerful nation, did it intend to wrest any advantages from China by force.

Implied though not stated, nor even always understood, the assumption underlying Caleb Cushing's important treaty was that the Celestial Empire of China as a sovereign state should and eventually would admit the ships and citizens of foreign powers. Special provisions of the Treaty of Wangshia permitted Americans to employ Chinese as teachers and purchase books recommended by Cushing's missionary advisors and interpreters.[10]

In 1856, the second Opium War led to the imposition on China by Great Britain and France of the Treaties of Tientsin (1858), to which the United States of America and Russia were also parties. China consented to unlock eleven more seaports, admit foreign legations to Peking, the Manchu Dynasty's imperial capital, permit foreign missionary activity, and legalize the importation of opium. In renewed hostilities in 1859, the third Opium War, British and French forces occupied Peking, burned the emperor's summer palace, and required the Chinese to grant additional concessions. Americans shared almost automatically in these newly won advantages, including the extraterritorial privileges of immunity from local law enforcement. The United States thereby became a party to the system of "unequal treaties," which Chinese nationalists of future days would resent so bitterly. Yet for years to come Americans assumed self-righteously that the Chinese favored them over Europeans because the United States government had not won their privileges by using armed force.[11]

American missionaries were the most likely source for this naivete. From 1829, when Elijah C. Bridgman and David Abeel, the first American missionaries to China, had arrived at Canton, urged to come out there by Dr. Robert Morrison, England's earliest Protestant evangelical in the Far East, and the Reverend William Milne, his assistant and the founder of a Chinese language-training school for missionaries, American proselytyzing developed inevitably apart from commerce and at odds with it, in fact, over the opium trade. The missionaries reported home regularly and at considerable length about Christian endeavors among the Chinese and the Western trading community to earn the support essential for maintaining themselves. To overcome the formidable obstacles of the Chinese language and script, American and English missionaries invented ingenious systems, based on local speech and dialects, for translating the Holy Bible with its gospel of individual salvation.

The missionaries shaped opinion at home positively during the Opium Wars by combining their observations and convictions with compassionate appeals. However, even the missionaries became imbued with the "old China hand" prejudices of British and American traders. Dr. Peter Parker and Samuel Wells Williams, for example, would share the merchants' frustrations at the stubborn Chinese unwillingness to understand and adopt Western ways of doing things. Incomprehension and condescension obstinately blended into American stereotypes of China and the Chinese people, impeding any attempt to formulate policies of mutual respect.[12]

Meanwhile the market at Canton, with its tantalizing hints of lucrative opportunities, was tempting Americans in growing numbers into Pacific Ocean enterprises. Trade in furs was held to be the legitimate key to the Chinese market. On the other hand, whaling, though carrying into the Pacific basin each year more seagoing Americans than any other industry, was important mainly for providing oil, tallow, and whalebone for home processing and consumption. The established route to China favored by shippers of domestic goods lay southeastward across the Atlantic Ocean around the Cape of Good Hope at Africa's southernmost point into the Indian Ocean, then far beyond India and the East Indies into the Pacific Ocean from the west and northward to Canton. The fur trade route involved at all times even greater risks and adventure-filled undertakings. Fur traders had to sail either in the opposing direction around South America's tempestuous tip to obtain their cargoes from the wild unclaimed islands of the subantarctic, or along North America's northwest coast from California and Oregon to Nootka Sound on the western shore of Vancouver Island or to Russia's subarctic Alaskan and Aleutian islands. From Boston, New York, Philadelphia, and lesser ports, ships seeking furs for the mandarins headed outward on a southeasterly plotting to the Cape Verde Islands off western Africa for water and provisions, then southwestward toward southern Brazil, continuing to the south past the Rio de la Plata and through the Strait of Magellan or, more probably, rounding dangerous Cape Horn itself farther south via Drake's Passage around South America to enter the Pacific Ocean from the east. Whichever the way, nineteenth-century voyages to China from the United States were incredibly long and hazardous.

The quest mounted for new items to sell to the Chinese. European, African, and South and Southeast Asian commodities reached Canton in American ship bottoms to augment the young republic's developing yet still limited economy. Sandalwood, *bêche de mer* (the prized sea slug delicacy, *Holothuria*), tortoise shell, pearls, and pearl shell came from the Polynesian and Melanesian archipelagoes, Australia, Fiji, and New Zealand; edible birds' nests arrived from Indonesia and the western Carolines. Between 1810 and 1830, the Hawaiian sandalwood trade led to virtually uncontrolled cutting of the islands' biggest and most accessible trees, from whose fragrant wood Chinese craftsmen contrived ornamental boxes, chests, and furniture; and joss sticks were made to burn as incense in Buddhist ceremonies. Trade with the Pacific islands included the supplying of ships with fresh water, firewood, vegetables, fruits, coconuts, and assorted provisions such as lumber and hemp for repairing vessels and rigging. By midcentury, plantations for growing coconuts were developed throughout the South

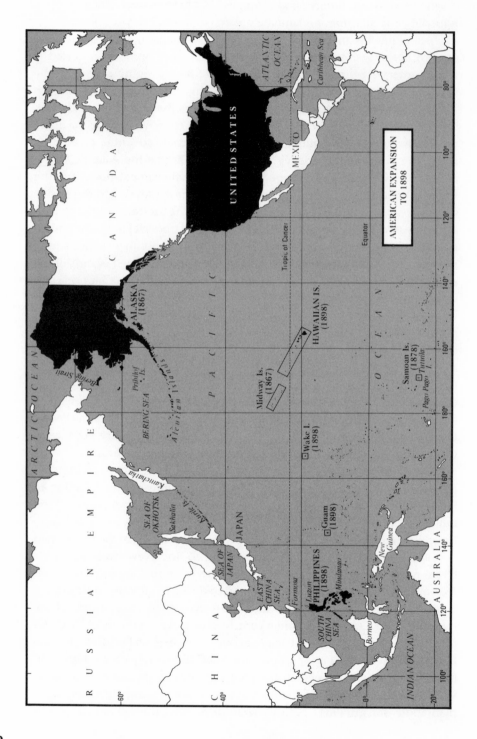

AMERICAN EXPANSION
TO 1898

UNITED STATES

CANADA

MEXICO

ATLANTIC OCEAN

Caribbean Sea

ALASKA
(1867)

Bering Strait

Pribilof Is.

Aleutian Islands

BERING SEA

ARCTIC OCEAN

RUSSIAN EMPIRE

Kamchatka

SEA OF
OKHOTSK

Sakhalin

Kurile Islands

JAPAN

SEA OF
JAPAN

EAST
CHINA
SEA

Formosa

CHINA

SOUTH
CHINA
SEA

Luzon

PHILIPPINES
(1898)

Mindanao

Borneo

New
Guinea

AUSTRALIA

INDIAN OCEAN

Guam
(1898)

Wake I.
(1898)

Midway Is.
(1867)

HAWAIIAN IS.
(1898)

Samoan Is.
(1878)
Tutuila
Pago Pago

PACIFIC OCEAN

Tropic of Cancer

Equator

80°

100°

120°

140°

160°

180°

160°

140°

120°

100°

60°

40°

20°

0°

Pacific. The British, French, and German governments took over one group of islands after another, brusquely excluding foreigners from land tenure in the latter nineteenth century's reawakening of an old-fashioned style of imperialism. Americans, on the whole, would play only limited roles in the copra or dried coconut meat business. Americans focused instead on the Hawaiian Islands in mercantile, whaling, and missionary endeavors at Honolulu on Oahu, Lahaina on Maui, and Kailua on Hawaii, the big island. The Hawaiian Islands border the northern fringe of the tropics, where coconut palms grow neither rapidly nor abundantly enough to sustain any economy so singularly based. Mexican-style cattle ranches for raising beef animals, and sugar, banana, and pineapple plantations, began to flourish there instead, selling their produce directly to California's gold rush population.

By the middle of the nineteenth century, the China market aside, Americans and Europeans cultivated a far-reaching trading economy spanning the Pacific Ocean to link its myriad islands with the bordering continents. American ships making for the sea otter coasts of the Northwest would tack up the western coasts of South and Central America followed by whalers and sealers. Seaport markets sprang up along the way from Valparaiso to Acapulco. Enterprising merchants eagerly sold provisions and exchanged copper or silver for American and European manufactured wares made more accessible by the amicable diplomatic relations between the United States and Latin America's newly independent nations than under Spain's restrictive colonial system. Americans could be found almost everywhere, but their share in the commerce was only a fraction of the total even of their own country's foreign trade, except in Hawaii, where American merchants, planters, and missionaries increasingly surpassed their British and French competitors. Hiram Bingham and the other American missionaries believed that if they themselves failed to help Hawaii's monarchs and chiefs resolve their mundane problems as well as their spiritual dilemmas, other nationals, presumably with less exalted motives, might intrude themselves into running this Pacific paradise.[13]

Whalers and sealers harried their prey from American, Hawaiian, and Asian ports and from the Arctic to Antarctica. A few ships combined seal hunting with whaling at first, but specialization arose because of the natural differences between their preys' habitats and the processing and marketing requirements for sealskins and whale blubber.

The fur seal quickly became a victim of the China trade. Fur seals were killed as early as 1783 on the Malvinas, or Falkland Islands, in the South Atlantic by a Yankee hunter from Stonington, Connecticut. The chase spread around Cape Horn into the high southern latitudes of the Pacific to the seal rookeries of the Juan Fernandez Islands off the coast of Chile and the islands below New Zealand and Australia. Sailors were put ashore on these bleak, rocky isles for many weeks and months at a stretch to club down the defenseless mammals while their ships sailed away to hunt elsewhere. Once an island's herd was extinguished or frightened away, interest in that spot ceased. Americans outdid themselves ruthlessly tracking down fur seals. In and around New Zealand and Australia, they caused such violent furors as to inspire Britons to claim all of Australasia. From one to three million seals were reportedly taken by 1805 from Mas Afuera in the Juan Fernandez Islands alone, exhausting nature's profligacy there. The frenzied hunt next raced away to more northerly regions of the Pacific along California's coasts and its offshore islands to Vancouver Island's Nootka Sound, where the search for sealskins would be combined with hunting the more highly prized sea otters and land animals of many kinds.

Still farther northward, the Russians had spread out a chain of fur trading outposts from Siberia across the Bering Sea along the Aleutian Islands down Alaska's shores beyond the apex of American and British activity as far as the mouth of the Columbia River. Certain enterprising Americans served as intermediaries in the subarctic, carrying Russian or British furs to Canton, thereby circumventing either the Chinese restrictions against Russian seaborne imports or the East India Company's monopoly. Similarly American merchantmen conveyed precious supplies to the outposts of the Russian-American Company, posing serious problems for the company's agents by trading firearms and rum for sealskins directly with the Aleut Indians. In 1810, with diplomatic ties newly in place, Russia's minister to Washington, Andre Dashkov, pressed the United States to halt the selling of guns by its citizens to the natives of Russian Alaska, while in St. Petersburg Count Nicholas Rumiantzov, the czar's foreign minister, proposed to John Quincy Adams, the newly arrived United States minister, to allow American ships to trade supplies for furs to carry to Canton (which they were already doing) in return for a pledge to trade only through the Russian company's agents. Hesitating to recognize, even implicitly, Russian sovereignty over little-known expanses of the northwest coast, Adams inquired as to the boundaries of "Russian America," and Rumiantzov at once backed down. Alarmed over Napoleon's latest threat to the peace of Europe, he dismissed the Alaskan fur trade as relatively unimportant, preferring to seek amicable relations with the United States.

In 1821, Congress bestirred itself. The House of Representatives formed a special committee under John Floyd of Virginia to uphold American fur trading interests and territorial claims in the northwest. Fur trader John Jacob Astor and explorer William Clark brought pressure to bear behind the scenes, and Missouri's Senator Thomas Hart Benton outlined an imperial vision for the Pacific basin and the Orient beyond:

Upon the people of Eastern Asia the establishment of a civilized power on the opposite coast of America could not fail to produce great and wonderful benefits. Science, liberal principles in government, and the true religion might cast their lights across the intervening sea. The valley of the Columbia might become the granary of China and Japan, and an outlet to their imprisoned and exuberant population. The inhabitants of the oldest and the newest, the most despotic and the freest governments, would become the neighbors and the friends of each other. To my mind the proposition is clear, that Eastern Asia and the Americas, as they become neighbors should become friends; and I for one had as lief see American ministers going to the emperors of China and Japan, to the King of Persia, and even to the Grand Turk, as to see them dancing attendance upon those European legitimates who hold everything American in contempt and detestation.

Ironically, at the very moment Benton was declaiming such far-flung ambitions, the maritime fur trade had begun to decline. Expansion was the nation's destiny, however. The primary basis for subsequent claims by the United States to territories on the Antarctic continent by right of discoveries was the fur seal trade.[14]

Even so, whaling was a more important industry than hunting and trading furs. The first United States vessel known to have killed whales in the Pacific Ocean was the *Beaver*, captained by Paul Worth out of Nantucket on a hunt from 1791 to 1793. Forty-six American whaling expeditions to the Pacific before 1800 are listed in Alexander Starbuck's history of the American whale fishery (1878). Early whalers concentrated mainly on the "onshore" fishery of the southeastern Pacific just off the western coast of South America, where not all dangers came from the sea. Americans continued to be distrusted as Englishmen by Spanish officials, who, though they ought to have known better, continued to seize American citizens and their property well into the nineteenth century. Spanish harassments notwithstanding, United States whalers, "Yankees" for the great part, found their quarries in the South Pacific, until 1820, mainly off Chile and Peru. The fresh water with the flesh and eggs of the giant tortoises of the Galapagos Islands afforded replenishment for many whalers after long months at sea. Far westward, where American whalers were also venturing, in the "middle ground" of the Tasman Sea between Australia and New Zealand, the War of 1812 temporarily suspended their activities. British controls imposed in the 1840s again curtailed American activity in the waters around Australia and New Zealand.

Other ships searched the waters surrounding the atolls and volcanic peaks of Polynesia. Honolulu hailed its first American whale ships in 1820. Soon the whale hunters were heading out from the Hawaiian Islands across the North Central Pacific westward to the fisheries newly discovered off Japan's eastern coast. Other fisheries were opened by 1835 in the North Pacific near Alaska and the Aleutian Islands, in the Sea of Ohkotsk in 1847, and in the Bering Sea and Arctic Ocean before 1850. The northern Pacific now afforded the major hunting ground for American whalers, with the Hawaiian anchorages its off-season epicenter. Whaling grounds as far away as the Philippines and the Indian Ocean were being fished regularly by ships and crews far distant from their home ports of New Bedford and Nantucket. Annually an average 419 whale ships were arriving at Honolulu. Six-sevenths of New Bedford's fleet based its remote operations there.

Between 1835 and 1855, the American whaling industry peaked. No fewer than 722 of the world's 900 whalers were American flagged vessels, while a few of the others were owned or operated by expatriated Nantucketers. The great majority fished the Pacific Ocean. Sperm oil from the gargantuan sperm whales was used for illuminating lamps, delicate lubrication, and making candles, while "whale oil," the cruder product extracted from the right whale and others, went for cheaper illuminating and lubricating. Whalebone from baleen whales, the toothless suborder of filter feeders to which the family of right whales belongs, created its own industry for the manufacturing of everyday utilitarian objects requiring both strength and flexibility, such as umbrella frames, riding whips, and ladies' corset stays, while ambergris from the sperm whale's intestines was sought after eagerly as a fixative for the most expensive perfumes.

The whalers' voyages soon lengthened from three on average to four or even five years. Their operating costs soared as the hunters killed the giant mammals in ever-growing numbers or drove the creatures farther and farther northward. The importance of Pacific havens for supplies and repairs rose correspondingly. Yet the isolationist kingdoms of Japan and Korea refused to allow Westerners to moor in their harbors, denying even rescue and succor to the tempest-tossed and shipwrecked, while China's facilities failed to meet the whalers' ordinary needs even after her treaty ports were opened.

The whaling industry's doom was final and abrupt, almost without warning. The Civil War interrupted or diverted American ocean shipping after 1861. Clipper ships and whalers alike were scuttled deliberately by the dozens to block Confederate ports, while a flotilla of rebel sea raiders harassed the remainder. Petroleum products for lighting and lubricating replaced whale oil; steel substituted for whalebone. The whaling industry's spokesmen were reduced within a few years to urging plaintively that the coast guard's lighthouses be required to use only whale oil illuminants and lubricants to keep American whaling alive. Grass grew in the streets and dockyards of New Bedford and Nantucket.[15]

Inevitably, when Americans first entered the Pacific Ocean, demands arose for naval protection. Shipowners and their captains backed suggestions for official exploring expeditions to lower the hazards of navigating unknown or inadequately charted waters. The United States Navy responded with limited and sporadic patrols as early as 1820, yet not for a long time on the scale being mounted by the British.

Captain David Porter, USN, without specific orders during the War of 1812, boldly sailed his frigate *Essex* into the southeastern Pacific, capturing and destroying a dozen and more British whalers, provisioning his vessel from their stores, and even, in the midst of his depredations, laying claim for the United States to the island of Nuka Hiva in the Marquesas. Porter was way ahead of his countrymen back home in such an aggressive policy, urging them as early as 1815 to send a naval expedition to Japan to force that cloistered nation's ports open to the world's commerce. Neither the administration of President Madison nor its successors for a generation shared Porter's enthusiasm for Pacific Ocean adventuring, so his schemes and territorial claims were largely ignored. In the 1820s, United States Navy patrols from the newly formed Pacific Squadron more or less regularly extended westward beyond New Zealand and Australia to Southeast Asia. This growing United States presence was capped by the establishment of the East India (later Asiatic) naval station in 1835 and guaranteed for the foreseeable future by the acquisitions of Oregon and California along the Pacific rim. The navy was undertaking the duties of a constabulary. The Stars and Stripes its ships flew expressed an emerging sense of national mission that symbolized or presaged imperialism itself in protecting traders, whalers, and adventurers wherever they chose to go.[16]

Indeed foreign policymaking was being imposed upon the United States, as it was upon Great Britain and France, by the growing numbers of its citizens active in the central and southern Pacific together with the increasing value of their properties there. The comparative abundance or lack of trade, then, created the policies to be formulated and enforced. Officially United States policy toward the Pacific islands to the middle of the nineteenth century was solely that of proclaiming (and occasionally maintaining) liberty and equality of opportunity for its citizens in trading goods, hunting mammals, and saving souls. The fur sealers' discoveries of the islands and coasts of Antarctica far to the south precipitated intense rivalries. Captain Nathaniel B. Palmer, an American, first sighted the Antarctic continent sailing the *Hero* southward through heavy snowstorms and immense icebergs between November 14 and 18, 1820, to behold "the shore everywhere perpendicular," yet he was never able to set foot upon it. This honor belongs to another American, Captain John Davis of New Haven, who went ashore on February 7, 1821. Maritime interests pressed President Monroe to protect these newly discovered American "rights" to the bottom of the world, but the extermination of the fur seals in that region reduced international tensions as quickly as they had flared. Only in Hawaii, where missionaries strongly backed the merchants and both parties had influential connections on the mainland, was "a form of international caveat enunciated," in Donald D. Johnson's apt phrasing, when President Tyler surprisingly invoked the Monroe Doctrine in 1842 to warn Great Britain and France explicitly against annexing the islands.[17]

The rivalry between American and British seal hunters reflected happenings across the Pacific wherever the two nationalities confronted each other. President John Quincy Adams called for scientific exploring expeditions comparable to those of Britain, France, and Russia to support the nation's commerce with sophisticated knowledge of the globe. At the same time, the British Admiralty turned its own efforts toward exploring the intervening waters of straits and surrounding islands. On one memorable voyage, HMS *Beagle* set forth, Captain Robert FitzRoy, RN, commanding, with Charles Darwin aboard as its volunteer naturalist.

In turn, for nearly four years, from 1838 to 1842, the Great United States Exploring Expedition, outfitted with the sloops-of-war *Vincennes* and *Peacock*, the brig *Porpoise*, the storeship *Relief*, and the schooners *Sea Gull* and *Flying Fish*—the grandest expedition any country had ever sent to sea at one time—cruised around the world to chart the seas under the command of Lieutenant Charles Wilkes, USN. A last-minute substitute, the arrogant Wilkes proved himself to be even a greater paranoid than the *Bounty's* notorious Captain William Bligh. Wilkes and his men headed first for Antarctica, determined to best Captain James Cook's voyage of 1774 to the highest southern latitude yet attained, 71°10' S. They sighted the southern continent, for a brief moment at least, before mist, sleet, ice, and high waves turned them back slightly short of their goal. The battered squadron, minus *Sea Gull*, which went down with all hands in a raging storm, sailed next to Chile and Peru, where Wilkes embarrassed his officers and deckhands in Valparaiso and Callao harbors by fouling ships from his own squadron and foreign vessels as well. Wilkes accused his officers of conspiring against him, and he brutally humiliated the surgeons, naturalists, and artists he was reluctantly carrying along. In mid-Pacific, Wilkes promoted himself to full captain, donning the resplendent new uniform he had brought along and running up the appropriate blue pennant. Wilkes was beyond control. Nevertheless, his squadron carried on to survey the equatorial island groups accurately: the Tuamotus, Tahiti, the Society Islands, the Samoans, Tonga, the Union Group, the Gilbert and Ellice islands, the Hawaiian Islands, the Marquesas, the Marshalls, parts of the Philippines, and the northwest coast of North America. Noting that Puget Sound was the region's ideal harbor, he stiffened James K. Polk's resolve in disputing its ownership with Great Britain. (Polk would campaign for the presidency in 1844 on a popular slogan of "Fifty-four Forty or Fight!") Thereupon Wilkes sailed back across the Pacific to Singapore, where he sold *Flying Fish* to an opium runner. The squadron rendezvoused at St. Helena in the South Atlantic after rounding the Cape of Good Hope to render Wilkes's personal homage to Napoleon Bonaparte at the exile's lonely grave.

Anticipating the official bitterness awaiting him at home because of his bizarre behavior, Wilkes slipped ashore inconspicuously from the pilot boat off Sandy Hook, New Jersey. He deserted the crews of his squadron, leaving them to land unsung and almost unnoticed after one of the most incredible adventures of all time. They had sailed nearly ninety thousand nautical miles, accumulating vast collections and charting hundreds and hundreds of islands, reefs, straits, harbors, and coastlines. They produced a stupendous array of charts for Antarctica and the Pacific Ocean, created the structures of modern anthropology, and contributed enormously to the institutionalization of science in the United States government. Wilkes and his men never realized the greatness of their achievement in their frustrations over its outcome and the outbreak of the Civil War. Instead Charles Wilkes would become renowned mainly for his blunder in forcibly removing two rebel emissaries en route to England aboard RMS *Trent* and almost singlehandedly bringing Great Britain into the war against the Union as the ally of the Confederacy.[18]

In truth, the half century after 1840 for the United States embraced intense competition with Great Britain and a series of confrontations at strategic points around the world, in North and South America, Asia, and the islands of Hawaii. Leaders of both political parties were hoping that the North Pacific Ocean might become, in William H. Goetzmann's words, "a vast American lake," the bridge to the wealth of the Far East from trading and whaling. Such men looked longingly for potential profits to the Japanese Empire. The few Americans there were systematically rebuffed, if not totally excluded, by both the Japanese and the Dutch at their Western trading monopoly on the sealed-off islet of Deshima in Nagasaki's harbor. Many Americans were convinced that Japan would be pried open before long by the British or the Russians to block their own prospects forever. The expansionistic American Geographical and Statistical Society of New York, backed by New England's whaling interests, was urging the United States government to install a permanent naval force in the western Pacific to strengthen its citizens' bargaining powers. Commodore Matthew Calbraith Perry's memorable expedition of 1853–1854 against Japan was the first step.[19]

Previous American attempts to deal with Japanese officials had been contemptuously spurned. Japan barred foreign shipping (except Dutch) from its harbors and coastal waters. In 1846, Commodore James Biddle, USN, with *Columbia* and *Vincennes* in Tokyo Bay, was suddenly surrounded by nearly one hundred Japanese war vessels, rudely towed out to sea, and expelled.

Perry's orders were to open up Japan by force if necessary. An unrelenting disciplinarian himself, the younger brother of Oliver Hazard Perry of War of 1812 fame, Perry favored a thoroughgoing show of strength. He would tolerate no indignities. He refused to allow any Japanese "sightseers" to board his ships nor Japanese guard boats to station themselves nearby. Two of the four black-hulled warships of his reorganized Asiatic Squadron, *Mississippi* and *Susquehanna*, were new and steam-powered. Spewing clouds of coal smoke on entering Tokyo Bay, July 8, 1853, this formidable pair afforded Perry a distinct psychological advantage. The Japanese had never before seen such terrifying apparitions.

Perry proved to be a firm yet patient negotiator. Well versed in the history and culture of feudal Japan, he knew that an agreement would take time to make, especially if far-reaching changes were to be involved. His sailors coolly rowed their longboats through Tokyo Bay each day, mapping it under the menacing, if archaic, guns and arrows of approximately twenty thousand shouting, armor-clad warriors and their batteries of antique cannons. Perry concealed himself aloofly in his quarters until the emperor's representative accepted his ultimatum to consider his treaty to open up Japan to American commerce and international tenets of behavior including diplomatic relations and the rescue of shipwrecked seamen. On July 14, to the din of a thirteen-gun salute, preceded by about four hundred armed officers and sailors and a ship's band playing "Hail Columbia!" and accompanied personally by two heavily armed black bodyguards, Perry landed from his barge to deliver President Millard Fillmore's letter to the emperor, in which Fillmore bragged, "Our ships can go from California to Japan in eighteen days." However, Perry was deflated when the Japanese rejected President Fillmore's "impertinence" and ordered him to depart. Perry promised to return for his treaty, next time with a larger show of force, and he rejected Japan's offer of joint trading rights with the beleaguered Dutch in Nagasaki.

On February 13, 1854, Perry reentered Tokyo Bay, fearing—needlessly, as it proved—that the British or French might have anticipated him. He commanded a beefed-up squadron of ten warships featuring three steam-driven frigates. His second ceremonial landing, on March 8, was even more impressive than his first: a seventeen-gun salute, "The Star-spangled Banner" shrilled proudly by three fully armed bands, and a courteous reception by Japanese officials. Sumo wrestlers and minstrels enlivened the crowds, while gifts were exchanged between the two parties—precious works of art from the culture-conscious Japanese; marvelous manufactures from the trade-minded Americans, including a miniature steam locomotive on rails, a telegraph system, telescope, clocks, and farming implements. Agreement was now at hand. Signed on March 31, 1854, the Treaty of Kanagawa provided protection henceforth for American castaways and opened the relatively inaccessible ports of Shimoda and Hakodate for obtaining coal and provisions, with consular privileges to be located there. Commodore Perry had opened Japan in fact, though just barely. He had won the most-favored-nation treatment for his country, but no guarantee for commencing trade. However, in 1858, Townsend Harris, the clever United States consul at the isolated port of Shimoda, wrested a second treaty, not by another demonstration of force but through skillful "personal diplomacy," wherein Japan opened more trading ports, agreeing at this time to freedom of trade and a schedule of tariffs. Harris was elevated to the rank of minister, inaugurating the first United States legation in Tokyo; in 1860, the first embassy from the Tokugawa shogunate arrived in Washington. Soon the leaders of the Meiji restoration would launch Japan on a dramatic course to abolish the anti-foreign remnants of feudal rule and modernize the nation toward world power, and Japan would move together with the United States and European powers toward the tumultuous events of the twentieth century.[20]

While Perry was forcing the United States into Japan's affairs, President Fillmore dispatched another great scientific and hydrographic undertaking, the North Pacific Expedition. The expedition's orders were to chart the coasts and explore the waters of Japan, the China Sea, and the North Pacific Ocean to make these vast regions safer for whalers and merchantmen. The Coast Survey, the Smithsonian Institution, and the Naval Observatory cooperated to advance the science of the oceans. Lieutenant Cadwallader Ringgold, USN, commanded the expedition, seconded by Lieutenant John Rogers, USN. Ringgold had captained one of the ships in Wilkes's fleet, while Rogers, who maintained liaison with the scientific community, hailed from an influential navy family. Ringgold's flotilla consisted of two veterans, *Vincennes* and *Porpoise*, the tender *John Kennedy*, the leaky harbor steamer *John Hancock*, and the tiny sloop *Fenimore Cooper*. Ringgold's ships sailed from the Chesapeake Bay on June 11, 1853.

Lieutenant John Mercer Brooke, USN, a southerner, was the expedition's ablest officer. His deep-sea sounding invention was responsible for the success of Matthew Fontaine Maury's earlier Atlantic Ocean charting expedition, and he would one day design the famous ironclad *Merrimack* for the Confederacy. Brooke retrieved tiny marine animals north of Australia from the bottom of the Coral Sea two and one-half miles down to disprove the popular theory that an "azoic zone" at great depths precluded the possibility of deeper life in any form. Some scientists until then held that ships and sailors drowned at sea floated suspended forever at an intermediate depth above the ocean's floor.

Lieutenant Ringgold was overtaken by the same sort of mysterious malady that befell other solitary commanders in the lonely wastes of the Pacific, like Bligh and Wilkes before him and Ahab in *Moby Dick*. After a quick search to lay out the fastest commercial route between Australia and China, correcting a few of Wilkes's charts along the way, Ringgold unwarrantedly sent *Porpoise* to fight a fleet of pirate junks with HMS *Rattler* of Hong Kong, and commanded his flagship *Vincennes* to Canton to aid the Manchu government of China against rebel forces, thereby taking sides in a civil war. Paranoically, he overhauled his ships repeatedly, then came down with delirium, which led Perry, on returning from Japan and convening a medical court of inquiry, to judge him insane and send him home.

Lieutenant Rogers assumed command over the North Pacific Expedition. *John Hancock* and *Fenimore Cooper* surveyed the huge Yellow Sea on his instructions. *Porpoise* went down in a typhoon as she and *Vincennes* headed for Okinawa and was lost with all aboard somewhere between the Formosa Strait and the East China Sea. Rogers was anything but a diplomat. More than once, he remonstrated furiously with Japanese officials for failing to uphold the terms of Perry's treaty. Laughing uproariously, he and his men several times fired their pistols at local dignitaries and kicked the haughty bureaucrats in the balloon-like seats of their puffy pantaloons. Fortunately relations improved with the arrival of Consul Harris after the expedition had sailed elsewhere. Meanwhile the gasping *John Hancock* chugged northward past the Sakhalin Islands and all around the Sea of Okhotsk to survey the mouth of the Amur River in Siberia. Her captain and crew spent weeks ashore with Russian representatives of the czar, who welcomed them warmly as fellow Anglophobes, this being the time of the Crimean War. *Fenimore Cooper* mapped the foggy Aleutian Islands chain and searched futilely for the missing whaleship *Monongahela*. Rogers, at Maury's request, sailed *Vincennes* far north through Bering Strait to approximately seventy degrees north latitude hoping to enter the open polar sea, but the ice packs of the Beaufort Sea forestalled him. The North Pacific Expedition ended on October 16, 1855, with a rich harvest of returns for science and spectacular mapping and hydrographic results, but the Civil War prevented publication of any reports on the scale of those of the Wilkes expedition.[21]

One important official who never forgot the North Pacific Expedition was its sponsor in Congress, Senator William H. Seward of New York. Seward, as secretary of state, would contrive to purchase Alaska for the United States from Russia in 1867. Seward's ambition for Alaska was to further American commerce with the Far East.[22] But strategic interests, as developed by the nation's political and military planners, would come by the twentieth century to outweigh any commercial considerations. Then, the spirit of manifest destiny would somehow span the Pacific Ocean to promote imperial goals for the United States. Much later, throughout the Cold War period after 1945, an anti-Communist militancy directed against the Soviet Union, Red China, and their cohorts elsewhere in Asia would command American policy.

There's a land where the mountains are nameless,
And the rivers all run God knows where;
There are lives that are erring and aimless,
And deaths that just hang by a hair;
There are hardships that nobody reckons;
There are valleys unpeopled and still;
There's a land—oh, it beckons and beckons,
And I want to go back—and I will.

Robert W. Service[1]

2

THE ALASKA BARGAIN

The czar of all the Russias, Alexander II, made up his mind in December 1866 to offer Alaska to the United States. Advising the emperor in St. Petersburg were his brother, the Grand Duke Constantine, who was urging him to sell, Prince Alexandr M. Gorchakov, the foreign minister, and Baron Eduard de Stoeckel, the longtime Russian ambassador to the United States. The czar's decision was prompted by at least four considerations, though it is not entirely clear which was foremost. (1) The Americans, in Russia's leaders' view driven ever farther afield by their manifest destiny impulses, would seek before long to take over Alaska as they had already taken Oregon, Texas, and California, so Russia herself ought to benefit from this inevitability before the opportunity was lost. (2) Any money to be obtained from selling Russian North America would enrich the imperial treasury, already depleted by the costs of the Crimean War of 1854–1856 against Britain and France and threatened even more by the vast railroad building enterprises Russia was undertaking. (3) The United States with Alaska acquired would become Russia's friend against Britain in the rampaging competition among Europe's great powers for empire and influence in the Middle East and Eastern Europe. (4) Freed of her unprofitable Alaskan colony, Russia could turn her energies toward Asia, where her true imperial destinies arguably beckoned in eastern Siberia, Mongolia, Manchuria, and even Korea. Enough was enough. Czar Alexander ordered Baron de Stoeckel to open negotiations immediately upon his return to the United

States and, if he could, maneuver the Americans into offering to buy Alaska.[2]

Stoeckel contacted Secretary of State William H. Seward on reaching New York City, probably through Thurlow Weed, a powerful New York Republican politician and Seward's close friend. Discussion commenced between Seward and Stoeckel on March 11, 1867, and ranged gingerly over various concerns at first. Stoeckel rebuffed Seward's request for fishing rights in Russian American waters. Seward eventually wondered if Alaska itself might be for sale, a question first tentatively raised by Secretary of State William L. Marcy in 1854 and occasionally since until quashed by the turmoil of the Civil War. Feeling that an affirmative reply would fulfill his instructions, Stoeckel responded that Alaska was indeed for sale. Seward thereupon hastened to President Andrew Johnson in Washington to urge him to agree to purchase the territory for the United States. Professing to have no opinion on the subject, Johnson consented in short order after consulting his cabinet, whose members strongly backed Seward's request.

Seward spent a week with Stoeckel going over the particular features of their proposed transaction, then Stoeckel cabled St. Petersburg to gain his government's approval to initial the treaty for the sale of Russian America to the United States. A few days later, on Friday evening, March 29, Baron de Stoeckel presented himself at Seward's home, according to the secretary's son Frederick, with the czar's permission in hand. Dramatically announcing that his emperor was willing to sell Russia's colony to the United States, Stoeckel suggested meeting the next day to complete the deal. Seward was so eager to obtain Alaska, however, that he asked why they should delay any longer to conclude their business. The two men went at once to Seward's office at the Department of State, where they worked with their hurriedly assembled assistants throughout the night to draw up the treaty before signing it early on Saturday, March 30, 1867. The price ultimately came to $7.2 million in gold, estimated roughly to be two and one-half cents per acre.

The formalities were eventually resolved. The debate in the United States Senate over ratification was unusually brief and took place only ten days after President Johnson submitted the purchase treaty. Senator Charles Sumner of Massachusetts spoke in support for three hours on April 9. Sumner on this occasion fastened the name Alaska to the entire territory, assuring his colleagues that it was adapted from the native name of Al-ay-ek-sa, meaning a great land. The Senate ratified the agreement on the same day, persuaded in large measure by Sumner's fact-filled argument and manifest destiny sentiments. Only two senators voted against it. Ratifications were exchanged between the two governments on June 20, with proclamations of the shift of sovereignty forthcoming on the same day. The actual transfer of territory took place at New Archangel on Sitka Island, October 18, 1867, when Russia's flag came down in military ceremonies for the last time and the Stars and Stripes was raised in its place. The United States House of Representatives delayed appropriating the funds required by the treaty, however, because certain members were miffed at the Senate's failure to consult them, and others, as evident below, opposed the purchase altogether. Finally, on August 1, 1868, the full amount due for Alaska was paid to the Russians, and its receipt was duly acknowledged.

Andrew Johnson's enemies promptly derided the purchase of Alaska. The czar, they gloated, had duped the president into buying an inaccessible, frozen wasteland for an outrageous sum of money. "Russia has sold us a sucked orange," complained the *New York World* (April 1, 1867), noting the fur trade's decline; "a dreary waste of snow and ice," added Chicago's *Evening Journal* (April 1, 1867). Then longer perspectives prevailed. Numerous observers predicted major gains for the United States from its territorial acquisition at Britain's expense, not Russia's. The American purchase of Alaska hemmed in Canada so narrowly on its Pacific coastline that it was being predicted that she would eventually lose British Columbia to her southern neighbor. Meanwhile the hated Hudson's Bay Company had been blockaded. "It is an advancing step in that manifest destiny," the *New York World* trumpeted (April 1, 1867), "which is yet to give us British North America." As for Secretary Seward himself, a genial, gregarious politician of forceful intellectual powers driven by unlimited expansionist dreams, his foresight would never be celebrated during his lifetime. Alaska was fated to be scoffed at throughout the next generation and longer as "Seward's Folly" or "Seward's Icebox." Alaska's advantages were scarcely obvious to the general public. Average citizens distrusted any grandiose governmental ventures for which in due course they would have to pay.

At this time also, on July 1, 1867, the Dominion of Canada was formed out of British North America's eastern provinces as an independent national confederation, and the following year the newly constituted Canadian government bought out the proprietary holdings of the Hudson's Bay Company, which, known as Rupert's Land, covered much of the west. By 1870, both British and Russian sovereignty had coincidentally vanished from the Yukon basin to leave control over North America henceforth to the Americans and the Canadians.[3]

So what was American Alaska? What was the newest United States territory on the Pacific Ocean like? Who were its inhabitants? How would they and their land fare under American rule?

Nature, it is said, created six Alaskas, not just one. The southeast region is the panhandle, over 560 miles in length. This is the narrow strip of mainland and the offshore islands travelers first encounter when coming

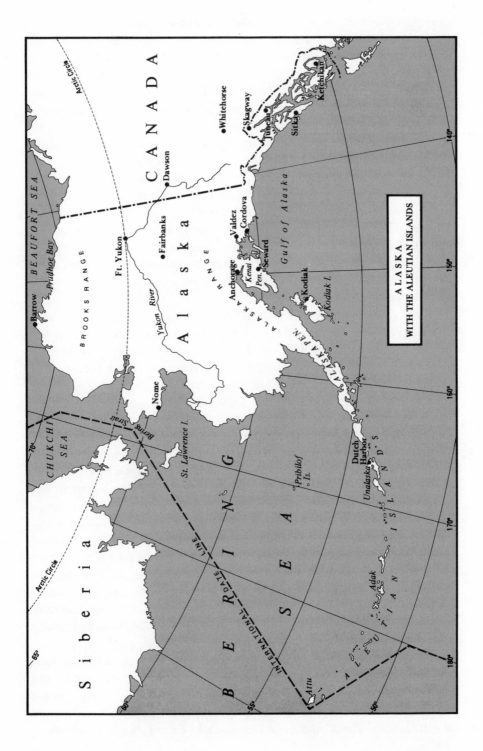

ALASKA
WITH THE ALEUTIAN ISLANDS

from the lower forty-eight states. Isolated from the rest of North America by the towering Saint Elias and Coast mountain ranges, the region is the home of Juneau, the state's capital, and boasts more than a thousand islands offshore, including Baranof Island, the site of Sitka, the former Russian capital of New Archangel. Precipitation is heavy, averaging 100 inches each year and ranging from a mere 26 inches at Skagway, the gateway to the Klondike gold rush of 1898, to 227 inches at Little Port Walter on Baranof Island. Adjacent lies the south-central gulf coast region, sandwiched between the Alaska Range and the Gulf of Alaska, stretching westward from Yakutat to Kodiak Island, the Kenai Peninsula, and Cook Inlet, which opens to today's population concentration around Anchorage. The mainland topography resembles a roller coaster of lofty peaks and broad river valleys. The comparatively mild climate is like the southeast's except at the harsher altitudes, while average precipitation approaches 200 inches in extreme locations and 100 inches overall. The south-central region along the Gulf of Alaska provides a habitat useful for the thirsty vegetation and the wild animals that abound.

Alaska's interior region, the "real" Alaska for purists, is best defined in superlatives. The topography is dominated by two gigantic mountain ranges, the Brooks Range to the north and the jagged, glacier-topped Alaska Range to the south. Towering above all, on the region's southern border, soars Mt. Denali, "the great one" (formerly named Mt. McKinley); its South Peak at 20,320 feet, and its North Peak, at 19,470 feet, are the highest elevations in North America. The Yukon River, nearly nineteen hundred miles in length and totally navigable, rises in British Columbia and Yukon Territory, then flows about fourteen hundred miles through Alaska's mid-section to the Bering Sea. The Yukon and its equally majestic tributaries, the Porcupine, Tanana, Koyukuk, Klondike, White, and Pelly, led explorers, trappers, and miners into Alaska's vast interior. The interior is dominated by mountain ranges and characterized by an inhospitable climate of scanty precipitation, wide temperature extremes, and stagnant, almost windless air masses. In the Yukon basin, local distributions of both flora and fauna are determined largely by altitude, and wildlife generally is abundant. A wilderness for the greatest part, little altered by humans, the interior sprawls across one-third of Alaska, though it is home to less than one-third of its population. Forests and tundra (Russian for treeless) ground coverings extend everywhere beyond the limits of vision.

The external margins of Alaska embrace three regions in all, the Aleutian Islands and Alaska Peninsula, the Bering Sea coast, and the Arctic. The Aleutian Islands separate the stormy waters of the North Pacific and the Bering Sea to form a thousand-mile-long rocky causeway between Asia and North America. The Aleutians and their Alaska Peninsula abutment belong to the volcanic "ring of fire" that surrounds the Pacific basin. The 124 Aleutian islands, the longest archipelago of small islands in the world, are actually the crests of gigantic submarine volcanoes rising from the ocean floor. Twenty-six of the chain's fifty-six volcanoes have erupted since 1760. Their eruptions and earthquakes pose chronic dangers, as do the tsunami (tidal waves) and landslides they cause.

Northward the Bering Sea coastal areas of western Alaska are bordered by Kotzebue Sound to the north, Bristol Bay to the south, and the interior region inland to the east. Below Kotzebue Sound, the Seward Peninsula juts out two hundred miles to the west pointing toward Siberia. Just above Nome, Cape Prince of Wales, the peninsula's tip, reaches seaward toward Little Diomede Island, a hair's breadth east of the International Date Line, and Big Diomede Island, which is Russian territory less than three miles away. The mighty Yukon River sweeps around the hills below the Seward Peninsula, where, augmented by the Kuskokwim River, its silt-laden water forms one of the world's major coastal flood plains, the Yukon-Kuskokwim Delta. Remotest of all, the Arctic region is divorced from the rest of Alaska by the mountainous crests of the Brooks Range, rising in the Yukon Territory of Canada and stretching for hundreds of miles to the Chukchi Sea just south of Kotzebue. The Arctic's climate is windy and bitterly cold for most of the year, with only a light precipitation. Gently the mountains and river valleys slope northward to the coastal plain, which is covered by tundra vegetation growing atop bog soils frozen solid by permafrost that starts but a few inches below the surface and extends downward as much as two thousand feet.

Human invaders first crossed the Bering land bridge, which for ages linked Siberia to North America, thirty-five thousand years ago or more. These Asians of unspecified origins, advancing in successive waves over thousands of years, moved eastward and southward, probably through the Yukon River corridor, toward new hunting lands. In time they distributed themselves from north to south and east to west, from one extreme of the Western Hemisphere to another, to settle every region and inhabitable climate.

These ancestors of the New World's Indians, as they would be mis-named by European discoverers, together with the Aleuts and Eskimos, constituted three separate ethnolinguistic stocks. The latter-day descendents of each group were hunting and fishing for their subsistence through-out the great territory later called Alaska when it was discovered for Russia in 1741 by Vitus Bering. Bering, a valiant Dane, explored eastern Siberia and the North Pacific Ocean in the service of Czar Peter I (Peter the Great) and his successors. The Indians encountered by the Russians comprised two different kinds, both of them speaking languages classified much later as

Na-Dene. One group, including the Tlingits, Tsimshians, and Haidas, inhabited the wooded islands and mainland of the southeast; the other, the Athabascans, lived in the interior, their domain extending far into Canada. The remaining two stocks, the Eskimos and Aleuts, spoke languages descended across bygone ages from Eskaleut, the parent tongue. The Eskimos occupied almost the entire coastline, hunting sea mammals from the Arctic Ocean in the north to Tlingit country, including Kodiak Island, the Alaska Peninsula, and Prince William Sound, in the south. The Aleuts, the fewest of all, lived lonely, scattered lives along their weather-beaten archipelago. When the Russians arrived, to be followed within a few decades by other Europeans and the newly independent Americans, no migrations from Asia into the Western Hemisphere had occurred for at least five thousand years. Tribal settlement patterns were characteristically stable, even if sparse, yet the native communities differed substantially from place to place. The Aleuts proved to be the first Alaskan natives to succumb to the Russian fur trappers and traders, who overran their hunting grounds, brutally wiping out their villages and enslaving whole families.[4]

The Russian period of Alaska's history would span 126 years. The Russians' fur trading posts and settlements were sprinkled along the southern islands and coastal areas. A few bold adventurers and hunters penetrated the hinterland to explore the wild Yukon River and its tributaries, but they left little permanently other than the ravages of smallpox among the tribes they encountered. At most, fewer than eight hundred Russians lived in Alaska at one time, while only handfuls settled permanently there. Furs from sea mammals and land animals almost wholly explained the Russians' presence in Alaska. Little else was there to lure them so many thousands of miles from European Russia. When Alaska was sold at last, in 1867, the czar's subjects were accorded the choice to return home to their fatherland or to become citizens of the United States of America. American officials did not encourage the latter option. Many Russians, if not most, chose to go home.

For a half century after Bering's discovery, the first Russians in Alaska were venturesome private individuals mostly seeking to profit from hunting and trading furs, especially the glossily soft, dense pelts of sea otters. Russia's rulers far away in St. Petersburg evinced little interest in their enterprises. Soon a lucrative market developed in China for the Russians' Aleutian pelts, admitted through the Mongolian border entrepôt of Kyakhta. The fur hunters themselves, the *promyshleniki*, were a coarse, hard-drinking, quarrelsome bunch; they enslaved the native Aleuts, forcing the men to take to their sea-roving *baidarkas* (kayaks) to hunt otters and seals for them and subjugating the women to their lusts. By 1770, only a few major merchants survived to dominate the fur industry because costs had risen sharply as the hunt was extended farther and farther from operating bases. Spaniards from Mexico, Britons, and Americans were sailing into Alaska's coastal waters meanwhile to raise the spectre of threatening competition. Place names aside, Valdez, Cordova, and Malaspina notably, the Spanish left almost nothing behind. In 1778, Captain James Cook entered the region on his third and final exploration, visiting the Aleutians, exchanging navigational data with the Russians, and mapping the Alaskan coast along "the backside of America," as Sir Francis Drake had labeled it in 1577–1578. Like the Spanish, the British left mostly place names to mark their transit. Cook departed for the Hawaiian Islands bearing a cargo of sea otter skins he had obtained from trading with the natives, only to be slain himself on the Big Island. His crew carried on to Canton under Captain James Clerke, where they reaped spectacular prices for their furs. A bit later, in 1784, Russia's leading fur traders, Grigory Ivanovich Shelikov and his partner, Ivan Golikov, led a company of 192 men to Kodiak Island and founded Russia's first permanent settlement. Shelikov brought with him his wife, Natalya, reputedly the first white woman in Alaska. He failed to persuade his empress, Catherine II (Catherine the Great), to grant him the monopoly of the fur trade he sought, even though the unrestricted private enterprise phase of Russia's Alaskan venture was obviously wearing itself out. So Shelikov departed from Alaska in May 1786, entrusting his successful business on Kodiak Island to the management of an extraordinarily astute Siberian merchant, Alexsandr Andreyevich Baranov.

Baranov would dominate Russian Alaska for the next three decades. He initially supervised the Golikov-Shelikov interests. Then, after 1799, he managed their successor, the Russian-American Company, a fur trading monopoly chartered for twenty years in that year by Czar Paul I. He won the respect of the Russian roughnecks working for him. He fought the fierce Tlingit Indians to a standstill and drove the conquered Aleuts against their will to hunt sea mammals on distant expeditions. On one occasion, in 1803, Baranov furnished an American, Captain Joe O'Cain, with a company of fifteen or twenty Russians and thirty or so Aleuts to hunt sea otters in California waters, beginning a practice of supplying labor to foreign vessels that became common in the years ahead. His authority over the natives was often compromised by the contrary influence of the zealous monks sent to Alaska to convert them to Orthodox Christianity. The monks accused Baranov of maltreating the natives and condemned him as a drunkard and sinner for living with a native woman while he himself was still married to a Russian woman left at home. Baranov carried out his instructions responsibly, nevertheless: to gather furs for Russia's increasing share of China's seemingly insatiable market. With the supply of furs diminishing at Kodiak, he sought fresh resources elsewhere, but a settlement attempted at Yakutat failed from its founding. On Sitka Island, Baranov finally crushed the Tlingits in a week-long pitched battle. He built New Archangel into the biggest town and capital of Russian America. He also carried out orders to expand beyond Alaska, if only to gain dependable food supplies for his trading posts. In the face of Spanish protests, he established Fort Ross in California in 1812, a Russian outpost just north of Bodega Bay that persisted for over thirty years; he also set up a fortified trading post on the Hawaiian island of Kauai, in 1815, that was quickly abandoned.

Pragmatic to the core, Baranov even turned the Anglo-American War of 1812 to profitmaking. John Jacob Astor had hastily sold his holdings at Astoria on the Oregon coast to the British-owned Northwest Company, fearing their seizure otherwise, and the American fur trading ships raced to Sitka to escape confiscation. Baranov bought several of the Yankee ships, leased others, and reflagged them all as Russian vessls to safeguard them from the British, who were the czar's allies now in the war against Napoleon. The American deckhands were unmatched in their seafaring skills, so Baranov employed them to the hilt. His company's earnings grew handsomely from the booming trade among Russian Alaska, the Hawaiian Islands, and China. Yet Baranov himself was no empire builder, which disappointed the court circles at St. Petersburg. He was first and foremost an entrepreneur seeking profits from fur trading. Even incidentally, he did little to introduce Russian civilization into North America. His forced retirement, at the pressuring of top bureaucrats in 1818, ushered in the third and final phase of Russian Alaska.

Thereafter, the Russian-American Company shaped Alaska into an imperial colony. Baranov's successors, who were specially assigned naval officers, as stipulated by the company's revised charters, concentrated on administrative matters, not on the fur trade itself, though some bureaucrats grew concerned also to foster the welfare of the natives. Czar Alexander I's reaction to the arrival of American and British fur traders in Alaska was a short-lived attempt to exclude them altogether. In 1821, Alexander closed Alaska to all outsiders. All trade was forbidden. No furs could be exchanged with them, while only Russian vessels could be allowed to provision the territory. Worse still, an imperial ukase stretched the Russian-American Company's boundary claim southward to 51° north latitude, nearly 250 miles into the Oregon country, which Great Britain and the United States had claimed and jointly occupied under their treaty of 1818. But the Russian government soon reversed itself in the face of British and American protests and the economic havoc its policies wreaked on the Alaskans themselves. The United States and Russia signed a convention in 1824 recognizing 54°40′ north latitude as the southernmost boundary of Alaska. Great Britain subscribed to this demarcation the following year, and agreed with the

Russians also to recognize 141° west longitude as the boundary to divide eastern Alaska from western Canada. Thereupon, the Russians accorded both the Americans and the British the right to trade along Alaska's coasts for a period of ten years. In addition, the British won the freedom to navigate the Yukon, Stikine, and other rivers flowing through Alaska to the Pacific from their lands in the interior. When the joint ten-year trading period expired, the Russians ousted the Americans, leaving the Hudson's Bay Company at liberty to compete on its own turf with the Russian-American Company for the fur trade.

The two companies wrangled and threatened for several years to harm each other before they compromised their rivalry amicably through the leasing arrangement of 1839. In return for annual payments in furs, food-stuffs, and manufactured goods, then in cash after 1859, the Russians agreed to the use by the Hudson's Bay Company of their mainland territory south of Cape Spencer down the panhandle. The Hudson's Bay Company occupied most of Alaska's panhandle for almost the next thirty years, even during the Crimean War of 1853–1856 between Britain and Russia, until the company was expelled by the sale of the territory to the United States. Both the Hudson's Bay Company and the Russian-American Company profited greatly from their compact.

The Russian fur trade changed dramatically during these years because of reductions in the supply of pelts from overkilling and a decline in China's markets, while Alaska itself underwent significant transformations. The capital city of New Archangel, dubbed "the Paris of the Pacific" by Yankee skippers, enjoyed a glittering, if provincial, social life in St. Petersburg style, led by successive governors and their wives. Schools were organized for the sons and daughters of company employees. The Orthodox Church dedicated St. Michael's Cathedral in 1848. Headed by Sitka's Bishop Innocent (Father Ivan Veniaminov, later to become Metropolitan of Moscow and Saint Innocent the Apostle to America), a strapping six-foot three-inch giant, gentle and pious as observers saw him, the church founded schools for the natives at New Archangel, Kodiak, and Unalaska halfway along the Aleutian chain, though most of the priests considered education to be secondary to rescuing the native heathen from the prospect of eternal damnation. By the mid-1830s, Sitka's population had grown to thirteen hundred, yet most inhabitants dwelled in crowded, dark, damp log buildings and subsisted on meager daily rations. Meanwhile, Russian Alaska was noticeably slumping, economically and into imperial disfavor as well. A number of new ventures failed. Coal was mined, but sold at a loss in San Francisco. Ice sold to California did turn a profit, yet on a small scale only at three thousand tons per year. Discoveries of amber, copper, and petroleum failed to lead to industrial production. As the Russian-American Company drifted perceptibly toward bankruptcy, the shifting imperial concerns of Russia's rulers began to overshadow their interest in Alaska. Company agents, in fact, were being dispatched to northeastern Manchuria to explore the Amur River region and endeavor to win over the natives. The czar and his advisors grew obsessed to take over eastern Siberia to support their designs on China. Alaska was made expendable and put up for sale.[5]

For many years, United States sovereignty scarcely changed Alaska. The czarist governments continued to support the Russian Orthodox Church. Few Americans were prepared even as well as the Russians to govern the vast domain. Yet Alaska was by no means unknown. Americans hunted and traded there for more than seventy-five years before the purchase. Foreign relations with Russia, as the result, had largely concerned Alaskan issues. In 1864, the efforts of the Collins Overland Company, a subsidiary of the Western Union Company, to string a telegraphic link from North America to Europe via Alaska and Siberia directed widespread attention to the North Pacific region, until Cyrus Fields's successful transatlantic cable in 1866 forced the cancellation of the telegraph project. Nevertheless, the extensive data gathered on Alaska's resources and climates by the telegraph scheme stimulated public awareness of Alaska's potential and undoubtedly contributed next year to the zeal for annexation.

Within Alaska, American rule manifested itself for a long time as military authority from headquarters in Sitka, through the army initially and then the navy. At Sitka, atop Baranov's Castle Hill, the first American flag was raised by a color guard from Company F, Ninth Infantry, to signify the transfer of sovereignty from Russia. General Lowell Rousseau, the official representative of President Johnson, formally took possession of Alaska for the United States of America from Prince Dmitrii Petrovich Maksutov, the last chief manager of the Russian-American Company. The Coast Guard revenue cutter *Lincoln* sailed into Alaskan waters. W. S. Dodge, the first U.S. Customs officer in Alaska, took charge of collecting tariffs. Brevet Major General Jefferson Columbus Davis, Twenty-third Infantry, assumed command of the occupying troops. A businessman, H. M. Hutchinson of Hutchinson, Kohl and Company of San Francisco, bought up many of the buildings, ships, and movable properties of the Russian-American Company. A Victoria, British Columbia, fur merchant, Leopold Boscowitz, took sixteen thousand sealskins at the bargain price of forty cents apiece. Gloom gripped the Russians, yet the Sitka social whirl continued unabated into January, until finally the elegant Princess Maria Alexsandrovich Maksutov, the chief manager's wife, departed for Russia accompanied by five children (three by Maksutov's first marriage, and two whom she had borne while in Sitka) and their nurse. Prince Maksutov stayed on a year longer to liquidate his company's remaining assets. Russia's dominion in America would soon be virtually forgotten.

Months earlier, on the treaty's ratification, President Johnson had recommended that Congress should provide "for the occupation and government of the territory as part of the dominion of the United States," within its authority (Constitution: art. IV, sec. 3) "to make all needful rules and regulations respecting the territory or other property belonging to the United States." Unfortunately for Alaska and its people, the beleaguered Johnson wielded so little influence that the legislators ignored his request, battling him instead over Reconstruction. Eventually, Congress conformed. By an act of July 27, 1868, it extended to Alaska United States Customs controls and the laws regulating commerce and navigation, while prohibiting the importation or sale of distilled liquor or breech-loading firearms. But no civil government followed for seventeen years. The army governed Alaska without interference or any significant impact. Soldiers never welcomed an assignment to Alaska, for boredom would afflict them more than hostile natives or wilderness dangers. Bound by water to one of a thousand islands and confined by dense forests to a small spot on that island, the troops were useless. Any malefactor was safe from apprehension when he pushed his canoe away from shore. Repeatedly the command's annual reports called for revenue vessels to replace the army's outposts and carry out the necessary policing functions. Then, in 1877, the troops were withdrawn to quell the Nez Percé Indian uprising in Idaho, which for two years left Mottrom D. Ball, the Treasury Department's toll collector, the only government official on duty in all of Alaska. Washington at last grasped the simple truth that two or three gunboats could keep order in coastal Alaska, where an army could not. The navy took over in 1879 and maintained one or more gunboats in Alaska's waters for the next twenty years.

In spite of the reluctance of Congress to appropriate funds for Alaska, the intrepid Lieutenant Frederick Schwatka of the United States Army conducted his own exploration of the interior in 1883. On an official census-taking mission to count the native population, Schwatka led a party of six men on a forty-foot-long wooden raft downstream from the headwaters of the Yukon River at Lake Lindeman in Canada, arriving four months later at Saint Michael near where the river flows into the Pacific Ocean. His book describing his adventure, *Along Alaska's Great River* (1898), intensified the feverish excitement of the gold rush.

Finally Congress passed the Organic Act of 1884 to make Alaska a civil and judicial district, and President Chester A. Arthur appointed John H. Kinkead, a former governor of Nevada, the first civil governor. Neither Congress nor President Arthur held any clear formula for shaping Alaska's government apart from agreeing that military rule ought to give way as simply and inexpensively as possible to civilian control. For the time being, Alaska would have to be designated a "district," they concurred, because the designation of "territory" would automatically introduce certain constitutional provisions and guarantees, which in turn would raise problems without precedents due to Alaska's noncontiguous location and the native majority in its population. The act explicitly forbade forming a legislature. Since Alaskans could not choose their representatives, taxation was also excluded. To assure the rule of law, the act bestowed on Alaska the statutory codes of Oregon, the state nearest to Alaska. (Washington was still only a territory at that date.) The governor of Alaska could exercise no real authority. The most important official was the district court judge, who presided over major civil and criminal cases, holding court alternately in Sitka and Wrangell. The district judge was assisted by commissioners sitting in Juneau, Unalaska, Sitka, and Wrangell. A district attorney, a marshal and four deputies, and the clerk of the court comprised the law enforcement staff. The Sitka-based commissioner served also as registrar of the Alaska land office. No provision was made for law enforcement in the interior.

Many Alaskans complained that the Organic Act denied their right to self-government and failed to meet their needs. The act recognized Alaska as a land district to be regulated by the mining laws of the United States, but no provision for privately owning land was authorized except up to 640 acres by mission stations. The act declared that natives must not be disturbed from lands they occupied, used, or claimed, and it provided for a special commission to determine what lands should be reserved for the Indians and what provisions should be made for their education. Congress at first appropriated funds for the general education of children without reference to race. Next it made additional funds available for Indian children of both sexes to attend industrial schools, which effectively introduced Alaska's characteristic system of racially segregated schools. The Reverend Dr. Sheldon Jackson, an energetic Presbyterian missionary, was appointed general agent of education to dispense the federal appropriations. Teaching missionaries from various churches opened schools at Sitka, Tongass, Howkan, Wrangell, Unalaska, Saint Michael, and Kodiak. The Moravians founded their mission and school far away on the Kuskokwim River, renaming the place Bethel, the House of God. Anglican and Catholic missionary priests endured the harsh privations of the Yukon interior to overcome the well-nigh impossible task of preaching the Gospel of Christianity to the Athabascan Indians, whose tribes spoke about sixty different languages in hundreds of distinct dialects. Even the Evangelical Mission Union of Sweden erected a mission school at Unalakleet. Other mission schools followed in short order at numerous locations. Conflict proved inevitable between the missionaries and civil authorities in the absence of home rule by Alaskans. Dr. Jackson was soon at odds with Governor John Kinkead and Governor Alfred P. Swineford, Kinkead's successor, over the citizenry's efforts to undo the prohibition of liquor and alter the administration of the natives, including their education. Their squabbles over the laws and political appointments for Alaska raged all the way to the nation's capital. The future was at stake.[6]

Instead Alaska's future until the Second World War would be determined economically, not politically, by commercial developments and by lumbering, mining, and fishing, but above all else by the great gold rushes at the turn of the century.

Real power lodged early in the Alaska Commercial Company, which was incorporated in 1869, absorbing Hutchinson, Kohl and Company, the Russian-American Company's buyer. The next year, amid charges of force, fraud, and corruption, Congress enacted a law ostensibly intended to protect fur-bearing seals. The law granted a monopoly for twenty years to the Alaska Commercial Company to hunt the pelagic mammals on their breeding grounds in the lonely Pribilof Islands. Such an exclusive mercantile privilege was anachronistic at best, but the company was the lowest bidder for the government's proffered favors. The company's leases at once became controversial, embroiling Congress in partisan conflicts. Balanced solutions were unlikely, if not impossible. Unhindered, the company efficiently extended its commercial empire over the Aleutians, Kodiak Island, and the Yukon River valley and, after the British departed, took over Fort Yukon, the Hudson's Bay Company's outpost. The company's influence increased exponentially. Its agents policed the interior, in the absence of any legal authority, and even equipped some villages with medical services and schools. Alaska's natives received better treatment from company agents than from the numbers of prospectors who were scrambling for immediate rewards. Dividends of 100 percent paid to the company's shareholders in 1880 reflected the great wealth accumulating from its sealing monopoly. But many blamed the company for discouraging immigration in favor of the fur trade, especially since Alaska's first census, taken by Ivan Petroff in the same year, could enumerate only 430 white men living in that vast territory. The exclusive twenty-year sealing franchise passed to the North American Commercial Company in 1890. By 1910, the herds were nearly extinguished, and control over the rookeries reverted to the United States government, which before long arranged a pact with Great Britain, Japan, and Russia to stop the unlimited hunting.

Alaska's timber industry strove to meet simultaneously the rising demands for lumber from salmon fishermen, packers, and canneries and from gold miners. Prospectors filtered northward from California and British

Columbia, sparking Alaska's first population boom. Juneau, which Joe Juneau and Richard Harris founded in 1880 following the gold discoveries along the Gastineau Channel, grew within a decade into a typical American frontier town boasting schools, a variety of stores and artisans, a hospital, nine saloons, and two breweries in spite of legal prohibition. Chinese laborers from British Columbia settled down to work in the hard rock gold mines, while every summer more and more Chinese sailed northward from San Francisco to work in close isolation in Alaska during the salmon packing season. They returned to China only, if they were fortunate enough, to retire and die. Even anti-Chinese rioting, which frequently swept the Pacific coast against the Orientals' docile readiness to toil for lower wages than white workers would accept, hit Alaska in the 1880s.[7]

Gold rushes turned Alaska into a bonanza to be immortalized in legend and verse. Gold had been found first by the Russians on the Kenai Peninsula in 1848, almost at the same time as it was discovered in British Columbia along the Stikine and Fraser rivers. Expectations heightened that more lodes were ready and waiting to be found. Gold deposits were discovered in 1872 near Sitka, in 1874 near Juneau at Windham Bay, at Gold Creek in 1880, at Fortymile in American territory on the Yukon River in 1886, at Yakutat in 1887, and on the Kenai Peninsula again in 1895. The Treadwell complex on Douglas Island near Juneau developed into one of the largest underground gold mines in the world, employing more than a thousand workers at its peak and operating continuously until 1944.

From 1896 for a decade or so, all hell broke loose. The stampede commenced with the Klondike strike in Canada's Yukon Territory. The Klondike region was most accessible through the Alaskan ports of Dyea and Skagway at the head of the southeastern panhandle and from the Bering Sea all the way up the Yukon River to Dawson City, the heart of the Klondike. The famous Trail of '98 into the Klondike led gold seekers across either the dangerously steep Chilkoot Pass out of Dyea or the White Pass out of Skagway and through the headwaters of the Yukon. Overnight Skagway, the prospectors' supply center, boomed into Alaska's largest town. Its notoriety for lawlessness owed a good deal to the violent feudal-like control exercised by Jefferson ("Soapy") Smith and his rough-and-ready gang of extortionists. Smith's cutthroats met their match ultimately at the hands of angry vigilantes, and Smith himself died from the posse's guns.

Alaska's own gold rush followed far to the west on the barren Seward Peninsula at Nome, only sixty miles from Siberia. Daniel Libby of the Western Union Telegraph Company had discovered gold there in 1866, but he was unable to return until 1897, when he brought three other prospectors with him, including a mining engineer and Louis Melsing, his brother-in-law. On September 22, 1898, Jafet Lindeberg, Jon Brynteson, and Eric

Lindblom the "three lucky Swedes," made their great strike at Anvil Creek. The rush started the following spring when the news reached Seattle. By October, more than three thousand men were frantically raking Nome's stony beaches, where more gold was discovered. Nome exploded into a wide open city of over twenty thousand by the middle of 1900, with generous complements of claim jumpers, swindlers, prostitutes, and gamblers mingling with the miners in at least one hundred saloons. The next great strikes took place in the Tanana River valley, near the site of modern Fairbanks. Italian immigrant Felix Pedro's find at Discovery Creek led to the stampede of 1902 and the gold mining industry of the interior, which eventually outproduced all other mining districts in Alaska. Fairbanks, which was named for Theodore Roosevelt's vice-president, Charles Fairbanks, early acclaimed itself as "the largest log cabin town in the world." By 1903, men were mining gold throughout Alaska, though the precious yellow metal became harder and harder to extract as placer deposits were exhausted, and the process required more costly mining machinery and greater capital investments year after year. Significant gold production still takes place at many localities throughout the state.

The gold rushes directed attention toward Alaska as nothing else had done since the purchase. During 1899 and 1900, Congress started to take Alaska seriously by authorizing new army posts at Eagle, Nome, Haines, and Tanana. The nation's coal mining laws were applied to the district, and the U.S. Geological Survey was directed to undertake detailed explorations and surveys. On June 6, 1900, Congress revised the stopgap Organic Act of 1884 and extended the Homestead Act to Alaska on a reduced scale by stipulating only 80 acres for each holding instead of the 160 acres customary elsewhere. The criminal and civil law codes were modified to suit Alaska's peculiar circumstances, with two new judicial districts formed to serve the growing population. Taxes were levied on businesses to meet the costs of government. Prohibition, though effectively a dead letter, was repealed and the sale of alcoholic liquor legalized, over the strenuous objections of Dr. Sheldon Jackson and his missionary associates. Congress decreed, in addition, that the capital should move from Sitka to Juneau, a larger town. Congress further determined that Alaskans deserved a measure of self-government, even the frontiersmen who cherished no government at all, by providing for the incorporation of towns. The gold rushes also brought to a resolution the long-festering dispute with Canada over the ambiguous Alaska boundary. A panel of jurists that included Great Britain's lord chief justice threw out Canada's claims to Skagway and Dyea, infuriating Canadians, who justifiably charged the British government with selling them out once again for Anglo-American imperial interests.

With population increasing, schemes arose to make Alaska less economically dependent on the outside. The federal government set up a number of agricultural experiment stations to promote farming, the first at Sitka in 1898, next at Kenai, Kodiak, and Fairbanks, and finally at Matanuska in 1917. Busy steamboats plied the inland waterways and the Yukon and Tanana rivers. However, dog sleds remained essential for Alaskans with so few roads or trails, until snow machines in the 1960s rendered them as obsolete as horse-drawn vehicles in the lower forty-eight states. Narrow-gauge railroads served local interests on the Seward Peninsula and in the Tanana valley, but only two sizeable systems succeeded—the White Pass & Yukon Railway between Skagway in Alaska and Whitehorse in Canada's Yukon Territory, and the Copper River & Northwestern Railroad linking the Guggenheim mining family's Kennecott copper mines with the port of Cordova·195 miles away. The Guggenheims and J. P. Morgan, with other financiers, had organized the Alaska Syndicate in 1906 to develop its rich copper ore deposits and discourage competitors. The syndicate's Alaska Steamship Company conveyed the ore to the Guggenheim smelter at Tacoma, Washington. The Alaska Syndicate also garnered near-monopolistic control over canneries and other enterprises.

Mining copper in Alaska for commercial export originated in 1900 on Prince of Wales Island in southeastern Alaska. After 1906, new workings of deposits opened on the Kasaan Peninsula on the southern panhandle, notably the Mount Andrews, Mamie, and Stevenson mines, and quickly outpaced the early producers. Copper production later shifted to Latouche Island in Prince William Sound southeast of Anchorage. Here the Beatson-Bonanza Mine (later known only as the Beatson after the lode's discoverer, A. K. Beatson) produced copper ore from 1904 to 1930. The Beatson Mine functioned as a tightly controlled enclave employing about four hundred men. Between 1900 and 1930, production totaled over two hundred million pounds of copper from just two mines in the Prince William Sound area— the Beatson on Latouche Island and the Ellamar on Virgin Bay, twenty miles southwest of Valdez. Overshadowing all other copper mines, the great Kennecott complex in the Wrangell Mountains of south-central Alaska was the most notorious and one of the richest in the world. The Kennecott development dated from 1885, when Lieutenant Henry T. Allen encountered Chief Nikolai on Dan Creek. The chief, whose people used native copper nuggets to make bullets and utensils, carried on his person samples of ore that assayed at 60 percent copper. The Chitina Mining and Exploration Company opened up the Nikolai deposits. By 1909, just as the push to electrify American industry and homes was getting underway, the Kennecott Copper Company had taken control of the area. The mill at Kennecott processed staggering amounts of high-grade ore, shipping the copper by rail to Cordova for transshipment southward by sea. In addition, more than

85 percent of the twenty million ounces of silver gleaned from Alaska before World War II was a byproduct of copper mining from the Kennecott mines in the Wrangell Mountains or a secondary yield from placer and hard rock gold mining elsewhere. Although its Alaskan operation shut down in 1938, the Kennecott interests drove ahead, using their Alaskan profits to acquire copper mines in New Mexico, Arizona, and Nevada and to develop copper mining prospects along Alaska's far northern Brooks Range worth more than $7 billion in 1980.[8]

Gold and copper mining, in fact, had a great deal to do with Alaska's progress toward self-government and, in the long run, statehood. Home rule came to Alaska by a set of curious chances. In the early insular cases (1901–1903), the Supreme Court held that the country's newly acquired possessions, including Puerto Rico, Hawaii, and Guam, were nothing more than unincorporated territories, possessions but not parts of the United States, to which the protections and guarantees of the Constitution did not apply. But the Supreme Court ruled in 1905, in overturning the conviction by a six-man jury of a Mrs. Rasmussen for running a brothel in Fairbanks, that Alaska had already been fully incorporated into the United States by the treaty under which it was acquired and by subsequent congressional legislation. The madam's common-law rights had been grievously violated because Alaska's six-man jury trials, authorized by the act of June 6, 1900, were, in the Court's reliance on the Sixth Amendment, "repugnant to the Constitution." Congress promptly changed the Judicial District of Alaska into the Territory of Alaska and gave Alaska the right to send a nonvoting delegate to Congress. But full territorial status for Alaska was not yet, and not for many years, a reality.

Meanwhile the publicity from the celebrated Ballinger-Pinchot controversy speeded up Alaskans' demands to govern themselves by fueling their argument that federal control both thwarted and corrupted Alaska's development. The Ballinger-Pinchot affair (1909–1911) disclosed a fundamental disagreement between conservationists and private enterprisers over the allocation and exploitation of the nation's natural resources. Early in the Taft administration, an order of former President Roosevelt setting aside certain water power sites in Montana and Wyoming for public purposes was canceled. Chief Forester Gifford Pinchot protested and charged his boss, Secretary of the Interior Richard A. Ballinger, with favoritism toward certain corporations seeking to exploit these water power sites. Pinchot also openly defended L. R. Glavis, a Land Office investigator, who was dismissed for denouncing Ballinger for encouraging the Guggenheim-Morgan Alaska Syndicate's claims to valuable mineral lands in Alaska. Pinchot likewise was fired. A congressional investigation exonerated Ballinger. But failing to overcome the public outcry, Ballinger resigned.

The Second Organic Act, signed by President William Howard Taft on August 24, 1912, provided a legislature for Alaska. Yet Alaska remained unique among the nation's territories in not gaining a judiciary of its own. The federal government retained control over Alaska's natural resources, and Congress kept for itself the legislative authority over local matters such as divorce, gambling, liquor sales, the incorporation of towns, and the formation of county governments. Alaska's early legislatures labored diligently nevertheless. Education and labor enactments occupied much of their lawmaking. Women won the right to vote. But schools remained segregated between whites and natives as they had been since 1905.

President Woodrow Wilson, Taft's successor, was explicitly active on Alaska's affairs. He urged Congress, in his first State of the Union message, to grant "full territorial government to Alaska" and authorize the federal government to build and operate a railroad "for the service and development of the country and its people." Still smarting over the wounds of the Ballinger-Pinchot affair, Congress balked at Wilson's proposal for full territorial status for Alaska, but it reopened the territory's coal resources to public entry and authorized the construction of a railroad from Seward on the tidewater to Fairbanks in the interior. Construction of the Alaska Railroad began in 1915. The work advanced only sporadically for several years, interrupted by the wartime shortages of men and materials during 1917–1918. It was completed at last in 1923. The railroad boom employed forty-five hundred men for construction at its peak and developed Anchorage from a temporary staging site into Alaska's largest city. Even so, Alaska was still treated as a distant colony, with only a limited degree of home rule. Congress maintained its control over the territory's resources. The Maritime Act, or Jones Act, of 1920 uniquely confined Alaskan seaborne traffic to American-registered vessels, excluding even the convenient Canadian ships altogether, a distasteful reminder to Alaskans of their near-colonial status.

The bituminous coal deposits of Alaska that gave rise to the Ballinger-Pinchot controversy were economically vital to the territory's development. They were never in Alaska simply an ideological bone of contention for the politics of the times, as they became in the lower states. Alaskans needed prodigious amounts of heat for their own domestic use and to thaw frozen ground for placer mining. Their need was met around the turn of the century largely by the coal output of at least one hundred small mine operators. Coal production was widespread wherever the abundant deposits were exposed to view, especially along the Yukon and other navigable rivers. The Russian-American Company had first mined coal for export to California in 1855 at Fort Graham on the Kenai Peninsula in southern Alaska. Coal interests, like gold claims, were bartered and sold before 1900, when the general mining laws of the United States were extended to Alaska. The Alaska Coal Act of April 28, 1904, permitted prospectors to claim coal as a locatable mineral without a precedent government survey. Claims were filed easily under this authority, which led to accusations of fraudulent claiming against "dummy entrymen" fronting for wealthy, land-grabbing corporations. These Alaska coal claims became a national sensation and contributed ammunition to the Ballinger-Pinchot controversy. Abruptly the legal processing of coal claims halted, frustrating both claimants and investors. Gifford Pinchot was burned in effigy in Katalla, then a booming center of several thousand, which hoped to serve as the railhead for Bering River coal. In Cordova, angry men dumped tons of expensively imported coal into Prince William Sound in a "coal party" protest reminiscent of Boston's Tea Party. However, the opening of the Alaska Railroad to the Matanuska coal field in 1916, and to the Nenana mines in 1918, created the transportation artery necessary for large-scale mine development and marketing. Between 1910 and 1940, production increased to a steady 174,000 tons per year. World War II and the two decades ensuing created the demand and profit opportunities necessary in the Anchorage and Fairbanks areas to open new mines. Production increased to 861,000 tons in 1953 and 925,000 tons in 1966. The transition to natural gas and oil for fuels doomed coal mining in Alaska, however, except for the Usibelli family's enormous stripping operation at Healy in the Nenana field, which continues to supply public utility and military demands in the Fairbanks area.[9]

The commercial and manufacturing prosperity of the 1920s scarcely touched Alaska. Alaska continued to lie outside the nation's main economy. The territory, for the same reason, suffered less from the Great Depression of the thirties, in spite of prolonged cutbacks in copper and lumber outputs and the reduced prices earned for salmon. Overfishing on the salmon grounds, which characterized the industry before 1900, alerted even the big packing firms based in Seattle and San Francisco to the imminent exhaustion of Alaska's fisheries. Secretary of Commerce Herbert C. Hoover, after extensive public hearings, persuaded President Warren G. Harding to set up the Alaska Peninsula Reserve in 1922, and the Southwestern Fishery Reservation several months later, to restrict the number of individuals and companies permitted to catch salmon. In 1923, President Harding journeyed to Alaska for the celebration to mark the completion of the Alaska Railroad from Anchorage to Fairbanks. Harding, who was accompanied by Secretary Hoover, drove the golden spike himself, on July 15, at North Nenana on the Tanana River. Hoover held hearings on location in several communities about the plight of their salmon fisheries. Then, most unexpectedly, Harding died in San Francisco on his way back to Washington. His passing cost Alaska "a great friend at court," mourned Ernest Greuning, who would become governor himself of the territory and Unites States senator (1958–1968) from the new forty-ninth state. Hoover continued in office as secretary of commerce to serve President Calvin Coolidge, and he persuaded Congress to pass the White Act of 1924 to fix fishing limits throughout Alaskan waters. Within a year, Hoover was being hailed for the evident success of his efforts to restore the salmon's abundance.

Transportation was still the big problem. Most of the funds Congress appropriated for transportation went to sustain the Alaska Railroad. The nation's only federally owned public railroad, it was troubled by chronic deficits, poor maintenance, and insufficient traffic until 1938, when Otto F. Ohlsen, its new general manager, turned out the system's first profitable year. But before long the airplane was proving to be more important than the railroad for Alaska's growth. Flying, the most flexible form of mechanized transportation, readily overcame Alaska's enormous expanses, its towering elevations, and the harrowing weather conditions that rendered roads and railroads more difficult there than elsewhere to build and operate. By the 1930s, Alaska's renowned bush pilots were taking off and landing on wheels, pontoons, and skis to fly into communities previously accessible only by dog sleds or boats and to connect the remotest places of that remote land to the world outside. Air mail service began to operate on a permanent basis in 1937, from the ninety-seven civilian airfields that the territorial legislature was intent on developing. Meanwhile the Depression was turning a good many thoughts toward Alaska as an opportunity to escape the country's ailing economy and rekindle the bygone life of pioneer self-sufficiency. Self-sufficiency, in fact, became the new Alaska's popular ideal.

The impact of Franklin D. Roosevelt's New Deal on Alaska was mixed and indirect, reflecting the territory's peripheral circumstances. Alaska was, as always, a distant concern. The 1937 report of the National Resources Committee prepared for Congress reaffirmed that there was "no clear need to speed the development of Alaska." Secretary of the Interior Harold L. Ickes, whose department supervised the territory's resources and native peoples, reprimanded Ernest Gruening, Alaska's delegate to Congress, by asserting, "Alaska ought to do more for itself than running to Washington for everything."

Still, several New Deal programs introduced new benefits and activities. Roosevelt's devaluation of the dollar inflated gold prices, which incidentally stimulated the gold mining industry to operate forty-eight dredges by 1940, nearly double the average of preceding years. The Civilian Conservation Corps built roads, trails, bridges, and recreational park facilities, which included restoring for posterity Chief Shakes's important Tlingit tribal house in Wrangell and preserving totem poles from numerous places. The National Youth Administration helped young students to continue their education by making part-time jobs available. The Public Works Administration and the Work Projects Administration employed men and women on construction, archival preservation, and other projects. A WPA guidebook to Alaska appeared as part of the landmark series.

However, the historic differences among Alaskans over natural resources management resurfaced in the salmon industry, when a sharp conflict erupted over Bureau of Fisheries Commissioner Frank Bell's efforts to apply the social engineering objectives of the New Deal. Bell succeeded only in uniting Alaska's articulate entrepreneurial groups against the government's latest efforts to circumscribe private access to a natural resource, accelerating the rising drive for statehood.

Perhaps the most exciting New Deal venture was its Matanuska Valley Colony, an agricultural homesteading enterprise along the railroad some forty miles above Anchorage, one of the Roosevelt administration's numerous resettlement schemes. Nationwide attention followed the 201 Matanuska pioneering families who were selected for their hardy, Nordic European origins from the rigorous climates of upper Michigan, Wisconsin, and Minnesota. Severe hardships awaited them in Alaska. Merely to survive by contemporary standards, the community required every facility at once. Matanuska grew into a minimal success at best, though it was never a failure.

In 1936, Congress extended the Indian Reorganization Act of 1934, the Wheeler-Howard Act, to Alaska's Eskimos and Aleuts. This law repudiated the long-standing policies of enforced assimilation of the Indians in favor of making generous tracts of public domain available to the natives to enable them to sustain themselves more satisfactorily and preserve their cultural heritages. Several Native American communities incorporated themselves under local government constitutions, and some villages launched their own commercial canneries. But Congress did not resolve Alaska's native land claims until 1971. It took the transformations wrought by the Second World War, the Cold War, and the civil rights enactments of 1964 and afterward to improve the status of the native Alaskans.[10]

The Second World War and the Cold War caused the biggest economic and population booms Alaska has ever experienced. The gains by both absolute and relative measurements were greater than from all gold rushes combined. The changes induced led directly to Alaska's statehood, granted in 1959, and to the exploitation by Atlantic Richfield and Exxon, commencing in 1968, of the enormous Prudhoe Bay oil field on the North Slope along the Arctic Ocean's shores. Overnight Alaska escaped from its historic backwater to enter the short list of the world's critically strategic and economically significant places.

World War II transformed Alaska. When the Japanese attacked Pearl

Harbor on December 7, 1941, Alaska was unprepared for war and almost undefended. Alaskans awaited the worst, with tiny garrisons here and there, a scattered array of undersize airfields, a handful of bombers and pursuit planes, an outmoded flotilla of World War I flush-deck destroyers and revenue patrol boats. Once more the prophets had been ignored. The controversial Brigadier General William ("Billy") Mitchell warned Congress in 1935 of Alaska's vulnerability to the Japanese: "They will come right here to Alaska . . . the most central place in the world for aircraft. . . . I believe in the future he who holds Alaska will hold the world, and I think it is the most important strategic place in the world." The territory's delegate to Congress, Anthony J. Dimond, later concurred. Pointing on a globe to the great circle route across the Pacific Ocean, where most likely any attack against North America would come, just south of the Aleutian Islands and two thousand miles north of heavily fortified Oahu in the Hawaiian Islands, Dimond pleaded for military bases. "I say to you, defend the United States by defending Alaska," he argued presciently. Dimond finally managed to persuade General George C. Marshall, the army chief of staff, and Major General Henry H. ("Hap") Arnold, commander of the army air corps, to strengthen Alaska's defenses. Even then, on April 4, 1940, only five days before Germany's invasion of Denmark and Norway and scant weeks before Belgium, the Netherlands, and France fell to Adolf Hitler's blitzkrieg, the U.S. House of Representatives denied funds to construct an air base near Anchorage. Belatedly Billy Mitchell's geography lessons hit home. Scandinavia, now Nazi-controlled, lay perilously close to North America by airplane over the North Pole to Alaska, Canada, and the contiguous forty-eight states beyond. By September 1941, naval air patrol stations and submarine operating bases were opening on Kodiak Island and at Dutch Harbor on Unalaska Island midway along the Aleutians. The main event was going to start immediately, yet Alaska was far from ready for whatever Japan had in store.

Japan readied herself to protect her northern sea approaches against the American retaliation anticipated for the attack on Pearl Harbor. Imperial headquarters commanded on May 5, 1942, that fleet and ground forces must "invade and occupy strategic points in the western Aleutians and Midway Island." Japan's attack against the Aleutians opened in the early morning of June 3, with planes from the carriers *Junyo* and *Rynjo* striking Dutch Harbor. Alerted the day before to the fleet's arrival by a patrolling navy PBY aircraft, the Americans responded with heavy antiaircraft fire, and Japan's task force backed away, leaving little damage behind. Japanese aircraft continued offensive bombing for a time until a virtually final attack was delivered on July 20. Japanese forces turned far to the west to occupy the outermost Aleutian islands of Attu and Kiska. It became evident that the Japanese had no plan to invade Alaska or the North American mainland but had determined, by late 1942, to hang on to the Aleutian island footholds more doggedly than ever. On the offensive at last, American planes from advance bases began bombing Japanese installations whenever weather conditions permitted. Then, on May 11, 1943, American troops invaded Attu, and by the month's end, they destroyed the Japanese garrison after extremely costly fighting. Aerial and naval bombardments saturated Kiska Island next. A colossal American and Canadian invasion landed on Kiska on August 14, only to discover that the Japanese had skillfully evacuated their forces two weeks earlier under the cover of fog. Japan's thrusts at the Aleutians were only diversions intended to lure major American naval units northward for Admiral Isoroku Yamamoto to intercept and destroy, and they fully alarmed the American commands. But the strategic costs proved fatal. Japan's attacks against Dutch Harbor required aircraft carriers she needed far to the south in the central Pacific. Unknowingly Japan lost the balance of sea power at Midway Island even as the battle was about to commence. Japan would never recover throughout the war from her disastrous defeat by the United States Navy at the Battle of Midway Island.[11]

At this juncture, the new realities of aerial distances and Alaska's closeness to the Soviet Union helped to establish the territory's course for the future. Alaska served once again, as in prehistoric times, as a bridge between the two hemispheres. Lend-Lease aircraft, ships, and supplies flowed into Siberia from Alaska from September 1942 until the war's end to assist the Allies' all-out struggle against the Nazis. The hurriedly constructed Alaska-Canada Military Highway (ALCAN) opened on November 20, 1942, to speed supplies and equipment fifteen hundred miles overland from Dawson Creek, British Columbia, to Fairbanks, Alaska, for deploying by the Alaska command and forwarding to the Soviet Union as well. After the fighting shifted away from the North Pacific theater and ended altogether, American ground force levels dropped in Alaska from a peak of 150,000 soldiers in November 1943, to 50,000 by March 1945, to only 19,000 by 1946. Bases were dismantled, and combat airfields relinquished for civil aviation.

Yet the effects of the war and its aftermath endured. The federal government's input of well over $1 billion between 1941 and 1945 left an enduring mark behind in newly constructed docks, breakwaters, roads, and airfields and the modernization of the Alaska Railroad. Civilian population figures rose from around 74,000 in 1940 to 112,000 in 1950, overloading Alaska's already insufficient schools, hospitals, housing, and other services. The cities of Fairbanks and Anchorage expanded rapidly to become the urban centers of postwar Alaska. Fairbanks grew from a gold mining settlement to a military center, the construction base for the trans-Alaska pipeline, and the home of the nation's northernmost university. Anchorage mushroomed into an international aerial crossroads for the jet age and recovered rapidly from the mammoth earthquake of 1964 to continue as Alaska's premier port. The Cold War rivalry between the United States and the USSR was demonstrating Alaska's strategic importance through a series of defense-installation construction booms and an enlarging military presence. Massive airfields, military bases, earth-based radar outposts along DEW lines (distant early warning) to detect strategic bombers, BMEWS (ballistic missile early warning systems), satellite monitoring networks for intercontinental missiles, naval bases, and coast guard stations, testified fearsomely to the nation's dependence on Alaska against the Soviet Union, America's recent ally.[12]

Three new issues now arose: statehood, aboriginal land claims, and oil. On January 3, 1959, the noncontiguous Territory of Alaska entered the Union as the forty-ninth state after years of dependency and frustration. Hawaii was admitted later the same year as the fiftieth state to conclude the balancing act in which President Dwight D. Eisenhower and Congress had engaged themselves for several years.

Although statehood was predicted for Alaska as early as 1869, by William Seward on visiting Sitka, no one realized it would take eighty-nine years. In 1916, Alaska's congressional delegate, James Wickersham, had introduced the first enabling measure. President Harding had declared in 1923 that the territory was destined for ultimate statehood, possibly in segments beginning with the panhandle, but Harding's partitioning idea failed, as did the separationist movement it encouraged. The outbreak of war in Europe in 1939 and Alaska's spectacular wartime development launched the territory toward statehood. Yet Congressman John Rooney (D–NY) reflected the continuing skepticism at Alaska's readiness. He charged that absentee fishing and mining interests controlled the legislature. Any citizenry, in his opinion, who allowed a major industry such as salmon fishing to take out about $60 million a year and retained only $1 million in taxes was not ready for self-government. So, in spite of nationally favorable public opinion polls and energetic lobbying year after year by Governor Ernest Gruening and Delegates Anthony J. Dimond (1933–1944) and Bob Bartlett (1944–1958), the statehood issue languished. At last, in July 1957, President Eisenhower announced his readiness for Alaskan statehood. Speaker of the House Sam Rayburn, a longtime foe of statehood for Alaska, changed his stance at Bartlett's urging, and Eisenhower, in January 1958, lent his full backing for the first time. At a critical moment, Hawaii's delegate, Jack Burns, helped the Alaska cause by urging the separation of the two statehood bills. The long contest had ended. President Eisenhower signed the Alaska statehood measure into law on July 7, 1958, and proclaimed the official entry of the forty-ninth state into the Union on January 3, 1959. The first forty-nine-star flag was raised on July 4, 1959, at Sitka, where the first American flag to fly over Alaska had been raised in 1867. The new flag was raised by a color guard, as the first Stars and Stripes had been, from the Ninth (now known as the "Manchu") Infantry. By far the Union's largest state, Alaska possesses an area in excess of 375 million acres, more than twice the size of Texas.

The federal government, which owned 99.8 percent of Alaska's land as statehood commenced, now gave the State of Alaska the authority to select 103,350,000 acres from the unassigned public domain for its own development over the twenty-five years to come. Next, in 1971, Congress passed the Alaska Native Claims Settlement Act, known as ANCSA. To extinguish their long-standing claims based on aboriginal rights, the Indians, Eskimos, and Aleuts of Alaska obtained legal title from Congress to forty million acres, compensation in addition amounting to $962.5 million ($462.5 million in federal appropriations and the balance from mineral revenues sharing), and the governing authority to form twelve regional corporations for administering this complex settlement. The secretary of the interior was empowered also to withdraw eighty million acres from the remaining public domain in Alaska for study and possible inclusion in national parks, forests, wildlife preserves, and scenic or wild river systems. The 1968 Prudhoe Bay discovery of a 9.6 billion barrel deposit of recoverable petroleum resources was followed by the opening of the Trans-Alaska Pipeline System (TAPS) in 1977, a hot-oil pipeline descending across eight hundred miles of wilderness from the North Slope on the Arctic seacoast southward to Valdez on Prince William Sound in the Gulf of Alaska. Alongside the pipeline, northwest from Fairbanks, the North Slope Haul Road, more than four hundred miles long, was constructed to Point Barrow on Prudhoe Bay, though this artery remains closed to public traffic. The pipeline led to still another boom for Alaska, the greatest in its history, and inevitably to a postboom bust as world oil prices fell and prosperity gave way to reduced circumstances. One fact was certain, the Great Land's colonial days were over.[13]

Once begun, Alaska's history evolved into a wonderful story of empire. The American purchase of Alaska was the product of Secretary of State William H. Seward's extraordinary zeal for a commercial empire and Czar Alexander I's amazing readiness to unload Russia's North American bridgehead in advancing his Asian and Middle Eastern imperial objectives. Effectively Alaska measures the highwater mark of Russia's eastern thrust and the United States' westward movement. Its sale fixed the boundary in time and space between the twentieth century's superpowers. The boundary held equally through their wartime alliance and their postwar confrontation. Oddly, Alaska's value to the United States remains predominantly economic rather than strategic, except for the military installations against Soviet threats for early warning and instantaneous retaliation. Pacific salmon, halibut, shrimp, crab, furs, timber, gold, silver, copper, petroleum, and other valuable minerals such as mercury, antimony, platinum, tin, lead, tungsten, and molybdenum constitute Alaska's bounty. The growing harvests from freely spending tourists afford Alaska an increasingly important source of revenue. But Alaskan politics at bedrock still arise almost invariably out of the uncompromised differences between exploiters and preservationists concerning the usage of natural resources in the wilderness.

Statehood has realized some of the hopes of Alaska's advocates. Senator Charles Sumner's dream has come true of expanding republican government in the United States, free from Europe's control, to reach to the farthest tip of the continent. For the commercial empire Secretary of State William Henry Seward envisioned, Alaska's role would be to guard the northern flank along the United States' approaches to Asia, while one day an isthmian canal would have to be opened to defend the southern corridor. Seward's oceanic highway for trading with China and Japan would extend directly between Alaska and the canal of the future, from San Francisco to Honolulu and beyond. In 1867, Seward arranged for the United States to take over Midway Island. Acquisition of the Hawaiian Islands would execute his next step. Yet this feat would not be accomplished as quickly as he hoped. Even so, the naval forces to advance the nation's imperial strategy for Asia and the Pacific would before long be based at Pearl Harbor.[14]

E Pele e!
Ke akua o ka pohaku enaena,
Eli'eli kau mai!

E Pele e!
O Goddess of the burning stones,
Let awe possess me!

Ancient Prayer[1]

3

THE HAWAIIAN ISLANDS

The unbroken continuity between modern Hawaii's epochs constitutes a remarkably singular chapter of American history in the Pacific. Nineteenth-century Hawaii before the United States annexation of 1898 was replete with Americans and American influences. Twentieth-century Hawaii after annexation is the history of the Territory and State of Hawaii.

The Hawaiian Islands stand up from the depths of the North Pacific Ocean three thousand miles south of Alaska's Point Barrow, the nation's upper extremity. They are more than two thousand miles from the nearest tip of the American continent, more than two thousand miles from the closest major group of islands still farther to the south, and four thousand miles east of Japan, making them the most isolated archipelago in the world. The Hawaiian Islands, north of the equator, constitute the apex of the Polynesian triangle, with the base's extremities, Easter Island to the east and New Zealand to the west, lying south of the equator. Ka Lae at the bottom of the big island of Hawaii marks the southernmost reach for the United States of America. Of all the fifty states, Hawaii is at once the newest and, in land area alone, among the smallest, though except for Alaska, it offers the greatest contrast to the others. In Mark Twain's oft-quoted recollection, the Hawaiian Islands are "the loveliest fleet of islands that lies anchored in any ocean."[2] Few would disagree.

The islands consist exclusively of the eroded peaks atop gigantic seabed volcanoes rising through tremendous depths. The globe's biggest volcanoes command the island of Hawaii. Snowcapped Mauna Kea is dormant, but Mauna Loa and Kiluea with their smaller offspring are among the world's most active volcanoes. The not-quite-extinct supervolcano Haleakala dominates a large part of the island of Maui. Bleak slopes and foreboding, lava-covered fields testify eloquently to the agony of their creation. The remaining terrain of the islands is characterized by precipitous inland mountains, the extinct or long-dormant volcanoes, with stream-coursed valleys leading down and out to alluvial flatlands and coral reefs scattered here and there in the shallow waters of the coastline. Far below the ocean floor, the earth continues over millions of years to create new surfaces. The shifting eastward of the crust's tectonic plates inexorably opens new rifts for molten magma to erupt from a "hot spot" through the earth's mantle to form new volcanoes and, in time as the peaks emerge, new islands. Coral reefs grow around the islands, enlarging themselves from the accumulated skeletons deposited by animal organisms and calcifying into rock-like barriers. Winds and rains erode these islands back into the sea as their volcanoes become extinct, to leave nothing above the waves ultimately except the familiar reef-encircled atolls of the Pacific Ocean. The Midway Islands (Sand and Eastern) about twelve hundred miles northwest of Honolulu, with their surrounding atoll, are, geologically speaking, the oldest islands in the Hawaiian chain, yet they are uninhabited save for American military and technical personnel.[3]

The Hawaiian Islands were the last Polynesian group and major archipelago in the Pacific Ocean to be encountered by Westerners. Until the nineteenth century, Europeans entered the ocean either by sailing southwest around the tip of South America, or to the southeast around Africa and across the Indian Ocean. The winds and current systems of both hemispheres made voyages incredibly lengthy, curtailing the possibilities for systematic explorations. Even Spain's astonishing failure to discover the Hawaiian Islands was explicable. For two centuries, the sixteenth and seventeenth, Spain's Manila galleons sailed from Acapulco in Mexico south of the islands to the Philippines, then far to the north on the voyage home. Sir Francis Drake crossed the Pacific Ocean from San Francisco Bay to Molucca, Celebes, and Java while circumnavigating the globe (1577–1580), the first Englishman to do so, but without a glimpse of Hawaii. The Dutch routinely entered the western Pacific from the Indian Ocean and the East Indies during the seventeenth century, never even remotely approaching the Hawaiian Islands. In the eighteenth-century Enlightenment, French and British navigators raced each other far into the Pacific Ocean. Their explorations and discoveries appealed to Western appetites for exotic accounts of faraway places. However, extraordinary isolation and the hazards of Pacific voyaging in tiny vessels—shortages of food and water, diseases,

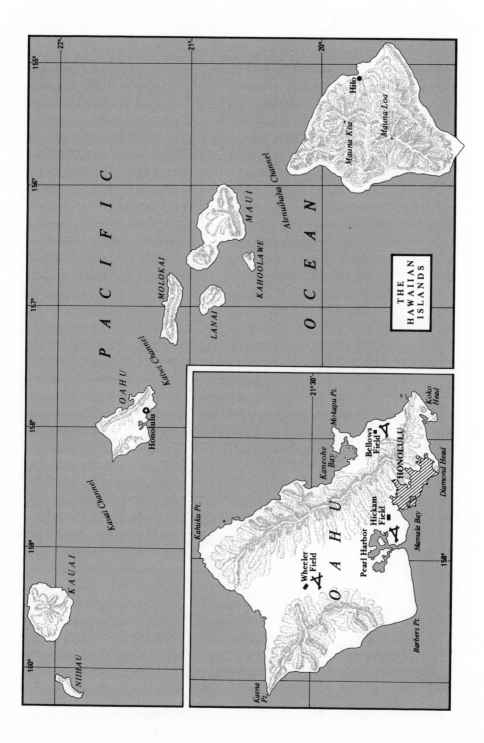

THE
HAWAIIAN
ISLANDS

PACIFIC
OCEAN

155°
156°
157°
158°
159°
160°

22°
21°
20°

KAUAI

NIIHAU

Kauai Channel

OAHU

Honolulu

Kaiwi Channel

MOLOKAI

LANAI

KAHOOLAWE

MAUI

Atenuihaha Channel

Mauna Kea

Mauna Loa

Hilo

OAHU

Kaena Pt.

Kahuku Pt.

Kaneohe Bay

Mokapu Pt.

Koko Head

Bellows Field

HONOLULU

Diamond Head

Hickam Field

Pearl Harbor

Mamala Bay

Wheeler Field

Barbers Pt.

21°30'

158°

uncertain navigating, storms, to mention only a few—left the Hawaiian Islands undiscovered by Westerners until Captain James Cook's third and final voyage of 1778.

Cook's goal was to locate a sea passage from the Pacific to the Atlantic, across the north of the American land mass. It was the age-old search for a Northwest Passage in reverse. One of the greatest adventurers of his or any time, James Cook was the consummate explorer, sailor, navigator, chartmaker, and leader of men. He had already discovered many of the elements for a detailed understanding of the South Pacific. The course for the Society Islands toward North America led him accidentally to the Hawaiian Islands. On January 18, 1778, Cook, with his two ships, HMS *Discovery* and HMS *Resolution*, sighted the three westernmost inhabited islands: Oahu, Kauai, and Niihau. Cook landed at Waimea on Kauai and remained there for a fortnight. While his crews provisioned their vessels, Cook and his senior officers set down the earliest Western descriptions of the Hawaiian natives. Captain Cook named his mid-Pacific discovery the Sandwich Islands after Britain's first lord of the admiralty. Then he sailed away, to spend most of 1778 vainly seeking the sea passage he had been sent to find. He coursed far to the north into Siberian and Alaskan waters. Late in November, after turning south to escape winter's icy clutches, he sighted the eastern islands of the Hawaiian chain, Maui and Hawaii. He spent the last weeks of 1778 and the first of 1779 coasting along the big island of Hawaii searching for the safest and best-supplied anchorage, sheltering finally in Kealakekua Bay. Tragically, this magnificent captain died there on February 14, stabbed to death by angry warriors when an altercation suddenly turned violent over their theft of the *Discovery*'s small boat.

Approximately three hundred thousand Polynesian Hawaiians lived in the islands at the time of Cook's discovery. Their ancestors had found their way centuries before to the Hawaiian Islands from the South Pacific. Linguistic, archaeological, and demographic evidence testifies that the archipelago was populated by two distinct waves of migration. The first arrived from the Marquesas as early as 600 or 700 A.D., the second from the Society Islands around 1100 A.D. Their seagoing, double-hulled canoes mounted a single claw-shaped sail. The double hulls afforded an outrigger's stability, while the sail steered the boats steadily on their course. A platform lashed inboard between the hulls provided living, cooking, and working quarters, with storage space for foods, plants, and domesticated animals. These Polynesian navigators were superior to the other skilled seafarers of their time. Boldly venturing far out onto the vast ocean to seek new homelands, they staked their lives on their familiar knowledge of the sky, the stars, the sun, and the moon, the clouds, the ocean currents and waves, the flights of birds, and sightings of fish and other creatures from the depths. Contact with the southern Polynesian homelands ceased eventually for reasons unknown, and the Hawaiians' culture evolved thereafter isolated from all others.

Hawaiian settlements were ordinarily small and dispersed from valley to valley in wedge-shaped slices of arable land reaching from the sea to the mountain slopes, within which all of life's necessaries could be obtained. Fish and poi, a nourishing paste pounded from taro roots grown in irrigated strips, were the Hawaiian staple foods, supplemented by coconuts, bananas, and other fruits and the flesh of pigs, dogs, and chickens. *Kapu*, or taboo, was the organizing principle of Hawaiian society. There were *kapu* people, places, things, and times. Any profanation of their sacred nature was severely punished by the *kahuna*, or priests. The high chiefs, the all-powerful *alii*, were believed by the people to be in touch with the four principal gods, all male—Ku, Kane, Lono, and Kanaloa. This quartet resembled the deities Polynesians worshiped elsewhere in the Pacific. They controlled all activities in the world they had created. In some temples human sacrifices took place. A detailed code for individual behavior regulated the relationships between Hawaiians and their contemporaries, between their ancestors and themselves, between them and natural forces and the universe at large. No single chief ruled even a single island at the time of Captain Cook's death. But the biological and cultural consequences of the Westerners' discovery of the Hawaiian people were devastating. The native population plummeted in a quarter century from three hundred thousand to just under two hundred thousand, decimated by foreign diseases including smallpox, measles, syphilis, and tuberculosis.[4]

In 1810, King Kamehameha I for the first time united all of the Hawaiian Islands into a single kingdom. Kamehameha (Maiha-Maiha) had been present as a young chief of about twenty-five at Kealakekua when Captain Cook's vessels anchored. He established his power after 1782, at the expense of his cousin Kiwalao, the heir designate, following the death of his aged uncle, King Kalaniopuu. An audacious warrior, Kamehameha aimed at conquest for the next thirteen years. He obtained a decisive arsenal of muskets and small cannons and pressed into his service a pair of English seamen, whose naval and gunnery skills greatly improved his prospects for victory. He swept through the leeward islands in 1790, overwhelming the local chieftains on Maui, Lanai, and Molokai. To seize Oahu in 1775, he commanded an immense, double-pronged fleet of canoes that landed an estimated twelve thousand warriors at Waialae and Waikiki. He trapped the island's defenders into a desperate last stand in Nuuanu Valley, forcing them either to surrender or to leap to their deaths from the precipitous cliffs of Nuuanu Pali. Finally, in 1810, the king of Kauai and Niihau accepted Kamehameha as overlord, completing the unification of the kingdom.

Kamehameha was fated to move the Hawaiian Islands from the Stone Age to the modern world, and before long the islanders' ancient ways were suffering massive changes. His final years found the aging conqueror hospitably welcoming all Honolulu-bound traders and explorers at his compound in Kailua, Hawaii. In 1816, the Russian naval officer Otto von Kotzebue came away most favorably impressed by the English-speaking king's friendliness, Westernized ways, and shrewdness in keeping his chiefs at his side to forestall any possible conspiracy.

Foreigners were arriving by then in swelling numbers, bringing domestic animals and plants previously unknown in the islands and deadly diseases together with alcohol and firearms. They also pressed young men into service to sail away on their ships as deckhands. The Hawaiians now began to die in fearful numbers, lacking immunity against the diseases the newcomers carried, the "future shock" induced by myriad wonders, novel problems, and baffling disappointments. The destruction of traditions and ancient practices brought on a melancholic loss of vitality akin to the dark despair afflicting native Americans on the mainland. An authentic autocrat, Kamehameha maintained the old-style religious and caste structures intact, keeping all the rituals, ceremonies, and *kapus* unaltered, but the common people were fast losing awe of the gods and respect for priests because of the imported customs afflicting them. While Kamehameha lived, however, his followers endured sufferings stoically and venerated their king as Kamehameha the Great, as history knows him.

Kamehameha had many wives; the two most important and influential who survived his death were his favorite wife, Kaahumanu, and the mother of his two sons, Keopuolani. These women quickly persuaded the new king, Liholiho, who ruled as Kamehameha II (1819–1824), to flout the *kapus* by sitting down in defiance of one of the deadliest prohibitions to dine with women. A skepticism about the *kapus* had grown up since Cook's discovery began to undermine the old ways. However, in the light of the *kapu* system's discriminations against women, it is not surprising that, when the attack against *kapus* came, it sprang from the female chiefs. Nor was it any surprise that the instigator was Kaahumanu. A six-foot, three-hundred-pound, strong-willed beauty, she had encouraged her much older husband in his campaigns. She bore him no children, but she managed to dominate the two sons born to the delicate Keopuolani. These succeeded him, in turn, as Kamehameha II and Kamehameha III. Politically ambitious, Kaahumanu next challenged the kingdom's *kapu* that barred her and others of her sex from taking any part in the decision-making councils, which often took place inside the temple enclosures, where no woman was permitted to enter no matter how distinguished her rank. Kaahumanu took to herself half of Kamehameha II's power on his accession, to become the first *kuhina-nui*, or prime minister, an office that would be exercised solely by women until it was abolished in 1866. With the collapse of the *kapu* system, Kaahumanu uninhibitedly exercised political authority.[5]

The comparative nearness of the Hawaiian Islands to the United States led to the rise of American interests that quickly overshadowed those of any of the rival powers, while any major development on the mainland invariably triggered repercussions in the islands. Merchants and sailors from the Atlantic seaboard first landed in Honolulu from the earliest China trading vessels before 1790, and the crews of whalers soon followed. By 1820, in the wake of the peace settlements of 1815, American commercial travelers, seafarers, and Christian missionaries started flocking into the islands to compete with their British and French counterparts for the trade and allegiance of Hawaii's Kanakas, as the Polynesians were generally known throughout the Pacific. The newcomers jostled each other for influence at the royal court of the kingdom's monarchs. The captains of whalers from far distant ports turned for repairing and reprovisioning ships to the sheltered waters at Honolulu on Oahu and Lahaina on Maui, while their crews recuperated after long months at sea. Both the gold rush in 1849 to California and the Civil War of 1861–1865 stimulated the demand on the mainland for fruits, vegetables, meats, and sugar from the Hawaiian Islands. The Civil War especially led to the spectacular growth of Hawaii's cane sugar industry, since the North was cut off from obtaining sugar produced in the South. Inevitably these developments combined forces to stamp Hawaii's social and economic institutions into patterns and shapes that had originated in the United States.

The earliest American missionaries to the Hawaiian Islands were especially important. These men and women were austere and zealous Congregationalists from New England dedicated wholeheartedly to saving lost souls from "the forces of heathenish idolatry." One of their own hymns expressed such hopes:

Soon may the heathen see the light,
Which dawns to close the pagan night,
And say with truth forever more,
Hawaii's Idols are no more.

The first seventeen missionaries sent out by the American Board of Commissioners for Foreign Missions arrived from Boston in the brig *Thaddeus* in 1820, led by the Reverend Hiram Bingham and the Reverend Asa Thurston, both of them trained in theology at Andover, Massachusetts. The Hawaiians had just abolished the age-old *kapu* system and dismantled the sacred temples (*heiaus*) and idols to carry out the drastic reforms of Queen Kaahumanu. Bingham, Thurston, and their cohorts could only credit this fortuitous timing to the direct intervention of the Lord. They promptly began to pronounce the inspired messages of New England's Great Awakening in popular Hawaiian terms, yet conversions came slowly at first. Having discarded their ancient beliefs, the Hawaiians were reluctant to substitute new doctrines for old; they seemed adrift and demoralized. Meanwhile the missionaries built their churches, worked hard, and demonstrated daily the spiritual dedication they carried within themselves. They learned the Hawaiian language and, assisted by the Reverend William Ellis, an English missionary from Tahiti, reduced it phonetically to written form. They established a mission press to publish the Bible and a hymnal in Hawaiian. They brought out a substantial body of literature both sacred and secular, even introducing a Hawaiian-language newspaper. They taught the Hawaiian people to read and write and to sing Christian hymns in their own language.

Cool to the missionaries for a time, Kaahumanu, now queen regent as well as prime minister, underwent a personal conversion after falling ill and being nursed back to fitness with missionary medicine. She became the kingdom's outstanding champion of puritan Protestantism. She became more and more zealous before her death in 1832, to the point of intolerance. She even expelled a number of French Catholic missionaries, severely damaging Hawaii's relations with France, while other Christian churches prospered only after her passing. Her example tipped the scales. Beginning in the late 1820s, a great popular enthusiasm produced mass conversions. Nearly twenty thousand Hawaiians accepted Christianity from 1837 to 1840, and by 1853 at least 30 percent of the population belonged to one Christian church or another. The most important white men in the islands during the twenty-nine-year reign of Kamehameha III (1824–1854) were Hiram Bingham, who had helped to bring in the first missionaries, William Richards, who left the mission to teach the chiefs the elements of Western-style government, and Dr. Gerrit P. Judd, a former missionary, who became the chief minister of the monarchy's government in the 1840s and early 1850s. The conception of enlightened progress for such men was to make over along American lines the kingdom's religion, laws, government, economy, and schools.

Most important, in addition to preaching their gospel of salvation, the missionaries helped the Hawaiian people to absorb the tremendous impacts of Westernization without entirely succumbing. The missionaries rapidly built churches and schools throughout the islands to disseminate their doctrines. By 1831, no fewer than fifty-two thousand pupils were learning to read and write in mission schools in order to uncover and propagate for themselves the principles of the Christian faith, but they were also studying several subjects not directly concerned with religion. Missionaries taught

Western agricultural techniques to develop plantation industries, especially raising rice to feed farm workers and sugar from cane to trade with the world outside. The missionaries undertook the kingdom's first census, and they applied medical skills to help stem the diseases being carried into the islands by the Westerners themselves. On the island of Molokai, the saintly Father Damien (Joseph de Veuster), a Roman Catholic priest from Belgium, devoted his life from 1864 to 1889, until he succumbed himself, to the alleviation of the physical and spiritual misery of Hawaii's lepers.

A number of the missionaries' phobias made them intolerant by anthropologically enlightened standards. Joyful sexual promiscuity on festive occasions and unclothed female breasts at all times startled the New Englanders into fears of suffering God's wrath over the Hawaiians' apparent restaging of original sin and their certain fall from paradise. These customary practices were repressed as quickly as possible. However, in striving to build a Christian community, the missionaries educated the Kingdom of Hawaii to govern itself along legitimate, constitutional lines safe from colonization, recognized by foreign powers, and respected by its own subjects, a considerable achievement in its own time. The missionaries primarily labored to save souls, but they saw themselves, in addition to being modern-day disciples of Jesus, as agents for advancing civilization. One was not possible without the other, in their view. To their detractors, the missionaries "came to do good and did well." But it was a greater glory to them that most of them strove to do good alone. The harm the missionaries did was a harm they could not have comprehended. They preached tirelessly to the Hawaiians about how depraved and ignorant they were as unredeemed sinners. They taught the Hawaiians, who heretofore had entertained no Judeo-Christian notions at all of mankind's inherently evil nature, to bear shame for their nakedness and carefree sexuality. Eventually, the missionaries proclaimed the Hawaiians a Christian nation, their task of conversion completed, but the price was higher for this triumph than anybody could imagine. The Westerners' ravaging diseases—cholera, measles, smallpox, syphilis, and tuberculosis—continued to drive the native population inexorably downward from an estimated three hundred thousand, when Cook discovered the islands to fewer than forty-five thousand a century later. The Hawaiians were fast deteriorating into a maimed race physically on the brink of vanishing altogether, while to the secular-minded they had been tragically deprived at the same time of their essential sense of worth or self-respect by their self-appointed spiritual rescuers. Culturally, demographically, and economically, the stage was set for the Kingdom of Hawaii now to gravitate toward the United States. Yet before 1898, when annexing the islands would be accomplished, American interests would have to tip in balance, away from commerce and whaling to grander strategic matters affecting national destiny, security, and expansion.[6]

In Hawaii, as throughout the Pacific, foreign nationals generally suspected their rivals of ulterior designs. Kamehameha I had complicated the problem in 1794 by his "cession" of the Sandwich Islands, as the archipelago was known on the outside, to Great Britain through his close friend and mediator Captain George Vancouver of the Royal Navy, and he still referred to himself as the "subject" of King George III as late as 1810, more likely for the protection it implied than for any reciprocal commitment. The Russians in Alaska posed an immediate threat from 1814 to 1820. At Alexsandr Baranov's instigation, the Russians turned to the Hawaiian Islands for fresh food supplies. Dr. Georg Anton Scheffer, a German employee of the Russian-American Company, appeared to have won control over the island of Kauai, with ambitions for Oahu as well. Neither his annexationist efforts nor those subsequent received any official backing from Czar Alexander I or court circles in St. Petersburg. In 1838, King Kamehameha III, the last son of Kamehameha the Great to rule, engaged the American missionary William Richards to advise him and the chiefs on affairs of state. A declaration of rights and code of laws was proclaimed the next year and followed by a written constitution in 1840, both actions stemming from the advice of Richards and the missionary party. Also in 1840, the rulers of Hawaii began a diplomatic offensive. As they saw it, their main hope of avoiding colonization such as New Zealand, Tahiti, and the Marquesas were undergoing at the time lay in persuading the United States, Great Britain, and France, the three most interested parties, to join in a common recognition of the kingdom's sovereignty and, if possible, its guarantee.

But the three powers were far from such an accord. French warships had more than once threatened to bombard Honolulu over the Hawaiian monarchy's exclusion of Catholic missionaries, until a declaration of religious toleration made in 1839 at Richards's urging ended the controversy. Then in December 1842, again at Richards's behest, President John Tyler, advised by Sir George Simpson, North American head of the Hudson's Bay Company, and Timothy Haalilio, an able Hawaiian, surprisingly invoked the Monroe Doctrine, which until then had been applied only to the Americas, to warn Britain and France specifically against annexing the Hawaiian Islands. In his formal statement Secretary of State Daniel Webster noted that "a great majority of the vessels visiting the Sandwich Islands were American" and went on to declare:

> The United States, therefore, are more interested in the fate of the islands, and of their government, than any other nation can be; and this consideration induces the President to be quite willing to declare . . . that the Government of the Sandwich Islands ought to be respected; that no power

ought either to take possession of the islands as a conquest, or for the purpose of colonization, and that no power ought to seek for any undue control of the existing Government, or any exclusive privileges in matters of commerce.

Webster's message went to Congress together with information on the recently concluded Opium War and the Treaty of Nanking to direct attention toward Pacific Ocean issues during the debate over sending a mission to the emperor of China. Suddenly news came that the French had seized the Marquesas and imposed a protectorate on Tahiti. To up the ante, Lord George Paulet, commanding HMS *Carysfort*, proclaimed a British protectorate over the Sandwich Islands on his own initiative, which deprived the Hawaiians of their independence between February 25 and July 31, 1843, until the Foreign Office, heeding Tyler's caution, repudiated Paulet's brash act. Happily the disturbance to Anglo-French amity caused by France's action in Tahiti and Britain's in Hawaii facilitated the making of treaties with both powers by the Hawaiians that formally recognized the kingdom's sovereignty and territorial integrity.[7]

The American missionary influence continued to show its strength. The Great Mahele, or land division, of 1848, endeavored to end feudal holdings, reapportion the land among crown, government, chiefs, and commoners, and introduce the Western principle of private title to rights in land. William Richards was one of the first five members appointed to the Land Commission to end the age-old system of land tenure. By 1850, it was lawful for a foreigner to purchase land in fee simple.

Nonetheless great holdings remained, and remain today, in private hands, some to descend over the years into *haole* (nonnative, especially white) ownership or corporate control. One of the world's largest today, the Parker Ranch operates on lands given by Kamehameha I to John Parker of Newton, Massachusetts, in gratitude for his advice and assistance. In 1847, the ranch began employing Spanish-American *vaqueros* from California, or *"paniolos"* as Hawaiians called them, to domesticate the dangerous wild horses and cattle rampaging everywhere, and selling beef to whalers and merchant ships. A revision of the constitution in 1852 broadened the franchise to draw voting eligibility within reach of universal manhood suffrage, although democracy continued to be offset by an upper house of the legislature for hereditary high chiefs and royally appointed nobles. French naval forces repeatedly demonstrated the precarious quality of Hawaiian independence, in one instance seizing the fort at Honolulu and the royal yacht to deliver demands to the king before sailing off. Finance Minister Dr. Gerrit P. Judd was dispatched to Paris via Washington and London to bolster Hawaii's independence. Judd, who took with him the two young princes in line for the crown, gained his major comfort from renewed

American expressions of support. President Zachary Taylor, in his first State of the Union in December 1849, restated the special concern of the United States for Hawaii and opposition to any outside attempt to win control there.

Secretary of State John M. Clayton told Judd that he would "notify France and England that his government will not look with indifference upon any act of oppression committed or any attempt to take the Islands. . . . The U.S. do not want the Islands, but will not permit any other nation to have them." President Millard Fillmore reiterated these sentiments two years later, in emphasizing the magnitude of United States commercial and whaling interests in the Hawaiian Islands, then Fillmore added that "they lie in the course of the great trade which must at no distant day be carried on between the western coast of North America and eastern Asia." King Kamehameha III presented a proclamation to United States Commissioner Luther Severance, to be kept secret unless needed, placing his kingdom under the protection of the United States of America to prevent a French seizure. Lacking any instructions for such a step, Severance could only assure the king that the United States would defend its flag in Hawaii, but he prepared the captain of the USS *Vandalia*, then in Honolulu, for possible action against French forces. In the meantime, instructions reached federal authorities in San Francisco to prevent filibustering adventures from United States soil against Hawaii by the restless crowd of rough-and-ready characters who were disappointedly shifting about after failing to strike riches in California's gold fields.

This threat, if threat it actually was, yielded shortly to the first serious attempt to annex Hawaii to the United States. Talk of annexation was commonplace in Hawaii and California, though Americans in the islands seemed divided on the subject and the missionary counselors to the monarchy were generally opposed. Senator William H. Seward advocated an inquiry into the possibility of obtaining the archipelago for the United States in 1852. Late in 1853, Secretary of State Marcy disavowed, to French and British inquiries, any annexationist plans on his part, but, he stated, "I will not conceal from you that it is highly probable that the Government as well as the Congress and People of the United States would be disposed to receive them." By August 1854, King Kamehameha III had agreed to the draft of a treaty annexing the Hawaiian Islands to the United States as a state "as soon as it can be done in consistency with the principles and requirements of the Federal Constitution," in return for annuities amounting to about $300,000 to be paid him and his principal chiefs. The agreement, which was opposed by Prince Alexander Liholiho, the heir apparent, touched off a tremendous uproar. Warships of four foreign powers appeared in Honolulu Harbor. The British government lodged a formal protest. Opposition to the treaty's terms arose in the Senate, in particular to the annuities and the unprecedented feature of instantaneous statehood. Abruptly, in December 1854, Kamehameha III died. His successor, Alexander Liholiho, the first grandson of Kamehameha the Great to rule, reigned as Kamehameha IV (1854–1863). Although Liholiho had accompanied Judd on his European mission, he and his Queen Emma showed a preference for English and French cultures and a marked hostility toward American influence and missionary tutelage. The new king promptly terminated the annexation negotiations, which, considering the growing likelihood of the treaty's rejection by the Senate, was probably fortunate for future American interests in the islands.[8]

At the same time, William Henry Seward of New York moved to the center of the stage. His vision of empire laid down over the next two decades, as United States senator and secretary of state, would shape American foreign policy for a century. A higher law, a law of Providence, Seward believed, had already propelled empire steadily westward for three thousand years from its Old World cradles across Europe and America, and its force must continue unchecked into the Pacific Ocean region and Asia. Seward's calculated endeavors to assist Providence on the westward course were to be frustrated for a decade or so by the Civil War, yet he would never lose sight of his farthest horizons. His goal was to prepare his country methodically for its imperial destiny. The contest for world power, he was convinced, would be won or lost in Asia one day, after commerce had brought the hemispheres together. The American empire must be launched from its internal bastions of economic might, then it must move by stages across the stepping stones of the Pacific to approach the final triumph in Asia. As Seward urged his fellow senators in 1853:

> Open up a highway through your country from New York to San Francisco. Put your domain under cultivation, and your ten thousand wheels of manufacture in motion. Multiply your ships, and send them forth to the East. The nation that draws most materials and provisions from the earth, and fabricates the most, and sells the most of productions and fabrics to foreign nations, must be, and will be, the great power of the earth.

Seward was equally certain that his continental bastion would in time incorporate Canada, Mexico, and Central America. It would be opened up by an isthmian canal linking the Atlantic and Pacific oceans, and it would be protected by American-controlled Caribbean islands on one flank and Alaska on the other. Mexico City, he considered, might serve suitably for the capital of the new empire because of its splendid location. Grandiose though his vision, Seward anticipated many of his countrymen, who, before the end of the century, would spell out the far-flung particulars of America's spreadeagle destiny across the Pacific. Hawaii, of course, afforded the next step.[9]

Economic changes ushered in a dramatic train of events. Whaling was being drastically diminished by the maritime disturbances of the Civil War, while the substitution of petroleum for a great many of whale oil's uses brought that industry to the point of extinction. The rapid growth of California's markets and the Union blockage of the Confederacy's sugar output stimulated the Hawaiian Islands' sugar industry to expand just as the whaling ships and their crews were vanishing from the ports of Honolulu and Lahaina. This extraordinary opportunity for the sugar industry commenced just as the Western-introduced killer diseases were reducing the Hawaiian people to the point of predictable extinction. The decline of their numbers signified that the sugar cane fields would more than likely lack the labor essential to work them. A shipload of Chinese "coolies," imported in 1852, marked the first effort to obtain adequate supplies of labor for the plantations.[10]

Large, though unrecorded, numbers of Chinese had already entered California on the way to the gold fields. There they were put to work in the mines, on construction jobs, at makeshift manufacturing, and in agriculture. Almost exclusively they were young male sojourners, whose intentions were to send money home and to return to China themselves one day. An individual Chinese man had been noticed in Kamehameha I's retinue at Kealakekua Bay in 1794, and legend has it that another Chinese male living on Lanai was crushing cane and boiling sugar in 1802. Between 1852 and 1856, several thousand "coolies" were introduced under contract to labor on the Hawaiian plantations. There were 6,045 Chinese counted in the islands in 1878, and 18,254 by 1884. A majority were Cantonese from the Pearl River delta near Macao, the focus of China's trade with the West. A sizeable minority came from villages close to Hong Kong. Speaking quite different dialects, the two groups communicated with each other in the Hawaiian language learned while toiling together in the sugar cane fields. By the terms of the Burlingame Treaty of 1868, initiated by Secretary of State Seward to gain cheap labor and the competitive advantage its products would bring, Chinese and Americans gained the right to migrate into each other's country and become naturalized citizens on the same basis as immigrants from the most favored nations. As soon as they fulfilled their indentures, most of the Chinese rushed off to Honolulu and smaller towns, where many opened small businesses and took Hawaiian wives, while the others pocketed their hard-earned savings to sail home to China.

The number of sugar cane plantations grew rapidly as sugar prices rose. In spite of the entry tariff that had to be paid at American ports, the Civil War proved to be a bonanza for Hawaii's sugar producers. Chinese workers were imported to clear and till the red volcanic earth in place of the dwindling number of Kanakas available. By 1866, Hawaii was exporting nearly eighteen million pounds of sugar, mostly to the United States, compared to only one and one-half million pounds six years earlier. Life was hard in the cane fields. Disobedience by a worker could be punished by imprisonment and forced labor. New varieties of cane superseded the original brought centuries earlier by the Polynesian settlers. New techniques of cultivating, harvesting, and milling were developed. To carry water to dry but fertile soils, tunnels were dug through mountains, and trestles and ditches were constructed for irrigating the expanding acreage under cultivation. The plantation villages were isolated settlements ordinarily remote from other towns or cities and surrounded by extensive cane fields. Mill structures dominated the small houses of the workers and their families. Mark Twain, on tour in 1866, exclaimed in amazement at the surpassing wonder of Hawaii's fertile land when put to growing sugar cane, "a land which produces six, eight, ten, twelve, yea, even thirteen thousand pounds of sugar to the acre on unmanured soil!" But the end of the Civil War threatened the profitability of Hawaiian sugar by reviving Southern production.

Therefore, to secure the sugar market for Hawaii's output became the cardinal feature of the kingdom's policy. To obtain a treaty of commercial reciprocity with the United States was the obvious answer. Sugar quickly became intertwined with Seward's larger strategy. While American planters generally favored proposals to ship Hawaiian sugar duty-free into United States markets in return for privileged access for certain American goods in the Hawaiian market, the undeveloped port capability of Pearl Harbor was a naval commander's dream. Seward attempted to conclude a reciprocity treaty with the islands, but his efforts succumbed to the squabbling in Washington over Reconstruction. President Grant's secretary of state, Hamilton Fish, finally concluded a reciprocity pact in 1875 for reasons that were remarkably like Seward's in design. Fish hoped to ward off any possible British threat to American traffic with the Far East by acquiring in the Hawaiian Islands "a resting spot in the mid-ocean between the Pacific Coast and the vast domains of Asia."

Under the treaty's terms, the United States virtually handcuffed Hawaii to the American economy. Hawaiian sugar could enter the United States duty-free provided Hawaii did not cede any of its territory to another power. The treaty immediately benefited the Hawaiian sugar growers and American refiners, especially refiners in California, while keeping sugar prices high to consumers. Sugar planting spread everywhere, surging over rice fields and taro patches. About twenty sugar plantations were evident in

1875, sixty-three five years later. "So ends the year 1876, praise God!" the head of C. Brewer & Company, one of the major sugar agencies, wrote in closing the firm's books. In 1877, Claus Spreckels, an unscrupulous San Francisco refiner, "cornered," or monopolized, the Hawaiian sugar crop. Spreckels next bought himself a position of extraordinary power over the imperious King Kalakaua (1874–1891) by lending great sums of money to the free-spending monarch. Going so far as to meddle in Samoan affairs, Kalakua dreamed of ruling a Polynesian empire himself with the Hawaiian Islands at its head. Between them, the pair nearly bankrupted the royal treasury before Spreckels left the islands.[11]

At the same time, strategic motives resurfaced. The change from considerations of commerce to considerations of political advantage was foreseeable. Edward McCook, the United States minister to the Kingdom of Hawaii, had written to Secretary Seward in 1867: "When the Pacific railroad is completed and the commerce of Asia directed to our Pacific ports, then these islands will be needed as a rendezvous for our Pacific navy and a resort for merchant ships." Major General John M. Schofield and Brevet Brigadier B. S. Alexander visited the islands on a confidential mission for the War Department and reported to Secretary William W. Belknap on the strategic and commercial potential of Pearl Harbor.

Reciprocity was helping the planters in Hawaii more than the commercial interests, as the drop in tariff revenues testifed. A number of merchants were restlessly reawakening their British connections. Secretary of State James G. Blaine, himself fast becoming expert at twisting the lion's tail, warned the British explicitly in 1881 to stay out of Hawaii, for, as Blaine put it, the islands were now a "part of the American system of states, and a key to the North Pacific trade." In 1887, the reciprocity treaty was renewed, and this time Hawaii conceded to the United States the naval rights for Pearl Harbor as a coaling station and repair base. Aroused, Great Britain appealed in vain for Hawaiian neutrality and a commercial open door to the kingdom's markets for all nations. President Grover Cleveland declared that the Hawaiian Islands outpost was "the stepping-stone to the growing trade of the Pacific" and that "America's commercial competitors" could never be allowed on Hawaii's "valuable ground." Secretary of State Thomas F. Bayard, borrowing John Quincy Adams's classic analogy, followed through in 1888, stating that the United States had only "to wait quietly and patiently and let the islands fill up with American planters and industries until they should be wholly identified with the United States. It was simply a matter of waiting until the apple should fall." Bayard did more to further American policy in the Pacific than await a Newtonian harvest. He and his successors won a significant share of the Samoan Islands for the United States.

The United States already held numerous pieces of territory beyond the

Hawaiian Islands. In 1856, during the craze that swept American agriculture for applying guano, or sea fowl excrement, as a fertilizer, Congress had enacted the "Guano Law" empowering the President to take over guano-rich islands in the Pacific and absorb them as "appertaining to the United States." Some fifty became "appurtenances" by 1880, most of them uninhabited volcanic islets, among them Howland, Baker, and Johnston islands. Guano would acquire an added importance later on as a source of phosphates, nitrates, and potassium for high explosives; later still, before the jet age, certain of the nation's guano islands would function as airstrips for transpacific flights. The United States Navy occupied Midway Island in 1867, but the coral atoll's lagoon bottom proved undredgeable, disappointing strategists' hopes for a deep anchorage far out in the Pacific Ocean.

Farther away below the equator, the Samoan Islands, a group of fourteen inhabited islands lying fifteen hundred miles southwest from Honolulu and four thousand miles from San Francisco, had enticed shipping and naval interests along the route from California to Australia ever since Lieutenant Wilkes's expedition surveyed them in 1839. A treaty concluded in 1872 between Commander Richard W. Meade, USN, and the local chiefs awarded exclusive privileges to the United States for the splendid harbor at Pago Pago. But the pact failed to win Senate approval in spite of the efforts of Henry A. Pierce, the United States minister to the Hawaiian kingdom, to impress all within earshot with the future value of the Samoan Islands. Then in 1878, after a goodwill visit to Washington by a Samoan prince, an agreement to similar purpose was negotiated and ratified. Not only did the United States gain the anchorages it sought, but it also acquired diplomatic good offices between the Samoan chiefs and the other Western powers.

The treaty with Samoa was soon put to a test. Germany was picking up colonies in the western Pacific in a belated race for empire. Already the strongest economic power in the Samoan Islands, Germany was attempting in 1889 altogether to dislodge the United States and Great Britain. Congress voted $500,000 to protect Americans and their Samoan property and another $100,000 to strengthen the naval station at Pago Pago. Warships of the three powers converged on the archipelago, and talk of war was rife. In the nick of time, a devastating typhoon struck Samoa and wrecked all but one of the warships sent there by the three contending powers. Resorting to diplomacy in June 1889, the Germans, led by Chancellor Otto von Bismarck, the British, and the Americans conferred in Berlin and formulated a tripartite protectorate over Samoa. But friction persisted throughout the ensuing decade, until Germany and the United States agreed to divide the islands between them. Great Britain received the Gilbert Islands and the Solomon Islands from Germany as compensation. The United States acquired Pago Pago and the surrounding region. Robert Louis Stevenson, who was living in Tahiti, derided the entire affair as a "furor consularis," a comic opera with threatening overtones. Walter Q. Gresham, Cleveland's secretary of state, worried over his country's unprecedented foreign entanglements far away in the South Pacific. Well might he worry. John Bassett Moore, who was third assistant secretary during the Berlin conference, reviewed the affair and realized its special importance: "There is no incident in the history of the United States that better prepares us to understand the acquisition of the Philippines, than the course of the government toward the Samoan Islands." He subsequently added: "The significance of the Samoan incident lies not in the mere division of territory, but in the disposition shown by the United States long before the acquisition of the Philippines, to go to any length in asserting a claim to take part in the determination of the fate of a group of islands, thousands of miles away, in which American commercial interests were so slight as to be scarcely appreciable." It was their strategic consideration that determined the islands' fate, as Moore knew, and it continues to do so almost a century later. The unincorporated territory of American Samoa consists of the six eastern islands; Pago Pago, the capital, is on the island of Tutuila. American Samoa was governed by the United States Navy until 1951, when the Department of Interior took over. Western Samoa, by contrast, became an independent nation in 1962 and is a member of the Commonwealth of Nations.[12]

Samoa notwithstanding, Hawaii was the key to America's Pacific interests. Captain Alfred Thayer Mahan, USN, one of the most influential strategists, identified Hawaii centrally with the security of the United States. Hawaii would be central also to the defense of the as yet unbuilt isthmian canal, which, Mahan argued, was essential for the future of the American republic. The nation's security was being threatened, Mahan observed in 1890, by the current political unrest in the Caribbean, notably in Cuba and Central America, as well as in Hawaii. Hawaii and the canal in American hands were necessities of national well-being.

In Hawaii, the blessings expected from renewing reciprocity scarcely had an opportunity to emerge. Dominant business interests included a growing number of annexationists, who believed the Hawaiians incapable of self-government, exemplified by King Kalakaua's pretentiously corrupt reign, or too inept to protect their property and profits. Led by Lorrin A. Thurston, an attorney and newspaper publisher descended from one of the earliest missionaries, the *haole* establishment of white American planters and businessmen organized the Hawaiian League and militantly readied the members for revolution. After a mass meeting on June 30, 1887, with a brandishing of weapons, King Kalakaua accepted the league's framework for government, the "Bayonet Constitution," which severely limited his powers and disfranchised perhaps three out of every four native Hawaiians by its property qualifications for voting. In July 1889, angry Hawaiian natives staged an insurrection unsuccessfully, hoping to overthrow Kalakaua and install his sister Princess Liliuokalani to restore the power of the monarchy. His health declining, Kalakaua went to California, leaving Liliuokalani as regent in his place. The king suffered a stroke in San Francisco, dying there on January 20, 1891.

Meanwhile, the effects of the new McKinley tariff of 1890 were destroying Hawaiian prosperity by abandoning reciprocity. Reciprocity had brilliantly tied the islands' economy to the United States and prevented, in the language of the 1875 treaty, "any other great power from securing a foothold there." Sugar from the Hawaiian Islands now lost its duty-free status to an outburst of protectionism, while sugar from Louisiana and other former Confederate states on the mainland won a bounty of two cents per pound to encourage homegrown production. The shattering effects of the new tariff on Hawaii's one-crop economy increased the annexationist sentiments of the planters, who were unhappily flailing about to regain the privileged American market they were losing. Tensions heightened perceptibly as Liliuokalani became queen in 1891. An imperious monarch, she was outspokenly determined to regain, through a policy of "Hawaii for the Hawaiians," the royal power her brother had relinquished. The Americans of the islands were equally determined to prevent this ever happening. In 1892, a secret Annexationist Club was formed in Honolulu; its ranks included Lorrin A. Thurston and another descendent of missionaries, Sanford B. Dole. Both President Benjamin Harrison's secretary of the navy, Benjamin F. Tracy, and the new secretary of state, John W. Foster, assured Thurston of their support for annexation.

Liliuokalani cast the fateful die herself on January 14, 1893, when she prorogued the legislature in session and proclaimed her intention to promulgate a new constitution restoring the powers of the monarchy. A self-proclaimed Committee of Safety immediately formed a provisional revolutionary government. Its adherents armed themselves and took over the streets of Honolulu. United States Minister John L. Stevens commanded armed sailors to land from the cruiser USS *Boston* in Honolulu Harbor on January 16, ostensibly to protect American lives and property. Few shots were heard. No life was lost. No matter; within three days, the Hawaiian monarchy was at an end. American intervention had been crucial to its overthrow. Sanford B. Dole took the helm of the provisional government, hoping for early annexation. But Queen Liliuokalani yielded her authority only "until such time as the Government of the United States shall, upon the facts presented to it, undo the action of its representatives and reinstate me in the authority which I claim as the constitutional sovereign of the Hawaiian Islands."

For a time, it looked as if her claim might be realized. A treaty of annexation went off to the Senate, though the outgoing Harrison administration lacked time and strength enough to win its approval. President Grover Cleveland, back in office for his second term, withdrew the treaty from the Senate pending a thorough consideration of the circumstances and sent James H. Blount of Georgia, a former congressman, as a special commissioner to investigate the revolution and its outcome. Blount's findings convinced Cleveland that Minister Stevens's forcible intervention had guaranteed the revolution's triumph. Cleveland tried in vain to restore Liliuokalani to her throne. The provisional government held firm. On July 4, 1894, it brought a new constitution into effect, proclaiming the birth of the Republic of Hawaii, and designated Sanford B. Dole as president. Cleveland, comprehending that he would have to employ force to restore the monarchy, recognized the republic, but he spurned its appeals for annexation. In 1897, under President William McKinley, a new annexation treaty was endorsed, but the Senate rejected it, reflecting the members' mixed reactions to the country's spectacularly expanding imperialism.

The victory of the United States in the Spanish-American War reversed the public temper. Commanded by Commodore George Dewey (soon to be made admiral), the navy's Asian Squadron sank Spain's Pacific fleet at Manila Bay in the Philippine Islands on May 1, 1898. Overnight Hawaii's strategic importance became obvious. Congress rushed through a joint resolution to take control of the Hawaiian Islands unilaterally. President McKinley signed his approval on July 7, 1898, making the islands "a part of the territory of the United States," the first sizeable acquisition overseas.

Joyfully the *Pacific Commercial Advertiser* featured H. M. Whitney's improvement on Francis Scott Key:

> And the star-spangled banner
> In triumph shall wave
> O'er the Isles of Hawaii
> And the homes of the brave.

On August 12, 1898, the Hawaiian anthem, "Hawaii Ponoi," sounded its last official notes. The Hawaiian flag was pulled down, and the American flag formally went up in its place at the Government Building, formerly Iolani Palace. That manifest destiny had proved itself seaworthy was surprising perhaps, but it was unmistakably clear.[13]

No great changes disrupted everyday life at first. The commercial and naval importance of the islands had made the American flag a familiar sight to most Hawaiians. American economic interests had long dominated the economy. The laws of the Hawaiian republic, which were based to a large extent on American statutes and jurisprudence, were approved to continue in force until Congress superseded them with organic legislation of its own making. During the debate over annexing the Hawaiian Islands, Senator Henry Cabot Lodge of Massachusetts had promised his colleagues that the nation's new possession would assuredly become another state in time, notwithstanding its watery detachment. The antiimperialists directed their major attacks against retaining the Philippines.

Hence, an organic act was passed in 1900 to create the Territory of Hawaii. The hearings held on the measure made it clear that Congress was trying to avoid creating an exploitative plantation colony like Spanish Cuba or Puerto Rico. Yet the Supreme Court was soon defining a middle position in its rulings for the newly acquired Hawaiian Islands, and, as in late nineteenth-century Indian policy, the justices had to face the problem of whether the republic could legitimately govern alien subjects against their will. In deferring to the presidential and congressional view of the constitutionality of annexation, the Supreme Court upheld American imperialism. The Court outlined an anomalous position for the human beings involved as lying somewhere between citizenship and alienage, while it rejected arguments that the inhabitants of an annexed territory had no rights of their own that the government was bound to respect. Ultimately, the Court applied or refused to apply certain guarantees of the Bill of Rights to territorial possessions depending on its judgment of whether or not the territory was incorporated into the United States of America. For Hawaii and the Philippines, the Court denied that a grand-jury indictment and trial by a petit jury of twelve good men and true were required, because it held that these places were unincorporated territories (such indictments and trials were required in Alaska, as earlier noted, because Alaska was ruled to be incorporated). The Pacific strategists of 1898 had won their coveted Pearl Harbor and could now go for the isthmian canal to link America's coasts by water. The struggle was just beginning over the full and equal participation of the Hawaiian Islands in the American political system. In any event, Sanford B. Dole, the revolutionary president of the Hawaiian Republic, was appointed to become the first governor of the Territory of Hawaii under American rule.[14]

For the next forty years, Hawaii's political and social life would accurately reflect the islands' economy, which functioned steadfastly almost as one big plantation with a clearcut hierarchy of labor organized by race and nationality. Asians worked the fields and the mills. Ownership and management were controlled by white men. The Republican party dominated politics. The Republican party in the islands was a party of white men, and it had the backing of the Hawaiian and part-Hawaiian population, an alliance that was patently an anti-Oriental coalition. Through the decades from 1900 to the Second World War, the maintenance of these arrangements was not difficult. Even though immigrants dominated the population figures,

Asians among them were ineligible for citizenship, unable even to register to vote.

It has been charged that the annexation movement was nothing more than a byproduct of the Hawaiian sugar industry, yet the industry depended on plentiful infusions of Asian laborers, contrary to the preference for Europeans on the mainlands. After the anti-"coolie" outbursts of the 1870s and the hardening of prejudice against them, Chinamen were barred as immigrants altogether in 1882, and the ban became permanent until after the Second World War. The Hawaiian Islands were not affected by American restrictions until annexation took place. However, as annexation loomed as a possibility in the 1890s, the plantation owners made haste to import as many Asian laborers as they could before American prohibitions took effect. In 1885, under the Meiji restoration, Japan began to permit its subjects to emigrate, so the importation of Japanese laborers into Hawaii and California commenced in earnest. There were more than sixty thousand Japanese in the Hawaiian Islands by 1900, when United States law became definitive. The rise of anti-Japanese feelings on the West Coast culminated in the exclusionist Gentlemen's Agreement of 1907 and the Root-Takahira Agreement of 1908. Even afterward, Japanese continued to arrive in Hawaii and California, mostly women as "picture brides," until passage of the National Origins Act of 1924 virtually barred them. By 1920, almost 43 percent of the population of the Hawaiian Islands was Japanese. Not until the McCarran-Walter Immigration Act of 1952 lifted the barriers against Asians by establishing quotas for them, and the amendments of 1965 abolished both quotas and numerical limits for Asians, could any Chinese or Japanese lawfully immigrate into the United States without extraordinary dispensations.

The plantation owners finally found the numbers of workers they required for their labor-intensive sugar and pineapple fields from the Philippine Islands, which, very conveniently for their purposes, had fallen under American domination as a result of the United States victory over Spain in 1898. More then 120,000 Filipinos, males constituting the overwhelming majority, were brought into the Hawaiian Islands as contract laborers between 1907 and 1941, Tagalogs, Viscayans, and Llocanos, peasants one and all. Smaller contingents of other peoples swelled the totals. Between 1878 and 1887, 17,500 Portuguese contract field hands had arrived, mostly from the Madeira and Azores islands in the Atlantic Ocean, just as the Chinese were being turned aside. The Portuguese demanded higher wages than the Chinese and reputedly were less submissive. About 8,000 Koreans were imported as contract laborers between 1903 and 1906. When their country passed under Japan's control in 1907, the flow was halted, picture brides excepted, by the terms of the Gentlemen's Agreement. Puerto

Ricans were imported also, some 5,200 between 1900 and 1901 and 10,000 by 1950. A scattering of Polynesian Mormons came from Samoa before 1950. They were followed by an outpouring of 13,000 more Samoans by 1980, who largely were the displaced civilian personnel from a former United States Navy base on Tutuila and their families.

Over the years the labor policies of the great plantation companies created the demographic dynamics of the islands. Hawaiian society was the product of the magnates who ran the sugar industry and its offshoot, the pineapple industry. Power became concentrated in a handful of companies and their interlocking family directorates. The five major plantation companies were rooted in early trading ventures, but their fortunes pyramided as agencies for sugar production: Castle & Cooke, Alexander & Baldwin, C. Brewer & Company, American Factors (AMFAC), and Theo. H. Davies. A sixth, the Dillingham Corporation, rivaled the other five in size and strength, but it was not itself a sugar producer or agency.[15]

Commercial pineapple raising began about the middle of the nineteenth century at Kailua-Kona on the big island of Hawaii, not far from the spot where Captain Cook died. An early variety failed in West Coast markets due to its high spoilage rate. In 1899, James D. Dole, a Boston-born distant relative of Sanford B. Dole, established a plantation on Oahu's central plain, planting the variety of pineapple known as "Smooth Cayenne," which is still the standard type grown today, and he also opened a cannery next to his fields. Dole formed the Hawaiian Pineapple Company in 1901, and six years later he organized the Pineapple Growers Association of Hawaii, involving two mainland firms as well, to coordinate research, advertising, and marketing. Although sugar virtually sold itself as a staple grocery, pineapples had to be advertised to gain entry into the average household. Hawaii became known in the popular mind as a cornucopia brimming with exotic fruits and flowers, in large part because of pineapple advertising. More and more growers and canners entered the industry as public demand soared for the golden fruit. Libby, McNeill & Libby and the California Packing Corporation developed large pineapple plantations on Molokai and Maui. Dole's industry-leading Hawaiian Pineapple Company purchased the entire island of Lanai, to expand production in 1922, for slightly more than a million dollars. When Dole went broke in the Depression, he lost control to the sugar agency of Castle & Cooke. His company at the time was producing 40 percent of the combined pineapple and juice output of the territory and one-third of the world's consumption. By 1933, the pineapple had developed into the islands' second-largest staple food after sugar. The Pineapple Growers Association worked hand in glove with the Hawaiian Sugar Planters' Association to set labor and immigration policies. The pineapple growers and planters had hired surplus labor from the sugar plantations at first. Later the sugar association recruited labor for the pineapple industry on a fixed fee basis per laborer provided.

The Big Five sugar agencies were taking over Hawaii's economy, including the pineapple industry. The Big Five controlled 75 percent of the sugar crop in 1910, and 96 percent by 1933. They extended their influence through networks of interlocking directorates to dominate every enterprise associated with sugar and pineapples: banking, insurance, utilities, wholesale and retail merchandising, railroads, and shipping.

An oligarchy of blood and wealth had succeeded the monarchy. The names turning up on boards of directors and public commissions in governing authority were those of the missionary families of the nineteenth century. Every one of the Big Five had at least one director on its board directly descended from a missionary, and Alexander & Baldwin had six. Moreover, the missionary names—Judd, Wilcox, Dole, Damon, Thurston, Hall, and Chamberlain—appeared on the boards of every important firm doing business at Honolulu, while their relatives by marriage—Athertons, Frears, Tenneys, Galts, Waterhouses, and others—served with the "mission boys." Even Walter F. Dillingham, the "Big Sixth," the most powerful businessman in the islands in the twenties and thirties, was related to the missionaries through his mother. The major problem of Hawaii's oligarchy was to obtain and hold enough arable land for the plantations. Less than 10 percent of Hawaii's land is suitable for agriculture, and it is chronically subject to popular pressures for other usage. Yet the 1930 census showed that the *haoles*, either through corporations or as individuals, owned or managed 2.6 million acres, more than 16 times the acreage controlled by Hawaiians or part-Hawaiians, 45 times the holdings of Japanese-Americans, and more than 140 times the amount held by Chinese-Americans. Their control of the land afforded the mechanism for the members of Hawaii's oligarchy to conserve and expand its near-monopoly over the wealth of the islands for forty years.[16]

The oligarchy's domination of the economy was paternalistic. Plantation labor in Hawaii made higher wages than anywhere else in the world. Strikes of sugar workers in 1909 and 1920 had improved working conditions, but the colony-like nature of the plantations guaranteed that exploitation of the laborers would characterize their conditions of employment. In 1924, Pablo Manlapit led three thousand sugar workers of the Filipino Higher Wages Movement out on strike. Violence flared. The national guard came. Sixty strikers went to jail. Manlapit himself was banished from the islands. His was the last significant strike for many years. Even though the racial balance in the sugar and pineapple industries was shifting in favor of Filipinos away from the fecund Japanese, who were moving into towns of their own to launch industries or businesses, the tempo of plantation life appeared still to be defined by the daily routine of work and rest altered only by the changing seasons for planting and harvesting. For Filipinos and Koreans, life was simple. It was field work on an hourly, daily, or contractual basis. A Japanese might rise to supervise the field workers at close hand. A Portuguese might oversee the hours worked and the accountable results. Managerial jobs invariably were held by white men, who comprehended Western ways and lines of command. Only in the towns did the pace of change accelerate. The number of Japanese on the plantations dropped from thirty thousand to ten thousand from 1902 to 1932, which signified that more than one hundred thousand were living in towns by the Great Depression.

During the 1920s and 1930s, three powerful forces began to undermine Hawaii's outwardly unchanging ways. The first was the popularization of the Hawaiian Islands on the mainland as a subtropical paradise within easy reach. Tourist and pineapple promotional advertising familiarized Americans with Hawaii's exotic charms. Brown-skinned, barefoot men and women in grass skirts and floral leis danced the once-forbidden hulas to intoxicating rhythms for newsreel cameras to sell the romance of the islands throughout the mainland. The volcano Mauna Loa erupted spectacularly, if not always on cue, then sporadically at least and always on film. "Hawaii Calls," the radio program, reached millions of listeners thousands of miles away who thrilled to the haunting sounds of the surf at Waikiki and the melodies of "Sweet Leilani" and "My Little Grass Shack." Movies completed the job. Hollywood discovered Honolulu's clever detective Charlie Chan. Musicals were perfect against the island setting. A ukelele-strumming crooner and a long-legged tap dancer would fall in love under a gorgeous moon supported by a chorus line of hula dancers, while a band of smiling male musicians in aloha shirts instrumentally accompanied the heartbeats. Every mainlander, or almost, learned to long for Hawaii. Those who could afford the expense sailed from San Francisco to Hawaii aboard the *City of Honolulu* or the Matson Lines' beautiful *Lurline* to dock at the foot of the ten-story-high Aloha Tower and step ashore in Honolulu into earthly paradise. The war in the Pacific from 1941 to 1945 would cancel the tourist influx, of course, but only for the duration.

The second force for change arose from the controversy over Americanizing the Oriental population. The Asian-language schools, to which Chinese and Japanese youngsters were being sent by their parents after regular school hours for supplementary learning in the language and culture of their homelands of origin, were opposed by *haoles* as barriers to the children's education for American acculturation and citizenship. Laws were passed by the territorial legislature to ban such schools. In the lawsuits that followed, the Supreme Court in 1927 affirmed the legality and constitutionality of the schools, infuriating the Americanizers. Even so, the Asian-American children were visibly Americanizing themselves. The anxiety about the Japanese, who were emerging as the most populous single group in the islands, transcended the purely local concerns or diehard racist prejudices, because the expansion of the Japanese Empire onto the Asian continent and in Pacific Ocean regions was becoming perceived in Hawaii as the greatest threat to American interests there. Hawaii's Japanese were a part of a larger picture.

The third force for change was the increasing military importance being assigned by the United States government to the Hawaiian Islands. After the First World War, Pearl Harbor became the home of the Pacific Fleet, the base of the battleships, and Schofield Barracks the biggest army post in the United States. Over fifteen thousand soldiers, sailors, and marines were regularly stationed in Hawaii even during the days of near-disarmament. The armed services were big business in the islands, especially for suppliers, construction companies, and merchants in Honolulu at payday. The development of port facilities, including dredging and drydock construction, ran second in cost only to the Panama Canal in one estimate. Proprietors of small businesses, taxi operators, barbers, tattoo artists, barkeepers, and brothel operators made their annual profits whenever the fleet docked from maneuvers or the soldiers of Schofield invaded the towns. Estrangements persisted between the military and civilian communities, yet each lived symbiotically off the other.

The three forces inexorably converged. The Hawaii that was popularly romanticized in America's hearts and minds, the territory's expanding yet stifled Oriental population, and the military resistance to imperial Japan's Greater East Asia Co-Prosperity Sphere were all on a collision course. The date and time fixed for their encounter was Sunday, December 7, 1941, at 0700 hours. The place was Pearl Harbor.[17]

The Second World War abruptly and drastically changed the Hawaiian Islands, as it did Alaska at the same time, but nowhere in the United States did it introduce greater changes than in Hawaii following the bombing of Pearl Harbor and other military installations. The ruling oligarchy, unchallenged for forty years, was pushed aside within hours of the Japanese attack by military control. At 11:30 A.M. on December 7, 1941, Lieutenant General Walter C. Short proclaimed: "I have this day assumed the position of military governor of Hawaii, and have taken charge of the Territory." Governor Joseph B. Poindexter hoped that the army's rule would not last long, but martial law and military government continued until terminated on October 24, 1944, by President Roosevelt. Throughout the war and again during the Korean and Vietnam conflicts to follow, the Hawaiian Islands served as a major staging and training area for vast American offensives across the Pacific. There was scant possibility that the old plantation society could reassert itself in the face of the tremendous influx of military personnel, businesspeople, workers, tourists, and, above all, fresh ideas. Most evident as a sign was the greater activity and influence of the Asian-American population.

Fear and hysteria against Hawaii's Japanese gripped many islanders after Japan's attack, and a minority blamed the Japanese-Americans in the population for its disastrous consequences. Many Filipinos in the islands blamed Hawaii's Japanese for Japan's conquests in the Philippine Islands, and the Koreans, who had hated the Japanese since their country was annexed by them in 1910, gave expression to their pent-up bitterness. Publication of twelve Japanese newspapers and three magazines was halted, while the *Hawaii Hochi* and *Nippu Jiji* were permitted to continue only with close censorship. To crush the Japanese-language schools, the legislature of the territory threw the baby out with the bath by outlawing the teaching of any foreign language to children under ten years or to those under fifteen whose grades fell below average. Even so, the Japanese in Hawaii, whether aliens or citizens, fared much better than in California and other mainland states, where 110,000 were sent away to remote relocation centers without due regard for their legal rights. The total of internees from Hawaii during the war reached but 1,444, nearly 900 of them aliens, and only 277 were being held at the war's end. Slightly more than a thousand women and children left the islands to join their husbands and fathers in mainland relocation camps.

Eventually the War Department agreed to form a *nisei* combat group of native-born American citizens of Japanese parentage. The 100th Battalion of *nisei* national guardsmen and draftees from Hawaii was activated on June 5, 1942. The following year Hawaii's famous volunteer 442nd Regimental Combat Team was born. The 100th landed at Salerno to commence the bloody fighting that marked its slow progress northward through Italy. The 442nd invaded the beachhead at Anzio, Italy, and later moved to southern France to rescue the "Lost Battalion," mostly Texans, of the 141st Infantry. Between them they took 80 percent of Hawaii's casualties, three times the average of other infantry units. The 442nd became the Army's most decorated unit. Of the seventy-five hundred men on its rolls at one time or another, nearly six thousand won medals for combat, including about thirty-six hundred Purple Hearts for wounds suffered. Seven hundred died; another seven hundred were permanently maimed; one thousand were seriously wounded. Their heroism would elevate the power and status of the Japanese people of Hawaii in the years after the war and indelibly transform the political and economic life of the islands.

It came as no surprise that politics and labor would reflect the postwar changes. Asian-American voters and politicians naturally attached themselves to the Democratic party, and by 1954, the Republicans lost their traditional control in the islands. The modern Hawaiian labor movement arose after the end of wartime martial law. The National Labor Relations Board, in key determinations for organizing purposes, classified Hawaiian workers on the mechanized plantations as industrial rather than agricultural. This gave unions every chance to succeed. The International Longshoremen's and Warehousemen's Union emerged as Hawaiian labor's champion and entered into the new mass politics of the Democratic party so vigorously as almost to take over the party altogether. Led by Jack Hall, whose experiences in the Marxist-tainted maritime strife along San Francisco's docks prepared him to take on Hawaii's Big Five companies, the ILWU called a number of spectacular strikes on the plantations and paralyzed Hawaii's seaborne commerce completely with a long and bitter waterfront shutdown in 1949. Hall's strongarm tactics proved to be too extreme even for a good many Democratic politicians. In the Red-baiting climate of the Cold War, Congress launched a series of investigations into communism in Hawaiian labor organizations. Representative Francis Walter (D–PA) expected the people of Hawaii to search out the "hideous conspiracy" in their community. Thirty-nine witnesses, Jack Hall included, took the Fifth Amendment against self-incrimination, achieving a brief immortality thereby as "the Reluctant Thirty-Nine." Eventually, in 1953, Hall and six others (the "Hawaii Seven") were tried and convicted under the Smith Act for conspiring to overthrow the government, though their convictions, like so many others from those times, were tossed out later on appeal. This question of communism plagued Hawaiians' hopes for statehood.

The idea of statehood for the Hawaiian Islands had taken a long time to gain the backing it needed to succeed. Hawaii's population figures exceeded those of many states at the time of their admission. Hawaii's taxes paid into the national treasury outweighed many states'. Hawaii had been a territory for a longer time than any other before admission to statehood. Congress, with its constitutional authority to "make all needful rules and regulations" for United States territories, could revise the crucial sugar tariffs at will or even whim, and indeed had done so for a brief period in the 1930s. The federal government could even suspend Hawaii's territorial form of government, and this had happened under the martial law laid down after the attack on Pearl Harbor. It was Hawaii's wartime record that swayed public opinion. Hawaiians' loyalty could never be regarded as deficient. Yet the power of the labor unions, the issue of communism, and the mixed racial complexion of the population combined to retard statehood. Alaska's plea was before Congress at this time, as earlier noted. Hawaii's congressional delegate, John A. (Jack) Burns, proposed admitting Alaska as the forty-ninth state to open the way for Hawaii to enter the Union as the fiftieth. On March 11, 1959, the Senate passed a statehood bill, and the House of Representatives followed on March 12. A plebescite in the islands ratified the measure, with the island of Niihau, the privately owned Hawaiian enclave, the only precinct opposed. Hawaii officially became the fiftieth state on August 21, 1959, "the last and the least" in its detractors' view. Jack Burns, a champion of Japanese-American participation in politics, would serve as Hawaii's governor from 1962 to 1974 and see his protégé, George Ariyoshi, become the state's first governor of Japanese ancestry.[18]

Since then, the Hawaiian Islands have grown more populous and prosperous than ever before. Sugar and pineapples are supplanted today as the leading revenue producers by tourists and federal spending primarily for military purposes. Commercial jetliners, which bring in businesspeople from the mainland, Japan, Canada, and Australia and each season's hordes of tourists, have influenced a new migration to take up year-round or vacation residences. A prospect looms that one ethnic group will one day constitute an absolute majority of the population, but whether it will be American or Japanese remains for the future to disclose. Although laid-back by American standards, the Hawaiian style of life is becoming indistinguishable from the mainland's. The passage from discovering this Polynesian paradise to statehood took fewer than two hundred years. Nevertheless, the Hawaiian Islands, like Alaska, remain only a distant concern for most Americans, for the same reason—distance. Much more distant, on the other hand, the Philippine Islands have written a chapter in the history of the American Pacific that is brief in comparison, different by contrast, ostensibly ended, but still astoundingly alive.

Take up the White Man's burden—
Ye dare not stoop to less—
Nor call too loud on Freedom
To cloak your weariness;
By all ye cry or whisper,
By all ye leave or do,
The silent, sullen peoples
Shall weigh your Gods and you.

Rudyard Kipling[1]

4

DESTINY IN THE PHILIPPINES

The Portuguese explorer Ferdinand Magellan, this time financed by King Charles I of Spain, arrived in the Philippine Islands in March 1521, landing first on Samar, the most westerly island in the Visayas and, after Luzon and Mindanao, the third largest in the archipelago. He named the islands the Felipinas for the heir to the Spanish throne, Prince Felipe, the future monarch Philip II. Since the Turks had made older trade routes unsafe, it became imperative for Europeans to discover alternate routes to the spices of the East that aristocratic palates required. Portugal's navigators, commencing with Bartholomeu Dias in 1487 and Vasco da Gama a decade later, chose the route down the coast of Africa and around the Cape of Good Hope, while Spain's captains sailed southwestward instead across the South Atlantic Ocean and through the strait at South America's tip later named for Magellan, its discoverer, to enter the Pacific Ocean and reach the Philippines. That Cape Horn itself could be rounded was unknown until 1616.

Europe's rising prosperity was making such costly enterprises possible, but the hazards were boundless. Magellan himself was killed on Mactan, the tiny neighbor of the island of Cebu, while aiding one band of natives in a fight against another. His opponent, the native chief LapuLapu, has become a modern hero as the symbol of Filipino resistance to foreign invaders.

Magellan's expedition conclusively demonstrated that the earth was round, not flat, fixed the relative proportions between land and water, and proved that the Americas constituted a new world unto itself, distinctly separate from Europe and Asia. Among the five vessels of Magellan's expedition and their crews totaling about 265 men, only the *Victoria* with eighteen survivors managed after three years from start to finish to complete the first circumnavigation of the globe. The *Victoria*'s cargo of spices, when sold in Spain, not only covered the expense of the entire adventure, but returned a profit. In the wake of the Magellan expedition's discovery, Spain would proceed to claim and colonize the Philippine Islands. The colonial history of the Philippines commenced on April 27, 1565, when an armada commanded by Miguel Lopez de Legaspi anchored off the island of Bohol, and Legaspi solemnly claimed the entire archipelago.

Unknown to Europeans, before the Spaniards arrived Muslim seamen, traders, and missionaries had already established themselves in the Philippines and converted the coastal peoples of the southernmost islands of the Sulu archipelago to the faith of the Prophet Mohammed. The Islamic sultans of Sulu would successfully defy Spain's efforts to establish complete imperial control or convert them and their subjects to Roman Catholic Christianity. Misled perhaps by Ferdinand and Isabella's triumphant expulsion of the Moors in 1492, Spain's governors vainly expected Mindanao's "Moros" to destroy their own culture. Occasional internecine rivalries among the Muslim tribesmen enabled the Spaniards to serve as arbiters, but invariably, whenever trouble loomed, the Moros joined together to confront their common Christian enemy.

Miguel Lopez de Legaspi established the first Spanish post in the Philippines on Cebu in 1565, then, moving northward, he defeated the Muslim army of Rajah Sulayman. In 1571, he established a base at May Nilad (on the site of modern Manila) to guarantee Spanish control. Philip II (1557–1598) became thereupon the earth's first monarch able to boast that the sun never set on his realm; when dawn broke at Madrid, as time was measured, it was but still early afternoon of the preceding day in Manila. Spain governed the Philippine Islands until 1821 through the viceroy of New Spain (Mexico), who himself was subject to the Council of the Indies in Madrid. Twice each year for two centuries the fabled Manila galleons carried Mexico's silver from Acapulco to Manila to pay for the luxuries of Asia cherished by kings, queens, and the aristocracy.

For the 327 years of Spain's effective sway over the Philippines, the major problem of governing the islands proved to be the instability of its policy, reflecting by its vacillations, as it came to do, the decline of Spanish power both in Europe and on the high seas. Outwardly, with the building of a fortress in 1635 at Zamboanga on the island of Mindanao, the stronghold of Muslim territory, Spain's conquest of the islands was completed. Yet unrelenting attacks by Chinese pirates forced a Spanish withdrawal to

Manila, which lasted until 1718, being aggravated by Dutch incursions and numerous local uprisings. The weakening of Catholic Spain's once great power on the European continent and the dismembering of her empire overseas arose, externally at least, from three sources: England's implacable enmity following the defeat of the armada, the equally intransigent Dutch republic in the Netherlands, and the Bourbon monarchs' efforts to thwart any Hapsburg encirclement of France. In the Philippines the great religious orders, the Franciscans, Dominicans, and Jesuits, acquired vast possessions and became mighty landowners. The friars' mastery of the land and the people within their domains recalled Europe's Middle Ages. Henceforth Spain's power spiraled self-destructively downward from preeminence to inferiority. Defeat compounded defeat from the War of the Spanish Succession (1701–1714) to the Seven Years War (1756–1763), when British forces actually occupied Manila for two years. The decline of Spain continued during the French revolutionary wars and beyond the titanic Napoleonic conflicts throughout the nineteenth century. Spain's attention to her colonies grew distracted at best. Governors came and went, averaging less than three years in office during this troubled period. Except for the islands of Cuba and Puerto Rico, Spain's American empire broke up into an array of independent republics from Argentina to Mexico. At the end of the nineteenth century, the disastrous war with the United States would complete the Spanish empire's disintegration, for Madrid's belated attempts at colonial reform failed to prevail in Cuba and the Philippines against their national liberation movements.

Spun off from the China trade and the whaling industry, American enterprises, introduced by Nathaniel Bowditch in 1796, penetrated the Philippine economy. Yankee merchants began adventuring in Manila and before long were reaching southward as far as Mindanao. Merchants in Salem and Boston dispatched furniture, including pianos, to Manila; even winter-cut ice was available for the pampered families of wealthy *encomenderos* (holders of *encomiendas* under the land-grant system copied from Mexico) to enjoy in the subtropical heat. If comparatively only on a modest scale, the traffic such shipping stimulated in abaca, or hemp, for making ropes and bagging fostered a staple for the Philippine Islands' growing export economy. Renowned worldwide, Manila hemp and its products represented the top quality available. Americans served as the catalysts for the hemp trade, linking supply and demand between Manila, London, and United States ports, mobilizing capital, promoting production, and brokering shipping. Peale, Hubbell, & Co. thrived in this capacity from 1856 to 1875 to persist for another half century before going bankrupt. The company failed after the turn of the century amid the burgeoning nationalism of the times, bogged down by unfulfilled contracts and costly litigations. The

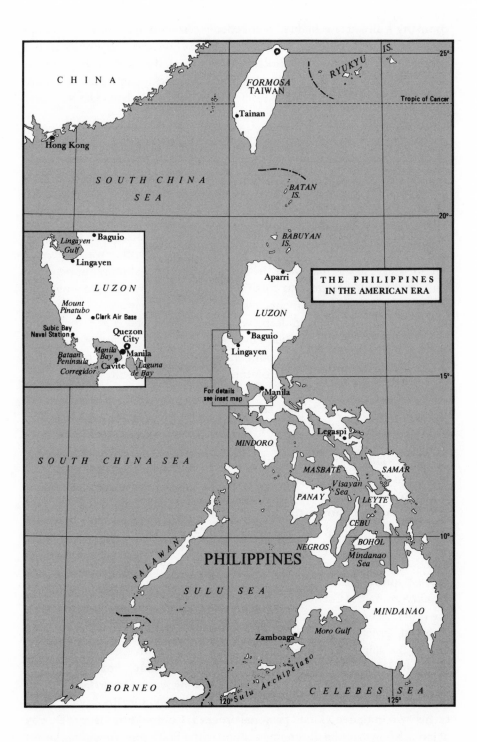

THE PHILIPPINES
IN THE AMERICAN ERA

Inset map labels:
Baguio
Lingayen Gulf
Lingayen
LUZON
Mount Pinatubo
Subic Bay Naval Station
Clark Air Base
Quezon City
Bataan Peninsula
Manila Bay
Manila
Cavite
Corregidor
Laguna de Bay

Main map labels:
CHINA
FORMOSA TAIWAN
Tainan
RYUKYU IS.
IS.
Tropic of Cancer
Hong Kong
SOUTH CHINA SEA
BATAN IS.
BABUYAN IS.
Aparri
LUZON
Baguio
Lingayen
For details see inset map
Manila
Legaspi
MINDORO
MASBATE
SAMAR
Visayan Sea
PANAY
LEYTE
SOUTH CHINA SEA
CEBU
NEGROS
BOHOL
Mindanao Sea
PHILIPPINES
PALAWAN
SULU SEA
Zamboaga
Moro Gulf
MINDANAO
Sulu Archipelago
BORNEO
CELEBES SEA

25°
20°
15°
10°
120°
125°

company's directors remained pigheadedly certain that it was easy enough to understand "the native" and that "Yankee enterprise" assuredly would succeed over local customs. Such ventures created little of lasting importance. The origins of the twentieth-century American empire in the Philippine Islands lay on the far side of the world in Madrid, Havana, and Washington.[2]

The Spanish-American War of 1898 broke out over the intervention by the United States on the side of the Cuban people in their uprising against Spain's domination. The explosion and sinking in Havana's harbor of the United States battleship *Maine* (February 15, 1898), presumably caused by Spanish agents while she lay at anchor there ostensibly on a goodwill visit, roused the American people to a fever pitch, capping weeks of excitement over lurid newspaper accounts of official tyranny and atrocities. Inflammatory news from Cuba, only ninety miles from Florida, was regularly splashed across the mainland. In addition, the long-simmering revolt in Cuba and Spain's attempt to crush it threatened many sizeable American fortunes. American investments in sugar and mining enterprises added up to $50 million. By 1893, trade between the United States and the island surpassed $100 million annually over and above the profits of shipping, banking, and insurance. By contrast, Spain's troubles with her Filipino insurgents on the other side of the globe were virtually unknown to Americans, while United States investments and trade in the Philippines were correspondingly trivial. Like President McKinley, most Americans could not have located the Philippine Islands upon a globe. A great many, a majority possibly, had never heard of the archipelago.

Spain's failure to modernize the colonial administration in the Philippine Islands would lead by August 1896 to the initial phase of an open revolutionary movement seeking national independence. Already by 1892, José Rizal, a medical doctor turned novelist and poet, had emerged as the Filipino nationalists' inspiring propagandist, and Andres Bonifacio was agitating for revolution through the Katipunan, a secret conspiratorial society he founded. Both were fated to die violently, shot by firing squads, Rizal by Spanish authorities and Bonifacio by rival revolutionaries commanded by Emilio Aguinaldo. On May 31, 1897, at Biak-na-Boto just north of Manila in the province of Bulacan, the twenty-three-year-old Aguinaldo, Bonifacio's archrival, proclaimed the birth of a Philippine republic, and five months later at the same place, a constitution was signed with Aguinaldo himself designated the republic's president. Moving quickly, Spanish officials halted the uprising before it could spread, bribing Aguinaldo to take himself into exile. Then, Assistant Secretary of the Navy Theodore Roosevelt, solely on his own initiative, issued personal orders to Commodore George Dewey at Hong Kong to strike the enemy at hand in the Philippines if war broke out with Spain. Dewey wasted no time. When the United States declared war on April 25, 1898, purportedly to free Cuba from Spain's misrule, Dewey drove his Asiatic Squadron down the South China Sea to the Philippines; in the lead was his speedy flagship, *Olympia,* an armored cruiser. Dewey's ships annihilated Spain's overage flotilla on May 1 at its anchorage in Manila Bay. Next Dewey seized the arsenal at Cavite, destroyed the fortifications at the mouth of the bay, and installed a blockade.

The Filipino rebellion was reignited. Aguinaldo hurried back to Luzon with a supply of arms to take command of the struggle for independence, and at Kawit, Cavite, on June 12, he once again proclaimed the Philippine republic. Together American sailors and marines, reinforced by soldiers, in maneuvers openly concerted with Aguinaldo's fighters, encircled Spain's garrison, which was entrenched in historic Fort Santiago inside Manila's fortified district of Intramuros, forcing its surrender on August 13. The "capture" of Manila, however, followed a secret understanding to save Spain's honor. Dewey and the Spanish commanding officer agreed to the surrender of the city after a show of resistance, on the significant condition that no Filipino forces would be permitted to enter the walled city.

Spain sued for peace, and both belligerents promptly proclaimed an armistice. President McKinley appointed a "peace commission" packed with imperialists led by Secretary of State William R. Day, a personal friend and obedient servant to the president's wishes. The talks between Spain and the United States began on October 1 in Paris and dragged on throughout the autumn. Meanwhile, McKinley's and the nation's appetite for territorial acquisitions grew by leaps and bounds. Originally Congress had declared that Cuba ought to be made free and independent, and it went on explicitly, in the Teller Amendment to the war declaration, to disclaim any territorial ambitions. Somehow America's horizons expanded, even while the fighting was continuing. Most probably Dewey's spectacular naval victory at Manila Bay toppled all restraints. On July 6, 1898, Congress annexed the Hawaiian Islands outright by joint resolution, in order to have Pearl Harbor for a naval base and coaling station astride the North Central Pacific Ocean highway to the Philippines. Next, in a drastic new step, McKinley demanded that Spain must cede Guam and Puerto Rico to the United States as his price for ending hostilities, and he further stipulated that United States forces would occupy the "city, bay and harbor of Manila pending the conclusion of a treaty of peace."

McKinley had at first held that annexing territory by the United States would constitute "criminal aggression." He was now saying: "While we are conducting war and until its conclusion, we must keep all we get; when the war is over, we must keep what we want."

Having launched hostilities against Spain solely to liberate Cuba, the

United States seized Puerto Rico and Guam as prizes of war, then seized the city of Manila as well. On September 16, McKinley told his negotiators to demand the island of Luzon, and by October 26, he was demanding the entire Philippine archipelago of more than seven thousand islands and its nearly nine million inhabitants. Spain refused, whereupon the United States delivered a blistering ultimatum on November 21, to which Spain helplessly acceded. Fears that Germany might take the Philippines if the United States did not (the admiral commanding the kaiser's Asiatic squadron having informed his superiors on May 12 of his readiness to seize the islands), and the evident assurance that Great Britain would not object if the United States did, encouraged the Americans to enlarge their demands. But President McKinley's own revelation offers an explanation as convincing as any other. McKinley had not sought the Philippines, he insisted to a delegation of Methodist ministers, but they dropped into his lap like "a gift from the gods." Not knowing what to do with them, having but recently learned where on earth they were, McKinley prayed for divine guidance:

> And one night late it came to me this way—I don't know how it was, but it came: 1) that we could not give them back to Spain—that would be cowardly and dishonorable; 2) that we could not turn them over to France or Germany—our commercial rivals in the Orient—that would be bad business and discreditable; 3) that we could not leave them to themselves—they were unfit for self-government—and they would soon have anarchy and misrule over there worse than Spain's was; and 4) that there was nothing left for us to do but to take them all and to educate the Filipinos and uplift and civilize and Christianize them, and by God's grace do the very best we could by them as our fellowmen for whom Christ also died.

Their labors finished, God and the president rested. As McKinley recalled:

> And then I went to bed, and went to sleep, and slept soundly, and the next morning I sent for the chief engineer of the War Department (our map maker), and I told him to put the Philippines on the map of the United States, and there they are and there they will stay while I am President!

So William McKinley, by his dramatic admission, which few believe to be the full story or even the true story, launched the most dubious imperial undertaking in his nation's history. The treaty, signed on December 10, ensured the freedom of Cuba and granted the Philippine Islands (for a $20 million payment to Spain) along with Puerto Rico and Guam to the United States. In the Senate debate over the treaty's ratification, the issue of acquiring the Philippine Islands overrode all other considerations. Senator Albert Beveridge of Indiana came to embody the annexationists' cause:

> We cannot fly from our world duties; it is ours to execute the purpose of a fate that has driven us to be greater than our small intentions. We cannot retreat

from any soil where Providence has unfurled our banner; it is ours to save that soil for liberty and Civilization. For liberty and Civilization and God's promise fulfilled, the flag must henceforth be the symbol and the sign to all mankind—the flag!

With the Senate debate in full swing, President McKinley pulled still another surprise by ordering the War Department on December 21, 1898, to extend its military occupation beyond Manila to the entire archipelago. Not knowing this, on January 2, 1899, President Aguinaldo announced the members of his cabinet of the first Republic of the Philippines. But when the news came, McKinley's latest move drove the frustrated Filipinos themselves to violence to determine the outcome. Aguinaldo's cohorts attacked United States forces on February 4, 1899, killing and wounding a number of American soldiers. This assault played into the hand of the annexationists already fearful over the treaty's doubtful fate. The outcry over the dead effectively ended any further debate over the destiny of the Philippines. Two days later, on February 6, the patriotically aroused Senate ratified the treaty of peace with Spain by fifty-seven to twenty-seven, a scant two votes more than the required two-thirds majority. Those Americans who had opposed the war from its beginning felt a renewed sense of outrage. The antiimperialist leagues marshaled every pressure in their power to defeat the annexation of the Philippines, even to scuttle the treaty itself. Arrayed against the antiimperialists, however, were the confident young orators of the war faction, overheated by victory and driven beyond reason to a superpatriotic self-righteousness. In time, Finley Peter Dunne, the nation's political wit, would let Chicago's best-known Irish saloonkeeper sort it out: "'Do ye think Hiven sint us to th' Philippeens?' Mr. Hennessey asked. 'I don't know,' said Mr. Dooley, 'th' divvle take them.'"[3]

But why?

Imperialists headed by Theodore Roosevelt transformed the War of 1898 fought to liberate Cuba from Spanish oppression, "the splendid little war" in John Hay's memorable description, into a Spanish-American-Cuban-Filipino war with ever-expanding bloodshed and bewildering complexity. The United States began the war on its doorstep with the self-disclaiming Teller Amendment against any territorial objectives, but almost heedlessly went on to capture a distant, polyglot empire of exotically mixed nationalities. The *Washington Post* noted a popular urge to demonstrate the nation's growing strength: "Ambition, interest, land hunger, pride, the mere joy of fighting, whatever it may be, we are animated by a new sensation. We are face to face with a strange destiny. The taste of Empire is in the mouth of the people even as the taste of blood in the jungle. It means an imperial policy, the Republic renascent taking her place with the armed nations." Duty-minded Americans prepared to take up "the white man's burden." They were intending to civilize and protect not only their close neighbors, the would-be independent Cubans, but the recalcitrant Filipinos, who, it was at last realized, dwelled seven thousand miles away from California on the doorstep of China.

The Treaty of Paris transferred sovereignty over the Philippine Islands from Spain to the United States without the Filipinos themselves being seriously consulted. Emilio Aguinaldo expected his newly acquired American allies would support the republic he had proclaimed, but he was quickly doomed to disappointment. So Aguinaldo, ably seconded by Apolinario Mabini, a brilliant lawyer crippled in both legs by polio, the Philippines' first secretary of foreign relations, formed "the dictatorship of Malolos" at a site thirty-five miles north of Manila. To draft a constitution, an assembly was summoned. Speedily drawn and ratified, the assembly's constitution went into effect on January 21, 1899. Aguinaldo intended to forestall any possibility of foreign intervention by demonstrating that his fledgling Republic of the Philippines could govern itself unaided.

During his exile of 1897, Aguinaldo had been sent aboard a United States naval vessel from Singapore to Hong Kong by United States Consul General E. Spencer Pratt. The two men were introduced by Howard W. Bray, a Briton, formerly a planter in the Philippines but now vengefully at odds with the Spanish authorities there for his severe financial setbacks. Bray persuaded Aguinaldo and Pratt that, in a suitable eventuality, the Filipinos and the Americans alike might benefit by pooling their efforts against the Spanish. Pratt advised both the State Department and Commodore Dewey of this prospect. Dewey apparently encouraged Pratt to send Aguinaldo to meet him in Hong Kong, but Dewey had already sailed for Manila Bay by the time the revolutionary arrived. While biding his time in Hong Kong, Aguinaldo and his aides met with United States Consul General Rounseville Wildman, who extended his advice and some assistance until they could proceed to Manila. Both Pratt and Wildman would later deny they had ever promised independence to the Filipinos when the war against Spain was ended. Yet Aguinaldo relied upon assurances such as Consul General Pratt in Singapore had made to him: "You need not have any worry about America. The American Congress and President have just made a solemn declaration [Teller Amendment] disclaiming any desire to possess Cuba and promising to leave the country to the Cubans after having driven away the Spaniards and pacified the country. Cuba is at our door, while the Philippines is 10,000 miles away!"

Aguinaldo also insisted that Dewey had guaranteed him, before he stepped ashore to take command of the Filipino rebel forces, that the United States would one day recognize him as the head of an independent Filipino republic under American naval protection. Dewey always denied having given any such assurances, complaining that "Aguinaldo and his people were forced upon me by Consul Pratt and Consul Wildman." As for Dewey himself, he naively assumed that his defeat of the Spanish fleet followed by the taking of Manila and the signing of the armistice with Spain were all the steps necessary for the United States to take possession of the Philippines. Obviously, there was no authoritative plan of any description, nor did anyone proclaim what the policy of the United States was or ought to be, least of all President McKinley. "If old Dewey had just sailed away when he smashed that Spanish Fleet, what a lot of trouble he would have saved us!" McKinley would exclaim before long.[4]

Instead the American Expeditionary Force of eleven thousand soldiers of the Eighth Army Corps, dispatched on McKinley's orders and led by Major General Wesley Merritt, began to land at Cavite during the summer of 1898 to take Manila. Insurgent forces by then controlled all of Luzon except Manila, which they were besieging, and immediately they learned to distrust the Americans' intentions because of their indefinite nature. American soldiers, for their part, quickly became apprehensive at the unexpected strength and determination of the insurgent "allies" confronting them. Outbreaks of violence grew increasingly frequent. Relations worsened between the two forces following the Spaniards' surrender of Manila and disintegrated entirely after Spain yielded her sovereignty over the entire archipelago to the United States. Aguinaldo's Philippine republic was formally inaugurated on January 23, 1899, two days after the adoption of the Malolos Constitution. On McKinley's insisting on United States sovereignty over the entire archipelago, the only remaining question was which side would fire the first shot.

On Saturday evening, February 4, 1899, Private William Walter Grayson of Nebraska fired on four blundering, probably drunken, natives. The so-called Philippines insurrection had begun. For ten months in 1899, American soldiers and marines fought one pitched battle after another against the determined Filipinos, until Aguinaldo switched his tactics to full-scale guerrilla fighting. Major General Elwell S. Otis, who had replaced General Merritt, rejected Brigadier General Arthur MacArthur's farsighted proposal for amnesty at that point. Otis pushed his own tactics of cautious military advance coupled with a pacification "policy of attraction," which emphasized the development of schools, municipal governments, public health, and public works to win over the Filipinos by acts of compassion and reform. Aguinaldo's determination indefinitely to prolong the struggle until the Americans would weary of their effort and go home began to inflict great costs on the combatants of both sides and on Filipino civilians. Unceasingly the guerrillas staged raids against supply trains and isolated patrols. They destroyed rail links and bridges, set ambushes and traps, and sniped at every opportune target. Himself discouraged by the spring of 1900, General Otis requested to be relieved of his duties, and the alacrity with which the normally torpid McKinley acquiesced suggested his alarm that, with any delay, the desk-bound Otis might regret his impulse and offer to stay. Instead President McKinley promoted Arthur MacArthur, Jr., to military governor and commanding general of the Philippines. The balance of power soon commenced to shift. MacArthur vigorously fought the war. He also granted amnesty to the rebels who surrendered, and he won over the wealthier Filipinos, who prospered handsomely by cooperating with their conquerors.

In March 1901, Aguinaldo himself was tricked into surrendering by General Frederick Funston. Shortly thereafter, he called on his compatriots to give themselves up also and swear allegiance to the United States, as he did on April 1. Many of them did so without delay, and more followed, though Macario Sakay chose to fight doggedly on for several years in remote regions. Aguinaldo, in spite of his newly declared loyalty, was deported to Guam with several other rebel leaders and imprisoned there for some time. President Theodore Roosevelt, who had succeeded the assassinated McKinley, announced on July 4, 1902, that the insurrection in the Philippines was over, and on September 8, the United States officially declared the war ended. Aguinaldo returned to public life in 1935, when he ran for president in the Philippines' first presidential election, but Manuel Quezon defeated him. Sadly, as Filipinos say, Aguinaldo lived too long to save his own reputation. In 1942, following Japan's conquest of the Philippines, Aguinaldo broadcast a demand to General Douglas MacArthur to surrender. Charged with treason at the liberation of 1945, Aguinaldo was once again publicly humiliated by the victorious Americans. Emilio Aguinaldo truly was the father of his country's independence. The tragedy of his life illuminates the fundamentally flawed nature of America's Asian empire in the Philippine Islands.

More often than not, Americans have depicted the war they fought to crush the fledgling Filipino republic as an insignificant, lawless insurrection against their legitimate sovereignty. It proved, in fact, to be a vicious all-out war lasting over three years, until 1902, against determined Filipino patriots. Two-thirds of the United States Army was engaged at the war's peak, around 70,000 troops; in all 120,000 Americans finally fought in the Philippines. After 1902, the fighting sputtered sporadically against stubborn Moro resistance in the southernmost region, which was finally crushed in the bloody battles of Bud Daho (1906) and Bud Dagsak (1913) on the island of Jolo in the Celebes Sea. The war's casualties greatly exceeded the Spanish-American War's. Nearly 4,200 Americans were killed and 2,800 wounded.

Fifteen thousand Filipino warriors were slain; altogether, as many as 200,000 natives, mostly noncombatants, may have died.

The American-Filipino War was ugly by any standard, featuring atrocities by both sides. Often the insurgents mutilated their captives, while the Americans' wartime bloodlust was intensified by homebred racist convictions of their innate superiority over the suddenly dangerous "little brown brothers" they were supposed to be civilizing. Exhausted and fearful for their own lives, insect-bitten, diseased, ill-nourished, and out of patience, America's soldiers at times turned brutal. They torched native barrios or villages and randomly bayoneted civilians, even bragging about hunting them down like birds or rabbits. Brigadier General J. Franklin Bell's concentration camps broke the resistance of the guerrillas and the villagers assisting them. To wrest intelligence about the guerrillas' hiding places and arms caches, American soldiers resorted to retaliatory killings and the infamous "water cure," forcing hoses down into their prisoner's throat, then jumping on his swollen belly to empty it quickly before he drowned.

Like the Indian Wars, the war against the Filipinos turned into a slaughter of unfortunates by an invading enemy equipped with modern weapons and hell-bent on destroying any resistance. Brigadier General Jacob H. "Howling Jake" Smith, an Indian fighter and recent veteran of the Boxer Rebellion in North China, ordered his men to kill every Filipino on the island of Samar over the age of ten. "I want no prisoners," he told Major Littleton Waller. "I wish you to kill and burn; the more you kill and burn the more you will please me. I want all persons killed who are capable of bearing arms." Savagely bent on avenging the Filipino massacre in Batangas of his Company C, Ninth Infantry, Boxer Rebellion veterans like himself, Smith would be court-martialed for his brutality after the war, as would Waller, the scapegoat. The army's chief of staff, General J. Lawton Miles, would be forced into retirement for his supervisory laxity. Ultimately the racism in American society, the conviction of Anglo-Saxon superiority, supplied the justification for the American conquest and most, if not all, of the uncivilized abuses against the Filipinos themselves. In spite of official policy to the contrary, the enlisted ranks adhered to their homebred prejudices, generally regarding the Filipinos as racial inferiors, as "gooks" or "niggers."

Overall, however, American officials facilitated the end of hostilities in relatively short order through co-option rather than coercion. Efforts to conciliate the peoples of the Philippines commenced from the beginning of their subjugation. Late in December 1898, President McKinley proclaimed to General Otis his policy of "benevolent assimilation." "It should be the earnest and paramount aim of the military administration to win the confidence, respect, and affection of the inhabitants of the Philippines by assuring them in every possible way that full measure of individual rights and liberties which is the heritage of free peoples, and by proving to them that the mission of the United States is one of *benevolent assimilation,* substituting the mild sway of justice for arbitrary rule." McKinley also instructed the members of the Schurman Commission, as the first civilian Philippine Commission was known, headed by Jacob Gould Schurman, the president of Cornell University, to emphasize "the just and beneficent intentions of the United States." Unless the United States would declare its intention to protect them against any possible aggressors, the Filipinos wanted only to be left alone to consolidate their revolution.

General Otis proceeded without delay to install a military government over the city of Manila under Brigadier General Arthur MacArthur, Jr. A youthful Medal of Honor winner for his gallantry at Chickamauga and a regular officer ever since, Arthur MacArthur was a brilliant choice. His leadership was outstanding from his landing at Cavite, south of Manila, commanding the third detachment of Merritt's invasion, through Manila's surrender. As governor of the demoralized capital during the Spaniards' transferral of authority, he tactfully restored the city's vitality. Earlier he had exercised a similar responsibility during Reconstruction days in the occupied South. Evincing genuine concern for Manila's populace, he resolved the accumulated problems of waste disposal, food and water supply, disease and rat control, crime, and education. His innovative system of primary education, replacing the religious schools conducted by the universally hated friars, was widely applauded. For three years, until yielding to civilians, Major General Arthur MacArthur (his rank by then) significantly shaped developments as the United States military governor of the Philippine Islands. Civilians would begin to replace the military officers even before the fighting halted. An augury arose in 1901 from Judge William Howard Taft of Ohio, the president of the Second Philippine Commission who would become the first American civil governor (1901–1904) of the Philippine Islands. Taft vouchsafed to predict home rule one day for the Filipinos, a government of their own "which shall teach these people individual liberty, which shall lift them up to a point of civilization . . . , and which shall make them rise to call the name of the United States blessed."[5]

Back home Taft's roseate forecast drew caustic ridicule from the still bitter antiimperialists, led by George Frisbee Hoar, the respected Republican senator from Massachusetts, in opposition to his own state's ardent imperialist, Senator Henry Cabot Lodge. Hoar was backed by Andrew Carnegie, Charles Francis Adams, Jr., and Charles Elliot Norton, among many others. William James, Harvard's renowned philosopher, and America's humorist Mark Twain exploded in anger. Thundered James: "We are destroying the lives of these islanders. . . . We are destroying down to the root every germ of a healthy national life in these unfortunate people. . . . No life shall you have, we say, except as a gift from our philanthropy after your unconditional submission to our will."

Mark Twain ridiculed "the Blessings of Civilization Trust," his contemptuous label for the nation's white man's burden bearers, in a scorching essay, "To the Person Sitting in Darkness." He lamented the opportunity lost to free the Philippines like Cuba, when by force the United States had annihilated Spain's sway over the islands and her claims of sovereignty. "It was then," Twain roared, "that we conceived the divinely humorous idea of *buying* both of these spectres from Spain!" The treaty with Spain bound the United States to maintain all rights of property, even the vast ecclesiastical estates known as "the friars' lands," which heavily taxed peasants through medieval-style exactions of labor and rent. "In buying these ghosts for twenty millions, we also contracted to take care of the friars and their accumulations," Twain complained. "I think we also agreed to propagate leprosy and smallpox, but as to this there is doubt. But it is not important, persons afflicted with the friars do not mind the other diseases." Worse, he concluded: "With our treaty ratified, Manila subdued, and our ghosts secured, we had no further use for Aguinaldo and the owners of the archipelago. We forced a war and have been hunting America's guest and ally through the swamps and woods ever since." What next? "And as for a flag for the Philippine Province, it is easily managed. We can have a special one—our States do it: we can have just our usual flag, with the white stripes painted black and the stars replaced by the skull and cross bones." Such outcries were largely ignored amid the novel excitements of empire. America's annexation of the Philippine Islands was an accomplished fact.[6]

"To the student of history and of social evolution," judged Yale University Professor Edward Gaylord Bourne in October 1902, "it will be an experiment of profound interest." Indeed it would. Ironically history records that the United States wasted untold lives and enormous treasure to crush the Filipinos' first independence only to realize quickly that the islands were not worth keeping, even dangerously indefensible especially against Japan, and to commence almost at once the process of freeing them. Nevertheless American sovereignty over the Philippines would persist for a half century with profound consequences for both peoples. Also the United States became an Asian power overnight, unknowingly to embark on a fearsome course of actions leading eventually to Japan's attacks of December 7–8, 1941, on Pearl Harbor and Manila. The Philippines, after more than three centuries of Hispanic rule, were to be diverted into still another mainstream of Western civilization, the Anglo-American variety, before they could ever realize their dreams of independence.

Spain's regime vanished to plunge the Filipino peoples into powerful modernizing currents. Rechristened in fire and blood, they would have to undergo an unprecedented struggle to retain their identity against American masters who tolerated no weaknesses and drove idleness or incapacity over the edge. Without hesitation, except for Muslims, the great majority of Filipinos maintained their Hispanic Christian names, remaining true, as baptized, to their Roman Catholic beliefs. Soon they would acquire unmistakable veneers of American acculturation, although they would never give up their Filipino traits of character or their folkways.

How could the United States' constitutional democracy govern them ten thousand miles away from Washington, D.C.? Might not the effort required transform America's citizens into provincial overseers, like Romans when that ancient republic converted itself into a far-flung empire? Had not African slavery in the South and manifest destiny westward already paved the way?

Imponderables aside, the foregoing and more, the American performance in the Philippine Islands evolved from the outset along uniquely straightforward lines. First, the so-called Taft Regime of civilians replaced MacArthur's military government; measures of Filipino self-rule were introduced, though initially limited to municipal and provincial levels but, after 1907, on a broader scale through a nationally elected legislative assembly. Second, the Jones Act, or Philippine Autonomy Act of 1916, authorized independence as soon as stable government could be established, and Filipinos themselves began to share in governing their country at home and representing their constituents in Washington through two resident commissioners seated in the United States House of Representatives. Third, the transitional commonwealth featured full-scale self-government under a United States high commissioner, who was akin almost to an ambassador, instead of a governor-general, and it lasted for a decade after 1935. However, the commonwealth was nullified for three years by Japan's wartime occupation and the sponsoring by the Japanese of yet another Filipino republic. The Allied victory over Japan introduced the independent Republic of the Philippines on July 4, 1946, as scheduled. Fourth, finally, the period to the present had been one of extremely close Filipino-American ties, though troubled by lingering sore points, chronic economic discords, and the anti-Communist, Cold War containment policies of successive American governments. All of these problems have been exacerbated by the Philippines' internal turbulence, which focused more and more on the inflammable issue of allowing the United States military and naval bases to continue.[7]

The Philippine Islands, as the Americans learned for themselves, lie off the southeast coast of Asia, constituting the northeastern fringe of the

Malaysian world. The influence of the western Pacific's deep, constantly warm seas is felt everywhere. Eleven of the islands account for most of the land mass and its population. The two largest are Luzon in the north and Mindanao in the south. Between them, in virtually inland seas, are the Visayas' eight main islands—Samar, Negros, Panay, Mindoro, Leyte, Cebu, Bohol, and Masbate—and other smaller islands. West of the Visayas is Palawan, a long insular strip of hills. In the far south, off Borneo, is the Sulu archipelago. The mountainous topography of the islands reflects their origins as the volcanic peaks of a submerged and still intensely active cordillera. With important exceptions—the plains of Cagayan and Bicol and the central plain on Luzon, the Cotabato plain and the Agusan valley on Mindanao, and the lowlands of western Negros and southeastern Panay— the Philippine flatlands are narrow and few in number. Almost uninterruptedly the eastern slopes of the islands drop down to the Pacific in precipitous scarps. Earthquakes and eruptions are frequent. The Philippines receive a high rainfall, particularly in the regions exposed to southwesterly monsoons. Overall the climate is enervatingly hot and humid, tropical or equatorial, with an exuberant vegetation of more than ten thousand species. Annually, between July and October a dozen or more oceanic typhoons wreak heavy damage from their violent winds and torrential downpours.

The Filipinos are basically Malaysian, though much interbreeding has taken place. Mestizos (mixed racials) may variously be blended products of Malaysians, Chinese, and Spaniards or other caucasians, including Americans. Of the enormous variety of languages and dialects, only eight languages are spoken by significantly large groups of people: Ilocano, Pangasinan, Pampangan, Cebuano, Bicol, Waray, Hiligaynon, and Tagalog. All these tongues, though often widely different from one another, belong to the Malayo-Polynesian, or Austronesian, family. Spanish was spoken exclusively by the educated elite until the Americans moved energetically to replace it by their own versions of English. Today English is still the language most used in administration, while Spanish has nearly disappeared, and Pilipino has become the national medium of expression. Pilipino employs Tagalog, which is spoken in the Manila area, for its structure and core vocabulary, being enriched by innumerable borrowings from other native languages and foreign expressions. To complicate the picture, the mountainous tribes were barely affected, if at all, by either the Spaniards' administration or their Christianity; indeed, many of these inhabitants would succeed almost as well in avoiding the Americans.

Even more resistant was the sizeable minority of Muslims, Sunnis of the Shafi'ite school in theory at least, who were concentrated in the southern Philippines. The first efforts by the United States to mollify them resulted in the so-called Bates Treaty signed with the Sultan of Sulu on August 20, 1899, based upon the prevailing accord with Spain. The Muslims of Sulu recognized the sovereignty of the United States in return for the latter's protection and promise not to interfere in their internal administration or customs, together with the payment from the army's payroll of annual subsidies to the sultan and his *datus*, or chieftains. To George Ade, the Hoosier satirist, this extraordinary pact officially sanctioned two peculiar Moro institutions, slavery and polygamy, anathemas outlawed back home, to provide clear evidence, in his opinion, of the absurdity of the entire imperialist adventure. Henceforth, Moro Province was made into a special jurisdiction over which the Philippine Commission exercised lawmaking prerogatives, and the provincial governor was an American military officer throughout the Taft regime. In 1913, Moro Province was changed into a ministry as the Department of Mindanao and Sulu expanded to incorporate the province of Agusan and its subprovince of Bukidnon, with a civilian governor for the first time, Frank W. Carpenter, who for several years had served as assistant executive secretary of the Philippine Commission.[8]

Upon annexing the Philippine Islands, the United States defined a twofold responsibility toward its new possessions. First, there was the necessity to provide a properly administered government, and the second need was to train the Filipino people themselves in the principles and practices of self-government through their own participation. To achieve the latter goal, President McKinley instructed the Taft Commission to give top priority to extending the system of primary education begun by the military, in order "to fit the people for the duties of citizenship and for the ordinary avocations of a civilized community." By 1913, at the Taft epoch's close, the American imperial system would be firmly fixed in place. In certain significant respects, the system harkened backward to the British colonial regime from which American independence sprang, while in education and self-government, the approaches tried out by the United States toward its Philippines dependency fairly sparkled in democratic novelty.

Early in 1900, President McKinley appointed his friend William Howard Taft to be president of the Second Philippine Commission to carry out the government's intentions for "benevolent assimilation." McKinley's desire to placate the Filipinos was plain. The timing was right. The frustrating rejection by Aguinaldo's Malolos Republic of Secretary of State John Hay's plan of May 12, 1899, the continuation of bloody fighting, and the return of the First Philippine Commission, the Schurman Commission, without its having facilitated, as instructed, the "most humane, pacific, and effective extension of [American] authority" throughout the archipelago, unhappily had left McKinley with little alternative, given his annexationist determination, but the force of arms. The Hay Plan sketched out a proposal for a

Philippine government headed by a governor-general appointed by the President; a cabinet to be appointed by the Governor-General; a general advisory council to be elected by the people, the qualifications of electors to be carefully determined and the governor-general to have absolute veto over the council's actions; a judiciary to be strong and independent, with the principal judges to be chosen from either natives or Americans, or both, based on their fitness to serve. The conservatives in the Malolos Republic wanted to accept the Hay Plan, but Apolinario Mabini and the irreconcilable General Antonio Luma blocked them.

Aguinaldo's switch to guerrilla warfare in November 1899, following the American's demolition of his army's pitched-battle resistance, renewed McKinley's efforts at reconciliation. Two steps were necessary: the substitution of a civilian administration for the military and the clearer formulation of Philippine policy. In a conciliatory gesture, the army on its own initiative established an independent judiciary. Taft's commissioners, in the months that followed, enacted over two hundred laws that would fundamentally affect nearly every aspect of life in the islands.

Then, upon the urgings of Commission President Taft and recommendations by Secretary of War Elihu Root, Congress, in March 1901, attached the Spooner Amendment to the Army Appropriations Bill empowering the president to establish a civil government for the Philippines until Congress could formulate a systematic policy of its own. General MacArthur resigned in bitterness as a result, even though President McKinley continued the War Department's supervisory role over insular affairs. On July 4, 1901, Taft was sworn in as the first American civil governor of the Philippines, while the other four members of the commission became cabinet secretaries in the new government. Three Filipinos were appointed to the commission in September, but they failed to be given any portfolios of executive responsibility. At municipal and provincial levels, trusted Filipinos, who usually were wealthy men from the social class known as *illustrados*, quickly began to assume local legislative, executive, and judicial positions, in keeping with McKinley's wish that Filipinos take over these duties without delay.

Taft moved into Malacañang Palace, and MacArthur sailed home. Inevitably the Senate conducted hearings. Both Taft and MacArthur testified. The general's global perspective foretold his son Douglas's panoramic speech to Congress in 1951, after President Truman sacked him. The Philippine archipelago was, Arthur MacArthur stated, the finest string of islands anywhere:

Its strategic position is unexcelled by that of any other position on the globe. The China Sea, which separates it by something like 750 miles from the continent, is nothing more or less than a safety moat. It lies on the flank of what might be called a position of several thousand miles of coast line; it is in the center of that position. It is therefore relatively better placed than Japan, which is on a flank, and therefore remote from the other extremity; likewise, India, on another flank. The Philippines are in the center of that position. It affords a means of protecting American interests which, with the very least output of physical power, has the effect of a commanding position in itself to retard hostile action.

For the moment, however, grand strategy was overshadowed by the subject of schooling for Filipino children.

Americans esteemed public education not only for themselves, but also for the peaceful, political development of the Filipinos. From Thomas Jefferson and Horace Mann to John Dewey, progressive education's zealous advocate for pragmatically improving society through the application of democratic practices in the classroom, the nation's faith in learning at public expense reflected the highest hopes for the future of generations unborn. Obedient to its mandate, the commission brought over its own agents of up-to-date pedagogy to bring the Philippines into line. The military transport *Thomas* disembarked some six hundred carefully selected American teachers on August 23, 1901, at Manila, the predecessors without their knowing it of thousands of latter-day Peace Corps Volunteers. Men and women alike, these hardy "Thomasites," as they became known, began at once throughout the Philippines to teach the English language and, as energetically as possible, to Americanize their youthful charges. The commission took over existing public schools and established many new ones. Within the limited available resources, American-style public schooling came to almost every Philippine barrio. Intermediate schools were established in the principal barrios (*poblaciones*) of municipalities, and at least one secondary school in each province. In Manila itself, a normal school for training teachers, an arts and trade school, a nautical school, and a nursing school were launched, along with an agricultural institute on the island of Negros. The University of the Philippines opened in Manila in 1908, patterned after the burgeoning state universities of America's Middle West—all of this accomplished in under ten years.

The introduction of American education instituted a sharp break with tradition. Its imperatives were secular, not religious, where the educational experience of the Filipino people had almost exclusively been under the control of the Roman Catholic Church, if not its auspices, and had emphasized for its pupils the overriding goal of glorifying God. The commission revised the curriculum along familiar American lines and continued the study of United States history begun under General Arthur MacArthur. (Mr. Washington Conner—read "one who cons"—satirist George Ade's secular missionary, who was shouldering the white man's burden among his considered inferiors, the brown-skinned Filipinos, lectured one of his hapless charges, a Mr. Bulololo Kakyak, that "he had become subject to the government of the United States of America, and it was not his right but his bounden duty to study the history of the country to which he owed allegiance.") For its climax, the commission sent about three hundred of the ablest high school graduates to the United States at government expense for higher education. Many of the *pensionados,* as these fortunate young men were known, later rose into government service or taught at schools and colleges throughout the Philippines.

On July 1, 1902, Congress passed the Philippine Organic Act to define constitutional authority. The executive power remained with the commission. Legislative power was to be shared with an elected assembly as the lower house, the commission serving as the upper house. The commission would retain control over any legislating that might pertain to the non-Christian tribes. The judiciary's independence was maintained. The act also provided for a bill of rights, the conservation of natural resources, and a delegation of two Filipino resident commissioners to the United States House of Representatives. Mr. Dooley glimpsed Taft's condescension behind the omission of trial by jury: "I have not considhered it advisable to inthrajooce anny fads like thrile be jury iv ye'er peers into me administhration. Plain sthraight-forward dealin's is me motto. A Filipino at his best has on'y larned half th' jooty iv mankind. He can be thried but he can't thry his fellow man. It takes him too long."

Three conditions had to be met before the organic act could go into effect: the complete restoration of peace, the taking of a census, and a two-year moratorium to follow publication of the census. Opponents in the United States Senate blocked the immediate creation of any elective assembly. The census was undertaken from 1903 to 1905. The figures enumerated some 7,000,000 Christian Filipinos and nearly 650,000 non-Christians. Two years later, slightly more than 100,000 men voted out of 105,000 registered for the eighty-member assembly. Taft, by then secretary of war, returned to Manila to open the first session of the Philippine Assembly on October 16, 1907. Sergio Osmeña, a young Chinese mestizo from Cebu, whose Nacionalista party took thirty-two seats, was elected speaker, a position he would hold throughout the life of the assembly until 1916, and for six more years after the establishment of the House of Representatives. The Organic Act of 1902 did not embody a veto, yet the American majority on the commission between 1901 and 1913 effectively gave the governor-general an indirect veto contingent only upon his ability to work in harmony with his fellow countrymen. The Jones Act of 1916 gave the governor-general the power to veto legislation.

No issue perplexed Taft more grievously than the issue of the friars' lands. The holdings of the great orders totaled over 420,000 acres, the best arable lands of the Philippine Islands, while article 8 of the 1898 Treaty of Paris with Spain required the United States to uphold "the property or rights which by law belong to the peaceful possession of property of all kinds." Taft wrote to his brother Horace, September 8, 1900: "In the assignment of subject" among his commissioners, "the most delicate matter of the whole lot—the friar question—has fallen to me. I made the assignment myself so that I have no reason to complain on it." Taft undoubtedly sought over this issue to win the support of the Filipino elite, the *illustrados*, the highly educated, patriotic professionals. Knowing their absorbing concern over the friars' power, Taft apparently made up his mind almost on arriving in Manila that somehow the friars must be ousted. Secretary Root instructed the Taft Commission to investigate thoroughly the friars' holdings. Taft personally conducted the commission's hearings, taking testimony both for and against the friars, who were themselves among the parade of witnesses. The commission reported the well-nigh universal hatred for the friars that permeated all social classes. "If we, the Americans, could rid the islands of the friars, the gratitude of the people for our action would be so deep that the slightest fear of further insurrection would be entirely removed," Taft wrote confidentially to Secretary Root. Meanwhile Archbishop John Ireland conveyed to President Roosevelt the Vatican's willingness to receive the proposals of the United States from any authorized representative.

So Taft, who was home on leave recuperating from surgery, proceeded to Rome late in May 1902, accompanied by Bishop Thomas O'Gorman of Sioux Falls, General James F. Smith, a Catholic justice of the Philippine supreme court and later governor-general, and Major John Biddle Porter as secretary. Taft's mission was to purchase the friars' lands and win their immediate recall from the Philippines. The Vatican was willing only to consider the sale of the lands and insisted that any such transaction must take place in Manila, flatly rejecting the American proposal to withdraw the friars. By December 1903, the United States managed to purchase the friars' estates for $7.5 million, and the proceeds were divided among the orders. However, religious problems continued. Repeatedly thereafter the Catholic hierarchy objected to the Americanization of the Philippines on such prickly issues as the arrivals of prosletyzing Protestants.

Between 1900 and 1913, the constitutional, educational, and landed property bases for American rule in the Philippines were laid down under William Howard Taft's leadership and the two presidents, McKinley and Roosevelt, he served. The corpulent, jolly Taft, as the president of the Second Philippine Commission, the first civil governor, and the first governor-general, then next, as secretary of war following Theodore Roosevelt's election in 1904, in direct charge of the Bureau of Insular Affairs, and finally as president of the United States, erected the enduring structures of America's empire. American administrators aided by Filipinos modernized governmental structures, revamping some of the Spanish legal codes, and introduced a new currency system, regular census-taking, and a public health service. They brought under "sympathetic control" the pagan tribes of the mountainous region of northern Luzon and the Muslims of Mindanao and Sulu. They built schools, seaport and irrigation facilities, roads, bridges, markets, and various public buildings. To escape Manila's sweltering heat, Taft removed the seat of government in the hot season to Baguio north of Manila, where in the cool highlands the celebrated architect Daniel Burnham laid out the town plan along American lines.

As civil governor, Taft employed the libel and sedition laws to quash hostility between two profoundly antagonistic groups, Manila's Americans and the Filipino nationalists. The capital's four English-language newspapers and their jingoistic readers, among them many U.S. Army veterans, were unqualifiedly anti-Filipino. Two American editors, Eddie O'Brien and Fred L. Dorr, had to serve six months in prison for libeling Benito Legarda, a member of the Philippine Commission, by publishing the news that he was corrupt and guilty of concubinage. The American colonial courts applied the same statutes more strictly when Filipino writers were charged, although the nationalist newspapers cautiously sought to avoid prosecution. But the Filipino theater felt the full force of colonial rule in two cases involving flags. In Juan Cruz's play, *Hindi Aco Patay* (1903), the raising of the Katipunan flag caused a riot by drunken United States sailors and led to the sentencing of Cruz to two years' incarceration. That same month, in Aurelio Tolentino's *Kahapon, Ngayon at Bukas*, the trampling of the Stars and Stripes by a character played by Tolentino himself also caused Americans in the audience to riot and the playwright to be sentenced to serve two years in prison for subversion. Evenhanded mediation gave way to confrontation, and blatant Filipino rebelliousness had to struggle for survival. Taft personally looked after Philippine matters, long after his years there, as secretary of war, then president; his successors as governors-general, experienced Philippines administrators themselves, followed his guidance: Luke E. Wright (1904–1906), Henry C. Ide (1906 for a brief time only), James F. Smith (1906–1908), and William Cameron Forbes (1909–1913).

In the expanding series of insular cases to 1911, the United States Supreme Court defined the relationship of the United States to its newly acquired possessions and inhabitants. The Court relied substantially on a brief by Charles E. Magoon, a lawyer in the War Department's Division of Insular Affairs (the BIA's predecessor) to rule, after some vacillating on whether or not the Constitution follows the flag, that the islands were possessions, though not parts, of the United States of America. The Court further ruled that inhabitants of the insular possessions were not inherently "bound and benefitted, privileged and conditioned" by the Constitution, but that Congress could extend such similar privileges as it wished to do, although Alaska's inhabitants, as noted in the *Rasmussen* case, soon acquired territorial privileges with constitutional guarantees. Hence Filipinos were declared to be citizens of the Philippines but mere nationals of the United States without the rights and privileges of American citizenship. Those who had feared the sentiments urging Philippine statehood could rest unworried.[9]

It fell to President Woodrow Wilson, a Democrat, to terminate the Taft era. In August 1913, Wilson nominated Francis Burton Harrison, a Tammany Hall veteran with no experience in the islands, to become governor-general, underscoring the Democratic party's 1912 platform promise of independence for the Philippines. Wilson also appointed Filipinos to a majority of seats in the upper house of the legislature. Most important, the Jones Act, or Autonomy Act of August 29, 1916, greatly enlarged Philippine powers of home rule and promised independence as soon as a stable government could be established.

From this time on, there arose between American authorities and the Filipinos a fascinating, yet paradoxical, system of collaborative colonialism exercised through the politics of mutual manipulation. The Americans cautiously moved ahead, unwilling too abruptly to yield the task they had begun of constructing a stable, self-governing, and comparatively self-sufficient republic. Governor-General Harrison (1913–1921) proceeded to Filipinize the civil service, the cabinet, and even his own executive powers. He leniently relinquished certain prerogatives to Manuel Quezon, the former guerrilla captain and resident commissioner to the United States (1909–1916), now president of the senate, and he yielded other rights to Sergio Osmeña, the leader of the legislature's majority. Accommodating themselves to increasingly complex patterns of assimilation, the Filipino leaders acquiesced in the promise of eventual independence, yet inside themselves grew reluctant to allow the United States to withdraw altogether.

Quezon, Osmeña, and the aristocratic Dr. Trinidad H. Pardo de Travera, leader of the Federalista party, exemplified Filipino collaboration in the highest degree. Pardo de Travera was appointed by Governor-General Taft to the Philippine Commission and went on to notoriety as a pamphleteer for secular public education, doggedly opposing the church as a bastion of superstition. Sergio Osmeña proved himself a consummate constitutional technician second only to Quezon in popularity, until he succeeded in 1944 to the presidency of the commonwealth just before independence. Manuel Luis Quezon, the most magnetic of the trio, brilliantly projected his patriot's wounded sense of frustrated national pride, even as he mastered the idiom and customs of his overlords to charm American investors and officials. Together these three and their cohorts charted a graphic line of diminishing hostility and increasing receptivity to America's imperial presence.

Senior United States officials, more often than not, originated from the ranks of political careerists bent on advancement back home rather than on progress for the Philippines. Taft's spectacular rise from the provincial judiciary to the presidency via the governor-generalship encouraged other ambitious men to recognize the Philippines as a stepping stone to higher fortunes. Success in the Philippines required the cooperation of Filipino leaders. The governors who went home covered with glory and goodwill were those who ingratiated themselves into Filipino confidence. Likewise, the Filipinos had to play the same game in Manila to win patronage jobs for their lieutenants and concessions from Washington to impress their mass followings.

By 1921, however, after eight years of Harrison's Tammany-style office and the distractions caused by the World War, the Philippines were tottering on the brink of disaster. Epidemics of cholera and smallpox went unchecked, and the corruptly mismanaged Philippine National Bank was virtually bankrupt. Reaction inevitably set in to delay the progress underway.[10]

Leonard Wood, Harrison's Republican successor as governor-general (1921–1927) and comrade-in-arms of Theodore Roosevelt from the 1898 campaign of the Rough Riders in Cuba, moved vigorously, if not always tactfully, to restore the standards of stability, honesty, and efficiency of his Taft-era predecessors. Sent to the Philippines in 1903 as governor of Moro Province, encompassing Mindanao and Sulu, and promoted to major general, Wood had crushed the lingering opposition to American rule, earning criticism for his ruthlessness. From 1906 to 1908, he commanded all United States military forces in the Philippines. He served in Washington as chief of staff from 1910 to 1914 but was refused a European command after the United States entered World War I, having provoked President Wilson's displeasure by his bellicosity during the difficult months of neutrality. He failed in 1920 to win the Republican nomination for president and reluctantly accepted President Warren G. Harding's appointment to govern the Philippines instead of the post of secretary of war for which he campaigned. Distrusting the natives' capabilities for self-government, on the basis of his earlier experiences with them, Wood high-handedly repudiated the Filipinization policies of his predecessor and reinstated substantial measures of military control, allowing but scant prerogative to the legislature.

In Manila for several months, Wood's troubles were routine in nature, but scattered grievances eventually crystallized into a constitutional crisis on July 17, 1923, with the resignation of the cabinet. A nationalistic storm ensued. This affair was not caused by Wood by any evasions of the Jones Act nor any conflict of temperaments, although Wood's uses of the veto power had offended a number of legislators. Manuel Quezon staged the cabinet crisis to revive his flagging political fortunes. Quezon was losing control over his party, as was evident by his urgent need to elect his own candidate to the senate and by the partisan opposition rising against him. Quezon turned his handpicked candidate's campaign into a veritable carnival of nationalist denunciations of Governor-General Wood as the autocrat of Malacañang. Quezon staged a triumphant comeback himself as the immediate result. But Quezon's was a pyrrhic victory. The bitter senatorial campaign left wounds too deep to heal. Yet the cabinet crisis became instrumentally useful to upholding Quezon's popularity. The Filipino leader was forced to maintain a superpatriotic posture toward Wood. It was no longer expedient to display openly any harmony between them. Worse still for the cause of Philippine independence, their rupture delayed, most likely by a decade, the movement toward home rule.

On behalf of the political leaders and legislators, Manuel Roxas (due to Quezon's illness) sent President Calvin Coolidge a memorial, January 8, 1924, condemning Wood's actions and seeking his recall. Coolidge replied to the Filipinos as if they were ill-mannered children. Upholding Wood, the president warned that any further intransigence would probably be received by the United States as a clear indication of their unreadiness to govern themselves. That same year, the Fairfield Bill for independence was making headway through Congress, until Quezon and Osmeña, apparently wanting to have things both ways, derailed it by their lack of support. When, in 1925, the Philippine senate unanimously voted to hold a plebescite for independence, Wood's veto only added to his reputation for retarding Filipino sovereignty. Quezon could complain like any good anticolonialist that he would "prefer a government run like hell by Filipinos to one run like heaven by Americans." His popularity thrived by criticizing the American governors more surely than it might if their responsibilities became his own. "Damn the Americans," he once exploded to a follower. "Why don't they tyrannize us more?"

Tyranny was not the problem, neither too much nor too little; the problem was economic. By fostering dependence in important instances, American economic policies ran counter to the Philippines' movement toward political autonomy. Congress early enacted progressive conservation and antitrust laws to prevent American and other foreign investors from constructing large plantations and cartels, while homegrown sugar, tobacco, and other agricultural interests joined in to protect themselves against potential competition from producers in the archipelago. Such policies inhibited the native economy, especially when coupled, as they were, with the conservative, family-controlled, landholding patterns of the wealthiest class of Filipinos. By 1913, the United States and the Philippines shared a free trade reciprocity, while tariff barriers kept out most foreign competition. Ironically the United States was imposing a closed door, neomercantilistic policy on its colony yet proclaiming the Open Door policy for China. Revenues from insular taxes failed to meet the costs of government, although expenditures for civil administration were less than for the European colonies in Southeast Asia as the Americans anticipated their coming relinquishment of power. Yet the government's outlays for education and health were higher for the same reason. The clannish activity of the Chinese and Japanese communities, which hardly troubled the Americans accustomed to absorbing immigration, caused increasing concern to the Filipinos fearful of Oriental competition.

United States military policy was generous toward the Philippines insofar as American taxpayers bore the entire burden of defending the islands, but it was inexcusably inadequate in the forces deployed. Theodore Roosevelt perhaps did more than any other individual to acquire the Philippines. He soon changed his mind, regarding them, in the absence of any Mahan-style grand imperial design, as "our heel of Achilles . . . all that makes the present situation with Japan dangerous." He recognized the incompatibility of sustaining a far-flung empire by means of a third-rate navy and a sixth-rate army. In a predatory world, policy needed to be backed by armaments. Yet the United States government after 1920 subscribed to naval tonnage limitations that left Japan's navy paramount in the western Pacific, while erecting humiliating and hurtful barriers at home against both Japanese immigration and Japanese trade. Either of two possible courses of action might have reduced the growing threat from Japan. A mobilization of military prowess might have converted the Philippines, as Leonard Wood wished, into the "spearhead of the great Christian effort" in Asia. Alternatively a program of economic development joined to the Filipinization of the government might have located East Asia's co-prosperity sphere in Manila well before Tokyo cornered the concept. Instead the United States wavered in between, unwilling to emancipate its colonials, yet blindly unprepared to defend them or even itself against Japan.

At considerable sacrifice of his political influence, Leonard Wood had reaffirmed some of the substantive powers of the governor-general's office, although the indigenous movement toward independence continued unabated. Wood's successor after his death was Henry L. Stimson (1928–1929). Himself a committed imperialist, Stimson held that a dominion-style government would best serve the interests both of the Philippines and the

United States. Stimson's familiarity with the archipelago dated back to his position as secretary of war in Taft's administration. Since Stimson would become President Herbert Hoover's secretary of state, his tenure as the Philippines' governor-general was necessarily brief, but he managed to set relations between the empire and its colony onto a constructive course. Following the advice he gave to Wood in 1926, he conceded to Filipino politicians the highly valued authority to select the members of the cabinet from the ranks of their majority party. His concession instantly restored Filipino-American cooperation, ending the obvious hostility between the two groups. Stimson, however, upheld the powers of the governor-general in law enforcement, finance, and public health, Stimson's Republican successors, Dwight F. Davis (1929–1931), a wealthy patrician from St. Louis, and Theodore Roosevelt, Jr. (1932–1933), his father's eldest son, faithfully tried to carry out Stimson's intentions. The brevity of their tenures of office weakened their effectiveness, while young Roosevelt's incessant campaigning betrayed his presidential ambitions and dissipated his potential.[11]

In 1933, the Democrats' return to power, led by President Franklin D. Roosevelt, made the forces urging independence for the Philippines stronger than ever. The Great Depression acted as the catalyst. The New Deal's autarchic programs for economic recovery were unifying the nation's workers and farmers against outside competition. Sugar growers resentful of tariff-free imports, dairying producers of animal fats hostile to coconut oil, and labor's spokesmen opposed to admitting job-busting immigrants from the islands joined the Democratic party's traditional antiimperialists to press for freeing the Philippine Islands as soon as possible. Together with foreign-policy-minded isolationists and the farsighted realists worrying over Japan's rising sun, the strength added by the protective economic lobbyists made the time ripe for establishing an independent Philippines. Pressure from the new protectionists outweighed the vested interests' defense of their long-standing privileges.

Predictably America's military leaders were opposed to independence, regarding the Philippines as an asset, not a liability. That the army should think so was astonishing. Its own estimates of 1928 predicted that Japan would be capable of landing three hundred thousand soldiers in the Philippines within one month. To meet this threat, United States forces would consist of eleven thousand regular troops including seven thousand Philippines Scouts, plus the Philippines Constabulary of six thousand, and an aerial component of only nine bombers and eleven pursuit planes. Reinforcements from Oahu and the mainland could not be guaranteed. The navy also was blindly sanguine in evaluating the Philippines as a "distinct naval asset" to the United States, notwithstanding that no major navy base had yet been constructed there. By 1931, Japan's destiny was becoming clearer. Powerful economic combines, *zaibatsu*, had forged a commercial and cultural enclave on the southern island of Mindanao in Davao Province. Japan's army was conquering Manchuria, launching the puppet state of Manchukuo. Together, these were ominous portents for the security of the Philippines, either as an American colony or an independent republic.

Eloquently Army Chief of Staff General Douglas MacArthur and Britain's Winston Churchill championed an American presence to forestall the expansionist Japanese. MacArthur, Arthur MacArthur's son, himself with several tours of duty in the islands, admitted later that the Philippines "fastened me with a grip that never relaxed." Worried by the threats to the British, Dutch, and French colonies in Asia, Churchill, like Kipling before him, derided the bookkeeping consideration of profit and loss in urging the United States to retain its Philippines possession, an issue which "can only be decided upon considerations of national duty, dignity, and honor, and upon its international repercussions." Clearly, MacArthur and Churchill spoke Secretary of State Stimson's language, but President Hoover was antagonistic to colonies in principle and the enormous navies required to maintain them. Independence for the Philippines was in the cards at last.

Congress, stricken by the Depression, was determined to abandon the Philippines. Only the details that would affect trade and strategic responsibilities in the future needed to be reconciled with the timetable being proposed.

The Hare-Hawes-Cutting Bill sped through Congress in January 1933. Independence was to be granted the Filipinos in ten years. Meanwhile they would govern themselves as a commonwealth. American business would continue in the interim to enjoy profitable privileges, and the products of the Philippines could still enter the United States under liberal terms. American army and navy bases would not be affected. Hoover futilely vetoed the measure in spite of his anticolonialist convictions, as violating "the idealism with which this task in human liberation was undertaken" and confronting Americans and Filipinos alike with "new and enlarged dangers to liberty and freedom." The House of Representatives, in two hours, swamped the president's veto, and four days later the Senate followed with equal vehemence. William Randolph Hearst, whose newspapers had helped to ignite the 1898 war with Spain and ever since decried "the yellow peril," desperately mustered support for Hoover, but to no avail. Jingoism had lost its allure, and with its demise, three decades of Republican custodianship for the Philippines expired.

But Manuel Quezon upset Filipino-American relations once more. He had dispatched Osmeña and Roxas to Washington to lobby for independence. Now he was fearing their return as heroes bearing the garland of victory, with Osmeña likely to win the forthcoming presidential election while he himself vanished into obscurity. Quezon persuaded the Philippines Assembly, which had to ratify the accord, that Osmeña, Roxas, and other moderates had sold out their fellow citizens on crucial matters of trade and sovereignty, so the outraged legislators rejected the bill. Quezon hied himself to Washington, promising to obtain a better deal. Before departing, he cleverly won the support of Roosevelt's newly appointed governor-general, Frank Murphy, Detroit's welfare-minded ex-mayor, by explaining that he merely hoped to stretch out the period for commercial benefits while shrinking the wait for independence itself. Senator Millard Tydings of Maryland, whose committee was responsible for Philippine affairs, was not fooled by Quezon's rank opportunism, but he comprehended that Quezon alone had the influence to line up the legislature in Manila. Tydings and Representative John McDuffie of Alabama freshly packaged the Hare-Hawes-Cutting Bill, and with Roosevelt's blessing, the Tydings-McDuffie Act of March 24, 1934, brought the promise of independence at last to the Philippines.

Manuel Quezon reached home in triumph exactly as he intended. In 1935, he easily won election to the commonwealth's presidency.

Americans never have understood the Filipinos' love of authority. Their new constitution entrusted the president with extensive powers, including the right to invoke martial law that Ferdinand Marcos exercised in 1972. "The good of the Filipino state, not the good of the individual, must prevail," Quezon explained the distinction between Filipino and American democracy.

Governor-General Frank Murphy (1933–1935), as the result of Quezon's elevation, was the last American to hold that office, becoming as well the first high commissioner (1935–1936) to the Commonwealth of the Philippines. Filipinos respected Murphy, a bachelor perennially under his sister's mothering care, for his Catholic faith, patriotism, and sentimentality. They themselves could readily identify with Murphy, and many who were like him, including Quezon, admired him for this energetic philandering. Murphy hoped to inherit Roosevelt's liberal crown and calculated every move in the light of his political aspirations. Paul V. McNutt (1937–1938), Indiana's former governor and Murphy's successor, was a macho personality who, for Filipinos, represented a familiar type of politician and, like Murphy, was also a presidential hopeful. Masterfully McNutt utilized the authority inherent in the high commissioner's office during the final stage of American sovereignty. He, like Murphy, fostered an intimacy with President Quezon, who reciprocated to both men by encouraging their presidential ambitions. Francis B. Sayre (1939–1942), Woodrow Wilson's son-in-law, was the last United States high commissioner. A stern moralist and professional diplomat, Sayre tenaciously maintained all the presumptive powers of his office. His austere personality and economic preachings were loathed by the mercurial and sensuous Quezon. Between regimes, a number of capable deputies served as acting governors and high commissioners, but only two—Joseph Ralston Hayden and J. Weldon Jones—could be fairly compared to their outstanding superiors. McNutt alone of the high commissioners upheld an American strategy for the Far East based on the Philippines.[12]

War in the Pacific would change everything.

From 1937, Japan attacked, first in China, seizing the principal cities and pounding by 1939 at the temporary capital of Chunking (Chongqing) deep in the interior in her effort to crush the Nationalist government of Chiang Kai-shek. Next, with the opportunity afforded by France's sudden capitulation to Germany in June 1940 and the Luftwaffe's blitz paralyzing Britain, Japan entered the Tripartite Alliance with Germany and Italy and signed a neutrality pact with Russia. The United States was now isolated as Japan's sole obstacle to the domination of East Asia. Germany's victories left the British, French, and Dutch colonies in the Far East helpless before Tokyo's determination to establish a "new order" under Japanese control. With German pressure, Japan won concessions from France's Vichy puppet regime to occupy seaports and airfields in northern Indochina, opening the way to the rubber, tin, petroleum, and other resources of Vietnam, Malaya, Thailand, Burma, and the East Indies. The Nazis' attack on the Soviet Union in June 1941 freed Japan from the long-standing Russian threat to her rear.

Antagonistically, step by irreversible step, Japan and the United States began to move toward hostilities. The United States was insisting on its Open Door principles of equal commercial opportunity, noninterference in the internal affairs of other nations, respect for territorial integrity, and nondisturbance of the status quo in the Pacific except by peaceful means. Japan was unable to accede to these principles without surrendering her goals and sacrifices in China, a dishonor none of her leaders could or would endure. Already by November 26, 1941, when Washington rejected Tokyo's latest proposal, Japan's war orders had gone out to strike everywhere almost at once. The Imperial Japanese Navy had first to destroy the United States Pacific Fleet at Pearl Harbor before Japanese forces could overwhelm the Hong Kong–Singapore–Manila triangle of Western colonial power and prestige in East Asia.

Back in 1935, at President Quezon's inauguration, Vice-President John Nance Garner and Secretary of War George Dern had led the United States delegation to Manila bolstered by forty-three members of Congress. President Franklin D. Roosevelt's message had conveyed his hope that Filipinos would learn to appreciate America's "benediction," while Quezon asked God "to give me light, strength, and courage." Quezon eloquently intoned the poetry of American democracy, but in practice he was an autocrat, as Filipinos expected him to be, eager above all else to maintain his own power.

Tall and erect nearby, his profile chiseled like a statue's, Douglas MacArthur stood out in his new role as Quezon's military advisor. Quezon had delivered into his good friend MacArthur's willing hands the formidable task of safeguarding his country's security. Quezon dreamily expected the former army chief of staff to mold the fragile Philippine defense forces into an army like China's, which he extravagantly admired. He assumed that the United States would guarantee his country's protection. In June 1936, Quezon appointed MacArthur a field marshal, making him the only United States Army officer ever to hold that exalted rank. As trouble loomed, President Roosevelt recalled MacArthur to active duty as a major general, on July 26, 1941, and promoted him the next day to lieutenant general, his father's highest grade. In December, MacArthur would become a full general, and by the war's end a general of the army wearing five stars. Long before then, his Philippine forces were made part of the active United States Army.[13]

On December 8, 1941, the same day that Pearl Harbor was bombed (on December 7, Oahu time), Japanese warplanes attacked the Philippines, striking from Formosa at Clark and Iba airfields to destroy over half of the modern aircraft of the United States Armed Forces Far East (USAFFE) with only minor losses to themselves. Admiral Thomas C. Hart and General Douglas MacArthur received the news of Pearl Harbor at 3:15 A.M., Manila time, and alerted their subordinates to avoid getting hit unprepared like the Hawaiian commanders. Nonetheless the American fighters and bombers were caught being serviced or taxiing on the ground. Only three or four P-40's managed to take off into the maelstrom. The aerial attacks were followed up by Japanese landings at various points in the archipelago. The main bodies of troops came ashore at Lingayen Gulf on northern Luzon. Admiral Hart meanwhile withdrew the Asiatic Fleet from Manila Bay, which he believed could not be defended, to bolster the Malay Barrier and the approaches to Australia. On January 2, 1942, Japanese forces captured Manila. It was an American debacle equivalent to Pearl Harbor.

The surviving elements of the USAFFE retreated against the onslaught of the Japanese to Bataan Peninsula and the island fortress of Corregidor, accompanied by President Quezon and his government. From January 9, the battle for Bataan raged between Major General Jonathan Wainwright's troops and General Masaharu Homma's Fourteenth Army. Few supplies reached the beleaguered Americans and Filipinos, while hopes for reinforcements dwindled. The Philippines were doomed. Quezon and Osmeña fled to Australia. Quezon slipped his signet ring onto MacArthur's finger, brokenly saying, "When they find your body, I want them to know you fought for my country." On February 23, President Roosevelt ordered General MacArthur to go to Australia, and on March 12, the general, his wife, their five-year-old son, selected members of his staff, and two naval officers embarked on two PT boats to Mindanao, flying from there to Australia.

The end was at hand. Wainwright gave up Bataan on April 9, and less than one month later, on May 6, Corregidor's guns fell silent after a horrendous six-month siege. The infamous Bataan Death March for Bataan's and Corregidor's survivors followed their defeat. As many as ten thousand Americans and Filipinos perished along the roads to their internment camps. In Sam Grashio's description of the ghastly ordeal, the march was "a macabre litany of heat, dust, starvation, thirst, filth, stench, murder, torture, corpses, and wholesale brutality that numbs the memory." Horrors likewise befell the thousands of Americans later shipped to Japan and Manchuria as slave laborers, and in Manila itself the venerable Santo Tomás University was converted into a cruel prison for American civilians.

Soon after arriving in Australia, MacArthur had issued a short statement to reporters, concluding with his fateful words: "I shall return." His dramatic promise buoyed Allied and Filipino hopes throughout the three years of the Japanese occupation. But the way back to the Philippine Islands for the Americans and their allies proved to be arduous and painful, from Pearl Harbor, the Coral Sea, Midway Island, Guadalcanal, New Guinea, New Britain, the Gilbert and Marshall islands, and the Marianas across the vast reaches of the southern and central Pacific Ocean.

The Filipinos, in the meantime, were trapped in a terrible dilemma by Japan's smashing victories over the United States and the empires of the French, British, and Dutch. Many Filipino politicians felt betrayed or abandoned by the outcome of a struggle not of their own making. What did Filipinos have to gain any longer fighting for the Americans? Hong Kong had fallen, next Singapore, next Manila. Was not the white man driven from Asia? Accepting Japan's principles for the Greater East Asia Co-Prosperity Sphere, Benigno Aquino denounced the American failure to defend the Philippines, and José Laurel expressed a legal viewpoint that "the sovereignty of America in the Philippines has ceased, as well as that of the Commonwealth Government." Japan went ahead to set up a government similar to the commonwealth, promising independence, which indeed was granted in October 1943. Japan's occupation proved rigorously repressive nevertheless. The economy disintegrated. Food shortages caused severe hardships, particularly for Manila's population. Guerrilla warfare against the Japanese intensified throughout Luzon and the Visayan Islands. In Washington, Manuel Quezon and Sergio Osmeña, never quite believing in each other's fidelity, organized a government in exile. Quezon died in

August 1944 in upstate New York from the tuberculosis he had long suffered.

Quezon's death came but weeks before MacArthur's promised return. Vice-Admiral William Halsey opened the onslaught. Naval and marine aviators from his fast aircraft carriers dealt devastating blows to the Japanese airplanes and pilots guarding Okinawa, Luzon, and Formosa. MacArthur's amphibious forces of soldiers, marines, and sailors stormed ashore (October 17–20) from an enormous fleet of warships onto the Visayan island of Leyte in the heart of the archipelago. The Americans were invading not far from where Magellan had raised the cross for Spain and Christianity in 1521, and where MacArthur himself four decades earlier served as a second lieutenant. Cameras caught MacArthur wading ashore with Sergio Osmeña, now the president of the commonwealth, while radios transmitted his proclamation of redemption to the pious Filipinos: "I have returned. . . . Rally to me! . . . The guidance of divine God points the way. Follow in His name to the Holy Grail of righteous victory."

Highly alarmed, the Japanese went for a knockout. Four major naval fights erupted into the Battle of Leyte Gulf (October 23–26), the greatest sea battle in history, involving 282 ships, hundreds of airplanes, and 187,000 sailors and airmen. The United States Navy destroyed the attacking power of Japan's Combined Fleet.

Yet the liberation of the Philippines had only begun. Japan had deployed a terrible new weapon during the naval encounters just ended, the *kamikaze* suicide pilots. Leyte turned into a grim tropical battleground, where superior American firepower ultimately overcame the Japanese. On January 9, 1945, Lieutenant General Walter Kreuger's army began landing on Luzon at Lingayen Gulf, accompanied by Douglas MacArthur. His return exhilarated the now five-star General of the Army. Impatiently he drove the troops toward Manila. "We must move fast . . . ," he told photographer Carl Mydans, "to save as many of the prisoners as we can." To dramatize his return, he commanded the retaking of Bataan and Corregidor. Surprised on Corregidor, the Japanese lost over four thousand men in wild efforts to drive off the American paratroopers, climaxed by detonating their own munitions in a mass suicide. The struggle for Manila raged for weeks in bitter fighting street by street and building by building. Trapped, the beaten Japanese vented a savage fury on the hapless citizens equal only to their 1937 rape of Nanking. But most civilian casualties and the near-total destruction of the city resulted from the Americans' aerial bombings and the withering artillery exchanges between the two sides, especially from Rear Admiral Sanji Iwabuchi's defense forces trying to deny Manila's strategic harbor facilities intact to the Americans.

Eventually the end came. Sergio Osmeña was ceremonially installed as the president of the Commonwealth of the Philippines. On September 2, 1945, in Tokyo Bay, General of the Army MacArthur presided over Japan's formal surrender as high officers from all of the Allied nations stood beside him on the deck of the USS *Missouri*. The sole representative of the Philippines was an honorary Filipino—Douglas MacArthur.

The spectacle that unfolded in Manila on July 4, 1946, in front of the monument to José Rizal, the martyred nationalist, was unprecedented. Paul V. McNutt, the former high commissioner and now ambassador to the Republic of the Philippines, lowered the Stars and Stripes. President Manuel Roxas, who had defeated Osmeña in the election just held, raised the flag of the Philippines. Bands played the national anthems. In from Tokyo, General MacArthur exulted, "America buried imperialism here today." Notwithstanding his sentiments and the uniqueness of the occasion, the Philippines were fated to remain almost as dependent on the United States as ever.[14]

Today, half a century later, the Republic of the Philippines continues to struggle against enormous odds. Internal divisions are perpetuated through the chronic underdevelopment of the economy and the government's dependence on American financial assistance. The prolongation of American military installations at Subic Bay, Clark Field, and elsewhere in the islands, to support the Cold War against communism in Asia, frustrated Filipinos into feeling they have not fully won their long-sought freedom. When Alaska and Hawaii were entering the Union as full-fledged states of the Republic, the Philippines emerged from colonial subjugation into an appurtenant form of nationhood. The old joke that the colonial history of the Philippines consisted of three hundred years in a convent followed by fifty years of Hollywood is spinning out an ironic sequel.

Still, between Bataan and Cavite, astride the narrow straits entering into Manila Bay from the South China Sea, lie Corregidor and the tiny islands nearby, with their war-shattered fortifications and barracks. Ghost-like, the skeletal ruins hauntingly evoke memories of tragic encounters in the Philippine Islands between Spain and the United States, between the United States and Japan. The self-proclaimed destinies of these nations urged them toward the rich prospects China excited in their minds. Each seaborne power, in turn, imposed its colonial empire over the Philippine Islands. Eventually they collided one after the other, staining red with the blood of their sailors and soldiers the waters of Manila Bay and the Philippine Sea. China's empire has outlasted them all.

The policy of the Government of the United States is to seek a solution which may bring about permanent safety and peace to China, preserve Chinese territorial and administrative entity, protect all rights guaranteed to friendly powers by treaty and international law, and safeguard for the world the principle of equal and impartial trade with all parts of the Chinese empire.

John Hay[1]

5

THE OPEN DOOR FOR CHINA

China, the Middle Kingdom to the Chinese, the center of human existence, was a world in itself. Throughout the nineteenth century, destiny, duty, and cupidity prompted countless Americans toward China's Celestial Empire with its ancient culture and hordes of people. Commercial and spiritual zeal glowed over the prospects both of sending goods made in America into China's supposedly limitless markets and of converting to homespun brands of Christianity the heathen Chinese. These visions provided a rationale for strenuous action. China's proximity, in fact, was the primary attraction the Philippine Islands held for the United States, but acquiring the Philippines after Spain's defeat contributed only a part of the picture. William H. Seward's half-century-old dream of building an American trading empire with China motivated the majority.

Worriedly leaders in Washington watched Japan and the European trading powers commence to divide China among themselves by putting in place spheres of influence with exclusive privileges for their own nationals. China, weakened by her long decline, was rendered helpless by the devastating defeat suffered in the Sino-Japanese War of 1894–1895. Japan obtained Formosa (Taiwan) from the victory and secured her foothold in Korea. Then the McKinley administration saw Germany lease the port of Kiaochow (Jiaozhou) with adjacent territory in Shantung (Shandong) Province, while Russia wrested a leasehold at Port Arthur (Lüshun) on the Liaotung (Liaodong) Peninsula. France, already erecting an empire in

Vietnam, leased nearby Kwangchow (Kuang-chou) Bay in southern China. Great Britain exacted leases for the seaport of Weihaiwei (Weihai) on Shantung Peninsula and the New Territories adjacent to Kowloon opposite Hong Kong. Britain also won China's promise not to alienate the Yangtze valley to any other foreign power, thus obtaining there a rich sphere of influence. The British acted after vainly appealing to the United States for joint support to uphold their long tradition of equal commercial opportunity for all nations trading in China. Alarmed businessmen from the newly organized American Asiatic Association, abetted by their missionary friends, began to clamor for governmental help.

Secretary of State John Hay thereupon circulated his famous "Open Door" notes. On September 6, 1899, his first note asked Japan, Russia, Germany, Great Britain, France, and Italy each to sustain a policy of equal trading opportunity for all nations within their spheres. Hay was relying for advice on William W. Rockhill, his advisor on Asia, and Rockhill's British friend, Alfred Hippisley of the Chinese Imperial Maritime Customs Service. Hay read what he wanted into the noncommittal, evasive replies received and proceeded brashly to proclaim international adoption of the United States' policy of the Open Door for China. Hay's second Open Door note, dated July 3, 1900, went out during the Boxer Rebellion amid widespread antiforeigner violence and the prospect that the powers might dismember China in retaliation. This time Hay appealed for China's independence. The "policy of the Government of the United States is to seek a solution," Hay declared, "which may bring about permanent safety and peace to China, preserve Chinese territorial and administrative entity, protect all rights guaranteed to friendly powers by treaty and international law, and safeguard for the world the principle of equal and impartial trade with all parts of the Chinese Empire."

Triumphant outwardly and popularly appealing at home, Secretary Hay's policy of the Open Door for China over the next four decades would harden itself into a sloganized American shibboleth. Yet time and again it would prove itself to be unenforceable and, finally, provocatively misleading about Asia's realities and changing circumstances. The Boxer Rebellion of 1900 was, in truth, the beginning of the end of the exploitation of China by outsiders, an augury of the nationalist and socialist revolutions of the twentieth century. Americans and Chinese had for some time been moving together toward this epochal moment.

The Treaty of Nanking of 1842, to conclude the Opium War between Great Britain and China, tipped the balance in favor of Westerners, and the American and French governments promptly, in 1844, won equivalent rights for their own nationals to trade and reside beyond Canton (Guangzhou). Within another decade, these three foreign powers were pressing the

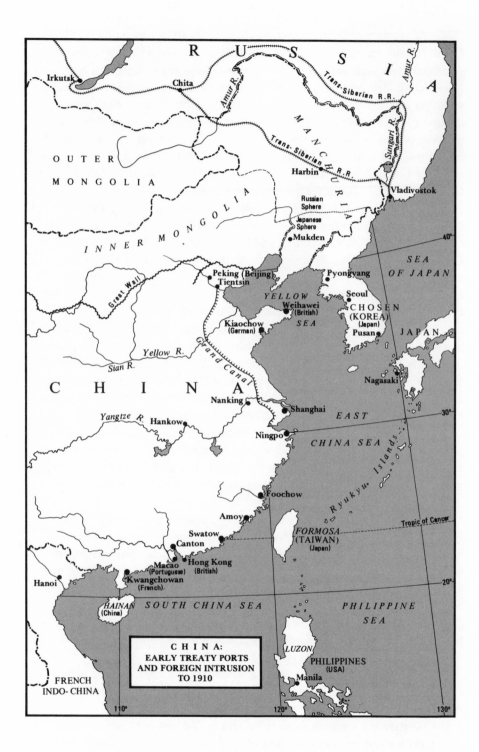

CHINA:
EARLY TREATY PORTS
AND FOREIGN INTRUSION
TO 1910

Chinese for treaty revisions to reduce existing restrictions on opportunities for commerce. Russia meanwhile thrust southward from Siberia toward Peking (Beijing) seeking, in addition to trade, territorial gains in Manchuria. The Americans, British, and French reinforced each other's claims. Their representatives joined in demanding lower tariffs, legations in Peking (where none but Russians were then admitted), opening of Tientsin (Tianjin) to traffic and residence, authority to purchase land in the interior, legalization of opium import, and abolition of inland transit duties. Unwilling to suffer further rebuffs, Dr. Peter Parker, the missionary American commissioner, made a solitary effort to reach Peking in 1854, but Chinese officials forestalled him at Shanghai.

The Second and Third Opium Wars of 1856 and 1859, fought by Anglo-French forces against the Chinese, finally gained the desired concessions. William B. Reed, a Philadelphia politician who once taught American history at the University of Pennsylvania, served as the United States plenipotentiary. Reed was instructed to cooperate amicably with the British and French and assure the Chinese that the United States entertained neither territorial nor political designs on their empire.

The Treaty of Tientsin of 1858, which Reed secured, and the Peking Convention of 1860 augmented the treaties of 1842 and 1844 to cement into place the so-called unequal treaties system. Together with subsequent agreements, through their encroachments against China's sovereignty by means of treaty port privileges, special concessions, leaseholds, and spheres of influence, they imposed a semicolonial servitude upon the Chinese people. Three stipulations proved particularly noxious: (1) the tariff fixed at 5 percent ad valorem, which precluded China's right to impose any protective schedule of duties in the future; (2) extraterritoriality, which allowed the foreigners to govern themselves under their own laws and customs administered by consular courts exempt from China's jurisdiction; and (3) the most-favored-nation clause, which granted to every treaty power all of the privileges gained by any one of them. Although the Americans by 1850 were carrying about one-third of China's oceanic traffic with the West, they trailed behind the British and French in obtaining diplomatic favors. Americans profited, nevertheless, by their piggybacking form of imperialism, from the derived blessings accruing to them as a most favored nation.[2]

Belatedly the Qing dynasty's bureaucrats conceded that the Westerners' victories at China's expense threatened greater dangers still to come and were not a mere historical accident. The unequal treaties perhaps were less influential than the foreigners thought, but without modernizing like Japan to save itself, the Celestial Empire would surely disintegrate. The rights of extraterritoriality, which originated in the 1840s to regulate about 350 Britons and Americans trading in 5 seaports, would expand over a century to encompass, in one way or another, 115 ports and some 350,000 foreign nationals. China's officials were endeavoring to appease the Anglo-French invaders as well as the Americans and Russians, their most-favored-nation beneficiaries, while at the same time striving to quash an assortment of internal disorders. The largest domestic upheaval, the Taiping Rebellion between 1850 and 1864, nearly overturned the dynasty.

The Taiping Rebellion burst unexpectedly out of Christian sectarianism, but it was also a classic peasant uprising. The Taiping's prophet was Hung Hsui-ch'uan. Hung preached a passionate gospel of Old Testament–based Protestant Christianity and a brotherhood of revolutionary nationalism and egalitarianism. Taiping Christianity blended Occidental and Oriental inspirations into a militant call for action that led to a civil war against China's Manchu overlords. For protection, Shanghai's rich merchants and businessmen desperately sponsored a foreign legion led by Frederick T. Ward, an adventurous Yankee from Salem, Massachusetts. The legion's successes against the Taiping earned from the grateful emperor the title of "Ever-Victorious Army," and Ward was given the rank of a brigade-general. When Ward died of battle wounds, his command fell to another American, Henry A. Burgevine, a shady conspirator who promptly purloined forty thousand silver dollars for himself. Burgevine was relieved of his duty by the famous British officer Charles George "Chinese" Gordon. The tremendous destruction of life and property included the burning of the Summer Palace in Peking by the British and French, who took advantage of the chaos to wrest additional privileges for themselves. Sated at last by the revision of their treaties in 1860 opening eleven more ports to them and granting freedom for their missionaries, the British and French thereupon backed the Manchus against the Taiping rebels. The Americans duly followed the Anglo-French lead, playing piggyback once again.

Somehow over the next forty years, the Qing dynasty made China's old system work by adopting a limited number of Western ways. Peking desperately aimed to achieve peace through diplomacy and accommodation. Self-strengthening was its long-term defensive program. Temporarily China managed to stymie the dual menaces of foreign invasion and internal rebellion.

Driven by co-regent Prince Kung, the imperial court established the Tsungli Yamen (Office for General Management) to consolidate the direction of foreign affairs. This office was arranged in five bureaus: Russian, British, French, American, and Coastal Defense. Two other agencies were attached to it: the Inspectorate-general of Customs and the College of Foreign Languages (the *t'ung-wen kuan*) to train interpreters. Robert Hart, an extraordinary Ulsterman, efficiently developed China's Imperial Maritime Customs Service into an international facility, and many outstanding foreigners served under him. These included H. B. Morse, a Harvard graduate, who later wrote important studies of Chinese trade, administration, and foreign relations. W. A. P. Martin, having just earned his doctorate at Indiana University, was installed in 1869 as president of the *t'ung-wen kuan* to introduce American-style college education. If it did not actually flourish as a foreign ministry, Tsungli Yamen came out fairly well as China's first modernizing institution. Unhappily, the self-strengthening movement restricted itself to equipping China with weapons, ships, machines, mines, communications, and light manufactures. China never attained an industrial takeoff point, as her defeats in the wars with France, 1884–1885, and Japan, a decade later, painfully show. Western philosophy, culture, and the arts were spurned as barbarian. Steadfast, in its own view, the Middle Kingdom was still the center of civilization.[3]

Back home in the United States, in the spring of 1861, President Abraham Lincoln and Secretary of State William H. Seward confronted the Civil War. The sectional crisis forced Seward to put aside his dream for the United States to play the major part in North Pacific and East Asian trade. Seward had to gain international support for the Union and forestall any outside assistance from reaching the Confederacy. He dispatched Anson Burlingame, an ex-congressman from Boston, to China as minister, under instructions to cooperate fully with the European powers there.

In 1868, Prince Kung appointed Anson Burlingame, who was retiring by then, to a diplomatic mission intended to discourage Europeans and Americans from hurrying the progress of modernization for China. Burlingame windily accepted: "When the oldest nation in the world, containing one-third of the human race, seeks, for the first time, to come into relations with the West, and requests the youngest nation, through its representative, to act as the medium of such change, the mission is not one to be solicited or rejected." Burlingame arrived in California, together with a Manchu and a Chinese as co-envoys, and grandiloquently announced that the hour had struck, the day had come, when China was prepared to welcome "the shining banners of Western civilization." He went on, in New York City, to proclaim that China was opening itself to missionaries "to plant the shining cross on every hill and every valley."

President Andrew Johnson received him, whereupon Burlingame, on his own authority, signed a treaty with Secretary Seward that committed the United States to noninterference in Chinese affairs. The Burlingame Treaty, as it became known, provided for the entry of Chinese consuls and laborers, with reciprocal rights for Americans in China of residence, religion, travel, and education. While not consulted beforehand, Peking was too pleased with its generous provisions to disown Burlingame's treaty, or the later pledges of restraint in treaty revising that the mission won in London, Paris,

Berlin, and St. Petersburg. Thirty long-gowned boys of the Chinese Educational Mission soon went off to Hartford, Connecticut, directed there by Yung Wing, Yale '54, to live with host families while attending schools in the Connecticut valley and learn, among other things, to play baseball. Altogether 120 boys were sent to America in four installments, 1872–1881, before the experiment was halted by conservative opponents on both sides.

At this time, racist agitation against the more than one hundred thousand Chinese workers in the United States was intensifying, even as antiblack violence terrorized the recently freed slaves. Brutality against the Chinese became commonplace, and the sentiment spread to favor excluding any more Chinese immigrants. President Rutherford B. Hayes vetoed a bill, as violating the Burlingame Treaty, to limit to fifteen the number of Chinese who could arrive in any one vessel. Both major political parties went on record, in their platforms of 1880, to oppose admitting any more Chinese immigrants. The United States forced a treaty revision on China to permit the suspension, though not the prohibition, of Chinese immigration, and Congress promptly enacted such an interruption for a period of ten years—the first step toward a permanent policy of exclusion. Anti-Chinese violence subsided, although in Wyoming twenty-eight Chinese miners were murdered in 1885, and lesser atrocities occurred sporadically, most of them in the west.

Meanwhile in China, the self-strengthening movement was faltering before reactionary resistance ordinarily expressed in anti-Christian agitation. The mandarins were holding onto their disdain for merchants and industrialists. Scholars, in fact, were directing the government's undercover opposition to any drastic modernization. Christians found themselves condemned by Confucians as superstitious and heterodox and resented by the landlord gentry in rural districts for taking over their traditional social welfare functions. Anti-Christian pamphleteering burst out, even as Burlingame was urging American missionaries to plant their shining crosses throughout China. The claim of the Taiping and other rebels to be Christians did not help, nor did the Christian practice of males and females worshiping together in mixed assemblies. Christianity's challenge to ancient customs was made notorious by the arrival in 1873 of the first woman physician, Lucinda L. Coombs, MD, of the Methodist Women's Society, who went ahead to build China's first hospital for women. And Kying Yuo Me, the first Chinese woman doctor, graduated in 1885 from the Women's Medical College of the New York Infirmary.

The missionaries proselytized for their Saviour, protected by foreign gunboats and bayonets as part of the hated treaty system. Many worked through pioneer agencies such as the London Missionary Society and the American Board of Commissioners for Foreign Missions. By the 1890s, these old China hands were being joined by shining-eyed newcomers in baffling sectarian profusion. Too often Chinese converts displayed a blatant intolerance for traditional beliefs and long-honored customs. They appeared to cast aside all respect for their elders. They refused homage to their ancestors. If they ran afoul of the law, they knew that missionaries would come to their assistance. Paradoxically the rivalry mushrooming among the imperial powers aided the missionaries and other favor-seeking foreigners.

In Japan's abortive invasion of Formosa in 1874, and her annexation in 1879 of the Ryukyu (Liu-ch'iu) Islands, China's vulnerability was evident. The British try at opening Yunnan in 1875, the Russian occupation of Ili in Sinkiang (Xianjiang) 1871–1881, and Japan's aggression in Korea were followed by the Sino-Japanese War of 1894–1895. Not only were China's modernizers becoming distracted, but precious resources were drained away from the self-strengthening effort. The scramble for concessions was threatening to partition China like Africa. Where Great Britain had long dominated the China trade, Germany and Russia now sought to monopolize entire provinces, and France was erecting a Southeast Asian empire at China's expense. Economic conditions were worsening throughout China. Demands for reform increased, yet most were rebuffed. Antiforeigner sentiments rose toward the boiling point. Anger was focused against the missionaries and their converts.

It was at this juncture, in 1898, that Commodore George Dewey hurled his flotilla from Hong Kong down the South China Sea to attack Spain's fleet in Manila Bay, and the United States moved forcibly onto China's threshold after conquering the Philippine Islands. The United States in East Asia was now a major power far across the western Pacific. Whether or not the Celestial Empire itself was about to be carved up by the imperial nations, or saved instead by the policy of the Open Door, remained to be seen.

More important, the Qing dynasty (1644–1912) was fast expiring, threatening by its demise to extinguish the oldest empire on earth. Yellow River floods in Shantung together with droughts in northern China added famine and its suffering on a vast scale. Disaster victims spread the superstition that their ancestral gods were punishing the Chinese people for the terrible wrongdoings of the foreigners. Secret antiforeign societies proliferated.[4]

The "Boxers" bore a nickname given by the governor of Shantung to their clandestine organization, the Society of Righteous and Harmonious Fists. Its members practiced so-called Chinese boxing, a series of exercises and postures intended physically and spiritually to ready them for combat, even making them supposedly invincible against foreign bullets. Like the Taiping rebels, the Boxers pursued both political and religious motives. Conservative Chinese officials welcomed the fervor of their antiforeign and anti-Christian slogans. In May 1900, the all-powerful Empress Dowager

Tz'u-hsi and several princes surreptitiously adopted them, when at least half of the army became Boxers. Alarmed for their safety, the foreign legations in Peking summoned an international force of armed guards from their navies moored off Tientsin. The guards were met on the way by the Boxers.

In the uprising of June, July, and August 1900, the rampaging Boxers, some 140,000 strong, pillaged and murdered their way across northern China, then laid siege in the capital to the diplomatic legations. They killed scores of Christian missionaries and thousands of their Chinese converts. They killed a Japanese diplomat and Germany's ambassador.

President McKinley quickly ordered twenty-five hundred United States troops from the Philippines under General Adna R. Chaffee to Peking to join the relief expedition of 15,500 soldiers, sailors, and marines from seven other nations. But Russia, in addition, supposedly to suppress the Boxers, sent about two hundred thousand soldiers into Manchuria. Russia's action especially irritated the Japanese because of both the great numbers of her soldiers sent into Manchuria and the protracted delay afterward in withdrawing them. Secretary of State John Hay, this time without consulting the other powers or the Chinese government, sent around his second Open Door note on July 3, 1900, to define the three pedestals of United States policy: (1) the protection of American lives and property, (2) the opportunity for open and impartial trading, and (3) the preservation of China. In sum, keep China intact to keep the trade door open. The international relief expedition defeated the Boxers, first capturing Tientsin, then entering Peking on August 14 to relieve the beleaguered legations before plundering and ravaging the city. The empress dowager and Emperor Guangxu fled to Sian (Xian). McKinley countermanded the orders he had issued assigning a ten-thousand-man American force to China, and transferred to the Philippine Islands two-thirds of the sixty-three hundred already there.

The Boxer Rebellion left a significant residue. By the Protocol of 1901, the expeditionary powers assessed China about $333 million for damages, which some of them, including the United States, later rescinded in part to educate Chinese students in their own countries. Foreign troops were authorized to remain in Peking to guard their legations, and to be stationed at various places between the capital and the seacoast. The United States even requested a parcel of territory for a naval coaling station at Sansha (Sanshawan) Bay above Fukien Province (Foochow), until the Japanese reminded Secretary Hay that this action would violate his own Open Door principles. Thereafter, louder than ever, American officials touted the Open Door policy for China. Even though fragile and insubstantial, the Open Door assumed considerable weight. Japan and the other powers, with the exception of Russia, feared that a catastrophic conflict might break out of

any scramble to partition China. The United States, more or less unconsciously adhering to Seward's dream of a North Pacific trading empire,
wanted to enjoy commercial opportunities in China without having to
commit itself. In the meantime, the prestige of the Celestial Empire sank
lower and lower. Foreign ambassadors dictated their governments' policies
to the Qing court, while on China's soil, without interference, Japan fought
Russia, 1904–1905, over Manchuria and Korea. The few reforms came
grudgingly, far too little and much too late. Many began to turn to the
republican movement led by Sun Yat-sen.[5]

Of course, the Open Door policy could not always succeed, but like the
Monroe Doctrine, it would lodge itself in the public mind as the morally
patriotic course for American foreign relations to take. In 1904, the United
States fixed the strength of its Peking legation guard at 305 soldiers and
marines. For emergency service in China, a force was designated of two
thousand soldiers stationed in the Philippines that could be expanded to
five thousand. An infantry battalion went to Tientsin following the revolution of 1911, and a second in 1914, to protect access routes to Peking. By
1902, the Asiatic Squadron had grown to forty-eight units, including one
battleship, two armored cruisers, and gunboats to patrol China's coastal and
inland waters. This fleet stood ready, the government proclaimed, to
guarantee "the interests of civilization and trade" and to administer, if
called to do so, "severe and lasting punishment" to anyone foolhardy
enough to threaten the safety of Americans anywhere in Asia.

The tempestuous climate of international rivalry aggravated China's
internal condition, though President Theodore Roosevelt consistently
strove to achieve a balance of power and a stable world order. Himself a
realist, though virtually hypnotized by Japan's muscle flexing, Roosevelt
hesitated to press his country's policy of the Open Door for China without
either the military power or the popular commitment at home to back him
up. He turned China's nationalists against him in the process. By March
1904, he was describing Japan's relationship with Korea, China's longtime
tributary province, as "just like we have with Cuba." The Taft-Katsura
memorandum of a conversation between his new secretary of war and
Prime Minister Taro Katsura, July 27, 1905, confirmed Roosevelt's stance,
while Katsura explicitly denied any Japanese designs on the Philippine
Islands. Roosevelt next terminated the Russo-Japanese War in the Treaty of
Portsmouth (New Hampshire), September 5, 1905, winning Russia's recognition of Japan's freedom of action in Korea and, in 1906, the Nobel Peace
Prize for himself. Roosevelt wrote that "our future history will be more
determined by our position on the Pacific facing China, than by our position
on the Atlantic facing Europe."

Nevertheless, Roosevelt's balancing act failed to benefit the United

States. China's nationalists denounced Americans for crushing the Boxers, the bloody extermination of the Filipinos, and the racist Immigration Act of 1904, which permanently barred any more Chinese from admission to the United States or its territories. Angrily, in 1904, the Chinese boycotted American goods and canceled J. P. Morgan's railroad franchise. Japan commenced to displace Russia as the leading outside power in northeastern Asia and, in 1905, renewed her alliance of 1902 with Great Britain. In 1907, Japan and Russia, the two recent enemies, secretly divided Manchuria between them into their respective spheres of influence. Russia acquiesced in Japan's determination to control Korea, and Japan, for a quid pro quo, recognized Russia's "special interests" in Outer Mongolia. In 1910, Japan, Russia, and Great Britain closed ranks against a blundering proposal by Secretary of State Philander C. Knox on behalf of a New York banking consortium to internationalize Manchuria's railways. Japan went ahead, that same year, to annex Korea outright. Effectively locked out of Manchuria and Korea by these developments, the United States government, on being informed, uttered not so much as a protest. It was in the nation's interest, ex-President Roosevelt explained, "not to take any steps as regards Manchuria which will give the Japanese cause to feel . . . that we are hostile to them, or a menace—in however slight a degree—to their interests." Obviously the Russo-Japanese entente was overriding the policy of the Open Door.

In a reversal, President Taft and Secretary Knox championed both the Open Door and Chinese nationalism. Taft, as Roosevelt's secretary of war, had once characterized China's market potential as "one of the greatest commercial prizes of the world." Willard Straight, United States consul general in Mukden, persuaded Taft in 1905, to support the Manchurian banking and railway scheme of E. H. Harriman, the railroad magnate. Taft and Knox, in due course, favored a policy for China of "Dollar Diplomacy." As Taft put it: "This policy has been characterized as substituting dollars for bullets. It is one that appeals alike to idealists of humanitarian sentiments, to the dictates of sound policy and strategy, and to legitimate commercial aims." The problem with Dollar Diplomacy lay in the reluctance of the American bankers, led by J. P. Morgan, to risk their capital in assuredly hazardous investments. So Willard Straight, now acting chief of the State Department's new Far Eastern Division, ordered Minister William W. Rockhill in Peking to demand American participation in the consortium of European bankers financing railway construction in China through the so-called Huguang Project. Pressed by the prince regent, the consortium duly admitted the American bankers, and in June 1911 the requisite loan was launched. But China's revolution, in part ignited by this latest foreign intrusion, delayed the start of construction for nearly two years. Dollar

Diplomacy, Willard Straight later admitted, "made no friends in the Huguang matter."[6]

Sun Yat-sen launched China's revolution of 1911. Sun grew up in the pro-Taiping, anti-Manchu region between Macao and Canton, the homeland for a great many overseas Chinese and China's longest-established foreign trading connections. He became a Christian, and commenced his personal Westernization in Honolulu, where he had gone in 1879, at the age of thirteen, to live with his older brother. At Iolani School, his Anglican teachers and schoolmates favored independence for Hawaii's kingdom against the threat of an American takeover. Sun, upon graduating, took the second prize for English grammar. He pursued advanced studies at Oahu College (today's Punahou School) until his brother sent him home to China. He promptly despoiled his village's idols and was exiled to Hong Kong. There he became a Congregationalist and began studying medicine under the British-trained Dr. Ho Kai, a reformer with an English wife. Sun turned to revolutionary nationalism. In Hawaii once more, he secretly organized the Revive China Society aimed at overthrowing the Manchus, restoring China to the Chinese, and instituting a republican government, and in 1895, he organized the Hong Kong branch to exploit the patriotic anguish over Japan's victory. An exile for years, Sun tirelessly traversed the globe agitating, speaking, and writing.

Dr. Sun Yat-sen's *Three People's Principles* (1903) preached nationalism, democracy, and socialism. In Chinese traditional terms, the principles meant people and race molded into a nation, people's rights, and people's livelihood—Henry George's antilandlord single-tax panacea to end peasant poverty, not Karl Marx's dialectical materialism. Sun was again raising funds in the United States when the Qing dynasty collapsed in October 1911, following the death of the empress dowager. Sun rushed back to Nanking in time to be installed on January 1, 1912, as president of the newly proclaimed Republic of China, but he offered to hand over his office to Yuan Shih-kai, the imperial army's commander-in-chief and reputedly a reformer, if Yuan would support the republic. Emperor P'u Yi, "the Last Emperor," the boy later known as Henry P'u-yi, abdicated on February 12, 1912, and Sun resigned in Yuan's favor.

Ruthlessly Yuan moved ahead to consolidate his power. He blinded the American missionaries to his cruelties by promising to tolerate Christianity. Wishfully they acclaimed China's new republic "the coming of the larger civilization of men which draws no national boundaries and which is controlled by good will." When Yuan turned to the United States for financial help, his self-proclaimed "Kingdom of God" wholeheartedly appealed to Taft's and Knox's pro-China bias. Knox even suggested expanding the bankers' consortium to include Japan and Russia. However, the

Tokyo and St. Petersburg governments in return demanded more concessions in Manchuria and Mongolia. Great Britain, France, Germany, and the
United States also attempted to extort additional concessions for themselves, refraining throughout 1912 from extending diplomatic recognition to
the infant republic.[7]

Immediately, in another abrupt move, President Woodrow Wilson,
newly inaugurated in March 1913, and his secretary of state, William
Jennings Bryan, expressed their opposition to the consortium's infringe-
ments on China's autonomy by canceling the American partnership. Just as
he would shortly do for the Philippines, Wilson reversed the policies laid
down by Presidents Roosevelt and Taft. Wilson, the moralist, and Bryan,
the Populist, mistrusted both Roosevelt's *realpolitik* and Taft's Dollar Diplomacy. Wilson renewed the United States government's commitment to
maintaining China's territorial integrity. It was a goal abandoned as imprac-
ticable by Roosevelt against the forcefulness of Japan's expansion; a goal
revived, though botched, by Taft; a goal being effectively countermanded
by Japan's deeds, if not by her words. To do less, Wilson and Bryan
reasoned, the United States would have to repudiate the honorable position
that John Hay secured by extending his Open Door policy in the midst of the
Boxer Uprising. Although Wilson misunderstood Hay's purpose, he felt "so
keenly the desire to help China," by putting pressure on the imperialists to
restrain themselves, that on May 21, 1913, he unilaterally granted full
diplomatic recognition to the republic. Wilson's supporters were delighted
by this display of his lofty moral principles, but the other powers, particularly Japan, were not.

A month later, civil war broke out across China between President
Yuan's forces and his parliamentary opponents of the Kuomintang. The
birth of the republic had done little to convert the Chinese masses to
nationalism. The country's regional leaders were still cultivating their own
ambitions rather than enhancing the nation's welfare. Several provincial
generals detached their military units one by one from Yuan's army to resist
his suddenly announced intention to make himself emperor. Yuan's American strategist, Dr. Frank J. Goodnow, who eventually became president of
Johns Hopkins University, declared that restoring the autocracy would
make China's movement toward constitutional government more likely to
succeed than if factionalism were to continue to prevail. Undeluded by
Goodnow's bizarre logic, Sun Yat-sen led the rising tide of anti-Yuan
agitation, and Yuan's own lieutenants forced him to give up his soaring
dreams of imperial glory. In June 1916, Yuan Shih-kai died, and the last
vestige of national government died with him. The age of the warlords had
dawned.

But China needed capital as much as unity. Woodrow Wilson's singular pullout from the consortium, together with the onset in 1914 of the Great War in Europe, left Japan undisturbed to play a foreign role in China's economic development. The Japanese, unlike the Americans, foresaw no useful purposes for themselves in fostering the modernization of China into a strong, self-reliant nationalistic society. Wilson's scuttling of the consortium followed by the guns of August left Japan in the position of becoming the sole source for the financial underwriting China so urgently required. The Japanese wasted little time in making this point crystal clear for President Wilson.[8]

The outbreak of war in Europe in August 1914 freed the Japanese to make their own way. Japan declared war on Germany on August 23, ostensibly to uphold the alliance with Great Britain. Japanese forces overran the German leaseholds of Kiaochow Bay and the port of Tsingtao (Qingdao) on the south coast of China's Shantung Peninsula, then occupied Germany's North Pacific colonies in the Marshall Islands, the Carolines, the Marianas, and Palau (Belau). The Tokyo government followed up its seizures by presenting China's President Yuan Shih-kai, in January 1915, the notorious Twenty-one Demands subdivided into five categories. China must agree to (1) recognize Japan's special interest in Shantung; (2) yield to Japan's demands for Inner Mongolia and Manchuria; (3) accept joint Sino-Japanese operation of China's iron and steel industries; (4) promise not to cede any coastal area to another foreign power; and (5) allow Japan to control the vital elements of China's internal administration including police, military, and economic affairs. By leaking these humiliating demands to the press, Yuan embarrassed the Japanese enough for them to put aside the fifth group for later consideration, but he was forced to acquiesce in the particulars of the first four. The Sino-Japanese treaties of May 1915 confirmed Japan's now dominant role over China's economy. Among the Chinese people, especially intellectuals and the moneyed middle class, the Twenty-one Demands touched off an outrage of wounded pride and boycotts of Japanese goods. No Western power came to China's defense. President Wilson was himself preoccupied with problems closer to home growing out of the war in Europe and Mexico's revolution.

The Wilson administration's initial reaction to Japan's Twenty-one Demands consisted merely of Secretary of State Bryan's declaration that the United States would refuse to recognize any agreement between Japan and China harmful to its treaty rights, to the rights of its citizens, or to the Open Door. Secretly, however, Japan's British, French, and Italian allies pledged themselves to support her demands at the peace conference for Germany's rights in Shantung. Diplomatically isolated, the United States alone could not help China against Japan's determination to expand in East Asia. But Japan became suddenly transformed into an ally in April 1917 by the entry of the United States into the World War. China, in August, also declared war against Germany, as urged to do by Great Britain and the United States, to counter Japan at the peace table. However, Secretary of State Robert Lansing, Bryan's replacement, in his agreement of November 2, 1917, with Viscount Kikujiro Ishii, conceded Japan's special interests in China owing to her "territorial propinquity," while, just as paradoxically, Ishii guaranteed his nation's support for the Open Door and China's territorial integrity. Japan's agents compounded the dismay of the Chinese by explaining away the Lansing-Ishii Agreement as an example of American perfidy concerning the Open Door policy for China. Intervening, President Wilson revived the international banking consortium he had earlier destroyed. To get Japan's cooperation, the consortium had to agree, as it had in 1912, to stay out of Manchuria. Wilson was thrown back where he started and where Taft had finished—thwarted in China by Japan. Worse, as it came out, the warlords governing at Peking had already signed protocols confirming Japan's rights as Germany's successor in Shantung.[9]

Between 1916 and 1928, China split itself into a decentralized country of warlord-dominated regions. Bully boys, the warlords themselves were little more than local military chieftains, though some actually governed their provinces. Their bloated armies rarely fought each other but scourged the peasantry by exacting taxes and intimidating the population. In turning against Yuan Shih-kai's intention to make himself emperor, eight southern and western provinces had seceded from Peking jurisdiction and delivered their destinies over to Yuan's lieutenants or other army commanders who turned into warlords. In 1917, Sun Yat-sen, with a cadre of former Kuomintang comrades and most of the Chinese navy, assembled a military government at Canton to rival Peking's, but the local warlords soon took charge. The Paris Peace Conference of 1919 compelled the Peking and Canton factions to present China's cause together, yet the country's fragmentation increased thereafter instead of diminishing. China's warlords, as Americans saw them, caused widespread popular suffering. The warlords provoked well-nigh universal resentment by extorting extralegal levies, inflating the currency, interfering with trade, and neglecting the upkeep of roads, railroads, and irrigation and flood control waterways. The deliberate revival of opium smoking was their worst offense. By imposing exorbitant taxes on farmlands, they ensured that no other crop but opium poppies could profitably be grown.

China's chaos of the 1920s stimulated a new nationalism out of a mixture of foreign influences and the Confucian tradition. Patriotic feelings had been heating up since Japan's seizure of Shantung and her notorious Twenty-one Demands. When the Chinese delegations discovered at the peace conference that Woodrow Wilson's Fourteen Points, including self-determination and open diplomacy, were not going to defend their country against Japan's blustering imperialism, China's frustrations boiled over. Wilson's yielding on the Shantung question to prevent Japan from bolting the conference, as she threatened, and to keep her a member of his cherished League of Nations, incensed not only Chinese patriots but also Secretary of State Lansing and many of the other American delegates. The Senate's repudiation of the Treaty of Versailles along with American membership in the League of Nations sidetracked the great-power cooperation in China for which Wilson had, as he saw things, only temporarily sacrificed the Open Door pledge of upholding the integrity of China against Japan's imperial ambition. Betrayed, from their standpoint, Chinese poured out their anger at the verdict of Versailles.

On May 4, 1919, several thousand students decrying the Shantung decision crowded together in front of Peking's Gate of Heavenly Peace (T'ien-an Men), and their assembly soon turned violent. Student and merchant demonstrations spread across China. The students won the support of Sun Yat-sen and the Canton government. Young Mao Zedong castigated Woodrow Wilson, in his first recorded attack on the United States, for undermining the Open Door pledge to sustain China's territorial integrity. The students launched a boycott of Japanese goods. They urged China's scholars and intellectuals to organize themselves for political action. In Paris, Chinese students physically prevented China's delegates from going to Versailles to sign the treaty. The May Fourth uprising and the students' ongoing program of political agitation grew into the complex nationalism of the "New Culture Movement." The New Culture Movement, in addition to its antiforeign overtones, attacked the Confucian hierarchies of both state and family, agitating for the emancipation of youth and women from their habitual subordination to parents, husbands, and rulers. The movement eventually came to express itself in the rise of Party dictatorship, the popularity of socialist thinking, and ever more effective resistance to imperialism. Scholars came from distant places to savor the fresh spirit of change in China. Philosopher John Dewey spent two years lecturing throughout China, often with Dr. Hu Shih of Peking National University, his former Columbia University graduate student, interpreting.[10]

Still, it was not the challenge of Chinese nationalism that prompted the United States to summon the Washington Conference of 1921–1922, but the Harding administration's pursuit of its independent policies of internationalism and armaments reductions under the leadership of Secretary of State Charles Evans Hughes. Having once again turned its back on European entanglements, this time by rejecting membership in the League of Nations, the American government turned to other arrangements in seeking security for itself, especially from the chronic troubles with Japan over China and the Red scare over bolshevism. Secretary Hughes welcomed a British suggestion to convene all of the nations with interests in the western Pacific, except for the outcast Soviet Union. He moved to halt the naval buildup before a naval race developed.

The Washington Conference produced several important treaties. The Five-Power Treaty of naval limitations restricted total tonnages for capital ships, including aircraft carriers, and established rations of 5 : 5 : 3 : 1.67 : 1.67 for Great Britain, the United States, Japan, France, and Italy. The Four-Power Treaty replaced the obsolete Anglo-Japanese alliance with a mutual agreement to respect each other's possessions in the Pacific and continue the status quo for fortifications, while Japan consented to relinquish Shantung to Chinese control, and Britain in time promised to restore Weihaiwei. In the Nine-Power Treaty, the five naval powers were joined by Belgium, the Netherlands, Portugal, and China to guarantee China's sovereignty, independence, and territorial integrity. Effectively the treaty internationalized the Open Door. For the Americans, the Washington Conference was an unqualified success, since naval equilibrium at low cost was achieved, along with, as they believed, an overdue affirmation of John Hay's Open Door policy. Japan, now assured of her navy's domination in the western Pacific, withdrew from mainland Asia, except for Manchuria and Korea.

But these British, Japanese, and American efforts to reduce competition among themselves failed to appease the Chinese. Nationalists chafed increasingly under the foreigners' control of their tariffs, the inequities of extraterritoriality, and the foreign troops, post offices, and other installations on their soil. On the eve of the conference, Harding's minister to China, Jacob Gould Schurman, the educator and diplomat who in 1899 headed the First Philippines Commission, had cabled Hughes of China's resentment against the unequal treaty system. Schurman advised a patient approach: "Only the Chinese can solve China's problems, and they will do it in a Chinese way." His advice was borne out by the attendance of Kuomintang and Chinese Communist delegates at the Moscow Congress, which reminded the other powers of Russia's continuing interest in East Asia.

Now newer strategic considerations arose to confound the traditional postulates that Americans held toward China. United States policy was forced to contend not only with Japanese imperialism but with the antiimperialist, nationalist Chinese themselves. American authorities were slowly realizing that a stable and united Republic of China was vital for the protection of the Philippine Islands, in a reversal from the axiom that the Philippines served as the nation's stepping stone to China. To guard its position, the United States garrisoned soldiers and marines in Chinese cities and patrolled gunboats up the rivers. Sun Yat-sen was angered when American warships helped thwart a Chinese takeover in Canton of foreign-run customs houses in 1923. Sun expostulated: "We might well have expected an American Lafayette would fight on our side in this good cause. In the twelfth year of our struggle towards liberty, there comes not a Lafayette but an American admiral with more ships of war than any other nation in our waters." The twin mirages of commerce and conversion still beckoned Americans toward China's potential for goodness. Theirs was but a "righteous infatuation," in Foreign Service Officer John Paton Davies's judgment, which originated from self-deluding missionary activity and a misapprehension that the United States was somehow esteemed over the other powers as China's best friend. In 1931, such romantic convictions as these were powerfully strengthened by Japan's greedy conquest of Manchuria and the popular success at home of *The Good Earth*, Pearl Buck's sentimental novel about China's struggling peasantry, which six years later was made into a cinematic triumph.

In truth, the vacuum in warlord-torn Peking almost subverted the Chinese government's claim to sovereignty. The civil strife between bandits and soldiers everywhere endangered the lives and holdings of the Chinese people and foreigners alike. The Chinese Communist party launched itself at Shanghai in July 1921 with Soviet assistance. Unlike the reforms being halfheartedly proposed by the treaty powers in response to Chinese pressures, Red Russia afforded a working model for revolution, and the Soviet government, for temporary propaganda advantages, renounced all concessions extorted from China by the czars. Many Chinese nationalists began to abandon their hopes of American benevolence and looked toward the Soviet Union for assistance. Michael Borodin, Moscow's agent in China, taught Sun Yat-sen how to centralize the command structure of the Kuomintang along Communist party lines. Confused by China's turmoil and feeling betrayed by developments, Americans could fathom neither what the nationalists wanted nor the use of Bolsehviks for their purposes. When Sun Yat-sen died in 1925, the violent outbursts on May 30 led to rampages against Americans and other foreigners throughout China, including the thousands of Christian missionaries living there.

The ferocity of the May 30 Movement forced new Secretary of State Frank B. Kellogg to attempt a fresh approach to American relations with China. His task was difficult. Shanghai's American merchants were screaming for gunboats and firm displays of strength. The United States minister, J. V. A. MacMurray, sensitive to the threat of communism, sided with the merchants, as did Britain's and Japan's representatives. Kellogg believed that the days of gunboat diplomacy were all but over and felt troubled at the likelihood of public and congressional protests if force were applied. Secretary Kellogg accepted the premises of Nelson T. Johnson, his advisor on Chinese affairs, that widespread disorders would be inevitable before the Chinese could emerge from their backwardness, yet he was worried at the visible influence of the Comintern over Chinese nationalism. The United States and the treaty powers, Kellogg and Johnson assumed, must prepare to restore China's full sovereignty without much delay. Idealistically Kellogg and Johnson were determined to uphold the image they cherished of the United States as China's most selfless friend. Nevertheless, the pressure from events beyond American control would require yet another recasting of the nation's policy.[11]

With Sun Yat-sen's death, the struggle to succeed him began. The ambitious, often ruthless Chiang Kai-shek, Sun's onetime military aide and commandant of Whampoa Military Academy, seized command of the nationalists' armed forces. In 1927 he destroyed Sun's alliance with China's Reds, either massacring them outright or driving them into hiding, thereby opening the long struggle between the Kuomintang and the Communists. Mao Zedong, the Communists' youthful leader, fled southward to establish a rival center of power. Chiang won control of the Kuomintang party and the Nationalist government. He established China's new capital at Nanking (Nanjing). Peking ("Northern Capital") was renamed Peiping ("Northern Peace") to underline the shifts of power. Uncertain of the outcome, the United States deployed gunboats between Shanghai and Nanking to defend American nationals and their property. Emperor-like, "Generalissimo" Chiang Kai-shek directed a three-legged structure of army, party, and government. His own personal bureaucracies in each branch counterbalanced the regional and rival factions.

Warming to Chiang, whose anti-communist zeal, they realized, even surpassed their own, the American authorities now returned tariff control to the Chinese and admitted China to the most-favored-nation treatment. Then, in 1930, Chiang Kai-shek announced his conversion to Methodism. He divorced his wife and gave up his two concubines in order to wed Soong Mei-ling, a Wellesley College graduate and sister of Sun Yat-sen's widow. Mei-ling, her brother, Soong Tzu-wen (known to Westerners as T. V. Soong), a Harvard graduate, and her two sisters, Ai-ling and Ch'ing-ling, both American college graduates, were the extraordinary children of Charles Jones Soong, a Vanderbilt University–trained Methodist missionary to his own country turned into a rich Shanghai merchant. Highly intelligent, poised, and beautiful, Madame Chiang Kai-shek enthralled Westerners. She and her husband, the generalissimo, appeared to fulfill in person the dream of American merchants, missionaries, and policymakers for a stable, Christian, Open Door China.

American influence grew by leaps and bounds. Chiang's well-placed relatives cultivated Western contacts in all the right places. Faculty members and administrators of China's major universities largely obtained their credentials in the United States. American technology dominated the Geological Survey of China, the research institutes of the Academia Sinica, the National Agricultural Research Institute at Nanking, the Rockefeller-underwritten Peking Union Medical College, and the national health service. Between 1901 and 1920, some twenty-four hundred Chinese students enrolled in American centers of higher learning, and between 1921 and 1940 some fifty-five hundred more enrolled in 370 institutions. An Americanized elite returned home to careers as engineers in industry or financiers in commerce or banking. Others utilized American research techniques leading to spectacular results, including the discovery by anthropologists of the fossil remains of Peking Man and the archaeological recovering of the earliest known written Chinese documents at the Bronze Age, Shang dynasty capital of Anyang.

Not surprisingly, the ranks of America's missionaries in China swelled, increasing to more than three thousand by 1930, representing sixty or so sponsors. The missionaries themselves shifted their endeavors away from saving souls to saving lives. Their social welfare programs enabled the YMCA, for example, to attract public-spirited Chinese men to its leadership. The China International Famine Relief Commission cooperated with rural officials to confront the damage caused by natural catastrophes. James Yen, a Yale graduate, started the Mass Education Movement to grapple with rural misery through a number of applied programs of agricultural science and general elementary education. Unfortunately, Yen's measures, and others of similar purpose, provoked resistance by landlords and their military friends. The government intervened. Chiang disarmingly adopted the YMCA's methods for his own plan of community regeneration. He established about thirteen hundred branch offices of his so-called New Life Movement, 1934–1937, to reaffirm the traditional virtues of righteous conduct enforced by the sense of shame. Behind this network, unknown to the doers of good deeds and their American backers, Chiang's cadres of Blue Shirts secretly mobilized a fascist-style apparatus for forcible social control along military lines.

The misery of the peasants was still China's fundamental problem. Without letup, peasant life continued to disintegrate. The Nationalist government, a one-party dictatorship by the Kuomintang under Chiang, virtually ignored the plight of the peasants, while its top subordinates vied with each other for power. The Communist party's remnants, led by Mao Zedong and Chu Teh, meanwhile were busy training Kiangsi's peasantry in the lowly art of guerrilla warfare. Whatever the future might yield was seemingly not yet theirs to determine, nor yet for Americans seriously to consider.

Unexpectedly developments in Manchuria magnified China's internal situation into a major international crisis. Notwithstanding China's structural chaos, Chiang, in the spring of 1929, subtly tried, by infiltrating hordes of settlers into Manchuria, to squeeze Japan out of the resource-rich northeastern province, where since 1904 she had labored to advance her "special position." The Japanese were outraged at China's boldness. Since 1926, with the reign of Emperor Hirohito, Japan's militarists had been expanding their influence, even installing army officers in classrooms to indoctrinate the boys and girls with patriotic fervor. Japan's Kwangtung (Manchurian) Army, based in Mukden, noticed its territory was growing more and more Chinese-populated day by day. American diplomats believed that Japan would defend her "treaty rights" in Manchuria, while, like Theodore Roosevelt, they preferred never to disturb the Japanese on Asia's mainland. Indeed the United States had long accepted Japan's presence in Manchuria through the Root-Takahira and Lansing-Ishii agreements. Nelson Johnson, the United States minister to China, if not fully comprehending Japanese feelings, wrote: "Manchuria becomes more Chinese everyday, but if Manchuria is destined to become part of Japan I do not see why that should necessarily embroil us."[12]

On September 18, 1931, the Kwangtung Army, on the initiative of its officers without orders from Tokyo, alleged Chinese provocation, captured Mukden within a few hours, and began the conquest of Manchuria. Quickly Japan severed Manchuria from China, founding the puppet state of Manchukuo the following year, and installed Henry P'u-yi, the last emperor of the Qing dynasty, as regent and emperor. From this point, Japan's militarists took their nation onto the road to Pearl Harbor.

President Herbert Hoover, whose administration was mired in the Great Depression, and Secretary of State Henry L. Stimson disagreed with each other how to react. Hoover opposed both military action and economic sanctions against Japan, fearing to risk either war or angry retaliation from a leading trading partner. So Secretary Stimson, on January 7, 1932, delivered to the Japanese government his own protest, which soon became celebrated as the "Stimson Doctrine" of nonrecognition. Borrowing from William Jennings Bryan's 1915 protest against Japan's Twenty-one Demands, Stimson declared that the United States would never recognize any impairment of her treaty rights in China, nor any violations of the Open Door principles, nor of the Kellogg-Briand Pact of 1928 outlawing war. Undaunted, the Japanese army marched into Shanghai. Stimson, who had been Taft's secretary of war and then colonel of the Thirty-first Field

Artillery in the World War, seemed more like a warrior than a diplomat. He badgered Hoover to reinforce the American garrison in Shanghai, then assailed Japan for violating her solemn obligations to uphold the Nine-Power Treaty's promise of China's territorial integrity and the Kellogg-Briand Pact. Obdurately he refused to recognize Japan's conquest of Manchuria. He threatened to fortify Guam and expand the navy's Pacific Fleet. Japan's officials were perturbed, though unrepentant. Chastened by the League of Nations' formation of the Lytton Commission to investigate the Manchurian incident, Japan withdrew from its membership in the league in 1933.

Stimson had failed to check Japan. Stimson was armed, he confessed in dismay, only with "spears of straw and swords of ice," If the Open Door could be slammed shut in Manchuria, could it be held open anywhere? The United States government still hoped to prevent war, protect China, and rekindle prosperity, as well as to ensure its own national security. Toward Japan, the United States could only moralize, not enforce its will, but foreign policy depended on power.[13]

In 1933, President Franklin D. Roosevelt continued Stimson's policy of nonrecognition and added the new pressure of naval construction, hoping that Japan's Manchurian adventure might falter under the financial and political strain of direct competition. Instead the president's authorization of thirty-two vessels, including two aircraft carriers, to be started in 1933 alone alarmed Japan's admirals sufficiently to induce their government to renounce the treaty limitations and resume building warships on its own. In 1937, Captain Claire Chennault retired from the United States Army Air Corps to join Chiang Kai-shek's air force as China's chief military aviation advisor. With tacit American blessing, Chennault proceeded to form the "Flying Tigers," a fighter wing flown by experienced American mercenary pilots. America's disapproval of Japan was unmistakable.

In July 1937, war broke out anew between Japan and China. This so-called China incident, or Second Sino-Japanese War, would stretch out over the next eight years, to end only in Japan's defeat by the Allied powers at the end of the Second World War. Declared an open city to save its treasures, Peking capitulated almost without a battle. Japan next took Shanghai, overcoming Chiang's army's spirited defense by massive bombings of hapless civilians. When Nanking fell, the Japanese army's entry into the capital city featured savage brutality mourned thereafter as "the rape of Nanking." Chiang hurriedly transferred his capital to Chungking (Chongqing). His troops in rearguard actions fended off the Japanese. Canton fell in the south, then Wuhan. Before the end of 1938, the major cities were all in Japanese hands, and her troops controlled most of northern, eastern, and southern China. Chiang's forces held only the less populous western interior. His prospects were approaching their nadir. A military stalemate ensued from this point, nevertheless.

More ominous for the Nationalists' future was the renewed vitality of the Communists. Mao Zedong's ragtail Marxist-Leninists had declared war on Japan upon her seizure of Manchuria and regularly railed against Chiang for, in their view, appeasing China's invaders. Indeed Chiang was prosecuting the civil war against the Communists more assiduously than fighting the Japanese. At one juncture, Nationalist forces almost trapped the Communist armies, but the Reds escaped by taking their epochal "Long March" of almost six thousand miles from their southern refuge to remote Yenan (Yan'an) in the northwestern interior. Unruly soldiers kidnapped Chiang himself in 1936, but he was released after the Russian and Chinese Communists convinced his captors that he was essential for resisting the Japanese. The outcome was that the Nationalists and the Communists put together a united front in 1937. Shaky from the start, the united front proved largely ineffectual to resist Japan, except for deluding Americans to believe what they yearned to believe about China—that China was now united, still friendly, and growing stronger in every way.

After the loss of Nanking, Chiang announced China's determination to resist Japan to the end. "The time must come," he predicted, "when Japan's military strength will be exhausted, thus giving China the ultimate victory." Frustrated, furious, and trapped in an expanding conflict without limits, the Japanese drove on deeper and deeper into the vastness of China.

Above Nanking, on December 12, 1937, Japanese warplanes deliberately attacked and sank the USS *Panay*, a Yangtze River gunboat convoying three small Standard Oil tankers. The clearly marked *Panay* endured bombing and strafing for two hours before sinking. Two British patrol vessels were also attacked. Admiral Yarnell had earlier advised the Japanese authorities where the *Panay* was going so they would not mistake her for a Chinese ship. The *Panay*'s surviving sailors and officers were machine gunned as they put off in lifeboats and even after they struggled ashore. Instigated by fanatically patriotic Japanese officers, the attacks, it later came out, originated from local operations levels, to show China that Japan had no fear of American or British reprisals. President Roosevelt demanded a full explanation and damages. Tokyo apologized profusely, contritely explaining away the raid as a grievous error and eventually paying $2,214,007 in indemnity. Many Japanese men and women called at the American embassy in Tokyo to express their personal regrets.

Japan's expressions of regret eased the tension. United States armed services, aware of the unfavorable disparity of combat strengths, were understandably loath to precipitate a showdown. The House of Representatives, in spite of the outraged oratory, reflected the public's fear of war by bringing to a vote the Ludlow Resolution to require a nationwide referendum before a declaration of war might take effect. The resolution lost by only twenty-one votes after heavy White House lobbying opposition. To reduce friction with the Japanese, as an extra outcome of the *Panay* sinking, the United States Army withdrew its Fifteenth Infantry Regiment. To the anguish of local prostitutes, the "Can Do" soldiers paraded out through Tientsin's streets serenaded by other foreign military bands and even by Japanese buglers. "Vinegar Joe" Stilwell sourly recorded his private judgement: "Japs apologize. 'Very sorry for you.' Couldn't see the insignia. The bastards."

Cautiously throughout 1938 and 1939, the Roosevelt administration, which was becoming increasingly worried by Europe's blackening war clouds, buttressed both the Chinese and American positions toward Japan. The United States Treasury purchased Chinese silver, not that its vaults needed any more, to enable China to pay for military equipment. Secretary of State Cordell Hull imposed a "moral embargo" against selling aircraft to Japan. Technical assistance was dispatched to improve China's transport network. The navy ordered the construction of two more aircraft carriers with a doubling of its fleet of warplanes, and occupied several more Pacific islands as potential bases. Japan's proclamation of a "New Order" for the Orient, the Greater East Asia Co-Prosperity Sphere, slammed shut the Open Door—"banged, barred, and bolted," an American trade representative in Shanghai described it. The United States abrogated the Japanese American Treaty of Commerce and Navigation of 1911, hoping to restrain Japan's advances, and authorized an additional naval construction bill for two more battleships.[14]

When the long-dreaded European war at last exploded with Germany's blitzkrieg into Poland in September 1939, Japanese-American relations ominously disintegrated. The United States was far more prepared to assert itself against Japan than in 1931–1932, when the Stimson nonrecognition doctrine was its only response. But its protests were still timidly couched, because American power was grievously limited. In the *I Ching* long ago, it was written:

> The strong disperse the weak; Kuai teaches so.
> Prospers the good man's way; to grief all small men go.

With the Japanese bombing of Pearl Harbor still two years in the future, American diplomats feared that a showdown was coming. The fall of France in June 1940 afforded Japan's leaders a golden opportunity to realize their dreams of empire, but it proved also for Japan the fatal point of no return.

*Evil customs of the past shall be broken off and everything
based upon the just laws of Nature.
Knowledge shall be sought throughout the world so as to
strengthen the foundations of imperial rule.*

In the name of the Emperor Meiji, the Charter Oath.[1]

6

JAPAN'S RISING SUN

Although history sets down in detail the long relationship between Japan
and the United States before the catastrophic warfare of 1941–1945 between
them, their interwoven tragedy is scarcely explained. One puzzles over the
unresolved whys and wherefores. That a number of frictions developed into
savage hostility—Japan's aggressive imperialism, competition for China,
and American racial prejudice against Orientals, to cite but three
examples—is obvious. Paradoxically, Japan and the United States shared a
number of vital interests that might have bound them together, for example
their important commercial connections and, following the Bolshevik Revolution, a fervent anticommunism. Yet they did not. Bondings such as these
were swept aside in 1941, by Japan's desperate attack on Pearl Harbor and
the United States' terrible revenge.

Commodore Perry's thrusts into Tokyo Bay touched off the Meiji imperial restoration of 1867, one of the most remarkable upheavals in modern
history, which almost overnight moved to end medieval feudalism in Japan.
For 225 years since 1639, with only Dutch and Chinese traders admitted to a
designated post at Nagasaki and Christian missionaries barred, Japan had
secluded herself from the outside world. Perry, we recall, extracted the
Treaty of Kanagawa from the Tokugawa shogunate in 1854, to open the
seaports of Shimoda and Hakodate to American ships and to station a
consular officer at Shimoda. The United States consul at Shimoda was
Townsend Harris, whose tenure in Japan may have inspired the "Madame

Butterfly" tale behind Puccini's charming opera. Tactfully and patiently Harris negotiated a more encompassing treaty, on July 29, 1858, wherein Japan and the United States established formal diplomatic relations, consenting to exchange ministers. Under duress and fearful of experiencing a fate like China's at the hands of the foreign barbarians, Japan agreed to open the ports of Kanagawa and Nagasaki to American commerce, and further, between 1860 and 1863, the ports of Niigata and Hyogo (Kobe) plus Edo (Tokyo) and Osaka for foreign residence, with extraterritorial privileges for Americans virtually to police themselves. The Japanese accepted moderate limitations, as well, on setting their customs duties. The Dutch, Russians, British, and French speedily negotiated equivalent terms for themselves while pressing on the Japanese still lower import duty restrictions. These one-sided treaties of 1858, especially the provision for extraterritoriality, when compounded by the shock of China's degradation, drove Japan's patriots in self-protection to overthrow the timeworn Tokugawa shogunate and commence building up the nation's military and economic strength.

Two artists had accompanied Perry's expedition. Their sketches of naked Japanese men and women bathing together appeared in his published report, causing a congressional furor and eventually their suppression. Perry himself characterized the lower-class Japanese as morally lax for enjoying pictures he deemed obscene. Cultural disparities of this kind would foster profound misunderstandings between the Japanese people and the Americans.

In the meantime, the Department of State chose Philadelphia for the initial visit outside Washington by the first Japanese envoys to the Western world. They had come to the United States to exchange ratifications of the treaty of commerce and navigation and set up their own legation. The seventy or so Japanese dignitaries and their attendants were ambitious to inspect American industries and, especially, the United States Mint. To Philadelphians, the Orientals themselves were the great attraction. "Japanese Fever" swept the city. Nearly a half million persons, estimates had it, from all over the Quaker City and far and wide across the country, thronged the streets, when the Japanese delegation disembarked their train from Washington June 9, 1860. For days after their arrival, the pavements adjoining Ninth and Chestnut streets around the Continental Hotel, the city's largest and newest, where the Japanese were housed, were packed with gaping onlookers. The crowd's favorite delegate, "Japanese Tommy," one of the interpreters and a ready wit, directed, it was reported, a number of flirtatious advances toward the ladies. The envoys took away with them as much as $100,000 worth of goods, an auspicious augury for commerce, and donated $3,000 to the police officers who protected them from the crowds—an unsettling forecast of municipal payoffs to come.[2]

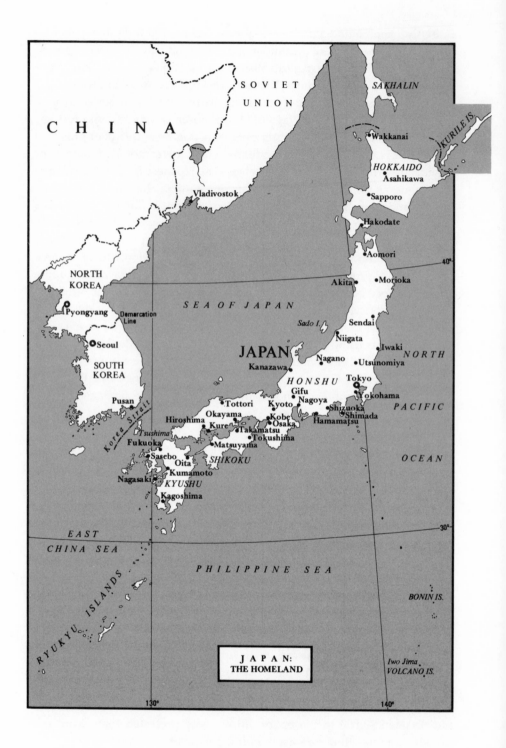

JAPAN:
THE HOMELAND

By the imperial restoration, fifteen-year-old Emperor Mutsuhito became, on December 9, 1867, Japan's highest authority, the mikado. He took for himself the name of Emperor Meiji. The creator of modern Japan, he would be venerated in time as Japan's greatest sovereign since Jimmu Tenno, the first emperor of Japan and, the ancient tales relate, the direct descendent of Amaterasu Ōmikami, the sun goddess. In 1869, Emperor Meiji moved the court from Kyoto to Edo and renamed the city Tokyo, "eastern capital."

In Emperor Meiji's name, Japan modernized herself within a generation. The emperor was surrounded by a talented array of young *samurai*, or warrior nobles, driving themselves to dismantle Japan's seven-centuries-old feudal structures. They pressed ahead to overtake the West to make up for Japan's lengthy isolation. The likeliest young Japanese went off to England, Germany, France, and the United States to learn all they could about modern technology. In the Emperor Meiji's Charter Oath of April 1868, the "evil customs of the past" were to be broken off and knowledge sought everywhere, "so as to strengthen the foundations of imperial rule." "The world was one vast school house for them," as Edwin O. Reischauer put it. "Students were carefully chosen on the basis of their knowledge and capabilities, and the countries where they were to study were selected with equal care. The Japanese determined to learn from each Western country that in which it particularly excelled." Among the American experts brought into Japan were postal, agricultural, and educational technicians to instruct the eager Japanese.

To elevate the people's intelligence, Kido Kōin, a zealous young *samurai* statesman, believed, they must become informed through newspapers about conditions in the West. "The other day one of your letters from New York reached me," he wrote to Shinagawa Yajiro in 1871. "As it contained news yet unknown to us, I submitted it to His Majesty's attention. That letter contained much that was highly instructive; and therefore I wish you to bear in mind my plans for a news office." Kido went on: "Kindly inform Mori Kinnojo, who has been dispatched to America, and Nawa Kan, who has accompanied him, about our plans for this newspaper office. If they will write about America, and on other matters of interest to our people, . . . I shall forward them for publication in the same newspaper." Shinagawa enthusiastically wrote back to Kido: "Immediately upon my arrival in America, Yamamoto Jinsuke and I went directly to a newspaper office to pay a visit. We were shown the printing presses and were told of the importance of the newspaper in the daily life of the people." Subsequent visits to England, Germany, and France confirmed his impressions. "Such was my enthusiasm in this regard," Shinagawa confessed, "that Oyama and others have been calling me 'Newspaper.'

Coveting the Westerners' trading gains in China, Japan's Foreign Office negotiated a treaty with the Chinese in 1871 to formalize their commercial relations and friendship. The two countries affirmed their equality by setting up a reciprocal extraterritorial system to cover their nationals abroad and, most significantly, by omitting to accord a most-favored-nation status to Japan. This spirit of mutual cooperation at the outset spectacularly manifested itself with the joint participation of the Qing and Meiji emperors during the signing ceremony. But Sino-Japanese harmony proved fleeting. Commencing at this point, yet almost unnoticed, was Japan's seventy-five-year effort to dominate Asia. Modeled on Western imperialism, Japan's plans were destined to unfold largely at China's expense. Although Meiji Nippon appeared to lag even more behind the times than Qing China, where both imperial authority and the centralized bureaucracy wielded visible power, the Japanese would far more effectively respond to the challenge of the West.[3]

Initially, American concerns over Asia were but marginal to the anguish over the Civil War and Reconstruction, or even to Western Hemisphere affairs. The United States Navy deployed only an obsolete warship to join the British, French, and Dutch men-of-war bombarding the Japanese port of Shimonseki for antiforeigner harassments perpetrated by the intransigent Choshu clan. Then, of the $3 million indemnity forced from Japan, the United States returned the $785,000 it received in 1883, as a face-saving gesture of mutual goodwill. Also, the United States moved only halfheartedly into Korea, China's wobbly dependency, though the "hermit nation" almost invited imperialist intervention. In 1866, Koreans burned the *General Sherman*, a merchant ship that had grounded in Korean waters, and murdered her crew. Not until 1871, a year after Japan acquired trading privileges, was a naval flotilla reminiscent of Perry's sent for redress to Korea, where it was fired upon. A battle erupted. Scores of Koreans and some American sailors were killed. The American gunboats demolished several Korean forts before departing without a treaty. More than a decade later, after two years of persistent efforts, Commodore Robert Shufeldt, USN, won a Korean-American treaty of peace, amity, commerce, and navigation. Soon American enterprisers established trading links with the Koreans. Even Thomas Edison negotiated a contract to install electric lights inside the king's palace.[4]

The Centennial Exposition of 1876 brought Japanese delegates back to Philadelphia for a second official visit. The Japanese this time were part of a cosmopolitan stream of visitors headed by Emperor Dom Pedro II of Brazil. Fifty foreign nations exhibited their wares alongside the displays of American machinery and ingenuity. The seven-hundred-ton Corliss steam engine dominated the exhibits, producing between 1,600 and 2,500 horsepower with the virtually silent perfection of a fine watch. By bringing two prefabricated buildings and the workmen to put them together, Japan's exhibitors perplexed Philadelphians. Equally puzzling to the Japanese were American tools and equipment. The workmen had never before used an American wheelbarrow, and they carried it with its contents instead of pushing it. The bystanders' ridiculing of the Japanese structures as overbuilt corncribs, particularly the beautiful house, yielded quickly to the esteem of Richard Morris Hunt, the leading American architect. Hunt praised the "graceful lines of roofs and porches, the perfect tile work, and the rich ornamental carving, altogether offering a capital and most improving study to the careless and slipshod joiners of the western world." Inside the buildings, the silks and porcelains dispelled all doubts about Japanese taste and skills.

The arts of Japan exhibited at the Centennial Exposition provided the primary measure for Americans for the achievements of Oriental culture since the artifacts brought home in the early China trading days. The Japanese exhibits made every other display look common by comparison, even bordering on vulgarity. The *Atlantic Monthly* judged: "The Japanese seem to possess the secret which the modern pre-Raphaelites have striven for without success, the union of detail and effect." In global competition for the first time, the cost of success was steep. Observed Fukui Makota, Japan's commissioner to the exposition: "The first day crowds come like sheep, run here, run there, run everywhere. One man start, one thousand follow. Nobody can see anything, nobody can do anything. All rush, push, tear, shout, make plenty noise, say *damn* great many times, get very tired, and go home."

American and European Christian leaders hankered for Japan's conversion meanwhile. The Tokugawa shoguns for two and a half centuries suppressed Christianity as traitorous. Now, in fresh circumstances, American preachers expounded their hope of saving Japanese souls. Inspired anew, the handful of American missionaries in Japan considered their work vital for Asia's future. As Asia's most modern nation, they argued, Japan must also be shaped into the most Christian. Once converted to Christianity Japan could march forward at the head of East Asia's peoples and, possibly, even lead a great crusade to convert them all. But the early results were most discouraging. Was it conceivable that Japan could borrow the technology and industry of Western civilization without assuming its basic religious beliefs? Incredible.[5]

In Lafcadio Hearn's life, the Western romance with Japanese culture culminated. Hearn, the Greek-Ionian island-born son of an Anglo-Irish surgeon major in the British army, himself a wayward British subject, immigrated in 1869 into the United States. He moved around at first, working as a printer, before settling down to write for newspapers in

Cincinnati and New Orleans. Japan's legends and traditions captured his imagination, and *Harper's Weekly* commissioned him to write about them in 1890. After he landed at Yokohama, Hearn spent the remaining fourteen years of his life infatuated with Japanese folklore and Buddhism. He married a kindly Japanese woman who had nursed him through an illness, and assumed her family name, calling himself Koizumi Yakumo. He taught in several Japanese schools and universities. He served for some time as editor of the Kobe *Chronicle* and wrote several books. In 1895, he acquired Japanese citizenship. Appointed the next year to lecture at Tokyo Imperial University, Hearn held the chair of English literature until just before his death in 1904, at the age of fifty-four.

Lafcadio Hearn became the outstanding interpreter of Japan to the West. His best books—*Glimpses of Unfamiliar Japan* (1894), *Kokoro* (1896), *Japanese Fairy Tales* (1902), and *Japan: An Attempt at Interpretation* (1904)—are, understandably, read in Japan today. He presented the Japanese people in their own terms, wherein, culturally speaking, they prefer to believe, they surpass all other peoples of the earth.

On the Shinji lakefront in the coastal village of Matsue, Lafcadio Hearn frequented a favorite noodle shop, often sitting there to capture the day's end. "Before me, the fair vast lake sleeps, softly luminous, far-ringed with chains of blue volcanic hills shaped like a sierra. . . . The sun begins to set, and exquisite astonishments of tinting appear in water and sky." But disenchantment flooded his soul. Lafcadio Hearn's Japan, a magical kingdom filled with temples and shrines, haunted by the ghosts of feudal days, and hushed by the poetic rhythms of rural life, was fast giving way to the modernized nation he hated. His expatriate romance turned sour. He wanted his adopted country to linger forever in the mists of antiquity. Cities, industries, navies, and armies were instead pointing toward Japan's imperial greatness. Hearn's dismay at the transformation anticipated the alarm of many Americans as Japan's challenge mounted.[6]

Diplomatically, throughout the 1870s and 1880s, Japanese authorities struggled against the unequal treaties imposed by the Western powers that implied their racial inferiority, confined their economy, and, in fact, hobbled their sovereignty. To complicate the changing of extraterritorial rights or inequitable tariffs, unanimity of agreement had to be achieved among the powers. The powers wanted to exchange any concessions they might yield for complete access to Japan's markets and population. United States Secretary of State Hamilton Fish feared that any departure from the policy of cooperating with the other powers would jeopardize commercial opportunities and endanger the safety of American citizens. More moderate than the British or French in employing their extraterritorial privilege, some Americans openly sympathized with Japan's petitions. Minister John A.

Bingham pushed for granting tariff autonomy to the Japanese as early as 1878, but the United States failed to persuade the other nations involved to concur. In 1879, former President Ulysses S. Grant on a goodwill tour ceremonially planted a tree (still standing) in Tokyo's Shiba Kōen, redeeming his promise to pay a state visit to Japan. Grant received a historic welcome featuring a personal call by Emperor Meiji himself. Ten years later, however, the new American minister, John Franklin Swift, a Californian with intense anti-Oriental prejudices, convinced Secretary of State James G. Blaine, in Benjamin Harrison's administration, that potential floods of Japanese immigration constituted the gravest danger. When Great Britain relinquished her rights of extraterritoriality in Japan in 1894, the United States followed suit, but Washington reserved the right to restrict Japanese immigration.[7]

Unfortunately, Japan's efforts to overturn the unequal treaty system coincided with the new waves of Western imperialism. The Japanese imitated the high-handed methods of the great powers, if only to gain parity with them in China.

Immediately upon concluding the treaty of 1871, jurisdictional disputes broke out between Japan and China over their conflicting claims to the Ryukyu Islands, Formosa, and Korea. China had lost control over these tributary areas, and Japan intruded into the opportunities at hand. Japan was searching for sources of food and raw materials, as well as outlets for her manufactured products and military bases to protect her spreading enterprises. Strategically, Korea's peninsular setting was vital, lying as it did on Japan's direct route to the rich resources of Manchuria. Korea became the unwilling cockpit for Japan's competition with China against czarist Russia's imperial ambitions.

Before 1895, few Americans objected to Japan's expansion at China's expense. Many Americans, indeed, admired Japan so intensely that her decisive victory over China in the war of 1894–1895 only appeared to add evidence of Japan's enlightened progress. Hilary A. Herbert, the secretary of the navy, proclaimed that "Japan has leaped, almost at one bound, to a place among the great nations of the earth," and Charles Denby, the United States minister to China, expressed the widely shared judgment that "Japan is now doing for China what the United States did for Japan. She has learnt western civilization, and she is forcing it on her unwieldy neighbor. The only hope in the world for China is to take the lesson, rude as it is, to heart." Neither President Grover Cleveland nor Secretary of State Walter Q. Gresham considered that Japan's defeat of China affected any substantial American interest.

Henceforth, Japan insisted that Korea was her own sphere of interest and required China to surrender suzerainty over Formosa and the Ryukyu

Islands. China under duress also yielded Port Arthur, Dairen (Lüta), and the strategic Liaotung Peninsula to Japan. But Russia, Germany, and France, in the so-called Triple Intervention, bluntly told Japan to give these places back, whereupon Russia seized this territory for her own empire to administer to Japan a lesson in cynical arrogance that the Japanese never forgave nor forgot. At a time when force was respected above all, Japan's easy triumph over China brought her the prestige she sought. Where in the 1850s Japan's military weakness invited conquest, her military strength in the 1890s brought international power and respect. Having picked up the stepping stones toward an empire in the Ryukyus, Formosa, and Korea, the Western powers now treated Japan as an equal. The Japanese learned their lessons well.[8]

Now the directions Japan and the United States were taking converged. Trouble surfaced in 1897 over the Hawaiian Islands, where an oligarchy of Americans ruled over a polyglot people including thousands and thousands of Japanese sugar cane laborers. To forestall imperial Japan's ominously rising influence among the local Japanese, the Republic of Hawaii's government in March of that year halted Japanese immigration. In strenuously protesting, Japan dispatched the warship *Naniwa* to Honolulu bearing representatives of the government, the press, and the emigration contractors. Rumors of Japan's plans to invade, or to forcibly coerce the Hawaiians, boosted the partisans of annexation. In June, President McKinley hastily sent a new treaty to the Senate for annexing the islands. Japan's minister to the United States formally protested the treaty as disturbing the tranquility of international relations in the Pacific and endangering the rights of Japanese workers in the Hawaiian Islands. The government of Japan, according to Foreign Minister Count Shigenobu Okuma, was well aware that the threat of supposed Japanese intervention was trumped up to facilitate American annexation. The State Department directed Minister Harold M. Sewall to observe as closely as possible the Japanese-Hawaiian negotiations getting underway. If Japan were to resort to force, Sewall was to proclaim a provisional protectorate by the United States and summon assistance from the navy.

Assistant Secretary of the Navy Theodore Roosevelt favored annexing the Hawaiian Islands without delay. Undaunted by the possibility of war with Japan, he requested the Naval War College to prepare plans for the defense of Hawaii against Japan and also for the emancipation of Cuba from Spanish dominion. But a sharp debate ensued in Congress, where the opposition comprising mainland beet-sugar interests and principled antiimperialists once again forestalled annexation. Hence, on receiving assurances that the United States would respect the rights of her subjects in case of annexation, Japan abandoned her objections, though grumblings persisted in the nation's newspapers. In the jingoist excitement following Dewey's victory at Manila Bay, Congress opted for the easier path of annexation by joint resolution, earlier taken for Texas, and managed at last to absorb the Hawaiian Islands under the sovereignty of the United States.

Nothing less than the balance of power was at stake in East Asia. The issue generated by annexing the Philippines dwarfed the confrontation with Japan over Hawaii. Cautiously the Japanese responded to the latest American advance, for with the dismemberment of China looming as a probability, Japan hoped for the preventative support of the United States, particularly against the Russians. Japan welcomed the Open Door notes. Japan also welcomed American participation in the relief of the legations trapped by the Boxers in Peking, when, once more, the Russians threatened to frustrate Japan's intentions. As the Japanese saw things, the Russians blocked their economic opportunities in Manchuria, posed a naval threat, and jeopardized their hold on Korea. In the Boxer crisis, eight thousand Japanese soldiers (about 42 percent of the total) were largely responsible for rescuing the legations. Japan hoped by her large-scale intervention to gain the equal treatment from the other powers she so desperately sought. In Manchuria, however, Russia planted nearly two hundred thousand soldiers to slam the door in Japan's face.

Distrust and enmity continued to heat up between Japan and Russia over their rivalry in Korea and Manchuria, until Japan broke off diplomatic relations, and without warning, on February 8, 1904, the Japanese navy attacked Russia's Pacific fleet based at Port Arthur. Quickly the Nipponese blunted the tremendous preponderance of Russian numbers. Japan's unbroken string of victories over Russia's forces culminated in the capture of Port Arthur and seizure of the surviving warships of the Pacific fleet, the bloody victory of Mukden, and the destruction of the Baltic fleet just as it arrived in the Sea of Japan. Initially President Roosevelt cheered, "Japan is playing our game," but he worried over the enormity of the Russian disaster. He hoped for an outcome "on terms which will not mean the creation of either a yellow peril or a Slav peril." "'It's hard f'r me to think iv th' Japs this way. But 'tis th' part iv prudence,'" added Mr. Dooley, Chicago's Irish saloonkeeper oracle. "'A few years ago I didn't think anny more about a Jap thin about anny other man that'd been kept in th' oven too long. They were all alike to me. But today, whiniver I see wan I turn pale an' take off me hat an' make a low bow.'"

Triumphant, the Japanese nevertheless were exhausted, and the European powers wanted the fighting stopped. Minister Kogoro Takahira asked President Roosevelt to take the initiative by inviting Russia and Japan to negotiate a peace treaty.[9]

Theodore Roosevelt sensed that the future pointed toward Asia, as few of his compatriots did. He himself had opened the campaign for the Philippines. He consistently endorsed the Open Door policy for China, while muting its interventionist implications concerning China's territorial integrity. Although he distrusted the czar's effort to colonize Manchuria and dominate Korea, he and John Hay realized there was little they could do except merely voice their opposition. He supported the 1902 alliance of Japan and Great Britain for contributing to East Asia's balance of power. He understood the hazards of playing Asian power politics without sufficient military power. By 1905, Roosevelt felt that achieving a balance of forces in East Asia would protect American interests better than any other likelihood. A Russian victory, if the outcome were reversed, would probably have excluded the United States from Manchuria given Russia's demands on the Chinese for a commercial monopoly, while Japan's victorious aggressors one day might even challenge the Open Door policy. It would be much better if Russia and Japan were to compete to moderate each other's ambitions.

Taking the opportunity to mediate, President Roosevelt called the Russians and the Japanese together in August 1905 for peace talks at the naval base in Portsmouth, New Hampshire. No Chinese representative was asked to take part, even though the issues intimately concerned China. Headed by future premier Sergei Witte, the Russian delegates simultaneously had to face up to the revolution of 1905 and the humiliation of their nation's defeat by Japan, yet they secured unexpectedly lenient terms. The Russians, without compensation, ceded their South Manchurian Railway to Japan. The Russians also agreed, in recognizing China's sovereignty, to Japan's demands for the evacuation of their troops from Manchuria, and acknowledged the independence of Korea subject only to Japan's "paramount political, military, and economic interests" there. Japan obtained the disputed Liaotung Peninsula with its prized harbors of Port Arthur and Dairen, the southern half of Sakhalin Island between the Sea of Okhotsk and the Sea of Japan, and offshore fishing rights adjacent to Siberia. At the czar's adamant insistence, Roosevelt rejected an indemnity for Japan. Roosevelt won the Nobel Prize for Peace in 1906 for his Portsmouth Treaty settlement.

Most likely Roosevelt's peacemaking efforts masked his true intentions. He hoped to solidify Japanese-American friendship. He approved Japan's drive toward East Asia's continental resources, in part because it would divert the ambitious Japanese from adventuring across the Pacific. The danger of a conflict between Japan and the United States lay not in China, Roosevelt reasoned, but in their profound racial and cultural differences, which were, he observed, agitated by Japanese migration to the Hawaiian Islands and the American mainland. In 1904, Roosevelt openly conceded Japan's priority in Korea. The secret Taft-Katsura memorandum of July

1905, initialed at Roosevelt's behest, reaffirmed that concession in exchange for Japan accepting American dominion over the Philippines. The United States also pledged to cooperate with Japan and Great Britain for stabilizing East Asia. When in November Japan declared her intention to absorb Korea, Secretary of State Elihu Root withdrew the United States legation from Seoul. Protests from Koreans, including young Syngman Rhee in Washington, were overlooked. Japan thereupon reopened Manchuria to American and European commerce, yet persistently discouraged foreign capital investments.[10]

Japan's dislodging of the Russians, a victory unprecedented in modern history of yellow Asians over caucasian Europeans, unsettled Theodore Roosevelt and many of his fellow citizens. Their alarm was heightened by China's surprisingly successful boycott of American goods to protest the racially motivated 1904 Immigration Act's permanent exclusion of all Chinese immigrants. Fears of a yellow peril reemerged in the United States. More virulent than before, the phobia this time assumed that Japan and China would someday unite themselves against the West. Nothing that American missionaries could write or say about the friendly responses they ordinarily encountered from the Japanese people could reduce the prejudices that bred anti-Oriental racism in America.

In fact, racial unrest in California ignited the fire. Pacific Coast inhabitants were already conditioned by the prevalent anti-Chinese attitudes to exaggerate the threat from Japan's aggressive rise to world power. California's governor referred out loud to the "Japanese menace" when crowds staged the first sizeable demonstrations against Japanese immigration. Japan's efforts failed to hold back the emigrants going to California, since the larger flow to Hawaii was not blocked, and many Japanese moved on from there to settle on the Pacific Coast. In 1904, about fifteen thousand Japanese entered the United States, causing alarmed Californians to express their fear at the inrushing horde. Anti-Japanese immigration movements gathered strength particularly in San Francisco, where the newcomers were concentrating. The demagogues heading the Union-Labor party excoriated both the yellow devils in their midst and the government in Washington that tolerated their entry. A Japanese and Korean exclusion league was born, while the legislature debated barring all Orientals from entering the state. On October 11, 1906, barely six months after the great earthquake and fire had ravaged San Francisco, the municipal Board of Education established the segregated Oriental School for the city's Chinese, Japanese, and Korean boys and girls. Sporadic rioting burst forth against Orientals living along the West Coast from Los Angeles to Vancouver.

Outraged, Japan's oligarchs, the *genro*, expected President Roosevelt to rectify the misdeeds of California's authorities and the unruly mobs their actions encouraged. The Meiji patriarchs had taken Roosevelt's oft-repeated assurances of goodwill at face value, having no clues to his personal racist ambivalence toward the Japanese themselves. In delivering his government's formal protest, Tokyo's ambassador, Aoki Shuzo, evenhandedly mixed a sense of relief with his dismay over California's actions. He recorded "that the hostile demonstration in San Francisco has produced among all people in Japan a feeling of profound disappointment and sorrow," then added: "Happily that feeling up to this time is unmixed with any suggestion of retaliation because it is firmly believed that the evil will be speedily removed."

Lacking foresight, President Roosevelt unknowingly embarked on more than two years of troublesome relations with Japan. He promised to employ his best offices to resolve the crisis, even as he patiently defined for the Japanese the constitutional limits of his powers over intrastate matters. He sent emissaries to California's governor and San Francisco's school board. He instructed the ambassador to Japan to deliver assurances that the United States "had not the slightest sympathy with the outrageous agitation" against the Japanese. Roosevelt sympathized well enough with labor's fears of unrestrained immigration, but he was angry at the rioters and "the idiots of the California legislature," who wanted to enact an all-inclusive Oriental exclusion measure. Japan's embarrassed leaders only wanted a quick settlement of the controversy. They were hoping for American support in their ongoing competition with Russia.

Unfortunately, Roosevelt and Root magnified the problem. They worried that the racially instigated disturbances in California might drive, in Root's characterization, the "proud, sensitive, warlike" Japanese to attack the United States. "The subject is not one of some far distant, possible evil," wrote Root, "but is an immediate and present danger to be considered and averted now, today." Instead of simply seeking congressional action to prevent Japanese contract laborers moving from Hawaii to the mainland, which was the mainland's major source of immigrants, Roosevelt and Root proposed a treaty to Japan for barring migration both ways. Patently unequal as affecting none but the Japanese, the measure was indignantly rebuffed by the Tokyo government. Roosevelt misjudged both the Japanese and the Californians. By undervaluing Japan's Manchurian aims, Roosevelt unwittingly incited the Japanese to escalate the immigration issue. Blustering at white Californians, he failed to measure their inflamed emotions on the Japanese question. To make matters worse, he himself was succumbing to a belief in the yellow peril. His apprehensions at Japan's militancy lent his outbursts an inflated urgency.

Nevertheless, a compromise took shape between foreign policy and domestic reality, as Roosevelt managed one step at a time to accommodate both the Japanese and the Californians. He invited San Francisco's mayor and the school board members to Washington to persuade them to repeal their Oriental school segregation ordinance. He convinced Congress to prohibit Japanese immigration from Hawaii to the mainland. He reached a "gentlemen's agreement" with Tokyo in March 1907 whereby Japan consented to halt the emigration of laborers to the United States and the United States promised to prevent discrimination against its Japanese residents. In May, however, relations once again deteriorated when anti-Japanese violence swept San Francisco during a bitter street railway strike.[11]

Pessimistic over his helplessness to reduce anti-Japanese tensions, Roosevelt worried more and more over the chances of war. The Hearst newspapers already trumpeted the possibility. Roosevelt confided to Taft his wariness of the "Japanese intention to force a war with us." He grieved at the vulnerability of the Philippines, "our heel of Achilles," he now realized, and thought about setting the archipelago free under "an international guarantee." He declared that he would "rather see this nation fight all her life than to see her give up to Japan or any other nation under duress."

Talk of conflict with Japan ran rife. Alfred Thayer Mahan, naval officer and historian of sea power, wrote of the "menacing appearance" of Japanese-American relations. Army Chief of Staff James Franklin Bell warned the president of Japan's war fever, while his field commanders assembled reports of Japanese espionage in the Philippines, Hawaii, and the United States. The navy's commanding officers until now had never seriously considered waging a war against Japan. They were concentrating on Germany's new strength in the Atlantic Ocean as a threat to the Western Hemisphere. The navy needed time to develop its proposed major base in the Philippines at Subic Bay thirty miles north of Manila. But prodded by Roosevelt, the navy's planners proceeded to analyze the Japanese danger to the stability of the Pacific. Their studies later evolved into the pretentious war plan "ORANGE," the code name for Japan. The ORANGE plan could not hope to save the Philippines in the event of hostilities, though it was destined to endure as a defensive strategy through countless revisions and refinements to the outbreak of the Second World War. The navy's lack of urgency was reflected by Admiral George Dewey when he wrote that trouble with Japan "would not reach a critical stage for a long time to come." Japan's main enemy was still Russia. Yet Japan, the once favored protégé, was rising up, in the minds of many molders of public opinion and ordinary citizens alike, to become a potential enemy of the United States.

President Roosevelt pressed ahead for an accommodation with Japan. Sensitive to his nation's weakness in the Pacific, he bullied Congress to authorize the construction of four new dreadnought-class battleships and to fortify Hawaii and Manila Bay. To his son Kermit he wrote: "I do not believe there will be war with Japan, but I do believe that there is enough chance of war to make it eminently wise to insure against it by building such a navy as to forbid Japan's hoping for success." Dramatically he ordered the navy's entire fleet of sixteen battleships of the line to embark on a goodwill cruise across the Pacific and around the world. Following calls in New Zealand and Australia, Japan welcomed the "Great White Fleet" to Tokyo Bay, where a rousing popular reception at Yokohama for its officers and sailors included rows and rows of schoolchildren waving American flags and trying to sing "The Star-spangled Banner."

On the day the fleet departed, Tokyo authorities sent instructions to Ambassador Takahira Kogoro in Washington to seek agreement with the United States on issues outstanding between the two countries. In the Root-Takahira Agreement of November 30, 1908, the two governments promised to (1) respect each other's possessions in the Pacific and maintain the status quo in the region, and (2) affirm the independence and integrity of China together with the Open Door principle of equal opportunity for the commerce and industry of all nations. In private conversations Roosevelt emphasized the peaceful intent of America's relations with Japan, and the emperor's emissaries declared that Japan had never even considered making war on the United States. The tenor of the talks pleased Roosevelt. The future seemed secure in March 1909, when he left office.

Appearances were deceiving. To Congress, at the moment of the Root-Takahira Agreement, Roosevelt castigated the Japanese as belligerent, in order to obtain the battleship building program he coveted. Then in February 1909, just as the Great White Fleet was triumphantly returning to Hampton Roads, Roosevelt had to marshal all of his influence to block the latest wave of discriminatory measures against the Japanese in California. The battleships of the Great White Fleet were already being denuded of their gilt ornamentation. Repainted they wore the menacing gray color of regular sea duty.[12]

President Taft substituted a legalistic idealism that favored China over Japan for the strategic and military supports underpinning Roosevelt's foreign policy and, in certain respects, foreshadowed Woodrow Wilson's approach to the world outside. Taft's secretary of state, Philander C. Knox, the president's alter ego, though not so corpulent, was a Pittsburgh corporation lawyer who brought into office little, if any, knowledge of foreign relations. While playing golf one day, a friend urged Knox to travel to China to see the revolutionary crisis for himself. "I'm just starting to learn this game," Knox joked, "and I'm not going to let anything as unimportant as China interfere." Taft was less wary of Japan than Roosevelt, and his benevolence toward China surpassed Roosevelt's, as did his conception of America's duties there. To advance the progress of Anglo-Saxon civilization, Taft and Knox felt obliged to employ the wealth and power of the United States for the benefit of mankind, especially in Latin America and China. A man of peace, Taft was at once less aggressive and less perceptive in dealing with world affairs than Roosevelt. His wide experience in the Philippines and throughout East Asia had conditioned him to understand events and circumstances largely in the light of his encounters. Taft and Knox attempted to shape the nation's foreign policies almost exclusively in terms of trade and investments. Unmatched by common sense, their good intentions failed to direct a disciplined realism toward Asia's inescapable actualities.

Soon, Taft and Knox announced their support for the Open Door policy and China's modernizing reform movement. In reversing Roosevelt's policy they challenged both Japan and Russia over Manchuria, Korea, and North China. The two recent enemies, Japan and Russia, blessed by their British ally, had secretly made a bargain in 1907, wherein Russia through its Chinese Eastern Railway could control northern Manchuria, while Japan with its South Manchurian Railway controlled southern Manchuria. To dislodge Japan and Russia, Secretary Knox put forward a "neutralization" scheme to induce the powers with interests in China to cooperate in buying up the Manchurian railroads and operating them under Open Door principles. The British and French, who needed Russia's and Japan's support against Germany, backed away in alarm. Russia and Japan drew together to thwart Knox and, in a timely dig at the United States, on July 4, 1910, signed a fresh treaty of friendship. Less than two months later, Japan formally annexed Korea. In Manchuria, Japanese cottons at once replaced the long-dominant American textiles. Likewise, in China's interior, Taft's and Knox's intervention came to naught in the ill-starred Huguang Railway consortium.

Taft and Knox responded calmly to ex-President Roosevelt's worried letters explaining his precepts for East Asian policy, but neither seemed to understand or share his concerns. Taft and Knox refused to see any connections between their own high-minded goals for China and Japan's interests in Manchuria, or the problems being provoked by Japan's emigrants to California. Their distrust of Japanese imperialism never seemed to influence their sense of mission toward China. Yet like Roosevelt, they leaned hard on California's politicians to impede the passage of restrictive legislation against the Japanese. In revising the Japanese-American Treaty of 1894, Taft and Knox realized that Japan would no longer accept a one-sided exclusionary provision, and agreed as a substitution to a Japanese memorandum promising continuing emigration restriction. They furthermore persuaded Californians to acquiesce in this new arrangement, so the Senate could proceed without delay to ratify the treaty.

When Emperor Meiji died, in 1912, he left behind in his name the revolutionary changes that transformed feudal Japan from a medieval society into an industrialized and militarized empire, but America's recent reversal of its policy toward East Asia was perplexing and provoking his empire's statesmen. Their once-cherished dream of peacefully expanding across the Pacific Ocean had given way against American resistance to fashioning a continental destiny on Asia's mainland. Suddenly, nevertheless, the United States was challenging Japan's hard-won position in Manchuria and preparing to compete for China's economy. The Japanese hope of sharing the development of the Pacific region yielded reluctantly before a realization that an inevitable collision with the United States lay ahead. Trade with the United States seemed not to count. More and more, it was becoming difficult on both sides of the Pacific Ocean to imagine a future without war. The idea of an inescapable conflict, long prevalent in American fears of the yellow peril, ineluctably entered into Japanese thoughts and anxieties.

In twentieth-century Japan, like the United States, the army and navy were constitutionally subordinate to civilian authorities, who controlled the purse strings and determined policies, but in practice the general military staffs managed to dominate Japan's foreign policies and political directions.[13]

During Woodrow Wilson's presidency, 1913–1921, many of the assumptions Americans held about world affairs in general and East Asia in particular came to grief. Wilson believed in enforcing the Monroe Doctrine to guarantee righteous conduct throughout the Western Hemisphere. He cherished the Open Door policy for China. And like Taft, Wilson trusted God, destiny, and duty to carry America's self-confident moral superiority and political enlightenment to the farthest corners of the earth. To Asia's revolutionary nationalism, Wilson compassionately responded. He favored independence for the Philippines. He wanted to assist and protect China against the ambitions of Japan, Russia, and the other powers. He pulled the United States out of the six-power banking and development consortium in China to go it alone, because he believed that the Japanese and Russians dominated its directions. Wilson's deep-seated Presbyterian faith and his connections with Christian missionaries convinced him that Christianity was the instrumentality of China's rebirth. He also, like so many other Americans, suspended the loftiest standards of morality to judge China's actions, but he severely applied them to Japan. Wilson and Secretary of State William Jennings Bryan were ill equipped for any crisis to arise with Japan, let alone for a succession of them.

In short order, Japan and the United States quarreled over (1) a renewal of anti-Japanese tension in California, (2) Japan's wartime seizures of Germany's holdings in China and the Pacific Ocean islands, (3) the Twenty-one Demands made by Japan on China, (4) American and Japanese intervention in Siberia against the Bolsheviks following the Russian Revolution of 1917, and (5) the Treaty of Versailles.

In May 1913, the state of California enacted an alien land law to bar Japanese residents from owning real estate, prompting Japan immediately to protest. Japan's anger surprised Wilson and Bryan, who had never attempted to understand the Japanese point of view, relying on flowery reassurances as necessary. Wilson and Bryan hid behind the narrow states'-rights constitutional argument that local enactments did not make a national policy of discrimination. Japan's protest precipitated a minor war scare. The American army and navy began planning for a Japanese-American war, and the navy recommended removing its ships from China to the Philippines. Wilson and Bryan thought that the alarm of the military chieftains over the yellow peril was preposterous, which induced several important army and navy advisors to deem them unqualified to define strategy for the Pacific. The alien land controversy was never settled throughout Wilson's presidency, embittering the Japanese.

The Great War in Europe between 1914 and 1918 afforded Japan a golden opportunity to achieve preeminence in East Asia and, rivaling the great powers, to gain an empire among the islands of Pacific Oceania. The British, French, Germans, and Russians could neither check Japan, as Woodrow Wilson hoped, nor maintain the stability and equipoise in China essential for the Open Door policy to function. None other than the United States could hope to forestall Japan's expansionist moves. But Mexico's revolution and Europe's war, especially along the Atlantic sea lanes where Germany's submarines were devastating Allied and neutral shipping, preoccupied President Wilson and left China virtually helpless against Japan. Japan, as Britain's ally, declared war on Germany, then conquered the kaiser's North Pacific islands and raced over the Shantung Peninsula to claim the German leasehold of Kiaochow. The outcome of Tokyo's Twenty-one Demands on China, January 8, 1915, greatly extended Japan's control, even after the demands became somewhat modified under British and American pressures. Japan acquired new political and economic rights in Shantung, southern Manchuria, and Mongolia.

Wilson's high-minded refusal to recognize Japan's ill-gotten gains was wrecked by the secret acquiescence of Japan's British and French allies and the collapse of his reinstituted banking consortium. The Lansing-Ishii Agreement, November 2, 1917, saved face for both parties. The United States recognized Japan's geographical position as giving her "special interests" in China, in return for Japan's reaffirmation of the "so-called 'open-door' or equal opportunity for commerce and industry" in China, and the two powers repeated their support for China's independence and territorial integrity. Unfortunately, President Wilson must have been so blinded by his wartime idealism as to overlook the unique opportunity, which his new secretary of state, Robert Lansing, wanted to take, to hammer out a realistic accord covering all outstanding issues including immigration and alien rights.[14]

Early in 1918, both the United States and Japan faced the possibility of having to send their troops into Siberia. The collapse of the Russian armies and the withdrawal of Bolshevik Russia from the war by the treaty of Brest-Litovsk (March 3) drove Great Britain and France frantically to plead for renewing fighting in the east to avert defeat on the western front. The French, moreover, were the chief casualties from the repudiation of Russian debts. Only the United States and Japan had enough resources for any significant effort. President Wilson turned down entreaty after entreaty by the Europeans to intervene. Although the president was convinced that the Japanese would, if they could, use the opportunity to grab portions of Siberia, he and his advisors resisted the Allied pressures, because they feared that a Siberian expedition would siphon away essential troops and supplies from the western front, where, they believed, the war was going to be won or lost. Japan viewed the problem entirely within an Asian frame of reference, where the Bolshevik triumph posed a drastic threat to Japan's holdings. Dreading to risk a prolonged struggle against the Bolsheviks while the United States saved its strength, Japan's army leaders opposed pushing beyond Siberia to join any counterrevolutionary intervention. In April, backed by the British and French, Japan moved troops into position along the Trans-Siberian Railroad.

American participation in Siberia became essential for the Allies' strategy to succeed. The issue plagued Germany's foes. In Japan, militant interventionists were rallying popular opinion. President Wilson's resistance crumbled. The plight of thousands of Czech soldiers trying to escape from the Red Army allowed him to intervene in Russia to safeguard their withdrawal and also, he hoped, to encourage democratic elements against the Communists. In July 1918, Wilson invited Japan to join the United States in a limited intervention of no more than seven thousand soldiers each. Wilson also consented to send several military units to the northwestern ports of Murmansk and Arkhangelsk to keep Allied military supplies stockpiled there out of Bolshevik hands. In September, three United States Army batallions disembarked in Siberia at Vladivostok to protect the fleeing Czechs and constrain both the Japanese and the Bolsheviks.

Japan's new leader, Prime Minister Haro Kei, a moderate who craved postwar understanding and cooperation with the United States, mistrusted the army's readiness to obey any limitations he imposed. Haro's fears proved justified. By November, Japan had deployed seventy-two thousand soldiers in Siberia, where they were openly engaged in the civil war. Enraged by the Japanese army's violation of its own government's assurances, Wilson and his advisors no longer trusted Japan. What began reluctantly as an Allied diversionary campaign against Germany was being transformed, in the wake of the Russian Revolution, into an adventure to prevent Japan from swallowing all of northeastern Asia and much of Siberia.[15]

With the end of the World War, United States interest in the Far East increased, while Japan's goal never faltered of gaining supremacy over China. At the Paris Peace Conference, Japan demanded recognition for her conquests in Shantung and the Pacific islands and strove to act as China's defender against the outside world. Also Japan tried, without success, to force a racial equality clause into the covenant of the League of Nations. For whatever reason, Wilson capitulated to Japan on Shantung. Probably he agreed with Colonel Edward M. House, his close advisor, that Japan, if refused Shantung, would reject membership in the League of Nations, or possibly he felt a twinge of guilt at rebuffing Japan's proposal for a racial equality clause. Angrily his peace commissioners and the public at large protested Wilson's surrender of his own principles. Wilson hoped that the controversial Shantung settlement, like many other unresolved issues, would in time be put right by his beloved League of Nations. On the defensive now, Woodrow Wilson grew terribly weary as he fought night and day for the Treaty of Versailles with its League of Nations covenant. Then, on October 2, 1919, he suffered the incapacitating stroke that effectively removed him from public life for the remainder of his term of office. With President Wilson in seclusion, the Senate twice rejected the treaty. Never would the United States join the League of Nations.

Japanese-American relations turned ugly. The two governments publicly disputed the terms of the Shantung settlement and the interpretation of the Lansing-Ishii Agreement. A new issue arose, whether Yap in the western Caroline Islands, a vital cable station, was included under Japan's trustee mandates. In the United States, hostility toward Japan approached epidemic levels. Again an anti-Japanese campaign swept California over alien land ownership. The immigration issue worsened after discussions failed to resolve it at the ambassadorial level. Military leaders directed their attention to the Pacific Ocean, where most of them now believed the next war would commence. With the battleships based at Pearl Harbor, the navy's planners began to think more and more aggressively of attacking Japan's fleet on the very coastlines of her home islands. Some Japanese openly expressed their fears of the United States. A few military leaders talked of instigating a war to defend Japan's empire, and the navy launched a major construction program in 1919. As the era of Wilsonian idealism drew to its conclusion, Japan and the United States appeared to be moving toward a dangerous encounter in their relations with each other.[16]

President Warren G. Harding and Secretary of State Charles Evans Hughes brought into office a soothing respite from Wilsonian excesses and the anti-Japanese prejudices rampant in government circles. The problem, as they construed it, was to reverse Japan's wartime gains and revive the Open Door policy, while coping with rival revolutionary movements in China and appeasing the Japanese. President Harding and Secretary Hughes knew that constructive measures were needed. For one, the old Anglo-Japanese alliance must end, as it afforded a British mandate for Japanese imperialism. Harding opined to a journalist that Japan would be "the most difficult point diplomatically for the next few years." The prospect of a naval race by Great Britain, Japan, and the United States greatly alarmed the American people, however, and inspired the Washington Conference of 1921–1922.

Under Hughes's leadership and Harding's prodding the Washington Conference produced an entirely new treaty system for East Asia and the Pacific. Japan's diplomats proved unexpectedly accommodating. The Five-Power Treaty among Great Britain, the United States, Japan, France, and Italy called for scrapping large numbers of their ships already built or under construction. The treaty limited maximum tonnages and set ratios for the signatories for capital ships including aircraft carriers. Another among those parties applied the rules of surface warfare to submarines and outlawed the use of poison gas. In the Four-Power Treaty, the United States, Great Britain, Japan, and France promised to respect each other's domains in the Pacific and maintain the status quo of naval fortifications in the western Pacific. Great Britain and Japan terminated their alliance. Japan consented to return Shantung to China, settled its quarrel with the United States over Yap, and announced an early withdrawal from Siberia. China also won multinational support for its territorial integrity in two Nine-Power Treaties signed by the Big Five, Portugal, Belgium, the Netherlands, and China itself. But the imperial powers thwarted China's calls for full sovereignty. They rebuffed China's entreaties to end extraterritoriality and regain control of her import duties. The powers fathomed neither the obsolescence of their resistance to change nor the accumulating hatred against foreigners behind China's demands. Further, their exclusion of Soviet Russia, the Communist pariah, invited trouble for the future. Yet by invoking the Kellogg-Briand Pact of 1928, through which sixty-two nations had renounced war as an instrument of national policy, they achieved a momentary reduction of tensions between China and Russia in 1929 over possession of the Chinese Eastern Railway.

Interestingly, it was the absence of international crises that characterized the 1920s in American–East Asian relations. Japan's leaders foreswore the nation's earlier goals of imperial expansion to turn instead toward peaceful economic growth within a parliamentary system. The Japanese hoped to increase their already large traffic with the United States, which was buying 40 percent of Japan's exports, and to push their commerce into the Middle East and Southeast Asia. As Japan strengthened its democratic institutions and weakened the military influence in society, the government moderated its pressures on China. Americans adopted a cautious optimism. Franklin D. Roosevelt, who in 1913, as assistant secretary of the navy, vented hardline views, now praised the Washington treaties for their naval limitations and the Japanese for their evident friendship. Japan and the United States, Roosevelt declared in 1923, "have not a single valid reason, and won't have as far as we can look ahead, for fighting each other." Sympathy and humanitarian relief poured into Japan from the United States following the earthquake that devastated Tokyo and Yokohama in September 1923, causing Ambassador Cyrus E. Woods to report the old mistrusts gone. "Everywhere I go I hear the opinion expressed that our countries at last understand each other, and that we are united in ties of friendship, more strongly than any paper treaty could possibly establish." American businessmen and bankers were hearkening to Japanese ventures with a fresh confidence.

Only the United States Navy's high command, the Hearst newspapers, and avowed racists remained outspokenly anti-Japanese. The navy's strategy was still to defend, or if necessary recapture, the Philippines far across the Pacific Ocean. Over all, however, there hovered the issue of racial antagonism. Most naval officers anticipated renewed challenges from Japan not only against China and the Open Door policy, but against American immigration restrictions and the whole of the white race.

For decades, the pressures to restrict immigration had been growing. Reactions against the World War and the Russian Revolution during the Red scare led to witch-hunt deportations for foreign-born radicals. The faith in assimilation, as sung by Emma Lazarus and inscribed on the Statue of Liberty ("Give me your tired, your poor / Your huddled masses yearning to breathe free / The wretched refuse of your teeming shore / . . . I lift my lamp beside the golden door"), crumbled over delusions of racial purity. In the Immigration Act of 1921, Congress adopted a quota system based upon national origins and favoring northwestern Europeans but upheld the Gentlemen's Agreement with Japan. In furthering restriction, the Immigration Act of 1924 completely closed the gates to any more Japanese, including picture brides, by debarring all persons ineligible to become citizens of the United States.

Outraged, the Japanese protested in no uncertain terms. Secretary of

State Hughes gloomily anguished that the law excluding the Japanese had "undone the work of the Washington Conference and implanted the seeds of an antagonism which are sure to bear fruit in the future." American diplomats in Tokyo and Peking shared Hughes's alarm. Even John V. A. MacMurray, the voice of the anti-Japanese faction in the State Department, worried at the damage to the peaceful new order emerging in East Asia. The uproar brought out extremists on both sides. Retired Rear Admiral Bradley A. Fiske shouted that war was imminent, though officials in Japan and the United States deplored such talk. Ultranationalists in Japan decried the United States Navy's maneuvers scheduled for the waters west of Hawaii. Hughes rejected a Japanese hint to cancel the war games, and Foreign Minister Shidehara Kijuro rebuffed Hughes's hope that the Pacific Fleet might be invited to visit Japan. Right-wing fanatics and many newspapers in Japan denounced the exclusion law, as well as their own government's too-timid quarrels over it with the United States.

To make matters worse, as critics charged, the promise of the Washington treaty system for a peaceful future and a collaborative development of China was in a state of virtual collapse. Chinese and Japanese troops battled each other in Shantung Province, while the United States and Great Britain were pursuing independent courses of action toward Chiang Kai-shek's Nationalist regime. The worldwide Depression struck Japan with particularly harsh effects. Exports dropped by half between 1929 and 1930, causing drastic hardships for workers and farmers. Swayed by military leaders and patriotic zealots, the Japanese people began to repudiate moderates in public life. The United States stood for that cooperation with the West, which, they argued, jeopardized the nation. Military leaders, who identified the United States as Japan's most likely foe, believed the time was ripe to redirect Japan toward bold new goals. Nonetheless, Ishii Kikujiro, the respected retired diplomat, insisted that the only real cause for trouble between Japan and the United States was neither the control of the Pacific Ocean nor the future of China, but the racial problem. The danger of war would arise, Ishii argued, if the United States were to stand up for white supremacy, leaving Japan to champion the nonwhite peoples of the earth. But Ambassador to Japan William R. Castle, a career diplomat, reported that Japan's current leaders themselves were certain that war with the United States could only begin over China. Both statesmen, in a certain sense, proved to be correct.[17]

When, in 1931–1932, Japan's Kwangtung Army seized Manchuria and incorporated the puppet state of Manchukuo into Japan's empire, the United States registered its intense disapproval through Secretary of State Henry L. Stimson's doctrine of nonrecognition. Alarm intensified when bloody fighting broke out in Shanghai between Japanese and Chinese forces. The Japanese navy's savage attacks on Shanghai infuriated Stimson. Stimson persuaded President Herbert C. Hoover over his naval command's objections to transfer the Asiatic Fleet from Manila to Shanghai to display the force behind American disapproval. In Tokyo, Stimson replaced Ambassador W. Cameron Forbes, the onetime governor-general of the Philippines, who was openly disputing his angry denunciations of the Japanese, with Joseph C. Grew, who agreed with him. Simultaneously, however, Hoover undercut Stimson's moves by calling for reductions in the navies of the big powers and stressing merely the moral indictment of Japan. Arrived in Japan, Ambassador Grew suspected that the American sermonizing over Manchuria and Shanghai was fortifying the aroused young army officers in control of Japan's government. Stimson's and Hoover's strictures seemed to infuriate the Japanese toward defiance. The Roosevelt administration continued the policy of nonrecognition, which originated from the Democrats' own Wilsonian principles. Japan went ahead fastening its hold on Manchuria and undermining the Kuomintang across northern China.

Nevertheless, the years from 1933 to 1937 were comparatively quiet in East Asia, while in Europe Hitler and Mussolini were opening up the lists for another cataclysmic war. In 1935, Italy invaded Ethiopia. In 1936, Germany reoccupied the Rhineland, and Spain's civil war commenced. Concern over East Asia shrank before the terrifying prospect of a second world war in Europe.

Behind the passivity toward East Asia of FDR's New Deal government, in which economic recovery and social reform programs were uppermost, the traditional American policies persisted, including the Open Door for China and resistance to expansion by Japan. Stanley K. Hornbeck, an experienced and clever bureaucrat who dominated the State Department's Division of Far Eastern Affairs for more than a decade, staunchly upheld its favoritism for China against Japan. Hornbeck and his protégés froze the nation's policy, refusing even to reconsider its tenets. The navy likewise opposed serious changes. Toward Japan, the ORANGE plan of 1911 still set American strategy. In the event of war, the navy would sail across the central Pacific to defend or liberate the Philippines as needed, then go on triumphantly to destroy the Japanese fleet and blockade the home islands. Against the almost certain inability of the navy to carry out the ORANGE plan and the army's eagerness to abandon the western Pacific as indefensible, it is a subject for wonder that American strategy should have remained so steadfast until 1937. After 1934, the United States built up its fleet toward treaty strengths, though new construction lagged behind Japan's navy's expansion. War between them was growing more and more unavoidable if, as the margin separating their navies narrowed, the United States continued to insist on maintaining China's integrity and obstructing Japan's imperial ambitions.[18]

In Japan, the army and navy took control. The effects of the global economic crisis, the danger from Chinese nationalism, and the exciting examples of European fascism dissolved the Japanese people's support for individualism, parliamentary democracy, and economic liberalism. Especially in army circles, Western-style ideals succumbed before a mystical spirituality extolling the emperor's sanctity and pan-Asian solidarity under Japanese leadership. The cabinet of Hirota Koki responded in 1936 by launching plans to build Japan into a militant garrison state. Top officials in the Foreign Ministry, led by Arito Hachiro, rejected Western demands for restraint and prepared to establish full Japanese hegemony over China. The navy's leaders demanded the abrogation of the Five-Power Treaty limitations and called for a mission southward to acquire the vital raw materials, commercial strongholds, and defensive outposts necessary for imposing Japan's ascendency throughout Asia. The army fought on, as before, to contain the Russians and dominate the Chinese.

Unexpectedly, a clash between Chinese and Japanese troops in July 1937 at the Marco Polo Bridge west of Peking, precipitated Japan into a full-scale war with China. This incident opened the Second Sino-Japanese War.

Officials in the United States government grew perplexed. They were unable to comprehend either China's strident nationalism or Japan's expanded imperialism. Roosevelt and the American people were unduly confident of American industrial superiority. President Roosevelt and the general public alike were fearful of Europe's descent toward war and unwilling to interrupt the hard-won process of domestic recovery and reform. Roosevelt bided his time waiting for public alarms over East Asia to arise. Ambassador Grew warned against altering the aloof and cautious policy in operation. These appearances of continuity were misleading. The menaces of Hitler and Mussolini, together with the new linkages of the Anti-Comintern Pact joining Germany, Italy, and Japan against communism and the Third International, deepened American anxieties. Hornbeck predicted that Japan, if not dissuaded, would one day descend on the Philippine Islands and the British, French, and Dutch colonies in Southeast Asia. Chiang Kai-shek's Nationalists' vitality improved both official and popular support for China's cause.[19]

The Japanese remained fairly confident that their moves in China would not cause hostilities with the United States. Absorbed in their own adventures, Nippon's leaders failed fully enough to weigh the effects of their actions. Their decision to move southward beyond China into Southeast Asia brought Japan and the United States into a bitter confrontation. Mao

Zedong, the embattled leader of China's Communists, had warned the Western powers as early as 1936 that the Japanese would aim their thrusts not only toward China but also against all the other nations holding interests in the Pacific. To Mao's ominous forecast, there was little response. Isolationism, bred by tradition and reaction against war or economic depression, continued to define American foreign policy. Britain and France worried themselves and each other over Mussolini's and Hitler's latest threats and moves. The Soviet Union and Nazi Germany, in a shocking turnabout, signed their infamous nonaggression treaty. Once more, in September 1939, Europe was going to war.

War in Europe would again redound to Japan's advantage. Germany's victories over the hapless Belgian, Dutch, French, and British forces in May and June of 1940 provided the opportunity. When France capitulated, the Luftwaffe's aerial blitzkrieg against Great Britain began. A German invasion of the British Isles loomed. The beleaguered British, Dutch, and French navies faced almost certain seizure or massive destruction. Hypnotized, the United States feared to repeat its experience of 1917. In the Pacific region, Europe's colonies and holdings lay at the mercy of Japan. On June 25, the Tokyo government demanded the right to land troops in French Indochina, and Japanese warships soon entered several ports there.

France's German-dominated government at Vichy, unwilling or helpless to resist, granted the use of three airfields and a number of seaports to concede Indochina's occupation. President Roosevelt leveled an embargo against Japan on aviation fuel and first-quality scrap iron. On September 27, Japan joined her imperial destiny to those of Italy and Germany by entering with them into the ten-year Tripartite Pact. The Rome-Berlin-Tokyo Axis partners pledged total assistance to each other in the event any of the trio became involved in war against a country not yet a belligerent, with the exception of Russia. Roosevelt extended the embargo to include all scrap metals. Japan and Russia concluded a Neutrality Pact on April 13, 1941, to safeguard themselves from each other along the Manchurian frontier, which freed Japan to advance southward. No one could mistake the obvious point that the United States was Japan's only probable enemy.

When Germany invaded the Soviet Union on June 23, to open a vast new stage in the war, the United States was the only nonbelligerent power remaining. Slowly America began to rearm. But its attention still focused on Europe.

Japan's military leaders had been preparing for a general war since 1932, even to holding air raid drills for the civilian population. The China war now turned into the means to the end. As Prime Minister Prince Fumimaro Konoye articulated his government's plans, Japan must first undergo a national purification by victory of arms, then direct East Asia toward a triumphant rebirth. Japan's new order would be based on the amalgamation of China and Japan and eliminate the Western powers. The Western powers scoffed at Japan's ambitions, and the Russians decisively defeated the Japanese army in a major border clash in 1938. The United States government, in order to warn Japan of the American public's rising animosity and show support for Great Britain and China, declared its intention to terminate the commercial treaty of 1911 between the two nations. By late 1939, Japan's forces were hammering away at Chungking's defenses, futilely trying to overcome the Nationalist government's inland capital.

Fortuitously for the Japanese, the fall of the Low Countries and France followed by the siege of Great Britain released them from China's morass for easier targets. Buoyed by its new Axis partners, Japan demanded extraordinary access to petroleum resources and trading advantages in the Netherlands East Indies, but the Dutch refused. The Japanese next forced Great Britain into closing the border of Burma to block outside supplies from reaching Chiang Kai-shek. Yet within three months, the British reopened the Burma Road from Lashio to Kunming, as soon as the pressure on them in Europe lessened. On July 24, 1941, the Japanese moved for the first time into southern Indochina.

President Franklin D. Roosevelt retaliated by imposing an economic blockade. Through his executive order, Roosevelt froze all Japanese assets in the United States and further curtailed petroleum exports to Japan. The president's reaction surprised and shocked the Japanese. Japan's war machine could only operate for about eighteen months without fresh imports of oil, while instantaneous paralysis confronted the nation's financial institutions. Nothing but war or a complete reversal of policy by both sides could break the blockade. Japan had reached the point of declaring war against the United States.

Diplomacy posed only the slimmest hope. Negotiations had been underway in Washington from early March until mid-July between Secretary of State Cordell Hull and Ambassador Kichisaburo Nomura, but these proved fruitless. Laboriously, at meeting after meeting, the pair went over and over the points of dispute. The long-running policies of their respective governments blocked every meaningful compromise. Hull told the Japanese to get out of China and renounce expansion by force into Southeast Asia, in effect to nullify the Tripartite Pact and reverse their grand imperial design. The Japanese wanted the United States to abandon the Open Door policy and end its aid to China, then to lift the economic blockade of Japan in order to restore normal trade. Secretary Hull presented his case in four points. Japan must agree to (1) respect the territorial integrity and sovereignty of other nations, (2) avoid interfering in the internal affairs of other countries, (3) respect the principle of equality, including equality of commercial opportunity, and (4) effect none but peaceful changes in the status quo in the Pacific.

Secretary Hull was doggedly reiterating the substance of the Open Door policy, to which the Japanese could not accede without altogether withdrawing from China. Even so, Nomura failed fully to impress his superiors with the commitment of the United States to its traditional China policy, while Hull believed that firmness based on moral rectitude would deter the Japanese. In truth, President Roosevelt's embargo on petroleum and his order freezing Japan's assets in the United States had virtually killed any prospects for diplomacy. From then on, as historian and onetime State Department officer Herbert Feis realized, "the oil gauge and the clock stood side by side."[20]

What is astonishing is that no genuine peacemaking efforts were officially put forward by either the Japanese or the Americans before Japan had to face running out of oil.

7

THE WAR IN
THE PACIFIC

Japan's army and navy leaders insisted either on obtaining immediate diplomatic success or going to war to get what they wanted. Their pressure impelled Prime Minister Konoye to propose a conference with President Roosevelt. If he could avert war, Konoye intended to retain Japan's special position in China, but to disguise its form. Unenthusiastically, Konoye appealed to President Roosevelt to receive him in Washington.

United States Ambassador Joseph C. Grew, an experienced career diplomat, urged the president to agree. Grew had persuaded himself that the American embargo was swinging Japan toward reason. Optimistically he expected Konoye to make important concessions to the United States that would before long bring about a lasting accommodation. Secretary of State Hull did not trust Konoye, and Hornbeck's Division of Far Eastern Affairs feared a betrayal of China. In the White House, Roosevelt concentrated on mustering support for the battered British and Russians. The U-boat menace and his meeting in Newfoundland with Winston Churchill, which produced the Atlantic Charter's moralistic statement of war aims, preoccupied him. Roosevelt hoped to postpone, if not forever avoid, a showdown with the Japanese. Neither he nor Churchill expected the Japanese to move beyond Indochina against British warships and the guns of Singapore. Roosevelt and Hull failed to sense the desperation in Japan's high command. Although Konoye's proposal was never rejected, Hull informed

Nomura that wider-ranging agreements must first be reached on a number of issues before a summit conference could take place.

Konoye's government responded with evident concessions on September 25, by tacitly abrogating the Tripartite Pact and promising neutrality for Southeast Asia for as long as Japan could obtain vital resources there. Japan also demanded the normalization of trade relations, including large-scale deliveries of American oil, and, to bring about peace, a halt in American aid to China. Japan refused to pull out of Indochina before peace was reached with China on Japan's terms. Japan's terms would require the United States to recognize Japan's sovereignty in Manchukuo and her overlordship in China. Only by abandoning Chiang Kai-shek might the United States block Japan's progress into Southeast Asia, and then only temporarily. By mid-October, Hull measured the distances between Tokyo and Washington as growing wider than ever before. The Japanese government's resolve was stiffening. Without oil, the nation would become impotent. On October 16, with no persuasive alternative to war to offer his military leaders, yet loath to lead Japan into hostilities against the United States, Konoye resigned.

Since no more civilian leaders remained to tame Japan's ultranationalists, Emperor Hirohito named General Hideki Tōjō, the war minister, to the premiership. The emperor hoped to avert war. He directed Tōjō to attempt peaceful efforts once more. Upon Tōjō's insisting they obey the emperor, the army and navy chiefs consented, but they stipulated December 1 for their deadline. If Japan did not reach a diplomatic settlement with the United States by that date, they would make war in early December. Nicknamed "the Razor" for his sharp discipline, Tōjō epitomized the army's militarists. He held that the United States would pay dearly to avoid a war it did not want.

Since late winter of 1941, however, Admiral Isoroku Yamamoto, the commander-in-chief of the Combined Fleet, a carrier enthusiast, had been developing his daringly innovative plans. Traditionally, the Japanese believed they could seize the resources of Southeast Asia and the East Indies before the United States would react in force. Then they could destroy the American fleet near their home islands in the decisive battle for which, since 1909, the Imperial Navy had theoretically planned. Holding against his skeptics that the United States Navy must first be nullified, if the drive into the Southern Resources Area were to succeed, Admiral Yamamoto insisted on first attacking the Pacific Fleet and the army air corps at their Hawaiian bases. By sheer force of personality, he finally, in early November, won acceptance by the top commanders of the navy and army for his risky scheme.

In November, Ambassador Nomura and Saburo Kurusu, a special

envoy, offered Japan's pair of plans for a diplomatic solution. Plan A unrealistically set forth an all-embracing settlement. Plan B reflected two factors: Tōjō's conviction that the United States would pay almost any price to avoid war with Japan, and Japan's own worsening situation due to Roosevelt's economic embargo. Conceivably, it might have introduced a *modus vivendi* short of war. Plan B proposed:

1. Both the Government of Japan and the United States undertake not to make any armed advancement into any of the regions in the Southeastern Asia and the Southern Pacific area excepting the parts of French Indo-China where the Japanese troops are stationed at present.

2. The Japanese Government undertakes to withdraw its troops now stationed in French Indo-China upon either the restoration of peace between Japan and China or the establishment of an equitable peace in the Pacific area.

In the meantime the Government of Japan declares that it is prepared to remove its troops now stationed in the southern part of French Indo-China to the northern part of the said territory upon the conclusion of the present agreement which shall be embodied in the final agreement.

3. The Government of Japan and the United States shall cooperate with a view to securing the acquisition of those goods and commodities which the two countries need in the Netherlands East Indies.

4. The Government of Japan and the United States mutually undertake to restore their commercial relations to those prevailing prior to the freezing of the assets.

5. The Government of the United States undertakes to refrain from such measures and actions as will be prejudicial to the endeavors for the restoration of general peace between Japan and China.

The United States rejected Japan's overtures on November 26. Secretary of State Hull regarded them as mere contrivances to obtain American backing for Japan's hegemony over the western Pacific and eastern Asia. By then, Japan's war orders, provisional on the outcome of negotiations, had gone out to the Pearl Harbor Striking Force. The Second Sino-Japanese War, which had begun in 1937 in the so-called China incident, and the general European war that began in 1939 in Germany's invasion of Poland, were joining together in the second world war of the twentieth century. On December 8, 1941, Tokyo date, Japan would attack. Hirohito's Imperial Rescript declaring war summoned up both the spiritual support and patriotic sacrifice required for sacred Nippon's coming ordeal: "The hallowed spirits of our Imperial Ancestors guarding Us from above, We rely upon the loyalty and courage of Our subjects in Our confident expectation that the task bequeathed by Our Forefathers will be carried forward, and the sources of evil will be speedily eradicated and an enduring peace immutably established in East Asia, preserving thereby the glory of Our Empire."

Ahead lay four years of terrible strife. Both nations would harvest the bitter fruits of their shortsightedness and complacent ignorance of each other. The Japanese grievously underestimated the catastrophic nature of the war they would have to fight after their opening attack. Those Americans, who on that fateful Sunday morning had never anticipated Japan's bombing, were everlastingly going to "Remember Pearl Harbor!"[2]

Furtively, on November 26, the Pearl Harbor Striking Force slipped away from its isolated anchorage at Hitokappu Bay in the Kurile Islands northeast of Hokkaido. The Imperial Japanese Navy had spent months training the crews of the striking force's more than sixty ships and 360 or so aircraft. Specialists had devised airborne torpedoes to run accurately in shallow waters, and armor-piercing naval shells were converted into aerial bombs. Pilots over and over practiced dry-run, low-level flying maneuvers. Vice-Admiral Chuichi Nagumo, the force's commander, acutely alert to the hazards facing his mission, was following extraordinary precautions to prevent detection. Nagumo's ships were running blacked out and on strict radio silence, not even discarding garbage overboard, while behind him the Kure Naval Air Station obfuscated its radio traffic to distract eavesdroppers. Through rough seas across the vast wastes of the northern Pacific, Nagumo's armada, concealed by thick fogs, coursed eastward along a great arc just south of the Aleutian Islands, exactly as Billy Mitchell in 1935 had predicted they would. Destroyers formed a defensive screen, while submarines patrolled two hundred miles ahead. Two modernized battleships and two heavy cruisers guarded the flanks. In the center, in paired columns, the six carriers steamed toward their destination. Led by Nagumo's flagship *Akagi* ("Red Castle"), the other carriers were the picturesquely named *Kaga* ("Increased Happiness"), *Hiryu* ("Flying Dragon"), *Soryu* ("Green Dragon"), *Shokaku* ("Soaring Crane"), and *Zuikaku* ("Happy Crane"). Tension aboard the ships ran high. All of the assurances of Admiral Yamamoto and the air officers, Minoru Genda and Mitsuo Fuchida, did little to override Admiral Nagumo's fears of impending disaster.

At last, on December 2, when negotiations failed, Nagumo received the prearranged coded signal from Yamamoto, CLIMB MOUNT NIITAKA, signifying "Proceed with the attack!" Undetected, Nagumo steered his Pearl Harbor Striking Force southward to its launching point 230 miles northwest of Honolulu due north of Midway Island. Tremendous excitement swept his crews on learning their target. Far away in Japan's Inland Sea, Admiral Isoroku Yamamoto, who had sent Japan's fleet away to a brilliant, if infamous, victory, penned a short verse:

What does the world think?
I do not care
Nor for my life
For I am the sword
Of my emperor.

On Oahu, early on Sunday, December 7, 1941, everything began at once to go horribly wrong. Sightings of midget submarines and possibly the mother boat near the mouth of Pearl Harbor alerted navy sea and air patrols, which attacked and sank several, but their inexcusably delayed reports, when finally sent, only fouled up communications and intelligence channels until too late. Shortly after 0700, Privates Joseph Lockard and George Elliott, two young army radar operators at Kahuku, the island's northernmost point, tried in vain by telephone to convince Lieutenant Kermit Tyler, the pursuit officer on duty at Fort Shafter's Operations Center, of the importance of the huge pattern approaching on their screen. Tyler assured them their sightings most probably were American aircraft, and no one advised the higher commands. Scouting ahead, likewise undetected, the pilot of a Japanese float plane from the cruiser *Chikuma* reported seeing no American carriers in Lahaina anchorage between the islands of Maui and Lanai, but he radioed exact locations for the big battleships lying alongside Ford Island inside Pearl Harbor. At 0733, the War Department's cabled message warning of an expected Japanese ultimatum had reached Honolulu's Western Union office, to which it had been sent because poor atmospheric conditions were impeding radio channels and no one in Washington thought to employ the telephone. Like everybody else, Tadao Fuchikami, the messenger on his motorcycle, was about to be trapped in a volcano of Japanese bombs. At 0755, the Pacific Fleet's duty sections were ceremonially preparing for Sunday colors. The ship's band on the battleship *Nevada* stood ready to sound out "The Star-spangled Banner." Some sailors noticed strange airplanes in the sky. Some of them appeared to be diving.

Commander Mitsuo Fuchida led the aerial armada. Nearing Oahu he flew west of the island, avoiding the northeastern mountains to attack from the south. Two Honolulu radio stations playing soft Hawaiian music unwittingly guided him onto his flight path. One signal enabled him to adjust his radio direction finder, the other gave him weather conditions. Visibility was good. Looking down and ahead from his plane, at 0753, Commander Fuchida dispatched the code signal *Tora! Tora! Tora!* (Tiger! Tiger! Tiger!) to proclaim prematurely that Japan's surprise assault had already succeeded. He would not have to correct his haste. What a target! Unaware, seven majestic battleships rode at their moorings: *California, Maryland, Oklahoma, Tennessee, West Virginia, Nevada,* and *Arizona.* There, also, were *Pennsylvania* in drydock and the target battleship *Utah,* together

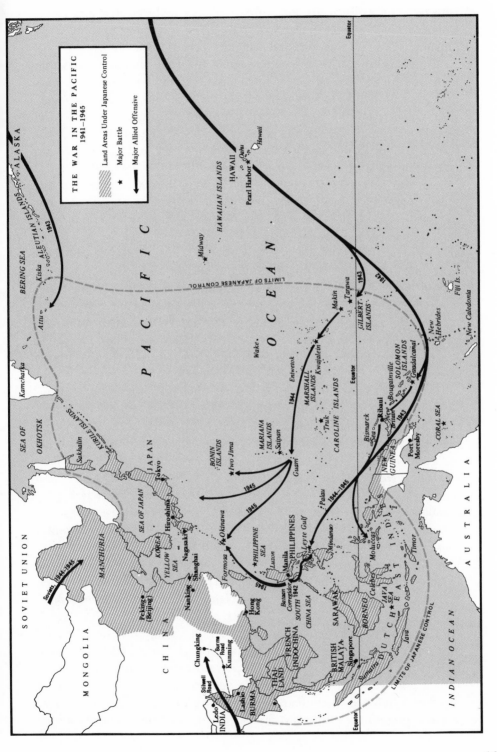

THE WAR IN THE PACIFIC
1941–1945

Land Areas Under Japanese Control
★ Major Battle
Major Allied Offensive

ALASKA

BERING SEA

ALEUTIAN ISLANDS 1943

Kiska

Attu

SEA OF OKHOTSK

Kamchatka

KURILE ISLANDS

Sakhalin

SOVIET UNION

MONGOLIA

MANCHURIA

Peking (Beijing)

Nanking

KOREA

Shanghai

YELLOW SEA

JAPAN

Tokyo

Hiroshima

Nagasaki

SEA OF JAPAN

CHINA

Chungking

Burma Road

Kunming

Stilwell Road

Lashio

Ledo

INDIA

BURMA

THAILAND

FRENCH INDOCHINA

BRITISH MALAYA

Singapore

Hong Kong

Formosa

SOUTH CHINA SEA

Bataan

Corregidor 1942

Manila

Luzon

PHILIPPINES

Mindanao

SARAWAK

BORNEO

Sumatra

Java

JAVA SEA

Celebes

Moluccas

Timor

DUTCH EAST INDIES

Soviet 1944–1945

Okinawa 1945

Iwo Jima 1945

BONIN ISLANDS

MARIANA ISLANDS

Saipan

Guam

PHILIPPINE SEA

Leyte Gulf

Palau

1944–1945

CAROLINE ISLANDS

Truk

Bismarck Sea

Rabaul

NEW BRITAIN

NEW GUINEA

Port Moresby

CORAL SEA

AUSTRALIA

Eniwetok

Kwajalein

MARSHALL ISLANDS

1944

Makin

Tarawa

GILBERT ISLANDS

Wake

Bougainville

SOLOMON ISLANDS

1943

Guadalcanal

1942

New Hebrides

New Caledonia

Fiji Is.

LIMITS OF JAPANESE CONTROL

PACIFIC OCEAN

Midway

HAWAIIAN ISLANDS

HAWAII

Oahu

Hawaii

Pearl Harbor

1943

Equator

INDIAN OCEAN

LIMITS OF JAPANESE CONTROL

169

with numerous destroyers and support vessels deployed here and there. Unbelievably Yamamoto's plan was going to work. Not a word escaped the impassive Zen Buddhist Admiral Nagumo aboard *Akagi*.

Commencing at 0756, the battlewagons tore open like tin cans. Within minutes after the first salvoes of aerial torpedoes and bombs struck home, the message went out to the world: AIR RAID, PEARL HARBOR. THIS IS NO DRILL. *West Virginia* sank in place. *Arizona*'s forward magazine exploded. The vessel took several torpedo hits, a heavy armor-piercing bomb through her second gun turret, and another bomb down her stack, rolling her over and entombing most of the ship's complement. All told *Arizona* lost 47 of 100 officers and 1,056 of 1,411 enlisted men dead or missing. Torpedoed five times, *Oklahoma* capsized. *California* settled to the bottom, leaving only her superstructure visible. Likewise, the *Nevada*, getting slowly underway, sank. *Pennsylvania* in drydock was severely damaged. *Tennessee* and *Maryland* were hit, but did not sink. Three cruisers, notably *Helena*, absorbed heavy beatings. Three destroyers and a minelayer sank. The heart of the prewar Pacific Fleet lay in ruins smoking and flaming. This was the worst day in the history of the United States Navy. Total destruction was avoided only by the courage and discipline of the officers and men frantically manning all available weapons while executing damage control measures. Within approximately ninety minutes, the Japanese finished Pearl Harbor's devastation.

Elsewhere, more or less simultaneously, dive bombers and low-flying, strafing aircraft struck Oahu's airfields. The Japanese quickly destroyed most of the first-line airplanes in Hawaii. Thirty-three of the navy's best planes, almost half the total there, were smashed at Ford Island Naval Air Station. Of the thirty-three Catalina (PBY) amphibian patrol aircraft at Kaneohe, twenty-seven were destroyed, six badly damaged. At Ewa the marines lost nine of their eleven fighters, eighteen of their thirty-two scout bombers, and all six of their auxiliary planes. The army fared just as poorly at Wheeler, Bellows, and Hickam fields. The Japanese pilots had easy hunting. Most American planes were parked in midfield, on runways wing tip to wing tip, to hinder sabotage. Much of the ammunition was tightly secured in storage bunkers for the same reason, out of a racially inspired fear of the Japanese islanders. The few planes managing to take off barely challenged the attackers.

There was no *coup de grace*, however. Back on the flagship *Akagi*, Admiral Nagumo rebuffed Commander Fuchida's appeals for a follow-up assault against the last vestiges of American power in Hawaii. Instead Nagumo turned northward at flank speed. He believed that he had fulfilled his mission to inflict as much damage as possible on the Pacific Fleet before withdrawing for the southward campaigns, and he feared retaliation from the American carriers, whose whereabouts were a worrisome mystery. The Hawaiian population meanwhile nervously prepared for more raids and possibly an invasion. As news of the catastrophe spread throughout the islands, the mood was grim. On the mainland, the initial shock gave way to anxiety and outrage inflamed by grief. The naval personnel lost totaled 2,008 killed or missing and 710 wounded; the army lost 218 killed or missing and 364 wounded; the marines lost 109 killed or missing and 69 wounded. Among civilians, 68 lost their lives and another 35 suffered wounds. But the rest of the fleet escaped. The aircraft carriers missed the attack, as did most of the submarines, cruisers, and destroyers. Ashore the repair facilities were still usable and the oil storages intact. The losses of aircraft, aside from personnel, were the most grievous for equipping the campaigns to come.

Almost unscathed, Admiral Chuichi Nagumo's fleet escaped. His task force lost twenty-nine airplanes, five midget submarines, and one large submarine. In Japan, the glorification as national heroes of the nine officers who went down with their toy boats ominously forecast future acts of suicidal bravery. Captured on Waikiki Beach, a castaway midget submariner became the first prisoner of war. Fortuitously, considering their fleets' unequal strengths, American searchers for the Japanese carriers looked southward instead of to the north. If only Lockard and Elliott's radar sightings had reached the navy's command before midafternoon, which they failed to do, the pursuers would have known what direction to take. Heading home on December 15, Nagumo dispatched the carriers *Soryu* and *Hiryu*, two cruisers, and two destroyers to the neutralizing invasion of Wake Island slated for December 22.[3]

For Americans, who struggled to account for the disaster of Pearl Harbor, the background of Japan's onslaught afforded important clues for understanding the United States' position in the Pacific region. Somehow Japan's secret attack explained much that had transpired beforehand, and similarly much of what has happened between the two powers since the Second World War.

Everyone, from the president down to the military commanders, knew for certain by December 1 that Japan was ready to move. In the Philippines, General MacArthur alerted his command, while the other outposts prepared for eventualities. On December 2, an unidentified submarine eluded searchers in the Pearl Harbor Restricted Sea Area. Next day the State Department advised the responsible authorities that the Japanese government had ordered its Washington embassy, the Honolulu consulate, and other posts to destroy secret codes, files, and coding machines. However, on December 5, the navy's War Plans Department decided that additional warnings to the service's subordinate commands were unnecessary, as enough had been sent. On December 6, through the top secret MAGIC interception of Japan's communications, code clerks deciphered the response to Secretary Hull's virtual ultimatum nearly a full day before its delivery to him by Ambassador Nomura. When President Roosevelt read the long transcription, he passed it to Harry Hopkins, his aide, who recalled him declaring, "This means war!"

But routinely and inexplicably, Army Chief of Staff General George C. Marshall's alarm concerning an impending attack against a United States installation somewhere in the Pacific, in which Admiral Harold Stark, the Navy's chief of staff, concurred at the last moment, went out to Honolulu only over RCA's commercial cable instead of by shortwave radio. In Hawaii also, it was Sunday morning business as usual.

When, early in 1941, Admiral Husband E. Kimmel became commander-in-chief of the Pacific Fleet and Lieutenant General Walter C. Short took charge of the army's Hawaiian Department, the basic United States war plan for the Pacific was designated RAINBOW 5; it was a revamping of the long-traditional PLAN ORANGE. The fleet, in the event of war, would proceed into the western Pacific to secure forward bases in the Marshall and Caroline islands, defuse Japan's navy, and drive into the Philippines. The army would defend the Hawaiian Islands, including the navy's shore-based installations and whichever ships were in port. Both officers keenly understood that Japan had never launched hostilities with a declaration of war, but only with an unannounced attack. Both officers were trying hard to cooperate with each other, but trying equally hard not to interfere with each other's responsibilities. Neither Kimmel nor Short, unfortunately, held overall authority, nor had anyone consolidated an aerial defense command from the forces assigned to them. The senior admiral commanding the Fourteenth Naval District encompassing the islands even outranked Admiral Kimmel.

Both commanders had worked hard to improve conditions. General Short emphasized training to guard against possible sabotage by the Japanese elements of Hawaii's population. Admiral Kimmel's fleet regularly sailed to sea on Tuesdays for battle exercises and returned on Fridays. On lengthier practice runs, Kimmel's fleet went out Friday and came home Saturday of the week following. (Kimmel's predecessor, Admiral James Richardson, angered navy wives and Honolulu's merchants by mooring his ships between Maui and Lanai in Lahaina Roads, where he could get his ships to sea in a hurry if need be.) Observing the fleet's schedule was one part of the Japanese consul general's duties, which scrupulously he did. On Sunday, December 7, Admiral Kimmel arose at 0700 to dress for his occasional golf game with General Short. Charged with safeguarding the security of the United States, these golf links–bound sentinels were blind to the self-evident. On them would fall most of the blame.

And blame there would be, more than enough for all to share. The horrendous failures to gather and assess intelligence had inevitably induced dreadful errors into judgments that ranged up and down through channels, from the commander-in-chief in the White House to the cabinet secretaries in the State, War, and Navy departments to the service chiefs and their theater commanders on the front lines. Institutionalized flaws and interservice rivalries throughout the chains of command resulted in divided authority, impeded communications, and a nearly fatal unreadiness. The soporific lulling from twenty years of peace had been scarcely disturbed by the hectic remobilizing occurring over the past two years. "My God!" exclaimed Secretary of the Navy Frank Knox in disbelief at the news from Pearl Harbor: "This can't be true; this must mean the Philippines." President Franklin D. Roosevelt, Secretary of State Cordell Hull, Secretary of War Henry L. Stimson, Secretary of the Navy Frank Knox, Army Chief of Staff General George C. Marshall, and Chief of Naval Operations Admiral Harold R. Stark, with their closest advisors or subordinates, were as culpable for Pearl Harbor as the officers and men who were caught on duty unprepared, if not more so.

At bottom, American self-delusions and mind-warping habits of thought help to explain, though not to excuse, the failure to defend Pearl Harbor. Three fixed mindsets were extremely harmful: first, the inability to comprehend the Second World War in Japanese and Asian terms as well as in European terms, and accordingly to prepare to respond to it as an unprecedented global challenge; second, the racist mentality that condescendingly, if not contemptuously, made it impossible to recognize the Nipponese as a worthy, civilized people in their own right possessing a military fighting machine fully equal, if not superior, to the finest Western armies and navies; and third, a purblind certitude that the Japanese would never foolishly provoke the United States into violent retaliation when, unopposed, they could advance southward in piecemeal fashion to gain the resources they required, bypassing the Philippines along the way. United States strategy rested upon predilections. Americans believed they knew what the Japanese would do, but did not understand what they were capable of doing, to shatter the American economic blockade. Actually, by mid-1941, unless changes were soon to transpire, Japan had either to abandon its imperial objectives or attack the United States to win them.[4]

Pearl Harbor's fate was harsh, yet even worse was to come. President Roosevelt, in denouncing Japan's "dastardly" sneak attack, characterized December 7, 1941, as a day "which will live in infamy," and Congress declared war against Japan. Germany and Italy, Japan's Axis allies, declared war against the United States. In response, Congress declared war on them.[5]

Against Japanese and Japanese-Americans in the continental United States, Japan's attack on Pearl Harbor unleashed an intolerant wave of popular anger. In 1941, about 127,000 Japanese, as the census taker categorized them, lived on the mainland, mainly in California. One-third approximately were Japan-born *issei*, most of them ineligible for citizenship. Two-thirds were United States citizens, either native-born *nisei* or their offspring. There were also a small number of naturalized citizens, mostly immigrants from Hawaii. Hysterically, many whites feared a Japanese invasion of the mainland after the raid against Hawaii. West Coast political and military leaders, led by Earl Warren, at that time California's attorney general, and John L. DeWitt, commanding general of the Western Defense Command, backed by President Roosevelt's executive authority, took steps to exclude all individuals of Japanese origin or descent from most Pacific coastal areas. President Roosevelt authorized the army to round up and "intern" such persons. Under the War Relocation Authority, which cruelly prohibited their voluntary relocation, some 110,000 evacuees found themselves being hastily apprehended and dispatched to ten isolated relocation centers scattered throughout the western states.

By the second week in June of 1942, the War Relocation Authority had designated eleven centers with an aggregate capacity for around 130,000 persons. Ten centers went into operation after initial processings of the dispossessed took place at various army posts: Manzanar and Tule Lake, California; Poston and Gila River, Arizona; Minidoka, Idaho; Heart Mountain, Wyoming; Granada, Colorado; Topaz, Utah; Rohwer and Jerome, Arkansas.

Internees were required to dispose of their property and household possessions before surrendering themselves for removal to the interior. Food and shelter were doled out to the relocated men, women, and children, even wages to those willing and able to work at maintaining the camps. Living conditions were neither comfortable nor humane. The Supreme Court, in the *Hirabayashi* (1943) and *Korematsu* (1944) cases, upheld the relocation of the Japanese by emphasizing their potential threat to the nation's security to justify depriving them of civil rights. Most evacuees remained at the centers until after December 1944, when the exclusion orders were countermanded. A minority of demonstrably loyal internees won early release. Some fought for the United States in the war. Kay Sugahara, an orphaned *nisei* entrepreneur from Los Angeles, who had been interned with his wife and children, actually enrolled in the supersecret Office of Strategic Services (OSS) and served throughout the Pacific, even, at the war's end, in Japan itself. Later on, Sugahara became a shipping tycoon and advisor to American and Asian leaders on numerous financial and public policy matters. The last of the centers, Tule Lake, housing the supposedly unrepentent, did not close until March 1946. On an unprecedented scale, the evacuated Japanese-Americans suffered losses of lives, liberties, properties, and their constitutional birthrights. An official apology, by President Ronald Reagan, would have to wait until 1988, and compensation until 1990, at $20,000 each for the living survivors.[6]

At war now, Americans girded for a worldwide struggle. General Short proclaimed martial law for Hawaii. Admiral Stark ruled that Guam and the Philippine Islands could not be reinforced. Soldiers and fliers in the Philippines, marines and sailors on Midway, Wake, Guam, and other lonely, American-held islands, awaited attack. Two Japanese destroyers shelled Midway Island right after the Pearl Harbor bombardment, but then withdrew. A regimental-size Japanese force overwhelmed Guam on December 10 and imprisoned the garrison's survivors. Wake Island's defenders, by means of shore batteries and four Wildcat (F4F) fighters, valiantly fought off the Japanese until December 23. After Wake and Guam fell, the aircraft carriers *Saratoga, Lexington,* and *Enterprise* put far out to sea to replace the captured islands as the outposts of American strength in the central Pacific.

Manila surrendered to the invading Japanese on January 2, 1942, after a debacle as humiliating as Pearl Harbor. Trapped on Bataan Peninsula and Corregidor Island without reinforcements, the American and Filipino remnants eventually gave themselves up to Lieutenant General Masaharu Homma's troops and to the horrors of the Death March, torture, and cruel imprisonment. From Australia, General Douglas MacArthur promised he would return one day to liberate the Philippines. Throughout the archipelago, guerrillas banded together to continue the fight. Many Filipinos felt abandoned by the United States' failure to defend them.

Manila, Hong Kong, and Singapore once stood for American and British imperial power in East Asia, but in short order Japan overwhelmed each place. Japanese aviators quickly obliterated Britain's obsolete Royal Air Force detachment in Malaya, then sank the unprotected battleships *Prince of Wales* and *Repulse.* On the day after Christmas, Hong Kong fell. Japan's armies under Lieutenant General Tomoyuki Yamashita stormed down the six-hundred-mile long Malay Peninsula to take Singapore on February 15, where the naval bastion's mighty guns waited pointing uselessly outward, like Corregidor's, anticipating the seaborne invasion that never came. Lieutenant General Arthur Percival surrendered the largest number of British troops ever to capitulate after a single campaign. Japan's forces, if still slowed by the valiant defenders of Bataan and Corregidor, could move now at will into Thailand, Burma, and India. In the Netherlands East Indies, outnumbered Dutch and Australian forces on Borneo, Sumatra, and Java proved no match for the swarming Japanese. Most decisive were the trouncings the Allied fleets took February 27 and 28, in the Battle of the Java Sea and the Battle of Sunda Strait, when the cruisers USS *Houston* and HMAS *Perth* went down with heavy losses of life.

From Burma, where he commanded the Chinese Nationalist troops protecting supply routes, Lieutenant General Joseph Stilwell of the United States Army led 114 war-battered stragglers out of the rugged north into neighboring India. Irascible "Vinegar Joe" blamed the equivocations of Chiang Kai-shek and the "stupid, gutless command" of both the Chinese and British. "I claim we got a hell of a beating," Stilwell affirmed. "We got run out of Burma, and it is humiliating as hell. I think we ought to find out what caused it, go back and retake it." Japan's successes in Burma and against merchant shipping on the Indian Ocean forecast an invasion of India. General Sir Archibald Wavell called it the subcontinent's "darkest hour."

By May of 1942, the prized Southern Resources Area lay wholly in Nipponese hands. Amphibious troops occupied the Gilbert Islands, landed in the Bismarck archipelago, and moved into the Solomon Islands to threaten Australia, New Zealand, the Fiji Islands, and Samoa. The Greater East Asia Co-Prosperity Sphere had simply to incorporate its conquered treasures. Japan needed, of course, to ready defenses against the Westerners' inevitable counterattacks, but for the first time, the Japanese began to relax. Tokyo's strategists made fresh plans to win the China war, then to assist Germany by attacking the Soviet Union. These plans relegated the Pacific theater to its original secondary, tactical role. Such intentions fatefully underestimated the furiously mobilizing United States.[7]

Roosevelt's and Churchill's strategy for the hastily formed Grand Alliance called first for defeating Germany and Italy in Europe before moving in full force against Japan. The United States Navy under new top commanders was already undertaking limited offensive operations in the Pacific. Admiral Ernest J. King, the snappish commander-in-chief of the United States Fleet, directed Admiral Chester W. Nimitz, the contrastingly quiet commander-in-chief of the Pacific Fleet, to protect the scattered surviving outposts and strike the Japanese wherever and whenever possible. On March 17, 1942, the United States agreed to defend the Pacific, while the Indian Ocean and the Middle East became Great Britain's primary responsibility. The Joint Chiefs of Staff defined two gigantic theaters of war. They designated General MacArthur to become supreme commander of the Southwest Pacific, which encompassed Australia, the Netherlands East Indies except Sumatra, the Philippines, New Guinea, the Bismarcks, the Solomons, and the waters surrounding. Admiral Nimitz took command of the Pacific Ocean Area (later Areas), overseeing its northern, central, and southern sections, though the waters washing Central America, South

America, and Antarctica were retained within the Western Hemisphere commands.[8]

Nimitz's submarines, with some Allied contributions, and the marauding aircraft carriers carried the attack. Unrestricted to warships, the subs sank over a score of Japan's merchantmen in April 1942, while Japanese I-boat (submarine) commanders inexplicably ignored German advice to attack cargo vessels. For agonizing months, America's undersea crews were frustrated by malfunctioning torpedoes that either ran ten feet too deep to strike their targets or failed to detonate upon impact. By November 1943, however, American and Allied submariners were surpassing their rivals and had reduced the Japanese cargo fleet below its tonnage level at the war's beginning. Meanwhile, the outnumbered aircraft carriers *Lexington, Enterprise, Yorktown,* and *Hornet* went to work. In drydock after being torpedoed by a submarine, *Saratoga* was under repair. The carriers' early forays, even if indecisive, afforded vital training for the inexperienced American pilots, while their hit-and-run tactics brought significant numbers of Japanese flattops and four army air groups racing back from southern seas into the central and western Pacific to safeguard Japan itself. Then, on April 18, Lieutenant Colonel James Doolittle's sixteen army air corps B-25 bombers flew off the heaving deck of the carrier *Hornet* (dubbed "Shangri-La" by President Roosevelt) to bomb Tokyo itself. The spectacular raid sufficiently shattered the confidence of Japan's high command to cause them to support Admiral Yamamoto's previously overridden, risky plan of confronting the American carrier threat by directly attacking Midway Island and, in direct retaliation, to launch hundreds of windborne balloon bombs against North America, the fantastic Fu-Go Weapon.

As the American and Japanese aircraft carriers maneuvered, strategists on both sides argued over their plans. Japan's army sought a final victory over China, while the navy undertook responsibility for two big jobs—the destruction of the United States Pacific Fleet at Midway and the isolation of Australia to protect the southern perimeter. Admiral King and General MacArthur insisted that the Japanese advance must be blocked, so, in spite of the policy to defeat Germany first, the army sent large forces to join the navy to defend the Pacific. Over many objections, including Brigadier General Dwight D. Eisenhower's, the army's top brass rushed ground troops westward, intending to concentrate thereafter on the war in Europe, but they soon learned that the war in the Pacific and Asia would not leave them alone. Newly tuned, the Japanese and the American strategies collided in the Battle of the Coral Sea.

The Japanese intended to install a forward seaplane base off the southeastern tip of New Guinea, and Admiral Nimitz, alerted by radio intercepts, moved to prevent the anticipated invasion of Port Moresby and the threat its capture would pose to Australia. Three carriers convoyed Japan's task force. Nimitz dispatched the carriers *Yorktown* and *Lexington* under Rear Admiral Frank Jack Fletcher, supported by "MacArthur's Navy" of American and Australian cruisers and destroyers commanded by Australian Rear Admiral John Crace, RN. The two carrier forces finally located each other after a string of missed opportunities and erratic calculations. "Scratch one flat-top!" came the exultant cry from Lieutenant Commander R. E. Dixon, as ninety-three aircraft swarmed over the sinking *Shoho*. But the *Lexington* was lost, as were an Australian oiler and the destroyer *Sims*, and the *Yorktown* damaged. In the Battle of the Coral Sea, the first carrier-versus-carrier engagement in history, Japan had won a tactical victory. Yet for the first time, a Japanese offensive was blunted. One enemy carrier was sent down, and two others crippled. Australians, on May 8, breathed in relief. Only two days earlier, Corregidor had fallen.

Admiral Yamamoto sought to seize Midway Island for a forward defensive bastion and was hoping, by his assault, to destroy the United States Pacific Fleet. He added an invasion of the Aleutian Islands to distract attention from his major goals. Unknown to Yamamoto, Admiral Nimitz held a lethal ace. Nimitz knew Yamamoto's plans. Commander Joseph Rochefort of the Combat Intelligence Unit in Hawaii, himself a breaker of Japan's naval code, had for some time been piecing together fragmentary messages that revealed units, ships, captains, courses, and schedules making ready for the Japanese attack. Rear Admiral Raymond A. Spruance, the last-minute replacement for ailing Admiral William F. "Bull" Halsey, took command of the three carriers in service, *Enterprise, Hornet*, and the damaged *Yorktown*. Spruance was ordered by Nimitz to husband his strength "by the principle of calculated risk," that is, to avoid attacking unless he could inflict greater damage than he would have to absorb. Refusing to be duped by Yamamoto's Aleutian diversion, Nimitz sent only a token force to counter the Japanese attacking there, while they wasted two sorely needed carriers to carry out the deception.

While illness and foul weather dogged the Japanese Combined Fleet, his intelligence staff's work paid off for Nimitz. Yamamoto himself fell sick, Fuchida underwent an appendectomy aboard ship, and Genda came down with pneumonia. Fog partially blinded the Japanese armada, but ominous sightings of reconnoitering submarines and airplanes alerted the lookouts that the Americans were ready for trouble. On June 3, Ensign Jack Read, patrolling in his Catalina flying boat from Midway Island, spotted and was spotted by Yamamoto's Midway Occupation Force, but Admiral Nagumo, zigzagging the carriers of the First Air Fleet, was not informed of the sighting. Nagumo had no clue that American carriers were lying in wait for his strike against Midway.

On June 4, mighty air battles raged. In spite of Spruance's advantages, Nagumo won all the early encounters. Five American air commanders died as their squadrons perished in unavailing assaults. The Japanese fliers ridiculed the unskilled Americans. Suddenly, the tide of battle turned. Lieutenant Commander Clarence McCluskey, the *Enterprise*'s air leader, found four Japanese carriers steaming ahead in an elongated diamond. Nagumo was caught off guard, with armed and fueled aircraft on the flight decks, with armed bombs and torpedoes lying around loosely scattered from earlier loadings. He had just ordered the next launching of airplanes when the Americans struck. The First Air Fleet's carriers faced mortal danger. Inside five incredible minutes, United States Navy and Marine Corps fliers killed the fleet's striking power. The carriers *Akagi, Kaga*, and *Soryu* went down, *Hiryu* later that afternoon, and, two days later, the new heavy cruiser *Mikuma*. But the *Yorktown* and an escorting destroyer were also sunk, by submarine torpedoes. Only the Japanese bombing of Dutch Harbor and the invasion of Kiska and Attu in the Aleutians marred the American victory. By June 6, 1942, the initiative in the Pacific Ocean passed to the United States.

The Battle of Midway was the second turning point after the Battle of Britain in winning the war against the Axis powers. Midway predated both the British victory at El Alamein and the Russian victory at Stalingrad. Ironically the victory at Midway saved Roosevelt's Germany-first policy, whereas Admiral Yamamoto's lackadaisical overconfidence after his stunning triumph at Pearl Harbor probably lost the war for Japan. Yamamoto wasted his chance to destroy the American carriers when he still had both the time and the opportunity.[9]

Before Japan could recover from Midway, Allied forces moved to thwart any offensive intended to isolate Australia in the Southwest Pacific. Japan's high command canceled plans to overrun New Caledonia, Fiji, and Samoa, but taking the forward Allied base at Port Moresby on New Guinea remained a top strategic objective. To anesthetize the Japanese air and naval base at Rabaul on New Britain Island, the United States invaded the southern Solomons. On August 7–8, the First and Fifth Marines stormed onto Guadalcanal, where a Japanese airstrip was being constructed, and Tulagi, Gavutu, and Tanambogo in the neighboring Florida Islands. Australians and Americans began slugging it out with the Japanese in the mountain thickets of New Guinea and the primeval jungles of Guadalcanal, where both sides were almost overpowered by heat, humidity, pests, dense vegetation, and diseases. Only four American aircraft carriers patrolled the Pacific: *Enterprise, Hornet*, the repaired *Saratoga*, and the new *Wasp*. Cautious about the risks of amphibious operations, the navy withdrew the carriers hurriedly, leaving the leathernecks high and dry without air cover and dangerously short of supplies. The marines fought for months on Guadalcanal to build and use Henderson Field for operational air support, while expanding their perimeter against suicidal counterattacks by the Japanese.

Naval battles raged offshore over reinforcing attempts by both combatants. The Japanese dominated the seas by night, the Americans by day. Within thirty-two minutes on August 9, in the Battle of Savo Island, Rear Admiral Gunichi Mikawa demonstrated his mastery of night surface combat, sinking four heavy cruisers and one destroyer while killing 1,270 crewmen and wounding 709, the worst defeat ever suffered by the United States Navy except for Pearl Harbor. Frequently warships escorting the "Tokyo Express" ran convoys down the "slot" through the Solomon Islands to maintain Japan's futile, though bloody, attacks. *Wasp* succumbed to torpedoes on September 15, and *Hornet* sank on October 26 after suffering vicious aerial assaults. The Japanese lost *Ryujo*. Both *Enterprise* and *Saratoga* suffered severe damage. Nimitz put the aggressive "Bull" Halsey in charge. From November 12 to 15, Halsey clashed with Vice-Admiral Nobutake Kondo in the naval Battle of Guadalcanal. The Americans held the sea, though ten warships were lost. American sailors and airmen wreaked havoc on the Japanese troop transports, sinking six and damaging four more already beached to unload. Featuring *South Dakota* (the unannounced new "Battleship X"), the fight closed with a battleship engagement, the first since 1916 off Jutland. Nevermore did the Japanese regain control of the sea or the air, and they soon abandoned Guadalcanal and their last opportunity for offensives to the south. Now, with a base at Guadalcanal and another in Papua on New Guinea, the allies could isolate Rabaul to advance toward Japan. Guadalcanal was the Pacific theater's El Alamein.

Thereafter, Japan's forces desperately strove to hold onto their oceanic shield. North and east of the Solomon Islands ranged Japan's easternmost conquests, the Gilbert and Marshall islands and lonely Wake Island. Fortified by diehard defenders, atolls such as Tarawa and Kwajelein swarmed with aircraft and bristled with gun emplacements. Westward of the outermost arc, closer to Japan's home islands and more heavily supported, the Palaus, the Carolines, and the Marianas likewise stretched from north to south. Saipan, Tinian, and Guam, the coming battlegrounds, lay among the Marianas. Closer still and vital for Japan's security, sulphurous Iwo Jima stood out over the Volcano Islands north of Saipan, while Okinawa dominated the Ryukyu Islands chain between Formosa and Kyushu at the southwestern tip of Japan's archipelago, the third largest of the home islands. The insular screen, more than three thousand miles long, guarded Nippon against invasions from the Pacific Ocean or the Philippine Islands.[10]

In January 1943, at the Casablanca Conference, President Roosevelt,

Prime Minister Churchill, and the Combined Chiefs of Staff ordered wide-ranging operations against Japan. The British were slated to attack Burma. United States forces were to seize Rabaul driving from there across the central Pacific to attack the Mariana Islands.

The meager resources available, with only scanty reinforcements likely, reduced these grand designs to taking small steps one at a time. MacArthur was designated overall commander in the South Pacific for capturing the Bismarck archipelago, with Halsey in tactical command. Any Pacific Ocean forces not required by Halsey would revert to Nimitz. Timing was left up to MacArthur and Halsey. Cleverly, MacArthur's command, using the code name CARTWHEEL, devised the strategy of "island hopping" to pass by as many fortified bastions as possible. CARTWHEEL would first advance the Allied bomber line toward Rabaul, then northward toward the Philippines, always protected by fighter covers and naval strength. The task of crossing the central Pacific remained in Nimitz's hands.[11]

Although the way proved long and hard, CARTWHEEL established the pattern for ultimate victory. Allied troops, picking their targets, assaulted the overextended Japanese here and there. After gaining tactical air superiority, the Allies would seize airfields and ports, or locations suitable for constructing the necessary facilities, then advance again under protecting umbrellas of land-based aircraft.

Progress was evident. Buna, opposite Port Moresby on New Guinea, fell on January 22, 1943, after bitter fighting, to serve as an advanced base. On April 18, after cryptographers uncovered Admiral Yamamoto's itinerary, Army P-38's intercepted his bomber and killed the mastermind behind Japan's attack at Pearl Harbor. From June 21, 1943, to April 26, 1944, the Allies took New Georgia and Bougainville islands in the Solomons and Salamaua and Lae on New Guinea, then secured New Guinea's Huon Peninsula and western New Britain. Scores of unsung battles raged. Ten thousand Japanese (of twenty thousand) died in New Guinea during their retreat to Modong. To the north in the Admiralty Islands, Seadlar Harbor was nabbed for a fleet base and Manus Island for heavy bombers. From Hawaii in the central Pacific, coordinated sea and air operations ranged westward to take over the Gilbert and Marshall islands in savage fighting between November 1943 and February 1944, as marines and sailors stormed onto Tarawa, Maki, Kwajelein, Eniwetok, and the neighboring atolls. Admiral Spruance next directed carrier strikes to neutralize Japan's naval stronghold in the Truk Islands.

The Japanese redoubts bypassed included Rabaul with ninety-eight thousand first-line troops, the remnants of the Sixth Division stranded on Bougainville, and scattered numbers of once-effective fighting units isolated on New Guinea. Bougainville was never actually cleared of Japanese. Australian replacements for the Americans continued to mop up stubborn pockets of resistance there until the war's end.

The perimeters of Japan's defenses cracked wide open. United States submarines were ranging far into the western Pacific to devastate naval and merchant shipping alike, severely constricting before long the island nation's economy. Wake Island was recaptured. By the summer of 1944, food rations for Japan's people were being drastically cut back, and fuel shortages developed. Admiral Spruance foiled a massive Japanese attempt to bolster the Marianas in the tremendous Battle of the Philippine Sea. In some of the war's bloodiest hand-to-hand engagements, Saipan, Tinian, and Guam, less than fourteen hundred miles from Tokyo, soon fell to the amphibious Americans. The Chamorro people, on the United States island of Guam, had suffered more cruelly at the hands of the Japanese during their occupation than any other indigenous American people. The cost to the marines, who liberated the island, was equally high. In twenty days of bitter fighting, the marines lost 1,435 killed and 5,646 wounded. Captain Louis H. Wilson, a future commandant of the marine corps, earned a Congressional Medal of Honor for his heroism on Guam. Likewise, after costly assaults, Peleliu in the Palaus succumbed. Giant B-29 Superfortress bombers launched massive incendiary raids from their Marianas bases, systematically leveling Japan's tinderbox cities.[12]

By this time, Japan had lost around fifty warships from her once-mighty naval forces, twenty-nine hundred aircraft and pilots, and one hundred thousand first-line troops. The Battle of Midway Island had set up MacArthur's and Nimitz's dramatic advances. American invasions now threatened the Philippine Islands and Japan itself.

In the China-Burma-India theater on Asia's mainland the war dragged on frustratingly, at times almost as a forgotten sideshow. Japanese invaders had driven General Stilwell out of Burma in 1942 and raced westward to India's frontier. To uphold Chiang Kai-shek's isolated Nationalist regime, Stilwell organized an Air Transport Command to fly supplies into China from Assam in northeasternmost India over the "Hump" of the Himalayas, and to carry out Chinese warriors for his men to train and equip. From October 1943 to May 1944, Stilwell led a reconstituted army of Chinese, Indians, Britons, and Americans back into northern Burma to break Japan's blockade of China. In operations involving Britain's Brigadier General Frank D. Merrill's Marauders and Brigadier General Orde C. Wingate's Raiders, Stilwell captured Myitkyina on August 3, after "a bitch of a fight." The air ferry henceforth could operate into China without having to fly over the Hump.

Stilwell owed his brilliant victory, in large part, to British Lieutenant

General William Slim, who tied down the main Japanese army throughout the months-long battle for Imphal just across the border inside India itself. In the fall of 1944, Stilwell reopened the Ledo Road (formerly the Burma Road) into China's Yunnan Province. But a successful Japanese counter-offensive thwarted the launching of B-29 air strikes from bases newly constructed inside China itself. The Japanese seized some of the airfields, endangered the terminus of the Ledo Road, and even threatened to storm Chiang's capital at Chungking. These disheartening reverses precipitated a crisis in Sino-American relations. Stilwell's openly expressed contempt of Chiang Kai-shek, for his reluctance to reform the army and deploy National-ist troops against the Japanese rather than against Mao Zedong's Commu-nists, impelled the generalissimo to demand his recall. Roosevelt had no choice but to comply. Nonetheless, Stilwell's successors, due to his dogged achievements, would eventually win the struggle he began almost alone to comply with General Marshall's 1942 order to "support China."[13]

By late 1944, Admiral Nimitz and General MacArthur had all but shattered Japan's outer defenses. Japan's defeat seemed inevitable, but the war was far from ended. When General MacArthur's soldiers invaded Leyte Island in the central Philippines (October 17–20), the Imperial Japanese Navy mobilized its remaining strength for a knockout effort against the Americans. Four major encounters merged overall into the greatest naval engagement in history, the Battle of Leyte Gulf. In sinking four Japanese aircraft carriers, the United States Navy and Allied fighting ships virtually terminated Japan's capacity to wage major warfare on the high seas. Japan's naval pilots turned suicidally to crashing their bomb-laden aircraft against Allied ships, especially onto the prime target aircraft carriers. Their fanatic example gave birth to the *kamikaze* corps ("divine wind"), improvised prayerfully to protect Japan from invasion, just as centuries ago a mighty tempest drove back China's Mongol emperor Kublai Khan. *Kamikazes* were to wreak a terrible toll of lives and ships. The Japanese, in this last desperate measure, invoked the spirit of the bygone *samurai*. By sacrificing their own lives, they were hoping to save their divine emperor and themselves from the inconceivable humiliation of losing to foreigners.

General MacArthur methodically extended his melodramatic, perhaps unnecessary, endeavor to restore American control over the Philippines. From Leyte's torrid jungles, MacArthur sent his forces into Lingayen Gulf, onto the island of Luzon, and back once again to bloodstained Bataan and Corregidor. Manila fell on February 23, 1945, after a horrible orgy of burning, raping, and killing by the trapped Japanese, coupled with system-atic shelling and bombing by both sides. One hundred thousand Filipino civilians died. Jesuit Father James Reuter shuddered at remembering "Ma-nila was flat!" Jaime Sin, a small boy then before becoming Manila's cardinal archbishop many years later, smilingly recalled the liberating American soldiers. "Uncle Sam gave us chocolates," said Cardinal Sin.

Unfortunately for American feelings, many Filipinos had, in fact, openly cooperated with the Japanese. One had to collaborate, as Stanley Karnow explains, not for love but for life. The occupation transformed the fabric of Filipino society and morality. Under the ostensibly independent republic's constitution of 1943, proffered by the Japanese authorities, José Laurel became president. (In 1986, Salvatore Laurel, his son, would become vice-president.) President Laurel's government declared war against the United States and Great Britain. Even the once great Emilio Aguinaldo, now a bitter old man, broadcast appeals to the Allies to cease their fight against Japan. The ancient University of Santo Tomás in Manila served as their prison for American civilians caught in the islands until American soldiers freed them. Throughout the occupation, sizeable numbers of Filipino guerrillas and handfuls of American military stragglers, especially in central Luzon's highlands, had resisted the Japanese. The strongest force of guerrillas, numbering some twenty-five thousand and led mostly by socialists and Communists, was the People's Anti-Japanese Army. In Tagalog, for short, the guerrillas were known and feared as the Hukbalahap, or Huks. Most Huks were landlord-hating, sharecropping peasants, whose rent-gouging landlords fled for their own safety to Manila. On May 28, the last important Japanese strongholds on Luzon gave up. Only fragmentary, ineffectual resistance continued throughout the Philippine Islands.[14]

American forces in the meantime went on to invade Iwo Jima and Okinawa, where in two campaigns they were to suffer a staggering toll of casualties—seventy thousand soldiers, marines, and sailors.

Shortly after daybreak on February 19, 1945, United States Marines of the Fourth and Fifth divisions began moving onto the black, volcanic ashes of tiny Iwo Jima in the Bonin-Volcano Islands. The Army Air Corps wanted Iwo Jima to field fighter escorts for the B-29 Superfortresses attacking Japan from Saipan and Tinian, and to land its crippled bombers returning from their missions. Choosing to hold the high ground at either tip of the island instead of resisting on the beaches, Lieutenant General Tadamichi Kuribayashi prepared an elaborate underground network linking together his gun emplacements and their crews to inflict enfilading fire upon the exposed flanks of the Americans. Kuribayashi expected his men to die in the end, but he intended to slaughter the American invaders at a ratio of ten to one, and he almost succeeded. For five hellish weeks on that godforsaken battleground, Major General Harry Schmidt's Fifth Amphibious Corps fought to wrest the twenty thousand Japanese defenders from cave after cave and hole after hole. All but a handful of the Japanese were killed. Of the invading marines, 5,885 died, while 17,272 were wounded but survived.

Altogether, American casualties amounted to one-third of the assault force of twenty-four battalions. On March 26, when the firing ceased, Iwo Jima, which was immortalized by the celebrated photograph of the flag raising on Mount Suribachi, overtook Peleliu and Tarawa in its grisly statistics as the United States Marines' bloodiest battle of the war.

At this juncture, the air campaign against Japan tremendously intensified. Major General Curtis LeMay's giant B-29 Superfortresses, escorted by Army P-51 Mustangs and Navy F-6 Hellcats, undertook low-level, incendiary bombing raids at night against Japan's important cities. Large numbers of damaged planes from these raids, carrying no fewer than 24,761 officers and men, would in the months to come wobble safely down onto Iwo Jima instead of ditching into the sea.[15]

The last chapters of the war in Asia and the Pacific were at hand. Allied forces had already smashed the Japanese navy and merchant marine, shredded her outer defenses, and isolated Japan itself from the essential resources of Southeast Asia and the East Indies. Japan's once formidable air power futilely endeavored to protect the home islands against United States bombers and fighters marauding almost at will. The "China incident," a quagmire for Japan, remained unresolved, and Russia, Japan's traditional enemy, was menacingly back. Regrouped along the frontier between Manchuria and Siberia, fresh from vanquishing Germany on the eastern front, massive Soviet armies were preparing to invade China and Korea against the depleted Japanese defense forces. The top secret uranium and plutonium nuclear bombs were being assembled for early deployment to the Pacific. Still untested, the atomic bombs would soon wreak cataclysmic destruction on Japan and the Japanese people.

Admiral Nimitz focused Operation Iceberg, his penultimate approach to Japan, on capturing the main Ryukyu island of Okinawa. Barely 370 miles south of the home islands, Okinawa's purpose was to serve as the Allied staging area for the forthcoming invasion of Kyushu in Japan itself. In preparing against the anticipated American assault, Lieutenant General Mitsuru Ushijima cunningly emulated Kuribayashi on Iwo Jima and Yamashita on Luzon, conceding the offensive advantage to the Americans and their allies. He could not equal their mobility, firepower, and airpower. Ushijima could, however, delay the attackers at great cost to themselves by requiring them to assail the fortified bunkers and entrenchments built into Okinawa's limestone maze of cliffs and caves.

Nimitz assigned his most experienced commanders to manage the largest invasion of the Pacific war. Raymond Spruance, a proven, meticulous overseer, became overall commander of the Central Pacific Task Forces. Marc Mitscher took command of the American aircraft carriers. Richmond Kelly Turner took over the Joint Expeditionary Force responsible for safely getting ashore the army and marine divisions. Vice-Admiral Sir Bernard Rawlings led a flotilla of newly arrived British aircraft carriers equipped, unlike the Americans', with *kamikaze*-resistant steel decks. Once on land, Lieutenant General Simon Bolivar Buckner, a veteran of the fighting in the Aleutian Islands, would take charge. All involved knew the Japanese intended to resist to their deaths.

From late March to the end of June, the struggle for Okinawa raged. The Japanese sent three hundred *kamikaze*-style torpedo boats and the mighty 18.1-inch-gun battleship *Yamato* (the sister ship of *Musashi*, sunk near Leyte) into the fray. Quickly, Mitscher's pilots sank *Yamato*, without her gigantic batteries ever having been fired in battle, killing all but 269 of her crew of 2,767. Japan's navy and army *kamikaze* pilots, not all of them by this time volunteers, caused havoc. Struck and heavily damaged by the suicide pilots were the carriers *Franklin*, the latest *Wasp*, *Intrepid*, the new *Yorktown*, *Enterprise*, and *Hancock*, and the battleship *Maryland*, a veteran of the Pearl Harbor attack. Ashore, the beleaguered Japanese launched night and day assaults against the American invaders. American infantrymen and tankers could scarcely maneuver across the rough terrain. They had to rely on "blowtorches" (flamethrowers) and "corkscrews" (inserted explosives) to rout the Japanese from their concealments. Everywhere Japanese soldiers died where they fought. Even with all their advantage in firepower, the Americans could advance only a few yards at a time. President Roosevelt died on April 12. The slaughter mounted. At last, General Ushijima's army started to disintegrate, crumbling into an undisciplined mob. Neither commander lived to the end of the Okinawa campaign. General Buckner fell on June 18, mortally struck, with victory in his grasp, and four days later, General Ushijima committed *hara-kiri*.

In haste, General Joseph Stilwell flew in to assume command of the war-torn island. Neither Stilwell nor the weary troops yet realized that Okinawa was fated to be the last battle, and only a few knew that General MacArthur planned to hurl them into the coming invasions of Kyushu on November 1, 1945, and Honshu on March 1, 1946. The fighting for Okinawa killed 12,281 Americans in action and inflicted nearly 40,000 other casualties. Okinawa was the costliest campaign of the Pacific war. Over 110,000 Japanese died. The United States lost 753 planes, hundreds of tanks, and, by *kamikaze* attacks alone, 36 ships. The Japanese damaged 368 other American ships, 164 by *kamikazes*, as well as four of the five British carriers there. Japan lost 4,155 aircraft including 1,900 *kamikazes*. Few veterans of Okinawa could have been eager to invade Japan and attack the Japanese on their home grounds.

While the fighting raged on Okinawa, submarines and bombing planes continued to attack Japan's logistical and industrial network, until the American submarines ran short of targets. Allied subs sank more than a million tons of merchant shipping in 1943 and almost double that total in 1944. The cost was calamitous. The United States lost forty-four submarines in the Pacific Ocean (plus two in the Atlantic) and 18 percent of its undersea officers and crewmen. The staggering toll of personnel—six submariners for every "blackshoe sailor"—grimly reflected the lonely dangers of undersea warfare. By 1945, Allied submarines, primarily American, had virtually isolated Japan from her outside sources of supply. Inexplicably the Japanese failed throughout the war, in spite of ample German advice, to counteract the submarine offensive against them.

In the daytime air, Major General Curtis LeMay's Twenty-first Bomber Command's B-29s boldly switched from high-altitude precision bombing raids to low-level (five to ten thousand feet) incendiary attacks. LeMay's 231-plane, Marianas-based assault against Tokyo on February 25 demonstrated the terrible efficacy of napalm firebombing. The three-hour attack by 334 B-29s on Tokyo, March 9–10, constituted another appalling success. Japanese officials counted 267,171 buildings reduced to ashes (one-quarter of Tokyo's total), 83,793 individuals killed, 40,918 wounded, and over a million inhabitants burned out of their homes. Demoralization was widespread among the people. In the days to follow, LeMay again and again sent his gigantic air armadas to attack Tokyo, Nagoya, Osaka, Kobe, Kawasaki, and Yawata. Then he shifted to Japan's medium-size industrialized urban centers. Aerial opposition and factory production alike began sharply to drop. By the end of June 1945, American bombers were roaming throughout Japan's skies without serious interference. Almost casually, they were picking their targets whenever and wherever they fancied. Between the submarine blockade and the incessant bombing, Japan could scarcely sustain the fight she began. The time seemed propitious to make peace. Yet peace did not come smoothly to Japan.[16]

Instead, the high command prepared to resist the coming invasion. The devastation of Japan's cities and the prospect of nationwide famine had failed to dampen the spirit of the anachronistic *samurai* in control. They marshaled the nation's defenses for a last defiant stand. The emperor, in private talks, endorsed the idea of peace following the American invasion of Luzon, then more openly after Okinawa was invaded. His peace advocacy gained strength in the cabinet. Germany's unconditional surrender on May 8 caused diplomatic feelers to go out, at the emperor's urging, to explore the good offices of Sweden, Switzerland, and the Soviet Union. Japan's authorities failed, however, to act decisively or directly enough to halt the war in June or July, and more than a month went by in futile efforts to obtain Soviet mediation toward a negotiated settlement. The truculent militants of the Supreme War Directions Council continued their policy of prosecuting the conflict "to protect the Imperial Homeland."

By late June, General MacArthur and Admiral Nimitz were assembling the largest amphibious force of the war for the invasion of Japan. Several State Department officials led by Acting Secretary of State Joseph C. Grew, the former United States ambassador to Japan, urged President Harry S Truman to accept a Japanese capitulation without overthrowing the imperial dynasty.

At the Potsdam Conference on July 16, President Truman learned that the world's first man-made atomic explosion had successfully taken place at Los Alamos, New Mexico. General Marshall and Winston Churchill recommended using the atomic weapons being assembled to end the war as quickly as possible. General "Hap" Arnold of the air corps doubted their necessity, and Fleet Admiral William D. Leahy, chairman of the Joint Chiefs of Staff, dissented on moral grounds. Quite casually, Truman informed an apparently unsurprised Premier Stalin, on July 24, of the test explosion of the nuclear device, and the Soviet leader expressed his hope that the atomic bomb would be dropped on Japan. Clement Attlee, Britain's newly chosen prime minister, concurred with Churchill's advice. On July 26, with Chiang Kai-shek's approval, President Truman published the Potsdam Declaration, a blunt demand for the unconditional surrender without delay of all Japanese armed forces, with no proviso for retaining the emperor. Declared Truman: "The alternative for Japan is prompt and utter destruction." Stalin informed Truman that he would reject Japan's plea for Soviet mediation. Truman expressed gratitude, but Stalin did not for some time advise the Japanese of his intention. In Tokyo, while the government procrastinated, Foreign Minister Shigenori Tōgō, a peace advocate, forlornly hoped for Russian mediation. On August 2, President Truman and the other Allied leaders left Potsdam.[17]

Already Truman had issued orders to drop the atomic weapon after August 3, unless he were to reverse his approval, but still the Japanese government made no response to his Potsdam ultimatum. The bomber group on Tinian Island readied planes and crews for its secret mission against one of four cities: Hiroshima, Nagasaki, Niigata, or Kokura, with Kyoto an alternate in the event of bad weather. The Pacific war was speeding to its *Götterdammerung*. Japan's ultimate tragedy loomed. Unknowingly, the Japanese were facing obliteration in cosmic thunderclaps brighter than a thousand suns.

On August 6, Colonel Paul Tibbetts's B-29, *Enola Gay*, dropped the "Thin Man" uranium bomb onto the industrial city of Hiroshima. Four square miles of the previously little-damaged city were incinerated. Approximately

130,000 men, women, and children were killed, missing, or wounded, and 90 percent of the buildings were destroyed. Beneath the towering mushroom cloud, a poisonously radioactive "black rain" showered over the devastated city. The epoch of the nuclear holocaust had dawned. President Truman, homeward bound from Germany aboard the USS *Augusta*, learned of the successful bombing of Hiroshima. He issued a statement taking full responsibility. He explained that the atomic bomb was used at his order to save lives by terminating the war as quickly as possible. Bluntly, Truman warned Japan's leaders again that if once more they should fail to realize their nation's impending catastrophe, "they may expect a rain of ruin from the air, the like of which has never been seen on this earth." Once again, Japan took no clearcut steps to avert disaster. The military leaders obtusely dismissed the Hiroshima bombing as an ordinary act of war.

In Moscow, on August 8, Foreign Minister Vyacheslav Molotov informed the Japanese ambassador, who was still hoping for Russian mediation, that as of the next day the Soviet Union would instead declare war against Japan. Dreaded for years, Russia's decision seemed to paralyze the Japanese high command even more completely than the bombing of Hiroshima. The Red Army quickly overran Japan's troops defending Manchuria, landed a force in northern Korea, and occupied Sakhalin Island between the sea of Okhotsk and the Sea of Japan. The Russians proclaimed that, after months and months of ineffectual bungling by the United States and its other allies, the Red Army had singlehandedly engineered Japan's defeat. Ominously, from Berlin to Tokyo, a sudden chill forecast the advent of the Cold War.

On August 9, another American B-29 dropped the second atomic bomb, "Fat Man," with a plutonium core this time, onto the beautiful city of Nagasaki. About seventy-five thousand people suffered death or injury in the leveling of one-third of the city. The bomb's blinding glare lit up the skies over China's coastal cities nearly four hundred miles away across the Yellow Sea.

In Japan, consternation ruled. The unclear fate of the emperor remained the key obstacle to peace. High officials feared the Allies' intentions to occupy their country and prosecute its leaders for war crimes. Meanwhile air attacks against Japan continued. At last, Secretary of State James F. Byrnes conceded that Emperor Hirohito could retain the throne subject to direction by the supreme commander of the Allied powers. Emperor Hirohito announced that he did not feel jeopardized by such an arrangement, and that he still wanted peace. On August 14 to 15, Japan's "longest day," militant diehards attempted to seal off Emperor Hirohito to prevent him speaking out for peace, and possibly to contrive a *coup d'etat*, but they failed. Hence, on August 15 at noon, the Japanese people heard their emperor's voice for the first time ever. Hirohito went on the air to broadcast by radio the news of Japan's capitulation to the United States, Great Britain, China, and the Soviet Union, and to appeal to his people for order. The Second World War in the Pacific had ended.[18]

At once, the Allied occupation got underway. Navy minesweepers cleared the approaches to Tokyo Bay, and units of the army's Eleventh Airborne Division under Lieutenant General Robert Eichelberger landed to take charge. Eichelberger had to rely on the Japanese army and local police forces to protect his own troops and the newly appointed supreme commander, General Douglas MacArthur. Arriving on August 30, MacArthur, with Eichelberger and staff commanders, motored slowly from Atsugi airbase to Yokohama and his headquarters in the new Grand Hotel. In fitting reception for their "blue-eyed shogun," the Japanese soldiers guarding the route of the motorcade turned their backs toward the supreme commander, just at they always had done for the emperor. In formal ceremonies aboard the USS *Missouri* in Tokyo Bay on September 2, 1945, V-J Day henceforth, General MacArthur accepted Japan's surrender.

Emperor Hirohito read the report of the capitulation proceedings prepared by Toshikazu Kase, a graduate of Amherst and Harvard and the secretary of Foreign Minister Mamoru Shigemitsu. Kase's final passage described his own tearful emotions on noticing the rows upon rows of tiny Rising Sun flags proudly displayed on the *Missouri*'s conning tower for the Japanese ships and planes downed by the battleship's guns. Members of the emperor's household observed that Hirohito dwelled on this poignant note for a painfully long time. Summoning Foreign Minister Shigemitsu, Hirohito announced an unprecedented decision. Japan's emperors, descended from the sun goddess, Amaterasu Ōmikami, had traditionally never called upon anyone, but he, Hirohito, the 124th direct scion of Jimmu Tenno, who ruled in the seventh century B.C., had determined to pay General MacArthur a formal visit once the supreme commander for the Allied powers established his headquarters in Tokyo. Overcome at the propitious portent of the imperial gesture, Shigemitsu delightedly bowed himself out.[19]

*The enemy will not perish of himself. Neither the Chinese
reactionaries nor the aggressive forces of U.S. imperialism
will step down from the stage of their own accord.*

Mao Zedong[1]

8

THE COLD WAR
SPREADS

The United States emerged from the war preeminent among the nations of
the earth. Its victorious land, sea, and air forces, atomic bomb monopoly,
colossally productive economy, and evident eagerness to shape the postwar
world elevated the United States to a peak of international influence never
before attained. Exhausted, on the other hand, the French, British, Dutch,
and Belgians faced massive tasks of domestic reconstruction troubled by
rising nationalistic pressures to relinquish their colonial empires in Asia,
Africa, and the Caribbean. Germany and Japan smoldered in ruins. From
Leningrad to Moscow to Stalingrad, the Soviet Union's cities and industries
spanned a desolated wasteland. Nevertheless, the United States found itself
confronting Russia. Galvanized by nationalism and communism, Premier
Joseph Stalin marshaled Soviet power to the maximum extent to ensure
security forever, if possible, against the Germans and the Japanese, and to
reconstruct his war-ravaged society. The Russians evenhandedly distrusted
their former enemies and allies alike. Their rude conduct in international
relations, and their even cruder language, angered many otherwise friendly
Americans, raising the spectre of trouble to come.

Wasting little time, former Prime Minister Winston Churchill, Britain's
bulldog, declaimed the unspoken. Churchill, at Westminster College in
Fulton, Missouri, on March 5, 1946, with President Truman approvingly at
hand, pronounced that Europe dangerously once again was dividing into
hostile camps. Declared Churchill: "From Stettin in the Baltic to Trieste in

the Adriatic, an iron curtain has descended across the continent." Much later Senator J. William Fulbright would realize that Churchill's stark depiction overly aroused his fellow citizens, many of them already fearing that the Russians were out to communize the world. Unmistakably the Cold War was underway.

In Asia, the old order had vanished or was disintegrating. Japan lay helpless, crushed and occupied. Korea, China's longtime tributary and recently Japan's colony, split into two sections along the thirty-eighth parallel, where Russians and Americans confronted each other from their northern and southern zones of occupation. China, torn between Chiang Kai-shek's Nationalists and Mao Zedong's Communists, still struggled in the throes of her interminable civil war. In India, Burma, Indochina, Malaya, and the East Indies, Europe's once mighty empires crumbled on the brink of collapsing. Debilitated by Japan's conquests, the colonial powers despairingly turned to the United States to save whatever could be saved. General of the Army Douglas MacArthur, the supreme commander for the Allied powers, ruled Japan magisterially, brooking little, if any, outside interference. Notwithstanding Soviet membership on the Far Eastern Advisory Commission, as befitted Japan's conquerors, MacArthur rebuffed repeated Soviet demands for sharing his power.

American military officers and civilian officials were governing hundreds of Pacific territories, among them the Mariana, Marshall, and Caroline islands, Iwo Jima, and Okinawa. On the Marshall atoll of Bikini alone, the United States would detonate no fewer than twenty-three nuclear blasts between 1946 and 1958 in a prolonged demonstration of the nation's strength. Likewise, Eniwetok in the Marshall Islands, a bloody battleground not long since, served as an atomic proving station, the site of test explosions in 1948, 1951, 1952 (first thermonuclear hydrogen fusion detonations), and 1954. To reduce outcries against wanton imperialism, the United States persuaded the United Nations Organization to consign Micronesia—the Mariana, Gilbert, Marshall, and Caroline islands—to an American-administered Pacific Islands Trust.[2]

China held the key to American hopes for East Asia. Already the special privileges and extraterritorial rights belonging to foreigners in China had ended. Secretary of State Cordell Hull and China's ambassador, Wei Tao-ming, signed a treaty on November 1, 1942, terminating American rights of extraterritoriality, and Great Britain's ambassador in Chungking signed a similar document. Japan did likewise for propaganda reasons. When Chiang Kai-shek joined Roosevelt and Churchill at the Cairo Conference in November, 1943, he bore the heightened prestige resulting from China's being, in theory at least, now a full partner in the war against Japan. Americans had long dreamed glittering dreams of commercial opportunities in China. Many hoped to Christianize the heathen Chinese. Many more considered China a special protégé to befriend and uplift. Japan's hostility, moreover, confirmed such convictions. Biased in China's favor, America's merchants, missionaries, soldiers, diplomats, and editors, the molders of public opinion in the United States, optimistically held that the Republic of China would become, with generous assistance, a great power in the postwar world. Free at long last from Western and Japanese imperialists and incursions, their prediction ran, Nationalist China would soon develop into an especially good friend. Grateful for the selfless American efforts, it followed that China would remain non-Communist, a valuable trading partner, a loyal ally, and indeed the keeper of East Asia's balance of power between Japan and Russia.

To further these ends, the United States in 1945 promoted China into one of the five permanent seats on the United Nations Organization's Security Council, together with itself, Great Britain, the Soviet Union, and France. Upon Japan's defeat, American airplanes and ships hurriedly ferried some half a million of Chiang's soldiers to northern China and into Manchuria's cities seeking to impede a full-scale Chinese Communist or Soviet takeover. Simultaneously 113,000 American troops, including 53,000 marines, hurried into northern China to lend the Nationalists the strength of their presence, while hundreds of American military officers and technical specialists fanned out to advise the ill-trained Kuomintang Nationalist armies.

If Americans had only made the effort at this critical juncture to understand China in Chinese terms, instead of through their own preconceptions and wishful thinking, they might have realized that Mao would probably win the struggle for China, and that whatever interfering assistance they might deliver, albeit well intended, would in the end prove unavailing and even harmful. "Vinegar Joe" Stilwell on Okinawa knew unequivocally what the United States ought to do about China. "We ought to get out—*now*," he wrote on August 19.

Ironically the Russians knew no better. Mao Zedong was too independent and peasant-minded for Stalin's liking. As revolutionaries, Mao and his followers failed to measure up to Marxist-Leninist standards. Stalin sneered that the Maoists were only "margarine Communists." The Soviets adhered to Stalin's Yalta pledge and concluded, in August 1945, a treaty of friendship with the Nationalist Republic of China. Devastated by Hitler's armies, the Russians needed time and tranquility to rebuild, and obviously, they preferred a weak, internally divided Chinese neighbor to a feisty, sectarian competitor along more than four thousand miles of Sino-Soviet frontier. Indeed relations between the Russians and the Chinese Reds became so unfriendly that United States Foreign Service Officers John Paton Davies and John S. Service reported from China that Mao could count on little, if any, assistance from Moscow. The Russians held the power to turn Manchuria over to the Chinese Communists, but they did not do so. They openly recognized the Nationalist Government's sovereignty there, and shipped home industrial equipment as booty of war worth hundreds of millions of dollars. On departing, however, the Soviet armies handed over some three hundred thousand rifles and fifty thousand machine guns to General Lin Piao's Maoist armies. Lin's soldiers immediately overran and occupied Manchuria's major cities.

In this Communist paradox, Major General Patrick J. Hurley, the United States ambassador to the Republic of China, saw a chance to assist Chiang to defeat Mao. Hurley, a swashbuckling soldier in both world wars, was a former secretary of war. He energetically pursued the Truman administration's pro-Nationalist efforts to persuade the Chinese Communist party (CCP) to collaborate with the Kuomintang government (KMT), in order to disarm the Red threat. But neither side trusted the other. The Communists sounded willing enough to cooperate, but only to contrive a stepping stone for themselves toward an eventual socialist revolution. The Kuomintang insisted that the Red Army must be disbanded. And both parties understood that, at some point, either the Communists would endeavor to seize control, or the Nationalists, with the Red Army eliminated, would be able to demolish the CCP. Neither side dared openly to offend the United States by opposing the goal of peace to be attained through their cooperation.

From August 28 to October 10, 1945, Ambassador Hurley managed to bring Chiang and Mao together for negotiations. Held at the Nationalist capital of Chungking, Hurley's talks led to a series of compromise resolutions between Chiang and Mao for bringing about (1) a new constitution based on Sun Yat-sen's three-stage principles to introduce democratic government, (2) phased reductions of their armed services; and (3) truce teams comprised of equivalent KMT, CCP, and U.S. representations to root out truce violations as they might arise. Yet each side proceeded to stall for time, purposefully neglecting to implement any agreements they made. Angrily, Hurley resigned. Storming home in November, Hurley accused the career diplomats on his negotiating team of favoring Mao Zedong and Zhou En-lai, Mao's foreign minister ("Mouse Dung" and "Joe N. Lie," Hurley reviled them), over America's true friend, Chiang Kai-shek. Hurley spat out his sensational accusations of sabotage, charging that "a considerable section of our State Department is endeavoring to support Communism generally as well as specifically in China." In fact, FSOs John Paton Davies and John S. Service were among the first United States government officials to perceive the changing nature of the Chinese revolution, and to become themselves the transmitters of unwelcome tidings. Before much longer, they would personally suffer for it.

Worried, President Truman sent General George C. Marshall, the much admired, retired chief of staff, to China to revive the agreements. Marshall arrived in Chungking in mid-December. The Communists still envisaged a coalition government, in which they might share powers with the Nationalists, but only as a nonviolent means to gaining victory for themselves. The Nationalists were determined to win a military solution over the Communists before working for political, economic, and social reforms. Most Americans simply longed for an outburst of patriotic unity to bring China's rivals together, but their perception of China was obsolete. Their frustration arose from a shallow comprehension of China's history and the Chinese civil war. Taken together, the intentions of the United States government after 1941 to use Nationalist China as a base to attack Japan, and after 1945 to forge China into a strong partner for policing the world, revealed the deep incapacity to think clearly about the Chinese revolution. Americans who personally had known warlord China or supported missionaries through their Christian congregations steadfastly placed their hopes in Chiang Kai-shek's Nanking government. Yet most young diplomats and many military commanders on the spot recognized the determination and popular appeal of the Communist movement and criticized Chiang as a corrupt and cruel reactionary. Their appraisal, with its implications, was scarcely different from that set down by the American journalist Edgar Snow in his best-selling book *Red Star over China* (1938).

But times were changing. Hurley's Red-baiting outburst swelled the nation's rising tide of Cold War anti-Communism. Hurley himself would shortly agree with Wisconsin's Senator Joe McCarthy that, if pro-Maoists in the United States Government had not sold out Chiang Kai-shek, the Chinese Communist revolution could never have succeeded. Few voices, in McCarthyism's fearful climate, would dare openly to disagree. Meanwhile, in January 1946, General Marshall reconstituted the cease-fire agreement between Chiang and Mao to win their consent to the structure of a coalition government. Nevertheless, his mission was doomed to fail. Marshall bought Chiang Kai-shek's cooperation outright by promising him a big, new loan. When Marshall went home to lobby Congress for appropriations to support his bargain, he lost command over developments in China.

Brashly, Chiang advanced his troops farther into northern China. Communist soldiers under General Chu Teh controlled most of the rural areas along with the rail network between the cities, and General Lin Piao commanded an additional 100,000 Red Army regulars in Manchuria. Chiang planned to invade Manchuria with 1,300,000 soldiers to be launched from a vast encircling arc seventeen hundred miles long. Grandiose at best, Chiang's fantastic scheme was undermined at the outset. Kuomintang armies caused mass unrest everywhere by ravaging and pillaging the cities ostensibly being liberated from Japanese occupation. Economic ills multiplied. In 1946, as currency values collapsed, consumer prices soared 700 percent in Kuomintang-ruled districts. A United States dollar, which, in 1945, bought one hundred and twenty Chinese dollars, would within three years be worth the staggering sum of eleven million Chinese dollars. Alarmed, General Marshall cautioned Chiang not to press his army forward. The Red Chinese, he judged, could not be militarily defeated, while the Nationalists' efforts were making economic and political circumstances grievously worse.

Chiang Kai-shek intended, nevertheless, to defeat the Communists quickly by force. In June 1946, open warfare broke out. Chiang's Nationalist Republican Army began to clear Lin Piao's troops out of the Manchurian cities they had occupied since the Soviet departure. The Communists retreated, preparing themselves for a lengthy struggle. In rural areas, they instituted land distribution programs enlisting hordes of grateful peasants into the Red Army. Mao Zedong proclaimed that his Communists would triumph within five years and released a remarkably accurate forecast analyzing exactly how and why the Nationalists would lose. When a deeply chagrined Marshall left China for the last time, on January 8, 1947, Chiang Kai-shek's Nationalists held all of the major cities of northern China and Manchuria, but the Communists dominated the vast countryside, waging a canny campaign of attrition. Inflation, starvation, and lack of money to pay his soldiers would devastate Chiang's dreams of glory.

At home, President Truman installed Marshall as Secretary of State, then, in July 1947, dispatched General Albert C. Wedemeyer to China to survey the prospects for forestalling a Communist victory. General Wedemeyer, a master strategist and Stilwell's successor in command of United States forces in China, noted the chaos prevailing throughout Chiang's command, but he urged even stronger support for Chiang than administration leaders advocated. To thwart the Communists' appeal, Wedemeyer recommended instituting a Truman Doctrine–style aid program, like that just getting underway for Greece and Turkey, with a United Nations peacekeeping commission to oversee Manchuria. Secretary Marshall scotched Wedemeyer's proposals, preferring to concentrate on United States efforts against the Soviet threat to European recovery. Marshall worried that extending the Truman Doctrine of anti-Communist assistance to China might require American military commitments for its protection. He hesitated to aid Chiang, fearing to provoke the Russians to compete openly in Greece, where the Americans were hoping to go it alone.

Understandably, President Truman's pro-Chiang critics were demanding why Greece ought to be defended from Stalin, yet not China from Mao. Neither Truman nor Marshall, in truth, knew what to do. Nor did the great majority of Americans. Although Marshall respected Mao's armies, he never could fathom their appeal for China's peasant masses. In yielding to critics, Truman and Marshall quietly released undelivered Lend-Lease equipment to the Nationalists and, in late 1947, sent them additional arms and ammunition and empowered the United States Army Advisory Group to train Chiang's combat soldiers on Formosa. A few months later, President Truman asked Congress for $570 million in aid for China. The China Aid Act of April 1948 provided the Republic of China with $400 million. Inadequate to uphold Chiang, the amount was more than enough to infuriate Mao Zedong. Some congressmen and journalists saw it as merely a futile gesture to deflect criticism from the Truman administration for failing wholeheartedly enough to sustain the Nationalist government. Complained Senator Arthur H. Vandenberg (R) of Michigan: "China aid is like sticking your finger in the lake and looking for the hole."[3]

In war-shattered Japan at this time, General Douglas MacArthur's occupation officials were trying to reform Japanese government and society while struggling to restore day-to-day life. Foreign Service Officer John K. Emmerson moved into his requisitioned office just as the previous tenant, a Mitsui Corporation manager, moved out. The executive indicated a map on the wall outlining Japan's Co-Prosperity Sphere. "'There it is,' he said, smiling. 'We tried. See what you can do with it!'" "The whole burden of American foreign policy in Asia hit me in the stomach," Emmerson realized. "What were we going to do with it?" It was a good question. Japan's civilian economy teetered on the edge of total collapse. The homeland was cut off from imports of food, fuel, and raw materials. In ashes, industrial zones lay burned to the ground. Government officials and their big-business, *zaibatsu* connections were hastily concealing stockpiles of supplies for their own subsequent profit. Inflation drove consumer prices skyward. Touched off by commodity scarcities and the extraordinary amounts of currency issued by the government to pay off its war contracts, the soaring costs of living were immeasurably adding to the people's agony. Moreover, defeat had marooned nearly seven million of its subjects throughout Japan's once-far-flung empire, most of them armed services personnel. The United States Navy organized their repatriation by a motley Japanese-operated fleet of nearly four hundred vessels. Most of these stranded, demobilized units reached home in 1946. Incredibly, American officials retained certain Japanese troops under arms to fight Mao's Communists in North China and the Marxist-tinged insurgents resisting the return of their former European masters to the Dutch East Indies and French Indochina.

Neither President Roosevelt nor President Truman had given much thought to occupying Japan. Their major concern had been to overcome Japan's military forces. Japan's surrender, when it came, afforded more than a sudden surprise. It was virtually unexpected. MacArthur's orders for conducting the occupation emerged only after frantic debates within and among the State, War, and Navy bureaucracies. War fever impeded any return to rational procedures. The fighting in the Pacific war reached barbaric levels seldom, if ever, equaled or surpassed. Racist bloodlust and an equivalent dearth of merciful compassion characterized the combatants on both sides. Japan's atrocities against civilians and war captives alike provoked horrified disbelief. Even President Truman depicted the Japanese as "vicious and cruel savages." Most Americans shared Truman's conviction that the Japanese richly deserved the holocaust of airborne fire and destruction they suffered at the war's end. The Japanese, it was agreed, even deserved the American atomic bombings of Hiroshima and Nagasaki. By their obdurate refusal to surrender when obviously defeated and facing invasion and possible obliteration, Japan's autocratic militarists brought the apocalypse on themselves.

As the supreme commander of the Allied powers, General MacArthur had to follow the guidelines set forth by the Potsdam Declaration to disarm and demobilize Japan's military forces and install a representative government. MacArthur was also the United States Far East commander. On September 6, 1945, President Truman approved the "Initial Postsurrender Policy for Japan" for MacArthur to put into effect. This document, the outcome of weeks of quarrelsome planning among the foreign policy bureaucracies, embodied twin goals of fostering a peacetime economy sufficient for civilian requirements, and instituting a reform agenda designed drastically to transform Japanese society. Before long, the fear of Japanese militarism would lead, in addition, to a constitutional prohibition against Japan's right to wage war, the celebrated Article 9.

MacArthur drove into Tokyo less than a week after Japan's formal surrender. "It was 22 miles from the New Grand Hotel in Yokohama to the American Embassy, which was to be my home throughout the occupation," he afterwards wrote, "but they were 22 miles of devastation and vast piles of charred rubble." More than two million homes had been ruined by American air raids, while Japanese defense forces themselves wrecked another half million to create firebreaks. Six hundred and seventy thousand civilians died in the bombings. Allied soldiers and sailors hastily erected field kitchens to feed the starving population. MacArthur cabled home for 3 million tons of food. In Washington, government officials demanded to know his reasons and details. The supreme commander immediately lashed off a second cable: "Give me bread or give me bullets!"

Thereafter, like a benevolent despot, Douglas MacArthur dominated Japan. His viceroy-like authority stemmed directly from the Potsdam ultimatum demanding Japan's surrender and his appointment by President

Truman and the Allied belligerents as the supreme commander. The Russians wanted MacArthur controlled by a four-power council with themselves included, but when such a body was finally created, MacArthur virtually ignored it. Indeed General MacArthur was the only United States official overseas who could make foreign policy without obtaining prior State Department approval. As President Truman had put it to him: "You will exercise your authority as you deem proper to carry out your mission. Our relations with Japan do not rest on a contractual basis, but on unconditional surrender. . . . Our authority is supreme." True to form, given a blank check, MacArthur interpreted his commander-in-chief's order in the fullest possible scope. He represented himself as solely responsible for administering Japan. Only the Russians protested. "Never before in the history of the United States," wrote an admiring Ambassador William J. Sebald, "had such enormous and absolute power been placed in the hands of a single individual."[4]

MacArthur intended to conciliate the Japanese nevertheless. To the consternation of Treasury Secretary Henry J. Morgenthau, who put forward punitive suggestions for humiliating the Japanese, not unlike the purgatory he urged for the Germans, MacArthur loftily responded: "If the historian of the future should deem my service worthy of some slight reference, it would be my hope that he mentions me not as a commander engaged in campaigns and battles, even though victorious to American arms, but rather as one whose sacred duty it became, once the guns were silenced, to carry to the land of our vanquished foe the solace and hope and faith of Christian morals." MacArthur's soldiers had expected to have to disarm the quarter of a million Japanese soldiers still dug into defensive positions on Kanto Plain surrounding Tokyo and Yokohama on the island of Honshu, but SCAP's General Order Number One instructed Japanese commanding officers to see to it themselves. (The acronym SCAP covered both the Allied occupation authority and the supreme commander himself.) He was saving face, MacArthur explained. To humiliate Japan's soldiers now would invite obstreperous behavior from them later as veterans. Consciously or unconsciously, he was avoiding an opportunity for cruelty like his brutal dispersal, while chief of staff, of the 1932 Bonus Army from the Capitol grounds. He spurned recommendations that he should command the emperor to appear before him. In time, he felt certain, Hirohito would ask to call on the supreme commander, if only out of his eagerness for peace and reconciliation. MacArthur overrode Admiral Halsey's order to prevent fishermen from crisscrossing Tokyo Bay to safeguard his ships against possible sabotage. The Japanese people needed the fishermen's harvest for food, MacArthur ruled. No sabotage occurred. The crushed populace began to take note. Ignoring Americans' sneers at his proconsul-like posturing,

MacArthur recognized the spiritual hunger among the demoralized Japanese to renew their faith in themselves.

With gusto, Supreme Commander MacArthur set forth to implant freedom throughout Japanese life. "I had to be," he recalled, "an economist, a political scientist, an engineer, a manufacturing executive, a teacher, even a theologian of sorts." He intended, he put it, to transform Japan into "the world's greatest laboratory for an experiment in the liberation of a people from totalitarian military rule and for the liberalization of government from within." MacArthur introduced American-style constitutional guarantees. He promulgated a bill of rights to uphold individual liberty and reforms to liberalize the domestic economy. Under his orders, the legislative Diet replaced Shintō (the way of the gods) with Minshushugi (the way of democracy). Freedom for religion, speech, and press were mandated, as were enfranchisement for women, free labor unions, democratic political, judicial, and educational systems, the decentralization of police powers, and the release of political prisoners. To revamp Japan's economy, Washington ordered MacArthur to widen the distribution of income and ownership of the means of production. SCAP officials endeavored to purge companies of their family-controlled, oligopolistic networks under the *zaibatsu* or money syndicates, by dissolving the manufacturing and banking combinations dominating Japan's trade and industry. The Americans also launched a peaceful agricultural revolution in tenant-landlord relationships. Some of these innovations endured, others proved fleeting. However, in moving to punish war criminals and their business allies, the United States government and the occupying authorities hoped to eradicate the autocratic bellicosity that had, since the late nineteenth century, driven Japan into far-flung imperialistic aggressions. SCAP's plans held out breathtaking promises of individual freedom and prosperity for the conquered Japanese. Knowing no other way himself, Douglas MacArthur intended to install democracy from the top down.

At last by appointment, at 10:30 A.M. on September 27, to end weeks of silence from the Imperial Palace, Emperor Hirohito, accompanied by two limousines full of household personnel, formally called on General MacArthur. The dramatic encounter took place at MacArthur's residence in the American embassy rather than his office at the Dai Ichi Insurance Building in Tokyo's business district. Major Faubion Bowers, an aide interpreter for MacArthur, remembered being told by his chief that it did enter his mind that Hirohito had come to avert the pressures from Washington to try him as a war criminal. Instead the emperor came to offer himself as a substitute for the lives of his countrymen accused of war crimes. He was proposing the *bushido* chivalric gesture of *migawari*, to put forward one's life in place of another. But MacArthur, in addition to his instructions based on the

surrender terms, had other intentions. Having assisted in the Allied occupation of the Rhine after the armistice of 1918, MacArthur had observed the
disastrous results of administering a war-devastated German population
shorn of its imperial authority. Hirohito, the 124th emperor in more or less
unbroken and, according to belief, divine succession, was not only allowed
to retain Nippon's Phoenix Throne, but he permitted himself to become
peacefully transformed with his dignity intact into a constitutional monarch. MacArthur admitted afterward to a fatherly feeling for the earnest
younger man, twenty years his junior, while Hirohito himself recalled the
meeting as "the most impressive event for me." "It was most fortunate for
Japan," Hirohito reflected, "that a person with a deep knowledge of
Oriental philosophy like MacArthur assumed the role of supreme commander of the Occupational Forces."

Nevertheless, MacArthur soon precipitated the angry resignation of
Naruhiko Higashikuni, an uncle by marriage of Emperor Hirohito and
himself an imperial prince, who had hastily formed Japan's first postwar
cabinet two days after the nation's surrender. An outspoken militarist when
commanding the home defenses, Higashikuni reportedly threatened to
execute all Allied airmen forced down into Japanese hands. His resignation
followed an order from the occupation authorities to abolish the Special
Higher Police.

MacArthur was omnipotent. He could overrule the emperor. He could
prorogue the Diet, ban a political party, and disqualify any individual from
holding office. Newspapers had to subject their pages to SCAP's censorship
and publish in full every SCAP directive. Diplomats presented their credentials to him, not to the emperor. He never returned their calls, and he
ordered them home if they displeased him. Businessmen could not enter
Japan without his permission, and SCAP supervised every step of their
visits. He prevented carping journalists from returning if ever they left his
domain. American money was useless until exchanged for army scrip at 360
yen to the dollar. The Japanese people seemed to welcome MacArthur's
mastery. Many feared for their lives from the American and British Empire
troops garrisoned in their midst. But the supreme commander ordered long
imprisonment for any American caught striking a Japanese, which led one
man, according to William Manchester, to observe, "That was when we
knew we had lost the war." J. H. M. Salmon, then a young New Zealand
army captain billeted on a former Japanese air force base at Onoda east of
Shimonoseki, later recalled that the Allied occupation forces routinely
referred to the remote and lofty MacArthur as "God," while SCAP's
bureaucrats demanded nine copies of everything.

Japan afforded a splendid theater for histrionics. If Douglas MacArthur
still nursed the presidential ambitions evident in 1944, which he did, he

possessed the complete independence as supreme commander to parade his dramatic talents. He relished the distance between him and his rivals or antagonists preoccupied in Washington by domestic politics and their European priorities. Like Manila earlier, Tokyo might serve him as his springboard to capture even greater honors. His words and deeds attracted as much attention in the United States as in Japan.[5]

Initially, Washington's directives to SCAP reflected the vitriolic vengefulness wrought by Pearl Harbor and the Pacific war, though this vindictive mood was mellowed somewhat by a New Dealish additive of liberal progressivism. During the first eighteen months of the occupation, MacArthur dutifully proclaimed an agenda far to the left of his own personal philosophy and the goals back home of his ultraconservative enthusiasts. Even so, he pulled the teeth of the reparations and antimonopoly objectives he was ordered to pursue. He did command the *zaibatsu* to relinquish their direct family control over Japan's great financial combines. But he evaded Washington's pressures to dissolve the industrial companies they controlled, and he allowed the reclassifying of their armaments factories as essential for civilian production and therefore exempt from Allied confiscation. In defense, he proclaimed his mastery of Japanese psychology coupled with a passionate anticommunism. It would be wiser, he insisted against his American or Allied critics, to leave real power in its traditional places, to encourage Japan peacefully to reclaim her "natural" leadership in Asia, than, by overzealous reforms, to invite the Soviet Union to sponsor a Communist revolution. At home, the postulates heating up the Cold War against communism sustained MacArthur's judgment. Skeptically, nonetheless, the independent-minded journalist I. F. Stone grew alarmed that the anti-Communist frenzy spilling from the old "pro-Axis" and "anti-Soviet" crowd might lead to unstoppable demands for "softer treatment for both Germany and Japan." Stone was on target. Assistant Secretary of War John J. McCloy, for example, hoped to erect right-wing bulwarks in Germany and Japan to stem any spreading of Soviet-backed revolutionary communism.

SCAP promulgated for Japan what it termed a "controlled revolution." Occupation officials, including the supreme commander himself, wanted to reform Japan, but never to unleash unpredictable forces for change that might unhinge the occupation. A concern for stabilizing conditions and restoring civilian life arose mutually out of routine dealings between SCAP and Japanese officials. On the anniversary of Japan's surrender, September 2, 1946, MacArthur reaffirmed his intention to lead the Japanese people toward "the great middle course of moderate democracy." To succeed, he grandiloquently declared, he was destroying what must be destroyed and preserving what must be preserved, in order to erect what must be erected for a peaceful, democratic future. Japan, as America's probable ally, Mac-Arthur predicted, could turn into "a powerful bulwark for peace" instead of reformulating itself into "a dangerous springboard for war."

Early in 1946, SCAP revealed to a startled government delegation the finished draft of a democratic constitution for Japan. Virtually mandated, the proferred fundamental law incorporated on an equal basis the civil and political rights of both sexes, strengthened the powers of the Diet and local government, outlawed the residual temporal powers of the emperor, and forbade the creation of armed forces or the waging of war. More than the document's liberal provisions, it was SCAP's readiness to submit the constitution to a nationwide, popular referendum, if necessary to win its approval, that terrified Japan's conservatives into a stunned acquiescence. Emperor Hirohito eased the constitution's ratification by repudiating his dynastic claims to divinity. "With him as a figurehead," MacArthur could confide to his closest advisors, "our job is so much more easy." Texas Congressman Maury Maverick hooted that Hirohito's real reason for declaring "he wasn't God was because he found out MacArthur was."

Also at this time, SCAP commenced purging Japan's political arena of the country's leading militarists and fanatic nationalists. The occupation authorities decreed the removal from public activity of politicians, bureaucrats, military officers, and police charged with aggression. Businessmen linked to imperial expansion found their names added to the lists, as well as local administrators notorious for war-related acts of wanton brutality. These purges provoked only a mild excitement. Conservatives, who viewed the war as an aberration not characteristic of Japan's normal conduct, wanted the nation's postwar atmosphere cleansed of its wartime leaders. The huge task of investigating some two and one-half million accused individuals mostly fell to Japanese officials, who inclined toward leniency for their countrymen. Still, some two hundred thousand persons, 80 percent of them military, lost their eligibility to hold offices and other political rights. MacArthur defended the process for forestalling a bloodier bath from drumhead justice. Among those banned from public life was Bin Akao, who, after the occupation, headed the Great Japan Patriots' Party of diehard extremists, dedicating himself to terrorist politics and violent deeds.

MacArthur evinced greater determination to nail selected offenders. He enthusiastically supported the prosecution in Manila and Tokyo of Japan's most notorious commanding officers (especially, in biographer Michael Schaller's caustic judgment, those generals who had successfully countered him on the battlefields) and government leaders. An eleven-nation tribunal in Tokyo, during 1946 and 1947, duplicated the Nuremberg war crimes proceedings. The jurists tried and condemned ex–Prime Minister Hideki Tōjō, who approved the attacks on Pearl Harbor and Southeast Asia, plus six other top officials for atrocities. Notorious were generals Masaharu Homma and Tomoyuki Yamashita, convicted for the savageries of their troops in the Philippines. On appeal, the United States Supreme Court rejected the defendants' claim that the international court lacked jurisdiction. Their executions by hanging quickly followed. Elsewhere military and civil courts handed down lighter sentences to about four thousand "war criminals." In return for highly secret information on Japan's preparations for chemical and germ warfare, MacArthur followed the instructions of War and State department officials to shield the medical doctors responsible for inhumane experimenting on Chinese civilians and Allied prisoners of war including Americans, and he spurned Soviet objections as mere Communist propaganda.

SCAP's reforms were democratizing Japan, especially in land tenure and politics, but, as MacArthur's liberal critics complained, form oftentimes prevailed over substance. The vaunted purges and innovations, they charged, were failing to upset either the oligarchic hierarchy of society or the alignment of ruling interests rooted in class and ideology. Two rightist conservative parties, the Progressives and the Liberals, controlled politics. The Progressives governed under the supreme commander's ever watchful eye from October 1945 to May 1946, led by Prime Minister Baron Kijuro Shidehara. Then Shigeru Yoshida, destined to become postwar Japan's outstanding politician, led the Liberals to take control. In his first term, Yoshida served as prime minister until May 1947, when he fell before the opposition to SCAP's controversial efforts to level the *zaibatsu*. Humiliated, Yoshida had to bear MacArthur's contemptuous characterizations of him as "inept" and "monumentally lazy." Ideologically, the two parties resembled peas in a pod. No distinctions other than personal differences or rival business motives divided them. The left-wingers' fragmentation and inexperience enhanced the conservatives' capacity to serve the Occupation authorities.[6]

Japan's economic recovery reintroduced a centralized control by the major corporations over the nation's regionally defined markets and networks. The framework of the new order, not surprisingly, approximated the old. Zealously SCAP's blueprint makers planned to institute a businesslike, conservative society. Little did they know that inside twenty-five years, Japan's economy would shake the earth.

To assist him, MacArthur called in civilian experts. Joseph Dodge, a Detroit banker, became the occupation's economic advisor. Inflation posed immediate dangers. Dodge managed to get a steep increase in income taxes, even on the rates for moderate incomes, and an exemption from all taxes on the interest earned on deposits up to three million yen per individual. Inflation halted within weeks; the rate of savings turned upward and continued to climb. Tax revenues began to increase almost at once.

Homer Sarasohn, an engineer with the Raytheon Corporation, was summoned to rebuild Japan's communications industry destroyed by American bombings. Sarasohn arrived in 1946 when MacArthur's men were striving to restart Japan's economy. "My first job," he later related, "was to get the communications equipment manufacturing companies back on their feet." Sarasohn's second job was to turn out radios for the Japanese to receive broadcasts by the occupation authorities. MacArthur wanted to enlist the populace's willing cooperation in reconstructing the country. Sarasohn's third task was to make Japan's communications industry profitable, a source of taxable income for the government, "so that the Japanese would not be a burden to the American taxpayer." "The first thing I taught them," he stated, "was how to produce quality goods. I taught them you could not have quality goods unless you had good quality management." Sarasohn and Charles Protzman, a Western Electric engineer, introduced a management training program through the Civil Communications Section of the occupation authority. Based on American techniques, their curriculum emphasized the social mission of the company. Sarasohn and Protzman stressed the importance of achieving quality over profits, treating each employee with respect, and defining a clear statement of the company's purpose. They underscored the necessity for cooperation among the departments and familiarizing managers with all aspects of operations. Sarasohn's and Protzman's students rose to head Japan's largest electronic companies, including the Sony Corporation, Mitsubishi Electric, Sumitomo Electric, Matsushita (Panasonic), and Nippon Electric. Excellent apprentices, the determined Japanese learned well what the Americans taught them. Their disciples would continue to teach the Americans' management course for at least the next twenty-five years.

Only the heated arguments of 1947 over the future of the *zaibatsu* and SCAP's proposals to curb their influence induced any troublesome outcry from the monied oligarchy against MacArthur's program. Even then, Japan's conservatives reconciled themselves to waiting for the fury of the conquerors to subside. That moment seemed certain to come when the Americans, in particular, would be impelled by events and new developments to reaffirm Asia's traditional realities of power.[7]

The Communist menace did the trick. The Cold War took over.

Fear-laced, a belligerent anti-communist mood engulfed the American people. The frenzy lay rooted in the Bolshevik Revolution of 1917, with its threats to overthrow bourgeois societies. The legacy of mistrust had on several occasions ruffled the wartime unity of the Grand Alliance against Hitler. Horrifyingly, the spectre materialized of a Third World War to come, the next time between the Soviet Union and the United States. Overnight the all too brief elation of victory evaporated. This Red scare arose, at least externally, over the USSR's intransigence in the wake of Germany's collapse and Russia's last-minute, self-aggrandizing entry into the war against Japan. Soviet outbursts in Security Council meetings at the United Nations in New York City were noisily dispelling the naive hope for a brave new world of peace and prosperity. The step-by-step uncovering of nuclear bomb spies and card-carrying commies or fellow travelers in sensitive government positions whiplashed initial alarms into a virtual panic. The additional shocks to come from the Chinese Communists' victory of 1949 and the Korean War of 1950 unleashed McCarthyism's full-fledged witch-hunt.

From 1945 to 1950, United States policymakers toiled diligently to navigate the nation's new global supremacy along an agenda of high priority targets. Three goals were uppermost: (1) a general recovery for Europe's and Japan's industrial systems; (2) the rehabilitation of world trade to pre-1930 peak levels or greater; and (3) the quarantine of the Soviets until they chose to accept the American rules of international relations. But the Soviet-backed Communist triumphs in Eastern Europe, with the likelihood of more ahead, dismayed conservatives and liberals alike. Americans in growing numbers hearkened to Churchill's outcry against the "iron curtain" now dividing Europeans, reawakening the prospects of global tragedy.

President Truman and Secretary of State Acheson led the reaction. In 1947, invoking the so-called Truman Doctrine, the United States government rushed military assistance and supplies to uphold the embattled conservative government in Greece, as well as to Turkey, Greece's wary, though as yet unthreatened, neighbor. The Marshall Plan launched the European Recovery Program in 1948, to foster a general economic recovery for the war-weary continent and the British Isles. Confined by Soviet objections to the Western nations, the ERP, as the program became known, effectively introduced the overall policy of containing communism. In retaliation, Soviet authorities blockaded all land and water communication to the four-power occupied, isolated city of Berlin, Germany's former capital. Berlin became a bone of bitter contention between East and West. For over a year, the Big Three powers, led by the United States, supplied Berlin by an airlift of provisions and fuel, until the Russians threw up their hands and lifted the blockade. In 1949, containment policy expanded under President Truman's Point Four to provide technical assistance for under-developed countries, and through the remilitarization of Western Europe for defensive purposes in the North Atlantic Treaty Organization. NATO constituted a permanent alliance with the United States its vanguard.[8]

Inside China, Mao Zedong's war of attrition reversed the tide of the civil war, thwarting Chiang Kai-shek's grand strategy. Some four hundred thousand Nationalist troops were killed or captured by mid-1947. Mao's force was redesignated the People's Liberation Army (PLA). The PLA's ranks swelled to nearly two million regular soldiers and guerillas, not counting its peasant militiamen. After an empty victory in seizing Mao's abandoned capital of Yenan, Chiang lost another hundred thousand of his best troops on their withdrawal to Sian. His American military advisors urged Chiang to fall back below the Great Wall, but stubbornly he refused. A retreat from Manchuria, he knew, would tacitly partition China between north and south, and amount to abandoning his prolonged struggle for China. The PLA initiated limited counteroffensives in central China against Chiang's overextended communications and supply lines. To exploit Chiang's predictable counterattacking, in December 1947 General Lin Piao struck hard against the Nationalist garrisons idling in southern Manchuria's cities. Quickly Piao's Fourth Field Army inflicted 150,000 casualties and trapped the Nationalist remnants inside the city of Chinchow. Only air drops could provision them. As the result, by the summer of 1948 Mao had achieved military parity with his enemy. Then Lin Piao, in four stunning campaigns, altogether smashed Chiang's northern forces, ejecting them from Manchuria and northern China and destroying the Nationalists' ability and will to fight effectively any longer. Chiang's ill-conceived Manchurian adventure had wasted some 470,000 of the Nationalists' best troops.

At the same time, PLA General Ch'en Yi's Third Field Army conquered the Shantung region, inflicting another hundred thousand casualties and seizing fifty thousand rifles. Together with General Liu Po-Che'ng's Second Field Army and four turncoat Nationalist divisions, Ch'en raced to surround most of Chiang's remaining army. Desperately Chiang brought up his elite armored reserves. When Chiang's tanks failed to break through the PLA's encircling ring, he ordered his aerial squadrons to bombard the trapped men to prevent their weapons from being captured by the Communists. The shocking proof that the generalissimo valued their equipment more than his soldiers' lives annulled their willingness to fight any longer for him. The encircled troops surrendered on January 10, 1949. Even before this great battle ended, Lin Piao swept southward to link up with General Nieh Jung-chen's North China (unofficially designated the Fifth) Field Army, overwhelming Peking and Tientsin. Within three months, Chiang had lost almost one and a half million men and their arms. The staggering total represented about one-half of the Nationalists' strength, but actually signified an unredeemable loss of the combat-hardened, best-equipped echelons.

The rest was epilogue. Chiang Kai-shek resigned the presidency of the

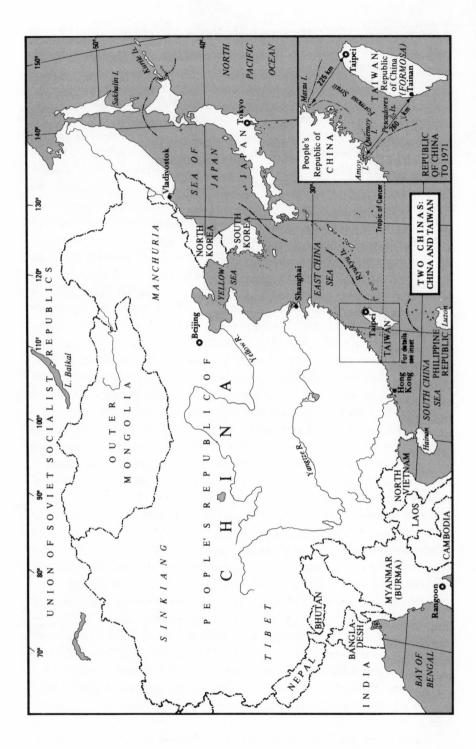

TWO CHINAS:
CHINA AND TAIWAN

Republic of China. He began to withdraw men and treasure to Taiwan. In April and May, the People's Liberation Army crossed the Yangtze River to sweep into Nanking, Nanchang, and southeastern China, while in the western sector, the cities of Wuhan and Changsha capitulated. On October 1, 1949, Mao Zedong proclaimed the birth of the People's Republic of China. Canton, the Nationalists' last capital, fell two weeks later, and in December, the last redoubts in Szechuan Province collapsed. Thirty-seven years of China's civil war had ended in the Communists' victory. Ended at the same time were 107 years of foreign intervention. Politically rather than militarily, the Kuomintang's defeat originated in its purblind insistence that China's Communists represented nothing more than Soviet Russia's pliant tools. By failing, when opportunity existed, to alleviate the miseries of China's wretched population, the Nationalists brought on their own undoing, which their catastrophic military blunders guaranteed. To no avail since V-J Day, the Truman administration had poured around three billion dollars into China to support the Nationalists against Mao's Communists.[9]

Washington's refusal to recognize the People's Republic of China prolonged the futility of United States policy. In June 1949, Mao affirmed that his revolution was inclining to the side of Soviet Russia against the "one great imperialist power," the United States. American officials were not surprised. They believed that the Chinese Communists were merely Moscow's puppets. President Truman rebuffed Mao Zedong's and Zhou Enlai's representations for diplomatic recognition and economic assistance made through Ambassador John Leighton Stuart and Consul General O. Edmund Clubb. Firmly Truman directed the diplomats remaining in China never to soften their position toward the Communists, but to judge their intentions solely by their actions.

Publicly, Secretary of State Dean Acheson washed the government's hands of Chiang Kai-shek in his notorious white paper sent to the president on July 30, 1949. Acheson insisted that American policies had not "lost" China. The "ineffectiveness of the Nationalist forces" caused the debacle, not any shortage of American aid or goodwill. "A realistic appraisal of conditions in China, past and present, leads to the conclusion," Acheson explained, "that the only alternative open to the United States was full-scale intervention in behalf of a Government which had lost the confidence of its own troops and its own people." Such an intervention, argued Acheson, "would have been resented by the mass of the Chinese people, would have diametrically reversed our historic policy, and would have been condemned by the American people." Americans, for the present, must face the reality of Russia's Communist victory. However, continued Acheson, "the profound civilization and democratic individualism of China will reassert themselves, and she will throw off the foreign yoke. I consider that we should encourage all developments in China which now and in the future work toward that end." With this, Truman and Acheson launched the policy of nonrecognition of Red China that would persist until 1979, while Mao Zedong, following a tirade against American imperialism, signed a treaty of friendship and alliance with the Soviet Union in February 1950. Truman and Acheson felt certain that Stalin had pulled Mao's strings.

In secret, late in April, Truman's advisors on the National Security Council expressed their alarm over a world increasingly challenged by Soviet expansionism. The National Security Council declared that none but American power, by means of a policy of "containment" backed up by superior military strength, could withstand the USSR's pressures. The Cold War, decided NSC Paper No. 68, is "a real war in which the survival of the free world is at stake." To defend ourselves and prevent all-out war, "we must by means of a rapid and sustained buildup of the political, economic, and military strength of the free world, and by means of an affirmative program intended to wrest the initiative from the Soviet Union, confront it with convincing evidence of the determination and ability of the free world to frustrate the . . . Kremlin design of a world dominated by its will." Following the outbreak of the Korean War, President Truman accepted NSC-68 as United States Policy. Then, early in 1951, stung by the setback in Korea, Assistant Secretary of State Dean Rusk hardened the nonrecognition policy against Red China: "The Peiping regime may be a colonial Russian government—a Slavic Manchukuo on a larger scale. It is not the Government of China. It does not pass the first test. It is not Chinese."

Earlier in Japan, when it appeared that Mao Zedong's forces might before long win control over China, SCAP's occupation authorities drastically shifted their strategy from reforming the onetime enemy's society to converting the country into an anti-Communist bastion of the Cold War, but only after a bitter struggle. The changeover commenced in Washington, when President Truman replaced Secretary of State James F. Byrnes with General George C. Marshall. For Truman and Marshall, the Soviet Union and its Stalinist satellites, in the lurid light of the Red scare, posed an imminent threat to free societies everywhere. Moreover, the Wedemeyer report of September 1947 reflected adversely on Chiang Kai-shek's ability to hang on to his own territory. George F. Kennan, Marshall's top policy planner and containment's architect, dared now to call upon Japan to recreate her empire over Southeast Asia to thwart communism's advance. The State Department's Japan-Korea economic division, under Edward F. Martin, recommended a bold policy to promote Japan's recovery, which was currently being held back, according to Martin, by unfavorable trade patterns and shortages of hard currency. Martin urged funding a $500 million pump-priming operation, reminiscent of the war-shattered Greater

East Asia Co-Prosperity Sphere, to stimulate a regionally-centered Asian prosperity around Japan's manufacturing industries and the commodities-producing economies of Southeast Asia, including Burma. To this end, ex-President Herbert Hoover, among others, discreetly advised canceling SCAP's intentions to confine Japan's industries under antimonopolistic definitions of small-scale enterprise.

Globally, the tide was ebbing away from vengeance, to favor reinforcing rather than dismantling the economies of Germany and Japan. To do otherwise, in the latest Cold War thinking, would invite a Soviet-orchestrated catastrophe. Germany's collapse must open the door to a Russian domination of Western Europe and the Middle East, while Japan, if prostrate, could not resist a Russian-backed effort to take over Asia. Yet President Truman, if for motives opposing Hoover's, hesitated for some time openly to balk the imperious MacArthur's determination to attack the *zaibatsu*. Earlier in the occupation, New Deal-minded officials had pushed MacArthur into launching liberal reforms for Japan, but the right-wing Democrats, whom Truman currently employed, were now pressuring him to convert Japan into a conservative, anti-Communist stronghold. Critics feared that the shortcomings of postwar policy were ushering both Germany and Japan toward economic catastrophes. Navy Secretary James Forrestal, Commerce Secretary Averill Harriman, Secretary of War Robert Patterson, Agriculture Secretary Clinton P. Anderson, and Undersecretary of State Dean Acheson were pondering together how to reverse what they now considered to have been disastrous occupation policies for Germany and Japan.[10]

The problem for General MacArthur was political, not ideological. He conceded the thrust of containment as valid, even if he distrusted its European emphasis and diminished support for China's Nationalists. His alarm focused politically on SCAP's inevitable loss of independence and the adverse reaction likely to follow any scrutiny of his economic overlordship. MacArthur worried that if SCAP were to join a *zaibatsu*-managed program of economic recovery, it would hamstring his hopes for a quick peace treaty to end the occupation and send him first back home in triumph and then, by popular acclaim in 1948, into the White House as president. Only three days after the White House, by invoking the Truman Doctrine, pledged assistance to Greece and Turkey and to any government fighting communism, MacArthur in Tokyo appealed for a peace settlement. He blamed Japan's depressed economy on world conditions and denounced the new schemes for recovery as certain to squander American resources. He urged a prompt termination of the occupation as successfully concluded. General Robert Eichelberger, who commanded the Eighth Army in Japan, observed later that this was his chief's means of "placing his hat in the ring for the presidency." To persist in attacking Japan's big financial combines, as MacArthur was determined to do, George F. Kennan now argued, would cause an "economic disaster" for Japan, which certainly was, Kennan added, what the left-wingers wanted as the surest road to communism.

MacArthur's futile efforts to gain a peace treaty for Japan before the end of 1947, while crusading against the *zaibatsu* in defiance of the Truman administration's revised Cold War tactics, reflected his vaulting ambition for the presidency. He naively hoped that his Asia First record and anti-monopoly principles would win the Republican nomination for him, begin-ning with the Wisconsin primary. As things turned out, he never came close. Thomas E. Dewey defeated Robert A. Taft to win the Republican nomination, and President Truman won over Dewey in the November election.

His political defeats signaled the close of MacArthur's glory days in Japan. In April 1949, an administration review board downgraded most of his orders to break up Japan's monopolies, and Congress appropriated huge sums to rebuild the nation's industry. At Kennan's urging, President Truman and the National Security Council approved a policy of encourag-ing economic growth to enable Japan to achieve political and military security. So MacArthur attuned himself to the administration's Cold War agenda. SCAP began to promote a conservative slate of economic and social goals, even to harass labor unions and minority political groups formerly its protégés. Ironically, MacArthur's rightward swerve reduced his policy differences with the president. In imitation of Truman's guidelines on loyalty, SCAP's Counter Intelligence Corps, under General Charles A. Willoughby, unleashed an intensive search for Communist conspiracies among leftists and liberals alike. Outwardly MacArthur and his cohorts continued to operate as though nothing had changed, though SCAP's staff dwindled after Japanese officials took on greater responsibilities for routine administration. Politically, it was easier for President Truman not to recall the vainglorious MacArthur providing he obeyed instructions. The out-break of the Korean War suddenly returned Douglas MacArthur to center stage.

Already Prime Minister Shigeru Yoshida had complained that the Amer-icans wanted Japan to accept a peace treaty, without either Chinese or Russian participation, that granted the United States permanent military bases in Japan. Although eager to end the tiresome occupation, Yoshida's right-wing backers and his left-wing rivals alike resented compromising Japan's sovereignty to placate the Americans' newly militant, anti-Communist stance. Cockily Yoshida forecast that "just as the United States was once a colony of Great Britain but is now the stronger of the two, if Japan becomes a colony of the United States it will also eventually become the stronger." Japan's economic recovery made Yoshida's point. In a spectacular case, Elmer L. Hann, an American shipbuilding executive, taught shipyard workers at Kure the methods of welding and construction that enabled the United States to turn out fleets of vessels in wartime. By 1958, Japan would surpass Britain as the world's leading builder of ships.

In December 1948, the USSR withdrew its forces from divided Korea, leaving the North Korean army heavily armed, while in June 1949, the United States likewise withdrew from South Korea, leaving only outmoded military equipment behind and about five hundred "advisors to the Seoul government." The Joint Chiefs of Staff had determined that South Korea was not vital to American security. Secretary of State Dean Acheson, Marshall's successor, in a public speech in January 1950, drew the perimeter of America's defenses in Asia, a line from the Aleutian Islands to Japan and Okinawa to the Philippines. Both Korea and Taiwan lay outside that line. Whether Acheson's hapless omission of Korea directly precipitated the bloody warfare of 1950 is unknown, as is whether the cause of the war's outbreak lay in Russia's or Korea's undoubted hostility to Washington's policies for rebuilding their Japanese enemy. Soon, in any event, the United States would have another Asian war to fight, this time over Korea. The Cold War struggles for Asia were clearly beginning.[11]

The peace treaty for Japan was signed in September 1951. By its provisions, which John Foster Dulles drafted, Japan bound herself firmly to the United States and the anti-Communist alliance. The American occupation ended in April 1952, yet American bases and military personnel would remain in Japan. Red China and North Korea had to be walled off, and disarmed Japan itself defended. John Gunther heard one Japanese foresightedly say: "Thank God for the disarmament provision in the Constitution! It means that taxation will be light, and we will promptly become the richest nation in the world!"[12]

The communist threat is a global one. . . . You cannot appease or otherwise surrender to communism in Asia without simultaneously undermining our efforts to halt its advance in Europe.

Douglas MacArthur[1]

9

CONTAINMENT IN KOREA

War erupted between North Korea and South Korea, along the thirty-eighth parallel dividing line, on Sunday June 25, 1950, when North Korean armored divisions invaded in force. The outbreak of hostilities at once produced a major Cold War confrontation between East and West, even to conjuring up the menace of World War Three and nuclear annihilation. As occupying powers, the Russians and Americans had divided Korea between their zones. Under Kim Il Sung, a onetime guerilla leader against the Japanese, the Soviets sponsored a Communist regime in the North at Pyongyang, Korea's oldest city. The United States set up its own regime in the South at Seoul under Syngman Rhee, a right-wing nationalist who had for a long time fostered an independence movement from exile in Hawaii and the American mainland. Fervent patriots both, Kim and Rhee, like their Russian and American backers, held antithetical ideas for unifying the frustrated Koreans.

More than most countries', Korea's history originates from its intermediate location. Largely mountainous, Korea occupies a six-hundred-mile-long peninsula pointed like a dagger away from its continental borders with China and the USSR across the Straits of Tsushima toward Japan to part the Yellow Sea from the Sea of Japan. The peninsula's climate descends dramatically from bitterly cold, dry winters in the north to monsoon rains and almost tropical, summertime conditions in the south. For over half a millenium, from 1392 to 1910, Seoul was the capital of Korea's ruling Yi dynasty. Korea became, during the latter half of this period, a tribute-rendering, vassal state of China's Manchu dynasty. Known as the Hermit Kingdom, Korea closed itself to the world outside.

Nineteenth-century imperial rivalries took over Korea's fate. Czarist Russia's interest stemmed from designs on China, as well as from Vladivostok's strategic location as the terminus for the Trans-Siberian Railway and chief Pacific naval base. In 1876, Meiji Japan forcefully opened Korea to the world, and after 1895, Japan utilized the peninsula as a bridge to East Asia's mainland. After the Russo-Japanese War of 1904–1905, Japan converted Korea into a protectorate, then formally absorbed the ancient kingdom into the Empire of Japan in 1910. Russia's expansionism in East Asia subsided, and terminated almost entirely during the Bolshevik Revolution. Uninterruptedly, as the result, Japan exploited Chosen, as Korea was renamed. From the Korean bridgehead, Japan conquered Manchuria in 1931 and absorbed the newly designated puppet state of Manchukuo into her growing empire. The Chinese Nationalists and Communists posed the only potential threat against Japan's Korean overlordship, until the Allied victory of 1945 transformed the situation. Roosevelt, Churchill, and Chiang, the Big Three leaders at the Cairo Conference of 1943, pledged independence for Korea to follow the war. The USSR blocked their intention, as well as United Nations efforts to hold elections to unify Korea.

In 1948, two rival governments were established, the Republic of Korea in the South and the Democratic People's Republic of Korea in the North. The Russian and American troop withdrawals precipitated their future into the hands of the Koreans themselves. Thereupon, the Truman administration announced that South Korea lay outside the vital defenses of the United States. President Truman and his advisors, including General MacArthur, believed that American air and naval power could sufficiently protect Japan, while South Korea, in their soon-to-be-overturned judgment, afforded "little strategic interest."[2]

Little strategic interest?

To Kim Il Sung, a lifetime opportunity had come. Kim felt certain now that he could unite Korea under Communist auspices with little, if any, risk of American intervention, and very likely Stalin concurred. Kim ordered the North Korean military forces to attack South Korea. Kim blamed South Korea for starting the war. Later, he accused American imperialists of provoking it. In 1990, Li San Cho, a former North Korean ambassador to the USSR living in exile in Moscow, contended that Kim Il Sung made use of a border incident to launch his invasion of the South.

Clashes frequently occurred along the boundary of the thirty-eighth parallel in 1949 and 1950, whenever the two sides probed each other's defenses to stir up guerilla warfare behind the opposing lines. Twice, in

August and October 1949, North Korean forces invaded the Ongjin Peninsula northwest of Seoul on the Yellow Sea, being repulsed only after heavy
fighting. The intelligence officers on MacArthur's staff in Tokyo, who were
responsible for assessing developments across Northeast Asia, discounted
the chronic skirmishing in Korea. They likewise overlooked the North
Korean assault units assembling all along the boundary.

Early Sunday morning, June 25, through driving monsoon rains,
massed North Korean tanks, a motorcycle regiment, several infantry divisions, and an array of amphibious assault units, some 75,000 troops in all,
tore into South Korea. Unforeseen, the invasion shocked United States
government officials, who at first knew next to nothing about the North
Koreans' intentions or even the size of their onslaught. Washington's
sketchy information depended on terse cables sent from Ambassador John
J. Muccio and the Korean Military Advisory Group in Seoul. Even General
MacArthur in Tokyo knew no more. Throughout Sunday in Washington,
thirteen hours behind Korean time, the military brass and foreign-
policymakers feverishly debated how the United States ought to respond,
while they waited for President Truman, summoned from his home in
Independence, Missouri, to arrive. With the crumbling of South Korea's
defense forces, the United States government faced a major crisis.

Obviously, Truman, Acheson, and the Joint Chiefs of Staff had overlooked the nationalistic significance of the Korean people's strivings for
reunification. Compromise between Kim in Pyongyang and Rhee in Seoul
was never possible. Each leader wanted to consolidate Korea, but exclusively on his own terms. By squarely fixing the North Korean invasion
within the context of the Cold War, as unhesitatingly they did, President
Truman and his advisors blamed the Russians for Kim Il Sung's attack, and
accordingly, they jumped to resist it. Although placed outside its defensive
perimeter by the United States government six months earlier, non-
Communist South Korea indisputably lay within the scope of the containment policy formulated to deter any spreading of Soviet influence. A
complete reversal of American policy for Korea promptly took place.[3]

To turn to the United Nations was the first step. Secretary Acheson
called for an emergency session of the Security Council. State Department
officials drafted a resolution to call North Korea to account for breaching the
peace. Explained Ambassador-at-large Philip C. Jessup: "We've got to do
something, and whatever we do, we've got to do it through the United
Nations." Even while President Truman was flying toward Washington, the
Security Council members who were present supported unanimously,
except for Yugoslavia's abstention, the American resolution to condemn
Pyongyang's actions. The USSR, which, as one of the five permanent
members, could have vetoed the United States resolution, was absent,

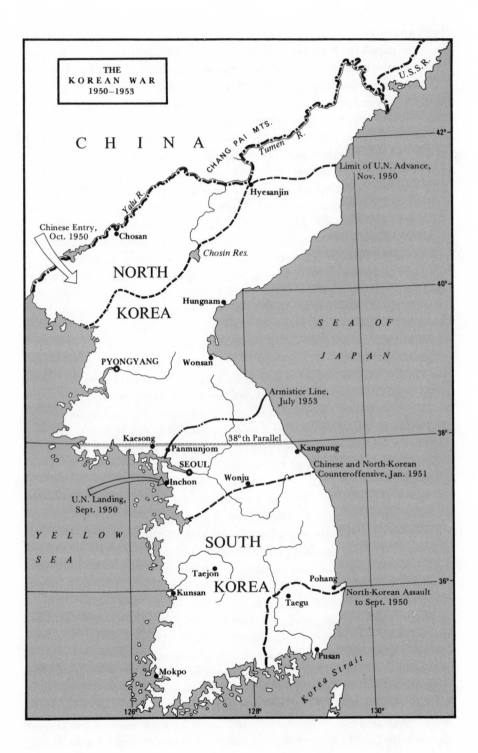

THE
KOREAN WAR
1950–1953

CHINA

CHANG PAI MTS.

Tumen R.

Yalu R.

Limit of U.N. Advance,
Nov. 1950

Hyesanjin

Chinese Entry,
Oct. 1950

Chosan

Chosin Res.

NORTH

KOREA

Hungnam

SEA   OF

JAPAN

PYONGYANG

Wonsan

Armistice Line,
July 1953

Kaesong

38°th Parallel

Panmunjom

Kangnung

SEOUL

Chinese and North-Korean
Counteroffensive, Jan. 1951

Wonju

Inchon

U.N. Landing,
Sept. 1950

YELLOW

SEA

SOUTH

Taejon

Pohang

Kunsan

KOREA

North-Korean Assault
to Sept. 1950

Taegu

Pusan

Korea Strait

Mokpo

U.S.S.R.

42°

40°

38°

36°

126°   128°   130°

maintaining its boycott resulting from the UN's refusal, at American insistence, to expel the Nationalists and seat the Communists in China's place. In his airplane *Independence,* Harry Truman's thoughts turned to history. "Communism was acting in Korea just as Hitler, Mussolini, and the Japanese had acted ten, fifteen, and twenty years earlier," he determined. This time there would be no appeasing the aggressor.

Sunday evening, at Blair House (the White House then undergoing a major restoration), President Truman and his national security councillors met over dinner and afterward to decide what the United States was going to do. No one doubted that Russia had pulled North Korea's puppet strings to launch the invasion of South Korea. Moscow's aggression, they all agreed, must be halted. The sole issue was what and where Russia's next move would be. Hastily, cables urging extraordinary precautions were sent out to all American posts overseas. Acting on his own responsibility as commander-in-chief, President Truman ordered General MacArthur to rush arms from Japan to assist the South Koreans, and to dispatch American warplanes to harass the North Korean invading columns. He also directed the navy to deploy the Seventh Fleet in the Formosa Strait to prevent hostilities breaking out between the two Chinas.

Speaking by radio on Monday morning to an aroused nation, President Truman grimly compared his actions for Korea with his earlier assistance for Communist-threatened Greece. "If we are tough enough now, there won't be any next step," he promised. But the news was ominous. Unchecked by that evening, the North Koreans were overrunning South Korea. Truman ordered American air and sea power into combat below the thirty-eighth parallel. He barred Formosa to mainland Chinese and authorized military assistance for the Philippines and French Indochina.

So far, this was "Mr. Truman's war." He had not, as critics would soon charge, asked Congress to declare war. Yet the public and its representatives apparently supported the decisions that their commander-in-chief was making. The United Nations endorsed yet another United States–sponsored resolution to urge its member states to aid South Korea. Talks commenced on whether American troops ought to be sent. On June 29, Truman ordered American aircraft to attack North Korean installations above the thirty-eighth parallel. To that purpose, he authorized army troops to secure the port of Pusan and a nearby airfield on the southeastern corner of Korea. Next day, on June 30, General MacArthur, after hurriedly visiting the battle zone and observing the disarray of South Korea's nearly leaderless defenders, asked President Truman to send American combat troops into Korea. His decision to do so, Truman would recall in his farewell speech of 1953, "was the most important in my time as President of the United States." By July 1, two reinforced rifle companies of the First Batallion,

Twenty-first Infantry Regiment, Twenty-fourth Division had landed at Pusan. Back home the United States strove to remobilize its martial strength.[4]

The Korean War would last for thirty-seven months. Hardly considered, amid the heated reactions of the moment, were the costs of President Truman's decision to intervene. More than thirty-three thousand Americans would die in the fighting, fifty-four thousand overall, together with untold millions of Koreans and Chinese. Nobody predicted that, four decades after the war's outbreak, Korea would be divided still, with thousands and thousands of American troops on standby alert alongside South Korean soldiers entrenched in deep, defensive positions. To one purpose after another, billions and billions of dollars were authorized, appropriated, and expended, without any end in sight. Nor could it have ever been imagined that the United States would tragically misapply the painful lessons of the Korean War to plunge head over heels into the revolutionary struggles for Laos, Vietnam, and Cambodia far to the south in French Indochina. There the costs would greatly outdistance Korea's.[5]

Until September 1950, victory lay within North Korea's grasp. The outlook for the defenders could scarcely have been bleaker. South Koreans, Americans, and small allied contingents battled against terrible odds to save South Korea from being overrun. The American detachments and the battered South Koreans had to confront nine North Korean divisions counting eighty thousand men. United Nations Secretary General Trygve Lie and President Truman moved in haste to connect the world organization to the battlefield by authorizing a combined command to operate under the United States government. Designated United Nations commander-in-chief, General Douglas MacArthur hoped to operate the port of Pusan until reinforcements could arrive. Hurriedly, he deployed the Eighth Army, then occupying Japan under Lieutenant General Walton H. Walker, to Korea, where, tragically, many of the soldiers, accustomed to peacetime idleness, would soon die for want of rigorous training and well-maintained equipment. President Syngman Rhee ordered his chief of staff to place himself and the army of the Republic of Korea (ROK) under MacArthur's command. The Fifth Regimental Combat Team was sent on its way from Hawaii, while the Second Infantry Division and the First Provisional Marine Brigade embarked from the mainland. While the North Korean army raced toward Pusan, MacArthur proclaimed there would be no "Dunkirk" withdrawal, and Walker ordered his Eighth Army to stand fast and fight. Walker established Pusan's defensive perimeter behind the Naktong River, effective August 1, to enclose a rough rectangle that stretched northward above the seaport for about a hundred miles and inland from the peninsula's east coast for fifty to sixty miles over its length. Walker's fortifications did not embrace continuous, coordinated positions. He organized scattered strong-points backed up by handfuls of local reserves.

The tide commenced to turn. Reinforcements moved up to the front as quickly as they landed. Five hundred newly arrived medium tanks dramatically altered the odds in favor of the American armored units. Naval gunfire shielded the perimeter's seaward flanks, and the air force took advantage of the confined area to afford close, tactical support to the soldiers and marines on the ground. By the end of August, the perimeter's defenders were unmistakably repelling the attackers. The North Korean onslaught raged until September 12, then faltered. The invasion was dribbling to a halt. Almost the entire North Korean army had been beseiging Pusan, and its supply lines were dangerously overextended. For a counteroffensive, the time was ripe.[6]

In a daring amphibious assault on September 15, MacArthur struck at the city of Inchon, the seaport of Seoul. Inchon posed formidable natural and tactical obstacles because of the harbor's prodigious tidal fluctuations. Landing craft could approach only at high water. Then, they must strand themselves vulnerably on the vast mud flats extending out from the shore. There were no beaches. The Fifth Marines (formerly the First Provisional Brigade) scaled the seawall to storm into Inchon, and the First Marines quickly followed. Both regiments dug in to await the counterattack, which never came. The North Koreans were helplessly outflanked. American units now swarmed far to the rear of the enemy troops besieging the Pusan perimeter. Next, the Army's Seventh Infantry Division landed without opposition and raced inland to cut off the North Koreans' escape routes. Beyond Inchon, the marines against bitter resistance plunged into Seoul. By October 1, the capital of South Korea was securely held. Marines fanned out north of the city to block any counteroffensives approaching from Pyongyang.

At Pusan, the weary Eighth Army managed after days of effort to break out of their perimeter onto the attack. The North Koreans began to withdraw on September 23, then completely fell apart. Hurrying northward, columns of Americans and South Koreans rounded up thousands of surrendering enemy soldiers. Near Osan, the First Cavalry Division (Armored) linked hands with the Seventh Infantry. At this juncture, the fighting for South Korea virtually ended. The only job left for the United Nations forces was to guard the North Korean prisoners of war.[7]

Already the United Nations Command had brilliantly accomplished its mission to uphold the Republic of Korea in repulsing North Korea's invasion, although next, being tempted to achieve an all-out triumph, it abysmally floundered. General MacArthur's dazzling victory fashioned by the Inchon landing intoxicatingly precipitated his fateful undoing. On September 11, four days before the Inchon invasion, the National Security Council and President Truman optimistically adopted the recommendation of the Joint Chiefs of Staff that, following the anticipated liberation of Seoul, MacArthur should cross the thirty-eighth parallel to crush the North Korean army and thwart any possibility that Kim Il Sung would reopen his aggression. MacArthur's units would not, they predicted, have to fight either Chinese or Russian soldiers. Yet to allay Chinese fears, only South Korean troops could be permitted to proceed all the way to the Yalu River boundary with Manchuria. Euphorically, after Inchon, Secretary of the Army Frank Pace prepared to shift supplies en route away from their Korean destination and redeploy some troops already there. What occurred next truly was a ninth inning overthrow of an apparently sure thing.

Early in October, MacArthur's soldiers went surging across the thirty-eighth parallel boundary line after the remnants of the North Korean army, at the same time intending to unify the country under Syngman Rhee's leadership. Arrogantly confident, General MacArthur flew off to Wake Island for a meeting with President Truman on October 15, to assure him that neither the Chinese nor the Russians would interfere. Concerning the Chinese, MacArthur declared: "We are no longer fearful of their intervention. . . . Now that we have bases for our Air Force in Korea, if the Chinese tried to get down to Pyongyang there would be the greatest slaughter." The Russians were stronger than the Chinese, but, MacArthur emphasized, they had no troops to spare for a Korean campaign. A problem might arise if the Russians were to provide air support for Chinese ground troops. However, he dismissed the thought: "I believe it just wouldn't work with Chinese Communist ground and Russian air. We are the best." As Truman remembered it, MacArthur promised: "Mr. President, the war will be over by Thanksgiving, and I'll have the American troops back in Tokyo by Christmas." Himself committed to the principle of self-determination, President Truman hoped that the Korean people themselves would at last be allowed to choose their own, presumably anti-Communist, government.[8]

What Douglas MacArthur had failed to grasp was that his army's entry into North Korea convinced the People's Republic of China to intervene to stop him. As emissary Wu Xinchnan would later explain in a speech on November 28, 1950, to the United Nations: "From the very outset the United States armed aggression against Korea gravely threatened China's security. Korea is about 5,000 miles away from the boundaries of the United States. To say that the civil war in Korea would affect the security of the United States is a flagrant, deceitful absurdity. But there is only a narrow river between Korea and China. The United States armed aggression in Korea inevitably threatens China's security." Hurriedly China set up a gigantic ambush.

Nothing of this was known to the Joint Chiefs preoccupied with the European problem. They, like MacArthur, believed the Korean War was just about over.

Worse still, MacArthur's campaign strategy was grievously flawed. Instead of engulfing the fleeing survivors of the Pusan and Inchon reversals, he planned to sweep gloriously over North Korea. He sent General Walton H. Walker's exhausted Eighth Army overland against Pyongyang, and the Tenth Corps into an amphibious flanking assault on the port of Wonsan. By October 26, North Korean opposition seemingly had evaporated. But Mac-Arthur's inexplicable strategy led to logistical nightmares, while his delay in starting wasted the precious time he needed. Though defeated, North Korea's soldiers managed to escape. Frustrated needlessly, even too late to block the North Korean defenders evacuating Pyongyang, MacArthur lifted all restrictions on the deployment of his forces. He recklessly disobeyed instructions forbidding him to move non-Asian troops into the Yalu River region proximate to Manchuria and the USSR. Some Pentagon staff officers realized that MacArthur had lost contact with significant portions of the enemy and faced serious shortages of supplies. But nobody cried alarm. Overall, Washington was ignorant of MacArthur's danger.

But Red China was already intervening. In backing the North Koreans, the Chinese had chosen to gamble their future. They risked global war.

In short order, UN field commanders learned for themselves. A savage counterattack against the Eighth Army's right flank battered the ROK Second Corps. A ROK regiment that had arrived at the Yalu River totally disappeared. The American Eighth Cavalry Regiment, the Tenth Corps, and the marines encountered aggressive resistance. The Seventh Marines at the Chosin Reservoir inflicted heavy casualties but had to fight for their lives before withdrawing.

China's Communist leaders had, in truth, tried to avoid confronting the Americans. Through India's diplomatic offices, the government of China, in late September and again in early October, warned that, if United Nations forces crossed the thirty-eighth parallel, the Chinese army would intervene against them. Foreign Minister Zhou En-lai stressed that China did not fear South Korea, only the United States. Zhou's threat was without delay conveyed through the British Foreign Office to the United States government. Soviet Foreign Minister Andre Vishinsky simultaneously appealed for a cease-fire in Korea, the removal of all foreign troops, and the establishment of a Korean coalition to run the country until elections. Secretary of State Dean Acheson rejected Vishinsky's proposal as a ploy to rescue North Korea's Communists. Over Peking radio, the Chinese restated their warning. Still, no one in authority in Washington or Tokyo conceived that the Chinese could mount a serious challenge. A Central Intelligence Agency estimate on November 6 placed at no more than forty thousand the number of Chinese Communist forces in North Korea, yet urged extreme caution lest the situation deteriorate. Unhelpfully, Major General Charles A. Willoughby, MacArthur's hapless intelligence chief, insisted that these Chinese could never restore Kim Il Sung's regime. MacArthur himself felt certain that China intended merely to safeguard its frontier.

Actually, 180,000 soldiers of the Chinese Fourth Field Army had furtively bridged the Yalu River by November 1 and were massing their formations against the Eighth Army. Marching only late at night and burrowing deep into the forested mountains by day, their sizeable presence was unnoticed by MacArthur's command. Nevertheless, to forestall Chinese reinforcements, MacArthur requested B-29s to bomb the Yalu River bridge at Sinuiju, which the Joint Chiefs at first refused, then consented to do. On November 25, the Chinese Army attacked. General Walker appraised their numbers at 200,000. Certain that China was bent on crushing his United Nations forces, Walker began pulling back toward safety. Defeat followed defeat. There was no stopping the human sea of Chinese. On December 5, Pyongyang was abandoned. Seaborne evacuations from Wonsan and Hungnam rescued 105,000 American and ROK combatants, together with 91,000 terrified North Korean civilians, 17,500 vehicles, and 350,000 tons of supplies. General Walker died in a jeep accident on December 23, as his soldiers retreated pell-mell. At MacArthur's request, Lieutenant General Matthew B. Ridgway, the heroic first commander of the Eighty-second Airborne Division, flew into Korea to take over. MacArthur told him: "The Eighth Army is yours, Matt. Do what you think best." Seoul had to be abandoned again. Below Osan, Ridgway's severely mauled army regrouped.[9]

Consternation reigned at home. Britain's prime minister, Clement Attlee, hastened to Washington. Attlee was highly alarmed by the battlefield setbacks and President Truman's hinted threats to resort, if necessary, to nuclear weapons in Korea. Army Chief of Staff J. Lawton Collins flew across the Pacific Ocean to confer with Douglas MacArthur. Between Attlee and Truman, reason and moderation prevailed. They unhesitatingly revoked MacArthur's plan to unify the Korean peninsula and reinstated the original war aim of merely upholding South Korea. They ordered the United Nations Command to halt the Chinese advance and to negotiate toward ending the warfare. Promptly the UN General Assembly called for a cease-fire. China bluntly refused, demanding instead, as its price, the immediate withdrawal from Korea of all foreign troops. The United States delegation thereupon introduced a resolution to brand Communist China an aggressor, which, though eventually adopted, exceeded the members' endorsement of Truman's and Attlee's scaled-back goals.

MacArthur in Tokyo was demanding major reinforcements meanwhile. He asked Collins for a naval blockade and aerial bombardment of the mainland, as well as permission for Chiang Kai-shek's Nationalist forces to invade South China from Taiwan. Otherwise, he insisted, evacuation from Korea would become mandatory to save his troops. MacArthur's truculence deeply disturbed President Truman and the Joint Chiefs. Within their Cold War strategy, they reconfirmed the newly limited war aims for Korea. Foremost was safeguarding Western Europe's security against the Soviet threat, while the Korean War must only be prosecuted on a prudently lowered flame. To MacArthur, Truman sent a carefully worded, personal letter, hand delivered to him by General Collins and Air Force Chief of Staff Hoyt Vandenberg. The president's letter underscored upholding the Republic of South Korea yet restricting the scope of the war. More important, Collins and Vandenberg determined by personal inspection that Ridgway was revitalizing the Eighth Army and could defend South Korea for so long as he was ordered to do.[10]

It was General Ridgway's war now. A strict disciplinarian, Ridgway had, within two weeks after taking charge, turned the Eighth Army around into a deadly aggressive weapon. The defeated soldiers under his leadership galvanized themselves into a professional army skillfully able to wage war for limited objectives and outwardly indifferent to the enemy's advantage of numbers. The Korean War now became a test of manpower against efficiently manned modern weapons. On February 10, 1951, the First Corps regained the Han River to neutralize Seoul by the recapture of Inchon and Kimpo Airfield. At Chip'yong next, the Twenty-third Infantry Regiment and the French Battalion, surrounded and provisioned solely by air, fought off wave after wave of attackers. Thereupon, the Chinese subsided, enfeebled by prodigious losses and shortages of supplies. As analyst David Rees later on observed, "The UN defense had triumphed, and for the remainder of the Korean War it would remain in the ascendent." Inexorably Matthew Ridgway's front-line "meatgrinder" rolled northward to drive the Chinese, by the end of March, into prepared defenses above the thirty-eighth parallel. MacArthur authorized Ridgway to pursue the Chinese to inflict heavy casualties on them and maintain the initiative. But Ridgway suddenly was appointed commander-in-chief of the Far East and United Nations commands. Lieutenant General James A. Van Fleet, a Second World War corps commander, took charge of the Eighth Army. President Truman, exasperated beyond patience, had fired Douglas MacArthur and summoned him home.[11]

His haughty arrogance and overweening pride brought Douglas MacArthur's downfall. Politics aside, the general and President Truman had clashed repeatedly, first about American policy concerning Taiwan, and second over the restraints imposed on his use of combat power. Still, their disagreements were private, until Red China's intervention in Korea jeopardized not only the UN Command but MacArthur's heroic place in history. When MacArthur complained openly through the press against the strategic restriction leveled on him, he directly challenged President Truman's authority. Sternly Truman, on December 6, issued an executive order aimed at MacArthur, which required all government officials to clear their statements on foreign policy with the Department of State and on military matters with the Department of Defense. But on February 13, 1951, MacArthur publicly declared that, unless he could attack the Chinese in their Manchurian sanctuary, he could never expect to move north of the thirty-eighth parallel to achieve victory, and on March 7, he thundered that a winning strategy for the war against the Chinese was yet to be devised. Both of MacArthur's pronouncements defied President Truman's executive order.

At this moment, President Truman believed the time was ripe to negotiate with the Chinese. Cheered by Ridgway's comeback, the president circulated to MacArthur and the allied leaders a draft proposal for halting the fighting and seeking a peaceful reunification of Korea.

MacArthur undercut the president's initiative. On March 24, he pronounced the Chinese forces incapable of victory and issued an "ultimatum" to end the fighting on United Nations terms: "I stand ready at any time to confer in the field with the commander-in-chief of the enemy." Confused and dismayed, the allied powers questioned who was speaking for the administration. Livid with anger, Truman understood General MacArthur's pronouncement as rank insubordination to his constitutional authority as commander-in-chief. Then MacArthur, in a letter to Joseph W. Martin, the Republicans' minority leader in the House of Representatives, got himself even farther out of step by expressing views on foreign policy clearly at crossed purposes with the president's. He emphasized his resentment of the nation's Cold War strategy by restating his convictions that Asia was as vital as Europe, and that the Korean War must be fought to a victorious conclusion. Martin, on April 5, released MacArthur's letter to the news media. Next day, a furious Harry Truman launched the process of firing MacArthur from his command that culminated on April 11.[12]

As Douglas MacArthur prepared to return to the native land he had never even visited in fourteen years, his resentment at President Truman boiled over. Never once had he disobeyed orders, MacArthur insisted to his staffer William Sebald, and he dismissed as irrelevant his letter to Joseph Martin. His removal he regarded as a part of Washington's underhanded intention to abandon Taiwan to Red China. In that event, he warned, the Philippines would crumble next to communism, and Japan would follow. He warned all who heard him of the darkening prospect for Asia's future.

The United States of America, where MacArthur headed after his long service in Asia, might well seem to him incomprehensibly strange. Upheavals wrought by the Great Depression and the Second World War, technological advances in electronics, medicine, and industrial automation, resentful stirrings of blacks, women, and the beat generation, would more than likely escape not only his sympathy, but even his attention and understanding. A large, friendly crowd bade him farewell from Tokyo. At San Francisco's airport, he answered a journalist's inquiry about his ambitions: "I do not intend to run for any political office. . . . the only politics I have is contained in a simple phrase known to all of you—God Bless America." He announced that all he wanted to do next, now that he had come home, was to see a baseball game and eat a hot dog. If MacArthur was not campaigning for political office, he was perilously close. Enormous crowds surged everywhere he went to catch glimpses of the fallen hero, while vituperative abuse swirled around President Truman for his clumsy dismissal. MacArthur, after all, was the last great commander of the Second World War to return home. Truman justified his action, in a message to Eisenhower at NATO headquarters, as disciplinary and necessary; MacArthur "asked for it, and I had to give it to him."

Not long after MacArthur left Japan, Red China's commanders fired a tremendous ground offensive against the United Nations forces, which Ridgway and Van Fleet, without altering either strategy or tactics, efficiently blocked. The Chinese expected to gain from the confusion following MacArthur's abrupt removal, but they underestimated allied resilience. Bloodily, from late April to the middle of May, the Chinese assaults were contained then beaten back, until their overextended supply lines began to fail under the heavy American pounding. Hungry Chinese soldiers surrendered in droves. The Americans unleashed their counteroffensive and smoothly advanced to the thirty-eighth parallel before halting for political reasons. Now, as the allied command had hoped would occur, Soviet diplomats were proposing talks between the belligerents to end the war. Negotiations got underway in July, in spite of Syngman Rhee's objections. Clearly, neither side wanted to fight any longer for Korean reunification. The talks were to drag on acrimoniously for two years, while outbreaks of bitter fighting would repeatedly interrupt the peacemaking. At home, the public mood turned angry. Born of alarms at communism's growth, the uproar over foreign policy was surging beyond tolerable limits. The firing of MacArthur capped the climax to the shock of Mao's victory in China and the frustrations of the Korean War. The debate swirled furiously, threatening to destroy the political process.[13]

MacArthur's justification of his actions generated a momentary triumph. On invitation, he spoke on April 19 to a special joint meeting of Congress, which was packed, not only by the legislators but by Supreme Court justices, cabinet officers, agency directors, and everyone important or fortunate enough to gain entry into the House of Representatives chamber. MacArthur's old-fashioned oratorical flourishes, authoritatively and resonantly delivered, riveted his audience's attention. His vast audience included millions of radio listeners.

Dramatically, MacArthur ridiculed the Europe-first policy of Truman and Acheson for containing communism. "You cannot appease or otherwise surrender to communism in Asia," he thundered, "without simultaneously undermining our efforts to halt its advance in Europe." Then, sweeping around the geography of the American Pacific like a schoolmaster in a classroom, he indicated the nation's interests most vital for security. Outward, he swept from the Hawaiian and Aleutian islands to Japan, now peaceful and democratic under his benign tutelage, to the brave and loyal Philippine Islands. He charged the administration with cowardly submissiveness to the Red Chinese for refusing either to sustain Chiang Kai-shek's Nationalist government, when it had the opportunity, or to unleash his Taiwan-based army of exiles onto the mainland. Of the fighting in Korea, MacArthur expostulated, "There can be no substitute for victory," and he denounced the combat restrictions imposed on him especially for China's "privileged sanctuaries." Every commander concerned with the Korean struggle, "including our own Joint Chiefs of Staff," claimed MacArthur, agreed with him, as did the Korean people, who entrusted him to deliver their plea to America: "Don't scuttle the Pacific!"

MacArthur's speech was great stuff. Wildly applauding, many tearfully crying, his audience roared its acclaim. Likewise 7.5 million everyday New Yorkers cheered Manhattan's ticker-tape parade. Disillusioned by the downturn of events and President Truman's inability to control them, MacArthur's adoring crowds applauded his simplistic doctrine of determination and duty to defeat communism in Asia and everywhere. Many wondered, at least, if Ambassador Hurley was not right all along about the loyalty of the nation's diplomats, and whether it was true, as California's United States Senator William Knowland had charged, Asia had "been frittered away by a small group of willful men in the Far Eastern Division of the State Department, who had the backing of their superiors."

The Senate's hearings on MacArthur's summary removal and the "Military Situation in the Far East," during May and June, posed a crucial test both for the administration's foreign policy and its outraged detractors. Senator Richard Russell (D–GA) chaired the joint sessions of the Foreign Relations and Armed Services committees.

MacArthur himself, as the first witness, testified for three days. Fault-less, by his own testimony, throughout every aspect of his political, military, and diplomatic conduct, MacArthur blamed his setbacks in Korea on poor intelligence from Washington and on China's "privileged sanctuaries." If he had been authorized to bomb Manchuria, he maintained, he would, with little risk of Moscow's involvement and nuclear conflict, have won the war, unifying Korea under Seoul's government. Again and again, he tried to shift the focus of the inquiry from Korean strategy to Asia's psychology and politics. He recycled his early stereotypes about SCAP's glorious reformation of the Japanese people's immature mentality, and he lamented once more the appearance of Chinese aggressiveness over the traditionally docile, Confucian traits of character. He expressed his confidence that neither China nor Russia would effectively intervene to oppose any American escalation of the Korean War. Republicans wanted Mac-Arthur's testimony to expose Roosevelt and Truman for their alleged softness toward Chinese communism. Democrats hoped the general would convict himself of gross ineptitude.[14]

The Democrats, who were coached by Senator Lyndon Baines Johnson, leveled a courteous, yet carefully synchronized, counterattack. Did he in Tokyo have better intelligence than the State or Defense departments, and if so, why keep it to himself? How did he know how Russia and China might react to American bombs or blockades of Asia's mainland? In view of the Nationalist army's disastrous defeats, what reason was there to deploy them once more against Mao's forces? The Democrats assumed that, as a mere theater commander, General MacArthur would protest that such matters exceeded his responsibility, which indeed they did. And that precisely was their point.

On the issue of strategy for Korea, Secretary of Defense George C. Marshall, who again had been called out of retirement, Secretary of State Dean Acheson, and the Joint Chiefs of Staff, led by Chairman Omar N. Bradley, flatly rejected MacArthur's argument. To expect Chiang Kai-shek's troops to bring about victory was fantastic. Why would the Nationalists fight for Korea more capably than they had fought for their own country? Bradley prophesied that, if unchecked, MacArthur would involve the United States "in the wrong war, at the wrong place, at the wrong time, and with the wrong enemy." Divided themselves, the Republican senators could only belabor the inflammatory theme of Roosevelt's and Truman's alleged treachery toward Chiang Kai-shek. Poor MacArthur! Even his justifiable insistence on the parity of Asia's importance with Europe's for United States foreign policy failed to win agreement. The battering Truman endured failed to turn into MacArthur's gain. True to his promise, the old soldier Douglas MacArthur soon faded away. But the issue of Korea would not.

Since 1950, when Secretary Acheson proclaimed the narrowed outline of the United States' defensive perimeter in the wake of Mao Zedong's takeover of China, the "Asia Firsters" in Congress, sparked by Senator Robert A. Taft (R-OH), "Mr. Republican" himself, had been bitterly attacking the Truman administration's foreign policy. Stimulated by ex-Ambassador Patrick J. Hurley's outcries, Taft claimed that the State Department was staffed by Communists and fellow travelers, who "surrendered to every demand of Russia . . . and promoted at every opportunity the Communist cause in China." Senator Joe McCarthy (R-WI), eager for a reelection issue, took up Taft's cudgel. On June 14, 1951, McCarthy delivered a sixty-thousand-word diatribe in the Senate against MacArthur's critics, in particular Marshall and Eisenhower, who, he proclaimed, comprised "a conspiracy so immense and an infamy so black as to dwarf any such venture in the history of man." Backed by NATO's commander, Dwight David Eisenhower, his "fast rising protégé," present Secretary of Defense General George Catlett Marshall, former army chief of staff and secretary of state, was, according to McCarthy, "with great stubbornness and skill, always and invariably serving the world policy of the Kremlin." Thrown onto the defensive, President Truman stiffened his administration's posture toward Asian communism. On the issues of Taiwan's status and China's United Nations membership, the United States adamantly opposed any alteration to favor Red China and urged the allies to tighten their economic squeeze. In postoccupation Japan, the Americans retained numerous military and naval bases and even began to press the disarmed Japanese to rebuild their armed forces. United States economic assistance to the French, who were fighting the Viet Minh revolutionary movement in Indochina, was dramatically increased.[15]

In July 1951, the negotiations for peace commenced, first at Kaesong, then at a more neutrally accessible site at Panmunjom. The Communists, to strengthen their bargaining position and score propaganda victories, provoked petty incidents one after another that delayed the start of meaningful discussions. Eventually, the United Nations delegation, headed by American Vice-Admiral Turner Joy, and the Communist delegation, headed by North Korean General Nam Il, agreed to an agenda: (1) to fix a demarcation line for establishing a demilitarized zone (DMZ); (2) to set up a supervising body for the cease-fire; (3) to exchange their prisoners of war; and (4) to develop recommendations to the nations involved in the war. Major problems arose from positioning the issue of the demarcation line first on the agenda instead of last, which lured the UN Command into a military stalemate and debilitated its power to bargain. The two sides spent the next twenty months haggling over details, while their infantry units waged a kind of static warfare occasionally punctuated by vicious outbursts.

To regain the initiative, General Ridgway turned his powerful air force and naval aviation squadrons loose. Ridgway's warplanes mounted an "active defense" to maintain the military pressure necessary for supporting his negotiators at Panmunjom. The aircraft methodically attacked North Korea's bridges, highways, seaports, railways, and supply bases. But Ridgway's shift from ground to air action proved a serious tactical error. After December 1951, the North Koreans and Chinese deftly switched from waging a military contest to political warfare. Debating every detail of the agenda, they purposefully dragged out the negotiations while seeking to discredit United Nations efforts in world opinion. They paraded brainwashed prisoners of war to charge the United States with imperialistic warmongering and bacteriological warfare. They encouraged the growing worldwide peace movement to adopt anti-Americanism for its central theme.

While the Panmunjom haggling went on, the war on the ground subsided. Little activity took place other than patrolling beyond the defenses and hurling artillery shells and sniper fire into enemy positions. Under General Van Fleet's guidance, the ROK army grew into a respectable fighting force, able to withstand heavy Communist probings and to give as much as it took. Boredom spiced with danger characterized the lives of most soldiers. Inside United Nations lines, South Korea's villagers strove to pursue time-hallowed ways. Yet, as author Ahn Junghyo depicts them in his antiwar novel, *Silver Stallion*, they could only succumb to outside pressures. American soldiers, noisily waving chocolate bars to corrupt the children and money to overcome the authority of fathers, husbands, and local chieftains, seduced, or on occasion raped, their women. In heavy boots and clothing, they frequented the brothels of "Texas Town," where the prostitutes became known as "Yankee wives."

How to exchange the thousands of prisoners of war now turned into the most perplexing problem. Most prisoners were held in South Korean stockades. The United Nations negotiators insisted on a policy of voluntary repatriation; the Communists wanted all of the captives returned, if necessary by force. To circumvent the impasse, both sides accepted the offer of the International Red Cross to identify those who wanted to go home and those who wished to stay where they were. But the Red Cross's tabulation shocked the Communists. Fewer than half of their soldiers and civilians held by the UN wanted to return home. Blaming the Red Cross and the UN for duplicity, the Reds refused for fifteen months to alter their stand. Then, General Mark Clark, the Second World War commander of the Fifth Army in

Italy, who relieved Ridgway in the summer of 1952, arranged for exchanging the sick and wounded. When both parties agreed that prisoners balking at going home could be handed over to a neutral repatriation commission, a general agreement seemed near. The Americans were weary of the wranglings and longed to sign. Moreover, the Korean War was no longer only "Mr. Truman's war."[16]

General of the Army Dwight David Eisenhower was now President Eisenhower. Eisenhower had enhanced his heroic appeal in the 1952 election campaign by a last-minute promise to go himself to Korea to try to break the stalemate and end the war, if elected. Ike kept his word. Yet no noticeable results appeared after his three-day inspection tour of the battlefront and the negotiations. MacArthur urged Eisenhower to conquer North Korea and to seal off the Chinese border by laying down a cordon of toxic, radioactive waste, but the new president wisely bypassed this bizarre adventure. In March 1953, the death of Stalin led to important changes for both Russia and China. Most likely, the new leaders grasped the opportunity to improve relations with the United States by closing out the Korean War. Whether in fact, as MacArthur's adherents claim, Eisenhower was threatening to escalate the war and even to employ atomic bombs in order to compel the Chinese and North Koreans to agree to peace terms is unclear.

At this point, Syngman Rhee registered his objection. President Rhee was gambling that the United States could never again desert South Korea. To demonstrate his leverage, he caused the stockade gates to be opened, June 18, 1953, to release some 25,000 North Koreans into South Korea, and he persisted, in spite of tighter UN security, to assist anti-Communist prisoners to escape. Exasperated, the United States government met Rhee's price. The deal was costly. The United States promised Rhee a mutual security pact, long-term economic aid beginning with an installment of $200 million, expansion of the ROK army to twenty divisions underwritten by the United States, and policy coordination thereafter between the two governments. While Rhee was winning a major diplomatic victory, the Communists tried for a last-minute battlefield triumph to improve their positions. On July 13, the Reds launched units of five armies at the ROK soldiers defending Kumsong. General Maxwell Taylor, Van Fleet's replacement, countered the Communists' attack but yielded some territory. At last, on July 27, 1953, frustrated though resigned, both sides signed an armistice, ending the Korean War. The last two of the war's three years had been spent trying to end the war. The United States and its UN allies did not win a unified Korea, neither in battle nor at the negotiations, but neither did North Korea and China.[17]

What did the Korean War signify? South Korea was virtually intact, but the peninsula remained bitterly divided. Communist China's international prestige had enormously increased, especially among the nonaligned states of the Third World. To Americans and West Europeans, the revolutionary intrusions of Moscow's "evil empire," to borrow Ronald Reagan's pejorative label, loomed more menacing than ever before. In part at least, owing to its unresolved outcome, the Korean War redefined international relations as a gigantic struggle ongoing between Communist societies and beleagured defenders of the so-called free world. The armistice did end the fighting, yet Korea's north-south division near the thirty-eighth parallel would mockingly serve for the future as a reminder of the original war aims of both the United States and China. Four decades later, the United States continued to deploy over forty thousand soldiers to protect the Republic of South Korea from North Korea. No peace was there, only an armistice.

Bad temper persisted between Red China and the United States. To complete China's reunification, Mao Zedong's government sought to absorb Taiwan once more as an integral province of China. American military units stationed on the island and the navy's mighty Seventh Fleet on patrol in the straits of Taiwan thwarted any prospect of invasion from the mainland and defiantly upheld Chiang Kai-shek's refugee regime. Successive American presidents followed Truman's example by maintaining the containment policy in opposition to the mainland Chinese. Then France, in July 1954, in the wake of her catastrophic defeat by the Viet Minh at Dien Bien Phu, consented to withdraw from Indochina. France's debacle further advanced the cause of communism and enhanced Red China's standing throughout Asia and the remainder of the Third World. Hurriedly, in September, Secretary of State John Foster Dulles wove together a joint defense network, the Southeast Asia Treaty Organization. SEATO embraced, in addition to the United States, Great Britain, France, Australia, New Zealand, the Philippines, Thailand, and Pakistan, and loosely resembled NATO. The United States also concluded, as promised, its mutual security alliances with the Republic of Korea at Seoul and the Taiwan-based Republic of China at Taipei. By 1955, when artillery duels broke out over the Nationalist-held islands of Quemoy and Matsu offshore from the mainland port of Amoy to instigate a new crisis, the United States opposed the Maoist threat with a wide-ranging counteroffensive.[18]

The long ordeal of Vietnam had already begun.

You can kill ten of my men for every one I kill of yours,
but even at those odds you will lose and I will win.

Ho Chi Minh[1]

10

THE VIETNAM WAR

The ordeal over Vietnam began long before most Americans knew where French Indochina was located, and before any suspicion arose that United States militancy in the Cold War against communism might one day involve them there. Such innocence is no surprise. At that distance, vast expanses of geography and history had to be comprehended. The origins of the Vietnam War were rooted, like Korea's conflict, in a civil war, in Vietnam's case in ancient ethnic rivalry and struggles to cast out foreign domination.

Indochina, as its name confides, blended multiple influences from Asia's largest civilizations, India and China. For ages traders, missionaries, and migrants pushed their wares and their faiths into the southeastern corner of Asia, introducing as well their languages, arts, and customs. Topographically the Indochina Peninsula features bewildering upheavals of peaks above plateaus, and climatically a tropical monsoon climate diversified sharply by local conditions. To the northeast is the delta of the Red River. In landlocked Laos and southward into Vietnam and Cambodia, the plateaus are ravaged by deep-cutting tributaries of the Mekong River flowing through thick forests to the alluvial and coastal plains. The earliest Austronesian tribes were overwhelmed long ago by the Khmer or Cambodians, who may have originated in western India, by the Lao from China's Yunnan province, who ethnically descended from the Thai, and by the Vietnamese from the lower Yangtze valley. Scattered remnants of aborigines have precariously survived into the present era in mountainous pockets harassed by their inveterate foes. Buddhism prevails, but its observance incorporates indigenous elements of Taoism, Confucianism, ancestor reverence, and animism.

The Vietnamese brought their labor-intensive system of wet rice agriculture from China. Growing wet rice depends on intensive irrigation and elaborate cooperation among the villagers. From time to time, Chinese emperors annexed Vietnamese territory, superimposing Confucian traditions atop tribute-exacting layers of bureaucracy, but the Vietnamese stubbornly maintained their distinctive identity. Like stones in fortress walls, Vietnam's rural villages, whenever threatened, afforded contiguous barriers of communal resistance to any invaders, even when the people's proclivities for unity succumbed to the competition for power among their leading families. Typically, the contest between North Vietnam and South Vietnam, after the French departed in 1954, reflected historic animosities tinted by the Cold War's ideological imperatives.

From 1862 to 1893, during Asia's colonization by the Western powers, France pieced together its Southeast Asian holdings to consolidate the confederation of Indochina. *Indochine Français* comprised, in order of takeover, Cochin China, Cambodia, Annam, Tonkin, and Laos. Hanoi in Tonkin was Indochina's capital city, a French governor-general the ruling executive. When France fell before Hitler's blitzkrieg in 1940, Japanese armed forces entered northern Indochina, and one year later, they advanced into the south. The United States, as we know, regarded Japan's movements as direct threats to the stability of the Pacific. Upon the freezing of Japan's assets in the United States, the two powers veered undeviatingly toward Pearl Harbor. French administrators continued to govern Indochina in a puppet regime under Japan's military control until the Japanese authorities, early in 1945, preemptively dislodged them. Then, in Paris, the government of liberated France announced its intention to incorporate Indochina into the newly proclaimed French Union, somewhat like a dominion of the British Empire. Cambodia and Laos accepted the proposal, but Vietnamese nationalists, led by Ho Chi Minh, himself a Communist, demanded full independence for Tonkin, Annam, and Cochin China as Vietnam.

When the Japanese gave up in August 1945, the independence-minded Vietnamese took over their country's government in Hanoi. On September 2, the date of Japan's formal surrender, Ho Chi Minh proclaimed the sovereignty of the Democratic Republic of Vietnam.

The son of an ardently patriotic mandarin, Ho Chi Minh became the father of his country. Ho had lived and worked in France for over twenty years within a colony of expatriate Vietnamese nationalists. In June 1919, Ho appealed to Secretary of State Robert Lansing, at the Paris Peace Conference, for support from the United States for the Indochinese people against French "terrorization and oppression." Following Lansing's rebuff, Ho joined the French Communist party. The Communists struck him as the only genuine antiimperialists. Known as Nyguyen Ai Quoc (Nyguyen the Patriot), he underwent training in the Soviet Union, then worked in succession for revolution in China, Thailand, and Vietnam. He launched the Indochinese Communist party in 1930, then provoked a sequence of nationalist uprisings that the French authorities brutally crushed. He came home to stay when the Japanese moved their troops into Vietnam. Unequaled at organizing, gentle in manner, and almost skeletally thin, Ho Chi Minh was a cold-blooded, intensely patriotic revolutionary. His Viet Minh (officially *Viet Nam Doc Lap Dong Minh*), the League for the Independence of Vietnam, a coalition of Communists and nationalists, grew under his inspiration into the spearhead of independence.

Vietnam's time was ripe. Japan's easy displacement of the French humbled their former overlords in the eyes of the Vietnamese. The maltreatment of the populace by the Japanese and their French hirelings, aggravated by a severe famine, fostered even angrier resentments. In the north, Ho Chi Minh and Vo Nyguyen Giap, a former history professor, marshaled five thousand Viet Minh guerrillas, who, upon Japan's deposing the French administration in March 1945, doggedly began to torment the Japanese. The Viet Minh warriors, with supplies and provocateurs infiltrated by the U.S. Office of Strategic Services (OSS, the CIA's predecessor), made life miserable for the Japanese in their final days in Indochina. One OSS agent heard Ho Chi Minh praise American ideals and predict United States support for Vietnam's freedom after the war.

On V-J Day, to a joyous throng of more than half a million people in Ba Dinh Square in Hanoi, Ho Chi Minh, as provisional president, proudly introduced the Democratic Republic of Vietnam. A handful of United States Army officers stood behind him on the platform. A band played "The Star-spangled Banner." Ho's declaration of independence closely paralleled the earlier American and French proclamations. Ho quoted Jefferson's immortal passages: "All men are created equal. They are endowed by their Creator with certain unalienable rights. Among these are life, liberty, and the pursuit of happiness." Broadly, this means, Ho explained: "All peoples on earth are equal from birth; all the peoples have a right to live, to be happy and free." Thereupon, General Giap hailed the Vietnamese republic's "particularly intimate relations" with the United States as "a pleasant duty to dwell upon." OSS agents counseled Washington that the Vietnamese were unalterably "determined to maintain their independence, even at the cost of their lives."[2]

However, the Truman administration spurned this opportunity for achieving peace and unity in Southeast Asia by consenting to the return of French authority over Vietnam, Laos, and Cambodia. Then, from 1950 to 1954 in the First Indochina War, the United States bankrolled France's military effort to restore her Indochinese empire, an investment that turned unwittingly into the first major American steps toward waging the Vietnam War. From 1950 to 1975, six presidents from Truman to Ford pursued the Cold War against international communism, as each one of them understood it, in Vietnam, Laos, and Cambodia. Since all of them would sidestep, as inconsequential or secondary, the nationalistic and ethnic strivings of the Indochinese peoples themselves, the outcome was foredoomed. No greater irony can be imagined than the unchecked disintegration of the Viet Minh's original friendship for Americans into bloody hostility.

Communism was the problem, of course. The State Department hoped to reinstate France in Indochina to forestall Russian influence. President Roosevelt, though personally more than willing to see the despised French lose their empire, never seriously considered Indochina's fate, except for expressing vague notions about an international trusteeship. At Yalta, Roosevelt kept his feelings to himself, because Churchill, it was clear, adamantly opposed any policy for Asia that might by its precedent undercut Britain's rule in India. Roosevelt conceded the postwar reconstruction of French Indochina on open door principles, which Ho Chi Minh's partisans could scarcely approve. At Potsdam, President Truman and Prime Minister Attlee agreed for convenience to divide Vietnam along the sixteenth parallel, with the British to occupy Saigon in the south and Chinese Nationalists to occupy Hanoi in the north. The United States avoided any direct participation, not even objecting when the British turned over some of their own Lend-Lease equipment to French military units for hasty transfer to Indochina. Thereby French authority, aided by British military intervention and American forbearance, returned to Indochina.

Helpless to prevent this development, the Viet Minh accepted "free" status in the French Union in March 1946. French armored columns swept northward from Saigon to take control of Hanoi from the Chinese. General Charles DeGaulle's government in Paris had no intention of granting home rule to the Vietnamese. Soon Viet Minh soldiers clashed with their reinstated masters. French naval guns bombarded the port city of Haiphong, killing thousands of civilians. Viet Minh guerrillas went into action. For eight years, Vietnam would be convulsed by Ho Chi Minh's efforts to expel the French.

Officially, the United States dismissed Indochina as France's problem. Ho Chi Minh wrote a series of letters to President Truman and administration leaders requesting support for the Viet Minh, but he never received a response. Ho Chi Minh's long-standing Communist affiliations cooked his goose in Washington's estimation. The Department of State by 1947 classi-fied Ho as an "agent of international communism." A number of Foreign Service officers saw Ho as an independent Asian, possibly likening him to Tito of Yugoslavia, but above all else, they defined him as a nationalist. In the near-hysteria over the Communists' takeover of China, Secretary of State Acheson settled the issue by pegging Ho Chi Minh categorically as an "outright Commie." When the French reinstalled Bao Dai as their puppet emperor of Vietnam in February 1950, Washington recognized this dissi-pated playboy and Japanese collaborator as legitimate. In June and July, jolted by the Korean War, the American government's equivocation over Vietnam ceased. The Truman administration dispatched a cadre of advisors and supplies and equipment costing $150 million to bolster the French. Thereafter, the ante rose steeply. By 1954 when the French gave up, the United States had contributed two billion of the five billion dollars expended to hold Vietnam in the French Union.

In March 1954, nearly fifty thousand of General Vo Nyguyen Giap's Viet Minh guerillas trapped thirteen thousand French airborne troops at Dien Bien Phu, a former French base in northwest Vietnam near the border of Laos. Desperately France pleaded for American intervention. President Eisenhower and his aides sharply disagreed over what to do. Vice-President Richard M. Nixon and Secretary of State John Foster Dulles urged sending a large-scale American expedition into Indochina, which Army Chief of Staff Matthew B. Ridgway opposed. Eisenhower appealed to Prime Minister Churchill, who had regained his wartime office, for "united action" to save the French. Eisenhower cited the "falling domino principle" to predict a dire succession of Communist seizures of power in Burma, Thailand, Malaya, and Indonesia if Vietnam should fall. In rebuffing Eisenhower's proposi-tion, Churchill expressed his firm doubts that the French could be rescued. The congressmen consulted, wary of another Korean imbroglio, likewise urged on the president a policy of caution. On May 7, the French defenders at Dien Bien Phu capitulated. France's new government, headed by Pierre Mendes-France, promised to stop the war at once. Ho Chi Minh's forces dominated two-thirds of Vietnam.[3]

The Viet Minh were assured at last of widespread diplomatic recogni-tion. France and the powers involved, including Russia, Britain, China, the United States themselves, and the Indochinese states, agreed provisionally at Geneva to terms for the future: (1) Vietnam would be divided temporarily along a demilitarized zone at the Seventeenth Parallel, and the French would withdraw below that line to shelter Bao Dai's Saigon regime. (2) Neither North Vietnam nor South Vietnam was to enter any military alliance, nor to allow foreign bases on Vietnam's territory. (3) Elections were planned to be held in 1956 to unify Vietnam, and elections would also be held in Laos and Cambodia as independent states. The United States refused to subscribe to the Geneva accords because of the Red scare's lingering alarms. Fearing McCarthyite or "Asia First" outcries, Secretary of State John Foster Dulles conspicuously absented himself from the negotiations, yet the Eisenhower administration promised to abide by the results if the elections were supervised fairly by the United Nations. The National Security Council characterized the agreements as a "major forward stride of communism, which may lead to the loss of Southeast Asia." The NSC's viewpoint prevailed. The alarm was growing that China and Russia would attempt to win over all Vietnam toward their presumed goal of worldwide Communist domination.

Unwilling to take chances, President Eisenhower flung up the barricades. Dulles and his allies assembled the Southeast Asia Treaty Organization in September 1954 to shield Cambodia, Laos, and southern Vietnam from Communist seizures. Imposed against the Geneva settlement, SEATO was intended to shelter South Vietnam virtually as a sovereign state. Meanwhile, as many as a million refugees from the north, most of them French acculturated, anti-Communist Roman Catholics, relocated themselves within the largely Buddhist south. In South Vietnam, the United States invested its hopes behind the non-Communist government of Premier Ngo Dinh Diem. Himself a Roman Catholic mandarin, Ngo Dinh Diem returned to Vietnam from exile in the United States in time to wreck the vestigal authority of Emperor Bao Dai. Diem refused to participate in planning the nationwide election scheduled for 1956 by the Geneva accords. Equally apprehensive that Ho Chi Minh would win any popularity contest, the Eisenhower administration concurred and instigated measures to strengthen Diem's government. American arms, economic assistance, and advisory personnel of many descriptions began flowing into South Vietnam. Washington also mounted support for the conservative Boun Oum regime in neighboring, landlocked Laos, where family disputes mostly defined politics, against the Communist, Viet Minh-backed Pathet Lao. "The important thing," John Foster Dulles declared, was to look optimistically ahead, "not to mourn the past, but to seize the future opportunity to prevent the loss in Northern Vietnam from leading to the extension of communism throughout Southeast Asia and the Southwest Pacific."[4]

But it was easier said than done, if only because the hostility between Red China and the United States deepened. American protection for Chiang Kai-shek on Taiwan, the wielding of the veto power of the United States to block the Beijing government from taking over China's seat in the United Nations, and the bloody warfare in Korea sustained the gravest threat of war. To the Communists, Chiang Kai-shek represented the possibility of a counterrevolution, and year after year Chiang, who was supported throughout the 1950s by an average annual American assistance program of $250 million, pledged to invade the mainland to overthrow them. In 1953, President Eisenhower "unleashed" the Nationalists, who proceeded to mount aerial pinpricks on China's coastal cities. In 1954, the United States signed a mutual defense treaty with the exiled Republic of China, and Congress overwhelmingly approved the "Formosa Resolution" to authorize the use of American troops if necessary to defend the island. In 1957, the United States stationed missiles on Taiwan capable of carrying nuclear warheads.

The tiny offshore islands of Quemoy and Matsu sparked major alarms in 1954–1955 and again in 1958. Chiang heavily fortified the islands and increased the defensive garrisons from sixty thousand to one hundred thousand troops. Both sides loudly threatened each other with invasions but merely exchanged thunderous barrages of artillery shells. President Eisenhower promised to defend Quemoy and Matsu. As Vice-President Nixon explained, these tiny islands were vital outposts in the defense of freedom against international communism. In 1958, Eisenhower insisted that to abandon Quemoy and Matsu would cause a "Western Pacific Munich," while Mao's government claimed "every right to deal resolute blows and take necessary military action" to oust the Nationalists from the islands. Once more China and the United States stepped back from the brink, but the antagonism remained. "Who would have thought that when we fired a few shots at Quemoy and Matsu," exclaimed Mao, "that it would stir up such an earth-shattering storm?"[5]

Twice in Laos, in 1958 and 1960, the White House vented displeasure at Prince Souvanna Phouma's nonaligned government, a coalition of nationalists and the Communist Pathet Lao, by unleashing the CIA to overthrow him. "The Americans say I am a Communist," cried Souvanna Phouma in fleeing his country. "All this is heartbreaking. How can they think I am a Communist? I am looking for a way to keep Laos non-Communist." Souvanna Phouma's mistake lay in evenhandedly accepting assistance from China and the Soviet Union to offset American patronage. Intolerant of such neutralist double-dealing, President Eisenhower and Secretary Dulles obtained funding from Congress for a major investment in the right-wing Laotian army, which by 1961 would reach the total of $300 million. Eisenhower declared: "The fall of Laos to Communism would mean the subsequent fall—like a tumbling row of dominoes—of its still-free neighbors, Cambodia and South Vietnam and, in all probability, Thailand and Burma. Such a chain of events would open the way to Communist seizure of all Southeast Asia."

President John F. Kennedy, Eisenhower's successor, saw Laos in much the same light. To demonstrate his opposition to the Soviet-backed Pathet

Lao, Kennedy ordered units of the Seventh Fleet to deploy southward off the Indochina coast. He alerted the troops on Okinawa and flew five hundred marines into Thailand just below the Laotian border. The several hundred American operations specialists already in Laos conspicuously donned their military uniforms. But the Bay of Pigs fiasco in Fidel Castro's Cuba abruptly diverted the superpowers to the mushrooming Caribbean problem. Fortunately, the Soviets consented to President Kennedy's appeal to negotiate a cease-fire for Laos, and at Geneva in June 1962, after a year of hard bargaining, the powers agreed to neutralize Laos under a coalition government. Souvanna Phouma once again took charge as prime minister. The distinction between the earlier neutralist regime that Eisenhower undermined and the Geneva-sponsored government of 1962 was glaringly evident, as French correspondent Bernard Fall acidly observed: "Instead of two communists in Cabinet positions, there would be four now; instead of having to deal with 1,500 poorly armed Pathet Lao fighters, there were close to 10,000 now well-armed with new Soviet weapons." Not surprisingly, both sides violated the Geneva settlement. The Pathet Lao continued to fight underground, and Washington covertly dispatched arms to Souvanna Phouma's faction. Then, in escalating his struggle against North Vietnam in 1964, President Lyndon B. Johnson authorized secret bombing raids against Pathet Lao forces. Not before 1974, when Souvanna Phouma signed a cease-fire pact with the Pathet Lao and American participation in the Vietnam war had virtually ceased, did the bloodshed in Laos end.

At the outset, however, John F. Kennedy had appeared more worried by Vietnam than the Laotian entanglement. "This is the worst we've got, isn't it?" he questioned Walt W. Rostow, the chairman of the State Department's policy planning council. "You know, Eisenhower never mentioned it. He talked at length about Laos, but never uttered the word Vietnam." Ike's silence was beside the point. Long ago, in 1956, when he was the junior senator from Massachusetts, Kennedy had lauded the non-Communist South Vietnam as "the cornerstone of the Free World in Southeast Asia, the keystone to the arch, the finger in the dike." On Laos, Kennedy was possibly dissembling for Rostow's benefit.[6]

Both Vietnams received major backing from the superpowers. In Hanoi, the Viet Minh government played off Russia and China against each other for maximum benefit, while Ngo Dinh Diem's regime in Saigon was getting about $300 million annually from the United States, mainly as military equipment. Prime Minister Diem repeatedly avoided Washington's urgings to mend his government's corrupt, repressive, and brutal ways. The Viet Minh sensed an opportunity in the growing unrest of South Vietnam's populace to organize its National Liberation Front in December 1960, which Diem pejoratively labeled the "Viet Cong," meaning Vietnamese Communists. Gullibly thereafter, the United States government downplayed the people's resentments against Diem's high-handed authority, characterizing the Viet Cong almost exclusively as Moscow's and Beijing's latest ploy.

Nor was President Kennedy immune. In spite of an extraordinary sense of history, he himself bore, in the apt term of James C. Thomson, Jr., "the legacy of the 1950s." Together with many Americans, the president painfully recalled the loss of China and the frustration of the Korean War. Smoldering residues from McCarthy's Red scare and Dulles's anti-Communist crusade could still roil his otherwise coldblooded political equilibrium. That communism was a Moscow-based conspiracy striving to undermine freedom and democracy everywhere, to topple governments like dominoes one after another while directing Red China's moves against Indochina, was a widely held viewpoint that Kennedy himself shared. His mindset guided him to strengthen SEATO, withhold recognition from Mongolia as Soviet-dominated, and expand Eisenhower's commitment to South Vietnam. Kennedy's willingness to raise the stakes in Asia also reflected the eagerness of his whiz-kid advisors to apply their novel theories of counterinsurgency to defeat the Viet Cong at guerrilla warfare. Although Kennedy was distracted by the Bay of Pigs invasion in Cuba and Kruschev's blustering over Berlin, he proceeded with caution deeper into Vietnam. Ike's concern over Laos made him wary of repeating France's misadventure in Indochina. Kennedy, moreover, distrusted Prime Minister Ngo Dinh Diem and Ngo Dinh Nhu, Diem's sinister brother, who controlled Saigon's security apparatus.

Yet Kennedy's escalation was evident. In January 1961, immediately after his inauguration, he approved funds to enlarge South Vietnam's army. In May, he sent Vice-President Johnson off on a fact-finding mission to evaluate conditions in Vietnam and Laos. In Saigon Johnson ostentatiously acclaimed Prime Minister Diem as the Winston Churchill of Asia, but he conceded on returning to Washington that his Texas-style exaggeration meant that Diem was "the only boy we got out there." Significant for the future, nonetheless, was Johnson's personal estimate that Vietnam and Thailand, not Laos, were "crucial" for the security of the free world. Vietnam and Thailand were threatened by an externally directed Communist conspiracy, argued Johnson, and the United States must help them "to the best of our ability." In October, President Kennedy sent out General Maxwell Taylor and Walt Rostow, his war hawks, to study the Viet Cong danger. Intelligence estimates counted seventeen thousand Viet Cong guerrillas, mostly local southerners. Taylor and Rostow urged Kennedy to send combat forces against them. Secretary of Defense Robert S. McNamara, Kennedy's chief whiz-kid, and the Joint Chiefs of Staff concurred. In November, in a further violation of the Geneva accords, Kennedy committed his administration to a sharp increase in American "advisors" in Vietnam. From 900 advisors when he assumed the presidency, the numbers jumped to 3,205 in December, to 9,000 by the end of 1962, and to 16,700 by November 1963 operating in direct combat-support functions.[7]

The problems multiplied. The "strategic hamlet" program, introduced in 1962, sought to forestall the Viet Cong from getting supplies and shelter from the peasants. Uprooted overnight by Diem's troops from their ancestral villages, South Vietnam's peasants found themselves being herded into some six thousand fortified hamlets ringed by barbed wire and bamboo spears. Diem's derangement of village life alienated the people whose support he needed. Rioting broke out next in the towns and cities as American-trained South Vietnamese Special Forces killed a number of unarmed Buddhists protesting Diem's decree against flying Buddhist flags. Buddhism at this juncture became an important vehicle for Vietnamese nationalism. Although South Vietnam was preponderantly a Buddhist land, the Catholic Christians dominating its government upheld the vestiges of French colonial rule. Prime Minister Diem, himself a Catholic, equated the Buddhist opposition to his government with revolutionary communism. Before horrified onlookers on a Saigon streetcorner in June 1963, an elderly Buddhist monk doused himself with gasoline and torched himself to death. Additional protests followed. Six more monks immolated themselves. Ghoulishly, Diem's sister-in-law, Madame Nhu, scoffed at these "Buddhist barbecues." The Diems unleashed military raids on Buddhist pagodas in Hué, Saigon, and other places. Sickened by the scenes on television, millions of American viewers expressed their outrage. President Kennedy publicly rebuked the Diems and briefly reduced aid to South Vietnam in pressing them for reform.

On November 1, 1963, rebellious South Vietnamese military officers seized and murdered Prime Minister Ngo Dinh Diem and his hated brother, Ngo Dinh Nhu. The leaders of the coup had disclosed their intentions to CIA agents but suffered no discouragement whatever from Ambassador Henry Cabot Lodge. Madame Nhu bitterly castigated United States officials for allegedly inciting the assassinations of her husband and his brother. Three weeks later, on November 22, John Fitzgerald Kennedy was also assassinated. Whether or not Kennedy could have avoided Vietnam's quicksands, or whatever he might have done if he had lived, can never be known. But President Kennedy passed on to Lyndon Baines Johnson a much deeper Vietnamese mess than he had himself inherited. President Johnson reaffirmed the policies of his slain predecessor concerning Vietnam and instructed all government agencies to support the nation's commitments there. The National Security Council, in National Security Council Action Memorandum 273 of November 26, 1963, transformed Johnson's

THE
VIETNAM WARS
1950–1975

243

pledge into the government's central objective to assist the South Vietnamese "to win their contest against the externally directed and supported communist conspiracy."[8]

That was not all.

Lyndon Baines Johnson opted to expand the nation's limited enterprise in Vietnam into an open-ended full-scale war to sustain the independent, anti-Communist government in Saigon. In making Vietnam into a terrible tragedy, Johnson would eventually destroy his presidency. So would President Nixon, his successor, though for dissimilar motives and an unlikely outcome. Yet President Johnson's policies for Vietnam scarcely deviated, except in magnitude, from the goals of his three predecessors— Truman, Eisenhower, and Kennedy. Like them, he sought to contain communism in Indochina. Johnson, in fact, depended for advice on Kennedy's ablest and closest counselors, especially Robert S. McNamara, Dean Rusk, Walt Rostow, and McGeorge and William Bundy. Ardent cold warriors of the White House inner circle, these dedicated public servants were, in David Halberstam's indelible characterization, "the best and the brightest." Together they held an almost unshakable faith in both the anti-Communist goals of containment and the Rand Corporation's escalation theory as the most efficient means for achieving them. The inconceivability of an American defeat virtually guaranteed that their recommendations to the president would prove to be, in James C. Thomson's devastating judgment, "regularly and repeatedly wrong." Escalation theory, like gambling with dice, dealt only with the odds and probabilities of succeeding by increasing or reducing the stakes and, therefore, the quotient of pain. Escalation never dealt with certainties, nor seriously enough with the possibility of failure.

For over a decade, from the initial engagements to the loss of Saigon to the Communists, the Vietnam War dominated the life of the United States and grew in time to divide the American people more angrily than any other issue since the Civil War. Controversy still plagues the history of the war. As Leslie H. Gelb and Richard K. Betts wrote in *The Irony of Vietnam:* "One picks away at the debris of evidence only to discover that it is still alive, being shaped by bitterness and bewilderment, reassurances and new testimony." The controversy first made headlines in the wake of the Buddhist crisis, when plucky newsmen on the scene, led by David Halberstam, Neil Sheehan, Stanley Karnow, and Bernard Kalb, disputed the Defense and State departments' claims of victory to report that the strategic hamlet program and the South Vietnamese army (ARVN) positions in the vital Mekong Delta were actually disintegrating against a powerful guerrilla buildup in battalion strengths. Once the "credibility gap" appeared, it never went away.

Nonetheless, in the stunned aftermath of Kennedy's assassination, President Johnson laid out his course of action—continuity, unity, and reconciliation. He set up a blue-ribbon commission to investigate the president's murder. He fired the opening salvos of the war against poverty, pressed for a tax cut, and determined to integrate civil rights. He knew that the grief at the memory of his martyred predecessor constituted his strongest political asset. Lyndon Johnson took "Let us continue" for his opening theme in his first presidential speech to Congress on November 27, an evocative twist on Kennedy's inspiring appeal, "Let us begin," to get America moving again.

South Vietnam's political turmoil and the worrisome increase of guerrilla warfare led to warnings in December by Johnson's foreign policy advisors, all of them Kennedy appointees, that unless these matters were brought under control an early victory for the Communists was predictably in the cards. They urged Johnson to retaliate with bombings against North Vietnam and to deploy American combat troops against the Viet Cong guerrillas in the South. That Johnson would in fact heed their advice did not mean, as critics later charged, that the formidable brilliance of McNamara, Rusk, Rostow, and the Bundy brothers intimidated him. He himself agreed with their analysis of the problems of containing communism in Vietnam, while, during the next three months, the situation worsened.[9]

In January 1964, General Nguyen Khanh, a young field commander, overturned the junta that had ousted the Diem brothers, and once again, this time in touting Khanh as his hope for stabilizing Saigon politics, Ambassador Lodge deceived himself. To Lodge, Vietnam was still only an operational problem. As he stated:

> We have everything we need in Vietnam. The United States has provided military advice, training, equipment, economic and social help, and political advice. The government of Vietnam has put a relatively large number of good men into important positions and has evolved civil and military procedures that seem to be workable. Therefore, our side knows how to do it. We have the means with which to do it. We simply need to do it. This requires a tough and ruthless commander. Perhaps Khanh is it.

Secretly, President Johnson turned up the heat. The Pentagon's Operation Plan 34A prepared to Americanize the struggle: (1) to conduct covert attacks on North Vietnam using South Vietnamese and Chinese Nationalist troops; (2) to replace the overoptimistic General Paul D. Harkins with a new commander, who must prepare bases for the arrival of American combat soldiers; (3) to retaliate against any North Vietnamese counterattacks for the covert actions, then shift by stages to sustained bombing of the North; (4) to use the arriving forces to defend the new bases and win control over the countryside; and (5) to obtain an open-ended resolution from Congress tantamount to a declaration of war and the essential appropriations. Contingency plans for retaliatory air strikes were drawn up. A supportive resolution was drafted to submit to Congress whenever opportune. In June, General William C. Westmoreland, one of Maxwell Taylor's soldier bureaucrats, assumed command of more than sixteen thousand American military advisors in South Vietnam. Antiwar demonstrations commenced with the May 2 movement in New York City and soon spread into a number of American cities. Next, in a "battle" on August 2 and 4 that very likely never took place, two destroyers, USS *Maddox* and *Turner Joy*, reportedly skirmished against North Vietnamese PT boats. President Johnson went on national television and denounced Hanoi's "attacks." United States Navy carrier-based airplanes raided North Vietnam in retaliation. Within three days with only two dissenting votes (Senators Wayne Morse of Oregon and Ernest Gruening of Alaska), a patriotically aroused Congress whooped through its Gulf of Tonkin Resolution, the administration document previously prepared, giving the president authority "to take all necessary steps including the use of armed force" to conduct the war.[10]

In the fall of 1964, for the first time but not the last, Vietnam became a presidential election issue. Vietnam threatened to sidetrack President Lyndon Johnson's dream of a Great Society. Johnson's platform for the Great Society proposed a utopian welfare state to assure civil rights, education, economic opportunity, and health care for all Americans. Divided over these domestic issues, Democrats and Republicans alike favored the nation's intervention against communism in Vietnam. The two parties differed only over the extent of the intervention and the methods to apply, but neither openly sought to widen the war. To the voters, President Johnson offered himself as the "peace candidate." He conducted an antiwar campaign against Senator Barry Goldwater, his hapless war hawk opponent, who was scorning the administration's efforts in Vietnam as a "no-win" policy. Johnson cunningly taunted Goldwater as a "mad bomber" brandishing nuclear weapons and, like Woodrow Wilson in 1916 and Franklin Roosevelt in 1940, pledged himself never to order United States troops into foreign combat. "We're not about to send American boys nine or ten thousand miles away from home to do what Asian boys ought to be doing for themselves," Johnson promised. Trusting him and fearing his fire-breathing rival, the voters on Election Day gave Johnson a smashing mandate to lead the country in his own right to victory on all fronts—toward the Great Society at home and a non-Communist Vietnam.

Hardly anyone could imagine that President Johnson had already authorized massive bombings of North Vietnam to follow his election, or that, during the four years of his second term, he would send 2.5 million American boys to Vietnam. Nor could anyone suspect that "Americanization" of the war in Vietnam would undo his cherished Great Society. He wanted the Great Society for the American people plus a victory over communism in Vietnam. His popular acclaim, he was certain, would exceed both FDR's and JFK's. Instead Lyndon Johnson contrived his own ruin. Supplies and military units arriving via the "Ho Chi Minh Trail" to bolster the Viet Cong were already spreading havoc throughout South Vietnam.[11]

Theory now escalated into practice. By early 1965, the twenty-three thousand American advisors had suffered serious casualties. Air force, marine, and navy aircraft were retaliating in force, attacking military depots and transportation lines across North Vietnam. The president approved the use of napalm. The United States built up its troop strength in Vietnam to 180,000. This figure doubled in 1966, and by 1967, the total of uniformed personnel went soaring toward an authorized one-half million. At Johns Hopkins University on April 7, 1965, Lyndon Johnson explained why Americans were fighting in Vietnam: "We want nothing for ourselves— only that the people of South Vietnam be allowed to guide their own country in their own way." Johnson promised that, with peace and stability restored, he would ask Congress to appropriate one billion dollars to develop the vast Mekong River to provide food, water, and power for the Indochinese peoples on a scale that would surpass even the Tennessee Valley Authority. But in the nation's capital, twenty-five thousand dissenters marched against the war in a protest demonstration called by the Students for a Democratic Society. Unswayed, Secretary of Defense Robert S. McNamara urged substantially larger military actions against the Viet Cong in the South and the Viet Minh in the North. Undersecretary of State George Ball disagreed, arguing that Saigon government forces were losing the war against the guerrillas. "No one can assure you that we can beat the Viet Cong or even force them to the conference table on our terms, no matter how many hundred thousand white, foreign troops we deploy." At this point, Secretary of State Rusk rattled the dominoes to insist, "If the Communist world finds out that we will not pursue our commitments to the end, I don't know where they will stay their hand." The deliberations subsided.

President Johnson forged onward, hewing to the course laid out for him by Truman, Eisenhower, and Kennedy. He sided with Rusk, McNamara, Rostow, and the Bundy brothers, who were carrying on the Cold War for Acheson and Dulles. Although unable to locate Ho Chi Minh's breaking point, they were unwilling to admit their mistake. Johnson opted for the nightmare of Vietnam over the dream of a Great Society.

Until 1968, escalations followed one after another. The May 1965 bombing halt proved fruitless. The Viet Minh refused to negotiate unless the United States unconditionally halted its bombings and withdrew from Vietnam. Washington's steadfastness reassured South Vietnam's President

Nguyen Van Thieu and Prime Minister Nguyen Cao Ky, yet the turmoil at home intensified. The Johnson administration dispatched so-called truth teams of bureaucrats and legislators to university campuses to persuade skeptically opinionated professors and students. Congress made burning one's draft card a felony with stiff penalties, a law that was promptly and widely defied. At the Pentagon, Norman Morrison, a young Quaker, father of three children, burned himself to death as the Buddhist monks had done in Vietnam. The Voting Rights Act of 1965 tightened up the Civil Rights Act of 1964 to guarantee voting to blacks. Yet only two weeks afterward, to President Johnson's shocked dismay, the predominantly black citizens of Watts in Los Angeles violently rioted against the misery of their lives. Watts resembled Vietnam. Television viewers could watch American marines torching the huts of villagers of Cam Re as rioters in Watts and cities elsewhere across the country could be seen destroying their own squalid surroundings.

From the autumn of 1965 to the spring of 1968, American participation in the Vietnam fighting increased sharply, with concomitant upsurges in battle casualties and domestic opposition to the war. Intensive bombing resumed, then was halted. On November 30, 1965, Secretary McNamara advised President Johnson to instigate "a three- or four-week pause" in bombing the North before increasing troop deployments or renewing the air strikes, in order to make it clear to the American public and world opinion that the government was doing its best to end the war by affording North Vietnam "a face-saving chance to stop the aggression." If no armistice resulted, McNamara recommended escalating American troop strength to four hundred thousand by the end of 1966, and possibly to six hundred thousand by 1967, while conceding that such increments would not by themselves guarantee victory. Air attacks ought to concentrate on lines of communication, petroleum storage facilities, power plants, and the mining of harbors. "U.S. killed-in-action can be expected to reach 1,000 a month," McNamara admitted, but "the odds are even that we will be faced in early 1967 with a 'no decision' at an even higher level."

Fault finders sprang up at once. The leftist Students for a Democratic Society (SDS) denounced the war as "immoral at its root . . . foreclosing the hope of making America a decent and truly democratic society." Carl Oglesby, SDS president, blamed the Vietnam War on those "not so human" liberals who safeguarded corporate interests above flesh-and-blood concerns while denying that the Vietnam War was, in fact, a revolution, "as honest a revolution as you can find anywhere in history." In February 1966, Senator J. William Fulbright, chairman of the Foreign Relations Committee, who was regretting his vote for the Tonkin Gulf Resolution, opened publicly televised testimony on the war. Officials before the hearings defended their goal of halting the spread of communism. Secretary Rusk blamed China most of all. Yet George F. Kennan, the persuasive architect of containment, argued that his doctrine of the 1940s for the Soviet Union ought not be applied to Asia in the 1960s. Kennan criticized the military commitment and urged withdrawal from Vietnam.

President Johnson and his aides refused to stop the bombing unconditionally, because the Viet Minh hurried men and supplies southward to the National Liberation Front (NLF) and Viet Cong guerrillas each time they did or constructed safeguards against renewed attacks. Throughout April 1967, according to the Central Intelligence Agency's assessment, the Rolling Thunder aerial assault severely hurt North Vietnam's industrial and military base and killed tens of thousands of civilians, but due to the "large infusions" of Soviet Russian and Chinese Communist equipment and supplies, the bombing damage had "not meaningfully downgraded North Vietnam's ability to continue the war in South Vietnam."

Italy and the Vatican tried to employ their good offices for peace from November 1965 to January 1966, and failed. Their efforts, nonetheless, defined the dispute. North Vietnam's NLF and the Viet Cong insisted that the United States must withdraw entirely from Vietnam, cancel its military ties with the Saigon government, and live up to the provisions of the 1954 Geneva accords for unification. The United States expressed a willingness to respect the Geneva accords, but only if the Viet Cong halted its guerrilla warfare beforehand. The White House refused to treat with the NLF as a principal combatant in the South. While American emissaries in foreign capitals were encouraging the diplomatic efforts underway, President Johnson halted the bombing of North Vietnam for the month of January 1966, but General William C. Westmoreland's troop strength in South Vietnam climbed uninterruptedly. Poland's peacemaking initiatives of December 1966 likewise failed, when American bombings intended to coerce the North Vietnamese to negotiate produced exactly the opposite effect. An attempt by British Prime Minister Harold Wilson and Russian Premier Alexei Kosygin early in 1967 collapsed for the same reason.

North and South, the bloodshed attained frightful levels. American and ARVN forces shelled, bombed, and incinerated thousands of villages suspected of harboring Viet Cong guerrillas. The black-clad VC "Charlies" lived off the land by day, attacking at night from cleverly concealed mazes of underground tunnels to defy the superiority of American firepower. Under General Westmoreland's strategy of "attrition," body counts of dead Vietnamese signified success. Helicopter-led "search and destroy" missions inflicted airborne terror on the countryside. Defoliants showered onto Viet Cong hiding places to devastate fields and forests and contaminate unsuspecting GIs or ARVNs nearby. Fiery napalm rockets killed or mutilated countless victims. Depravity multiplied. The massacre at My Lai, March 16, 1968, when United States soldiers led by Lieutenant William Calley mercilessly "wasted" more than two hundred helpless villagers, betrayed the vengeful frustration Americans were coming to feel against all Vietnamese. Rural villagers fled for safety into already overcrowded cities and "pacification" centers. Almost one-quarter of the South Vietnamese population, about four million men, women, and children, were uprooted. Many, torn away from family homes and burials, bitterly resented both the Americans and the Saigon authorities. In the imperial capital city of Hué, while firefighters idly watched, protesting mobs burned down the United States consulate. Twenty thousand political prisoners endured torture and horrible deprivation in government jails.

The half million Americans and the billions of dollars pouring into South Vietnam swamped the fragile economy and distorted the traditional order of society. Prices soared beyond reach before United States officials introduced scrip to pay military personnel. Ships and supplies choked docksides, while far out to sea long lines of heavily laden inbound vessels awaited their turn to unload. American goods inundated local markets, wrecking native industries and reducing the population to dependency. Urban wage earners mostly worked to provide services to the Americans. Sleazy bars and red-light districts sprang up near the mushrooming military installations. Criminals and corrupt officials enriched themselves. Currency manipulations and black market operations sabotaged all efforts to steady the economy. Ambassador Lodge and General Westmoreland worried that lodging overly strenuous complaints might offend the Saigon government, if not undermine it altogether.

To Washington's relief, South Vietnam's new constitution went into operation in 1967, and the Thieu-Ky ticket won a narrow victory in the September election. Skeptical Vietnamese dismissed the proceedings as "an American-directed performance with a Vietnamese cast." Here was an ideal moment for a deescalation movement by the United States, which proved in retrospect, to be only another lost opportunity. Still, President Johnson retreated somewhat, in his "San Antonio formula" for a cease-fire, from adamantly requiring the NLF to abandon its support for the guerrillas in return for a bombing halt, and ventured a novel willingness to deal directly with the Viet Cong. But no further would he concede.[12]

While victory eluded Lyndon Johnson, antiwar sentiment engulfed him at home. Neither force nor diplomacy was succeeding in Vietnam, while costs and casualties escalated proportionately to the scale of fighting. SDS, the Student Nonviolent Coordinating Committee (SNCC), and the Black Panthers rallied the growing opposition. Personnel recruiters for Dow Chemical Company, the leading manufacturer of napalm, and other targetable munitions makers were finding themselves boycotted nationwide on campuses picketed by student and faculty protesters. Hundreds of young men, eventually thousands, ignored draft calls, burned draft cards, or slipped away into Canada. On April 4, 1967, two years after winning the Nobel Prize for Peace, the Reverend Martin Luther King, Jr., before a congregation of three thousand persons at Manhattan's Riverside Church, delivered a profoundly moving sermon, "Declaration of Independence from the War in Vietnam," linking the civil rights movement to the antiwar movement. Dr. King spoke out again in New York City on April 15, to the hundreds of thousands marching against the war from Central Park to the United Nations, chanting, "Hey! Hey! LBJ! How many kids did you kill today?" The Resistance, an antidraft group, appealed for a national draft card turn-in. On October 20, a delegation of prominent citizens handed over to Justice Department officials a bag filled with more than one thousand draft cards, and five of this group, Dr. Benjamin Spock, Marcus Raskin, Mitchell Goodman, Michael Ferber, and the Reverend William Sloane Coffin, were subsequently prosecuted for their crime. Their widely circulated manifesto, "A Call to Resist Illegitimate Authority," supplied the necessary self-incriminating evidence.

Dissension spread. Antiwar ballads sung by Bob Dylan, Joan Baez, and the trio of Peter, Paul, and Mary infused the sound waves. Intellectuals, among them political scientist Hans Morgenthau, Jr., historian Henry Steele Commager, linguist Noam Chomsky, and the belatedly disenchanted Arthur M. Schlesinger, Jr., urged pulling out of Vietnam. Walter Cronkite, television's respected news commentator, colored his evening broadcasts with increasingly jaundiced reflections of the war. To sum up, as these critics charged, the war was costing too much in lives and treasure. America's young manhood was perishing, and the Great Society's much-needed reforms were vanishing into a miasmic rancor of greed, callous intolerance, and racial antipathy.

Lyndon Johnson's consensus was breaking apart. Assistant Secretary of Defense John McNaughton, a longtime hawk, agonized, "We are in an escalating stalemate." McNaughton had grasped the truth that his obtuse superiors were stubbornly demanding "capitulation by a Communist force that is far from beaten." Likewise disillusioned was McNaughton's powerful boss, Secretary of Defense Robert S. McNamara, whose own studies forced him to discredit the massive bombing of North Vietnam as ineffectual and the bombing of South Vietnam as catastrophic. McNamara now favored halting bombing above the twentieth parallel. Instead of the 206,000 additional troops requested by Generals Wheeler and Westmoreland for an "optimum force" level of 665,000 to expand the struggle into Cambodia, Laos, and North Vietnam, he recommended deploying only 30,000. Startled, President Johnson and the Joint Chiefs flatly rejected McNamara's proposals as tantamount to a "drastic" reversal of the government's fundamental policy. One hundred thousand stop-the-war advocates marched in protest in Washington, an impassioned horde, and many of them even besieged the Pentagon itself. Young people and their supporters were exploding in resentment.

On November 1, 1967, Secretary of Defense McNamara submitted a plan to "Vietnamize" the war by phasing out American combat involvement altogether, and when Johnson and the service chiefs again balked him, he announced his intention to resign in protest once a successor could be found. Already National Security Advisor McGeorge Bundy, Undersecretary of State George Ball, and Johnson's close protégé Bill Moyers had one after another departed after disagreeing with the president. Across the country, students and professors conducted teach-ins against the war in Indochina. Violent and nonviolent demonstrations interrupted processing procedures for conscripts at local draft board offices, and shocking numbers of draftees fled to foreign lands to avoid induction. Fatefully, McNaughton ranted, the administration was dividing the generations. On November 30, Senator Eugene McCarthy of Minnesota, a dovish liberal on Fulbright's Senate Foreign Relations Committee, announced his candidacy for the 1968 presidential nomination on a singular platform to end the war. One could not know for certain whether the little-known senator was himself seriously challenging President Johnson, or if, in fact, he was actually Bobby Kennedy's stalking horse. Beleaguered, his credibility gone, LBJ had floundered into deep political trouble. As Eric F. Goldman noted: "Increasingly he was seeing himself as the lonely traduced figure limned against history resolutely doing right, grimly awaiting the verdict of the future." He no longer mentioned his Great Society.

Harsh in judgment, the future would hold Lyndon Johnson responsible for wasting his last opportunity for peace. Hanoi's foreign minister, Nguyen Duy Trinh, in the diplomatic opener of a multifaceted offensive, announced at the end of December North Vietnam's willingness to hold direct talks with the United States for the first time, on the sole condition that the American bombing be halted unconditionally. However, Washington feared suckering itself into another Panmunjom-style siege of endlessly frustrating hassles and overlooked the deescalating significance of Trinh's offer. Once more President Johnson and his advisors convinced themselves that, given supplies and soldiers enough, they could bend the Communists to capitulate unconditionally. Right on schedule, on January 2, 1968, following the Christmas recess, the United States resumed the bombing. Fixated as he was, Johnson recognized no other direction to take that would not compel him either to confess error or concede defeat.[13]

Then, suddenly, the president's house of cards collapsed. Far away from Vietnam, on January 23, a flotilla of Communist North Korean patrol boats, seized USS *Pueblo*, an electronics-laden spy vessel idling off the port of Wonsan, capturing its eighty-three officers and crew members. In Saigon one week later, a daring Viet Cong band stormed onto the grounds of the United States embassy, blasting the stronghold for six hours with mortar fire and rocket-propelled bombs.

The assault on the embassy proved to be only a small part of Hanoi's far-flung Tet offensive. Masterfully coordinated with Tet, the holiday month introducing the Buddhist new year, North Vietnam's offensive caught the American and South Vietnamese intelligence services napping. The complex assault, as intended, lured retaliating American units into remote rural areas, while Viet Cong cadres slipped between and behind them into over one hundred and fifty unsuspecting cities, towns, and hamlets. Hanoi was hoping to inflict unacceptably high casualties on the widely scattered United States and South Vietnamese forces and to incite chaos enough in the streets for the Communists to gain a negotiating truce on favorable terms, that is, to obtain an all-Vietnamese coalition government and the complete withdrawal of American troops. Bravely Americans and ARVN forces rallied their superior firepower to decimate both the guerillas and the NLF regulars backing them. The Viet Cong and the North Vietnamese suffered, as General William Westmoreland declared, a severe defeat. But the setback was only for the short run. The Tet offensive dealt an overwhelming psychological defeat to the home front in the United States. Tet supplied the greatest victory for the Indochinese Communists since Dien Bien Phu.

Shown on color television at home, the scenes of violent fighting inside Saigon, Hué, and dozens of other places made hollow mockery of Johnson's and Westmoreland's victory forecasts and flabbergasted the American public. South Vietnam, the country that the United States was supposedly saving from a Communist takeover, was blowing up and burning down on living-room screens. An army major's account of the fighting for Ben Tre, "We had to destroy the town to save it," encapsulated a bewildering sense of the war's futility. The televised execution by Saigon's chief of police of a blindfolded, kneeling Viet Cong captive bared the savage thirst for red blood that underlay President Thieu's pretensions of civilized morality and humane restraint. "What the hell is going on?" Walter Cronkite exclaimed. "I thought we were winning the war."

Tet's effects mounted up. In the New Hampshire primary, Senator Eugene McCarthy barely missed beating President Johnson for the Democratic nomination by three hundred votes, an unprecedented rebuke to an incumbent. Senator Robert F. Kennedy, who had turned against the war after his brother's death, announced his own candidacy and looked like a sure winner. The new secretary of defense, Clark Clifford, himself a chastened war hawk, advised President Johnson that even if the 206,000 soldiers being requested by the army were sent to Vietnam, the war could not be won, which the March 16 massacre at My Lai all too vividly confirmed. On March 22, Johnson unexpectedly brought General Westmoreland home from Vietnam, kicking him upstairs, in Ambassador Ellsworth Bunker's wry verdict, to make him army chief of staff. But little else improved. The Wise Men, the president's senior advisory group, bluntly notified Johnson that in their judgment, his military commanders had entirely lost touch with reality. Their spokesman, Dean Acheson, himself once the government's outstanding cold warrior, declared: "We can no longer do the job we set out to do in the time we have left, and we must begin to take steps to disengage." "Unless we do something quick," Cyrus Vance added, "the mood in the country may lead us to withdrawal." Fumed Johnson, "The establishment bastards have bailed out."

Nevertheless, LBJ realized what he must do. He announced on March 31, in a televised address, that he had stopped most of the bombing of North Vietnam, and he appealed for negotiations to end the war. Then he astounded the nation by unequivocally taking himself out of the presidential race, which not long before he was expected handily to win. Radio Hanoi broadcast another surprise three days later by accepting the president's plea to talk. Paris was selected for the site after much wrangling, but the fighting continued as well as the dying.

The remainder of 1968 was nightmarish. A lame duck president now, Johnson immobilized himself in the White House, hoping against his despair to salvage whatever he could. One week after Johnson renounced his dream of reelection, James Earl Ray, a white assassin, shot and killed civil rights leader Martin Luther King, Jr. Infuriated blacks burned and looted neighborhoods and businesses in over 160 cities and towns. Their outrage led to a white backlash, and distrust between the races gravely deepened. Robert Kennedy was murdered next. In June, Kennedy had won the important California primary, putting him well ahead for the Democrats' nomination. Sirhan Sirhan, a fanatic Arab nationalist, shot and killed Kennedy to avenge his unflagging support for Israel. In Chicago in August, televised terror burst out once again during the Democratic National Convention, when Mayor Richard Daley's police officers brutally gassed and clubbed scores of antiwar protesters.

Both presidential candidates, Vice-President Hubert H. Humphrey, Democrat, and former Vice President Richard M. Nixon, Republican, pledged to wage the war in Vietnam until the stalled negotiations in Paris could untangle themselves. Trapped in his loyalty to Johnson and Rusk, Humphrey finally promised to "de-Americanize" the fighting in order to catch Nixon, who, like Eisenhower on Korea, was promising to end the war "with honor." At the last hour, President Johnson, who until then was still determined to win an independent, non-Communist Vietnam, ordered a unilateral bombing halt, without first obtaining a single concession from the enemy. His gesture belatedly boosted the lagging Humphrey candidacy. However, he commanded General Creighton Abrams, Westmoreland's successor, "to use his manpower and resources in a maximum effort" to convince the Communists that they "could never win on the field of battle." Too late, Johnson failed to alter either the war or the election.[14]

When President-elect Richard M. Nixon met with Johnson and his advisors to get briefed on the Vietnam War, the outgoing administration's failure painfully showed. "The travail of the long war was etched on the faces around me," Nixon remembered. "They had no new approaches to recommend to me. I sensed that, despite the disappointment of defeat, they were relieved to be able to turn this morass over to someone else." "We will not make the same old mistakes," Henry A. Kissinger, Nixon's chief foreign policy advisor, predicted. "We will make our own." Steadfastly upheld even so, the effort to stop communism in Indochina would also poison Nixon's presidency. Vietnam, during Nixon's first term, bogged him down, like Johnson, in a will-o'-the-wisp pursuit of an independent, non-Communist state, yet eventually he and Kissinger would manage to end the conflict and bring home both the American troops and the prisoners of war. With triumph at hand, Nixon, unlike Johnson, lost his touch with domestic reality. The unauthorized publication of the *Pentagon Papers* would unbalance his judgment. The ensuing Watergate scandal would destroy his place in history. By 1974, the "morass" of Vietnam claimed Richard Nixon as its second presidential victim.

Before taking office in January 1969, Nixon and Kissinger outlined a new world order to maintain American leadership. Their plan embraced minimal accommodations to reduce tensions with the Soviet Union and the People's Republic of China, as well as an honorable end to the war in Vietnam. To succeed, a withdrawal of the United States from Vietnam had to disguise even the hint of American defeat. They hoped to win a "fair negotiated settlement that would preserve the independence of South Vietnam," but prepared themselves to settle for assurances that afforded South Vietnam a fighting chance to survive. Their target, in truth, was unchanged from the goal that had eluded American statesmen since the fall of Dien Bien Phu in 1954. Supremely confident, Nixon and Kissinger believed they would succeed where preceding administrations had failed.

Outwardly, President Nixon appeared to be upholding his promise to terminate American military interference in Vietnam. A preliminary agreement lay on the peace table in Paris. Feelers put out for bettering relations with the Soviets and the Red Chinese, along with relaxing restrictions on Japan, afforded a fresh atmosphere for the Indochina problem. To compel an armistice, on the other hand, Nixon intensified the bombing of North Vietnam. Nixon was employing jugular diplomacy, in Kissinger's disquieting depiction. To show both Hanoi and Moscow the seriousness of his purpose, Nixon ordered massive, secret bombing raids upon neighboring neutral Cambodia against the camouflaged North Vietnamese supply routes and depots there. Over fifteen months, American B-52s dropped more than one hundred thousand tons of high explosives, killing thousands of Cambodian civilians. Next, Nixon launched his "Vietnamization" process. After placating President Thieu by strengthening Saigon's military capacity, Nixon commenced the withdrawal of American troops. Indeed, he shrank the total of American military personnel in Vietnam to 139,000 by the close of 1971.

Nixon's moves, for all that, failed to budge the North Vietnamese. Hanoi's delegation to the Paris peace talks dismissed his mixture of diplomacy and bombing as insufficiently altered from Lyndon Johnson's approach. The North Vietnamese negotiators pressed doggedly for an unconditional American withdrawal from Vietnam and for a provisional government to exclude Thieu's regime. They felt certain that the gathering opposition to the war in the United States would eventually require Richard Nixon to withdraw from Vietnam. They steeled themselves to wait and suffer.

Worrying more and more that antiwar protests at home might defeat his strategy to bludgeon the North Vietnamese into conceding peace on his terms, President Nixon set out to disarm his critics. He kept top secret the bombing of Cambodia. He appealed ingeniously, in his "silent majority" speech of November 3, for a broad, patriotic understanding of his objections to pulling out of Vietnam. He underscored the double necessity of averting a bloodbath and upholding respect for the nation's commitments worldwide. In spite of favorable public reaction, it was too late. Although he had defined a supportive constituency, Nixon failed to quash the antiwar outcries. Across the nation in October and November, hundreds of thousands of marching protesters demanded a moratorium to halt the bombing of North Vietnam and end the war altogether. On November 15, more than one-quarter of a million persons marched in Washington, D.C. Inside the White House, Nixon cautioned himself: "Don't get rattled—don't waver—don't react."

Indeed Nixon's self-control might have justified itself, for his policy of Vietnamization was apparently making headway. The Accelerated Pacification Campaign improved daytime security in rural areas to breathe new life into village redevelopment schemes. The Saigon government introduced a long-delayed land redistribution program in March 1970. The South Vietnamese army was now one of the largest and most modern war machines anywhere, and almost for the first time ARVN, with its militia units, fought skillfully and bravely against the Communists. NLF and Viet Cong units were recuperating from their Tet offensive losses. The insurgency, on the surface at least, seemed on the wane. Yet no progress could be reported from the peace talks in Paris, and General Abrams bitterly opposed the president's announced intention to summon home 150,000 more troops. In truth, Nixon's hope for success in Vietnam was fading fast.[15]

On April 30, 1970, President Nixon authorized a joint American and South Vietnamese invasion of neutral Cambodia to wipe out Communist troop sanctuaries and arms depots. Major targets were the Parrot's Beak, a slice of Cambodian territory only thirty-three miles from Saigon, and the Fishook base farther away to the northwest. The Cambodian "incursion," Washington's euphemistic designation, won a limited military success, but the enlargement of the war proved horribly tragic. Mounting anxiety over the lack of progress in Vietnam led the Nixon administration into a contemptuous disregard for the welfare of neutral Cambodia and its hapless population. While North Vietnam's intruders retreated out of range deeper into Cambodia, the murderous Pol Pot's Khmer Rouge, backed by Hanoi against Lon Nol's United States–backed government, set off the holocaust in "the killing fields," desecrating that once beautiful but defenseless land. Nixon's invasion of Cambodia reignited the domestic uproar. Students went on strike against the expanded war. Ill-disciplined Ohio National Guardsmen inexplicably shot and killed four protesters and wounded several other students at Kent State University. Local police officers and state troopers fired without warning into a dormitory at Mississippi's Jackson State University, killing two students and injuring nine others. Nixon denounced the outraged students as pampered "bums." At the same time, revolutionaries in deadly earnest robbed, bombed, and burned banks, businesses, and draft boards, skyjacked airplanes, and even on occasion accidentally blew up themselves.

To clamorous objections from Capitol Hill against President Richard Nixon's invasion of Cambodia, including Senate Minority Leader Hugh Scott's anxious foreboding, Nixon spat back furiously that there would be no more "screwing around," that if "Congress undertakes to restrict me, Congress will have to assume the consequences." Congress, at last, began to do just that. The Senate voted in June to annul the Tonkin Gulf Resolution of 1964 under which the Vietnam War was being waged. The Senate also voted to cut off funds for the military adventure into Cambodia, but the House of Representatives temporarily allowed the appropriations to continue. At the end of June, the president pulled the American troops out of

Cambodia, shutting down the issue. No matter; the peace talks in Paris remained deadlocked, the bombing continued in Vietnam, the protests at home intensified. Nixon angrily turned on his critics, the "madmen" in Congress, the "liberal" press, and the protesters in the streets. A state of siege settled over the White House.

Instead of reappraising the bipartisan Indochina policy of anti-Communist militancy, which had produced only a prolonged disaster, Richard Nixon throughout 1971 obstinately stuck to his Vietnamization strategy of bringing home the troops while bombing Hanoi enough to force it to concede the peace he wanted. In February, Nixon ordered an invasion of Laos, with the intention, as in Cambodia, of interdicting Communist supply lines. Unluckily, intelligence sources forecast only insignificant resistance, but Hanoi's astute General Giap furiously hurled his Russian-built tanks against the invading ARVN ground troops. Six weeks later, the battered and bloodied South Vietnamese withdrew, saved only by the U.S. Air Force cover overhead. At home, the antiwar demonstrations surpassed all previous levels. Vietnam Veterans against the War ceremonially cast away their medals and insignia. Violent mobs rampaged in the streets. The Mayday Tribe tried to shut down the United States government, sparking one of the capital's worst disorders. Police routed the veterans off the Mall and, without charges, jailed twelve thousand Mayday demonstrators. Nixon at this point ordered Lieutenant William Calley released from prison, while his lifetime sentence for mass murders of Vietnamese was still under appeal, in order to review the case himself.

President Richard Nixon's downfall began in June 1971 with the publication of the Pentagon papers. Four years earlier, Secretary of Defense Robert S. McNamara ordered a documentary record prepared of American involvement with Vietnam. Daniel Ellsberg, a former Pentagon official turned antiwar critic, had recently leaked the top secret report to the New York Times. The documents clearly revealed that both President Kennedy and President Johnson had consistently deceived the American people about their intentions and actions in Vietnam. Obsessively secretive himself and besieged by enemies, President Nixon feared that the Pentagon papers would be used by political opponents to attack his goals and policies. When the Supreme Court overturned the injunction he obtained to halt the publication of the papers, Nixon paranoically launched a vendetta to plug leaks in the government. His covert authorization of the criminal gang of "plumbers" to burglarize the Democratic Party's offices would before long erupt horrendously into the constitutional crisis of the Watergate affair.[16]

Meanwhile, throughout 1972, President Richard Nixon campaigned for reelection as a world statesman. He aimed to improve relations with the Soviet Union and China. He and Secretary of State Kissinger hoped to isolate North Vietnam, leaving Hanoi's leaders little alternative to peace and, in so doing, rescuing the administration from the domestic turmoil the Vietnam War was causing. In February, Nixon traveled to Beijing, and in May, to Moscow. His extraordinary journeys turned into elaborately staged and televised spectacles. In spite of the extravagant claims from all sides, neither trip yielded much more than extremely modest achievements. Yet the bitter climate of the Cold War commenced to ease off noticeably into détente. In Vietnam, on the other hand, a major North Vietnamese invasion of the south and the furious retaliation bombing by United States aircraft of the Hanoi-Haiphong area, with the mining of Haiphong Harbor, greatly escalated the stalemate. The Paris peace talks collapsed again, in spite of the first serious negotiations, over Hanoi's insistence on removing President Thieu from office, even by assassinating him if necessary. Just the same, to Nixon's advantage, the Vietnam War wound down. Mutual exhaustion and United States troop withdrawals were doing the trick. By September, the combat death rate for Americans drooped close to zero, and in late October, two weeks before the election, Kissinger exuberantly declared that peace was at hand. Kissinger's premature pronouncement undoubtedly helped Nixon on Election Day to beat bungling George McGovern, the Democrats' Pied Piper. Nixon's "silent majority," which embraced swarms of unhappy Democrats, overwhelmed McGovern's ragtail coalition of anti-war protesters, aging hippies, and fast-fading liberals. The Vietnam War proved secondary as an issue to the rise of threateningly radical lifestyles and riotous violence in the streets.

With the election behind him, President Nixon broke off the Paris peace talks, determined to resolve the impasse, if necessary, by force. Nixon and Kissinger were frustrated by North Vietnamese intransigence, and impatient at their inability to browbeat South Vietnam's President Thieu into accepting compromise terms. The Christmas bombing runs dropped thirty-six thousand tons of high explosives, devastating the Hanoi-Haiphong region and inflicting terrible casualties. Fifteen giant B-52s were among the twenty-six aircraft lost. The peace talks resumed. On January 27, 1973, Kissinger and Le Duc Tho signed a cease-fire agreement. Whether their pact resulted from the horror of the holiday bombing, as Nixon and Kissinger would later claim, or from Russian and Chinese reluctance to support North Vietnam forever, is still uncertain. Except for military advisors and aid program administrators, the United States agreed to pull its forces out of South Vietnam within sixty days, and consented also to the formation of a coalition government to include the Viet Cong. Acidly, analysts observed these same terms were available in 1969, and more than twenty thousand lives, out of the total of over fifty-nine thousand American wartime fatalities, could have been spared. To forestall the possibility of another Vietnam

War, Congress in November 1973 passed the War Powers Resolution restricting the president's authority to commit United States military forces abroad for more than sixty days without congressional approval. Long supine, the defiant action by Congress signaled the demise of the imperial presidency.

Both Vietnams promptly violated the cease-fire. Nothing had changed. From the North, the Hanoi government still fought to unify Vietnam along its own lines. Saigon fought to maintain in the South its independent, non-Communist republic. American officials, President Nixon included, encouraged South Vietnam's aspirations, but Nixon was unable, in the rapidly altering circumstances and war-weariness, to honor the promises he made to President Thieu. Fortunately, he persuaded the North Vietnamese and Viet Cong to return nearly six hundred prisoners of war for the only heroes' homecomings of the war.

Intervention in Indochina, which destroyed Lyndon Johnson's presidency, now led, in the mushrooming Watergate scandal, to Richard Nixon's downfall and his final days in the White House. The Pentagon papers documented America's clandestine involvement in Vietnam. Their unauthorized publication induced frenzied efforts in the White House to obstruct their damaging revelations and to uphold President Nixon's authority as chief executive and commander-in-chief to conduct affairs of state. Nixon's near-paranoia compelled him to subvert both the political and judicial processes of the Constitution. He permitted the law to be broken in his behalf, and in violating his constitutional oath of office to uphold the law, he proceeded to obstruct justice. Facing almost certain impeachment and conviction, Richard Milhous Nixon, on August 9, 1974, resigned his office, the only president ever to do so. Nixon was Vietnam's second presidential victim. Vice-President Gerald R. Ford succeeded him.

In the spring of 1975, when North Vietnam unleashed its anticipated offensive, the army and the government of South Vietnam abruptly collapsed. Congress rebuffed President Ford's appeal to send assistance. Hastily, helicopters rescued the Americans remaining in Saigon, including Ambassador Graham Martin, together with many, though not all, of their Vietnamese employees, snatching them to safety from the embassy rooftop. The thirty-year struggle for Vietnam had ended overnight. On May 1, Saigon was renamed Ho Chi Minh City in honor of the Viet Minh's deceased leader. The end of the Vietnam War left the United States where, if it had not intervened, it might have been in 1945. But three decades later, the nation was also wounded within and humiliated without.[17]

If the form of heaven is contemplated, the changes of time can be discovered.
If the forms of men are contemplated, one can shape the world.

I Ching[1]

11

THE NEW PACIFIC

It was time to take stock. Why Vietnam?

Whoever examines the nation's obsession with Vietnam will inevitably rediscover the terrible toll of lives, treasure, careers, and reputations, the humbling of self-esteem, the prolonged nature of the consequences, a defeat that could neither be readily explained nor accepted. The generation that lost tried to forget, until embittered veterans compelled public attention to them and their experience. The Vietnam Memorial, a V-shaped touchstone standing at the most emotion-laden spot in Washington, its glossy black marble wall inscribed with around sixty thousand names of the fallen, has helped to dissolve America's anger into sorrowful tears. The portion of that generation who in some sense or other ran away from the war has either trickled back or remains in exile.

Why Vietnam? Why Indochina? The nagging problem refuses to go away.

For that matter, even if solely in American terms, why Manila, Peking, Guadalcanal, Kiska, Hiroshima, Pusan, or Khe Sanh? And why Mitsubishi, Toyota, and Hyundai? What has resulted from all the American seafaring, hunting, whaling, adventuring, trading, and evangelizing in the Pacific? What came of exploration, salvation, greed, destiny, duty, the Open Door, and containing communism? Where in the Pacific Ocean's vastness, "the tide-beating heart of earth," are the primary clues for the westernmost reaches of American history?

261

To rethink the Pacific requires more than a regional outlook. Concepts such as "the Pacific basin," "Rim of Fire," "the Pacific rim," and even "the American Pacific" with its intrinsically nationalistic bias, focus less on the watery wastes linking the Western Hemisphere to the ocean's myriad islands and East Asia's mainland than whalers, explorers, and merchants had to do, or even the armada captains of twentieth-century warfare. American merchants and seamen first entered the China trade in 1784, when the *Empress of China* dropped anchor below Canton. Two centuries later, following the Vietnam War, the position of the United States in the Pacific basin was unsettled and difficult, if not impossible, to establish. Commercial opportunity was not everywhere apparent, as for Stephen Girard, Matthew Calbraith Perry, and William Henry Seward it once had been. Military forces were heading homeward from the imperial world that Dewey, the MacArthurs, McKinley, Teddy Roosevelt, Taft, Nimitz, Acheson, Dulles, McNamara, Rusk, and Johnson had made. Obsolete now, the stirring appeals of duty, the Open Door, and containment sound quaint to the ear. In every important aspect, change was overwhelming continuity. Pacific civilization at the end of the twentieth century seemed stunningly novel, almost wholly changed from the exotic worlds of Oceania and East Asia when the young republic's adventurers first arrived. The new Pacific is the American Pacific transformed.

Unchanging itself, the Pacific Ocean ranges across the equator from both polar regions west and east to the Americas and Asia, engulfing the Philippines, Indonesia, and the widely scattered archipelagos of Polynesia, Micronesia, and Macronesia, while overall there is no uniform or contiguous community of the Pacific's polyglot peoples nor any shared historical background. Folk loyalties and nationalisms are proving more durable than capitalism or communism, while religions steadfastly fortify ancient traditions. From the West, the peoples of East Asia's mainland and the Pacific islands borrow technology and popular culture, but except for money-making, they ordinarily spurn European and American value systems. As the jet airplane, electronic communications, and the thirst for consumer goods spun transpacific networks, Asians and islanders struggled to reconcile new circumstances with old. So did Americans.

The Second World War occasioned the rise and fall of Japan's empire, together with the destruction of the British, French, and Dutch empires in Asia and the Pacific. Imperial supremacy passed to the United States. The double threat of Soviet and Chinese communism led the United States, in its militant, anti-Communist containment policy, into the inconclusive Korean War and the morasses of Indochina. The Vietnam War, in retrospect, assumes more than a singular significance. For twenty-five years after 1950, the struggle for Indochina measured the limits in Asia of containment against communism. The fall of Saigon marks the tidal return of the American empire from East Asia and the western Pacific. Today, Japan's new economic power and China's colossal strength are reshaping world civilization. Japan's triumph may well be at hand. The future for China is less predictable. Independence for the Philippines, together with statehood for Alaska and Hawaii, have redefined American enterprise in the Pacific region in more conservative terms than before. Still, the far-flung possessions of the United States, the emerging commonwealths, and the newly self-governing microstates in free association, continue to express the vitality driving American interests far across the Pacific.

Rapidly international relations have changed to favor economic power. As the importance of military might subsided, though the superpowers—the United States, the Soviet Union, and China—remained heavily armed, the former Axis partners, Japan and Germany, abetted by the West's anti-Communist crusade, wrought miraculous economic recoveries for themselves. Japan, like the reunified Germany, was ideally stiuated to profit most from the expiration of the Cold War, even if she still lacked the natural resources to guarantee supremacy.

Japanese-American relations commenced to undergo a thorough reexamination at two extremely sensitive points. The first, from the American viewpoint, was the unfavorable trade balance between Japan and the United States, and the second, mutually troublesome, was resentment over the treaty-bound responsibility of the United States for Japan's defense. Around 1950, the United States produced 40 percent of the world's goods and services, with Japan contributing only 3 percent, but by 1990, the United States' share declined to 24 percent as Japan's rose to 13 percent. The transpacific trade had attained primary importance for the United States and become 50 percent larger than the transatlantic traffic. The imbalance for the United States of trade with Japan exceeded $50 billion per year, and the enormous profits of the Japanese led to wholesale purchases of American securities, industries, and real estate properties, awakening a mounting apprehension in the United States. Japan's investors financed important shares of the astronomic deficits of the federal and state governments. In truth, had the Japanese not purchased so many Treasury Department, state, and municipal securities, the trade balance would have reached still more alarming figures. Japan besides operated the globe's largest foreign aid program, owned fourteen of the world's fifteen largest banks, and employed a hard-working population that saved its earnings at a ratio four to five times that of Americans. Public opinion polls revealed that Americans regarded Japan's economic competition as more threatening than the military prowess of the Soviet Union.

The conviction grew in the United States that major manufacturing industries, such as steel, automobiles, electronics, computers, and semiconductors, were being unfairly undercut by government-backed Japanese competition, which sufficiently irritated the Japanese, as United States Ambassador Michael H. Armacost cautioned, to dismiss those Americans bashing them as only disguising their own shortcomings. At the same time, the demise of the Cold War and chronic budgetary shortfalls combined at home to reevaluate the rationale for stationing over 135,000 troops in the Philippines, Korea, and Japan. Fifty thousand soldiers, sailors, and air force personnel were garrisoned in 1990 in Japan alone. The virtual permanence of this enormous American military presence further inflamed the tensions over money matters, as did the discords about Japan's contributions to the costs of the Persian Gulf action in 1991. The central aggravation of the trade imbalance, as Americans generally understood the matter, was not that the United States imported too much but that Japan imported too little. If Japan itself could make or grow a particular item, it would not buy from abroad.

Willingly and without governmental restraint, Americans bought automobiles, cameras, television sets, and many other products from Japan, but as producers themselves, they feared Japanese competition and trade restrictions. During the 1980s, American consumers spent $350 billion more for Japanese goods than Japan bought from them. Washington's trade negotiators persistently pressed their counterparts in Tokyo to open Japan's markets freely to American rice, computer chips, and other goods and construction contractors. The hefty political power of farmers in Japan's Diet refused to admit imported rice into the country, even though homegrown rice raised on their miniscule plots cost 600 to 800 percent as much as rice produced in California or Arkansas. Similar special-interest barriers prevailed in many other areas. In President George Bush's free trade administration, retaliatory threats erupted. Secretary of Agriculture Edward R. Madigan reminded Motoji Kondo, his Japanese counterpart, in March 1991 that many American farmers drove pickup trucks and automobiles made in Japan. Did Mr. Kondo want two million American farmers to "band together against buying Japanese products?" he asked, but his outrage faltered at the unlikelihood of any such action. In spite of the friction, the close Japanese-American economic relationship had strong public support on both sides.

At the core of the problem lay different cultural peculiarities aggravated by the awkward language barrier. Mystification beclouded discourse between Americans and Japanese. Misunderstandings frequently occurred. The term "fairness" in American English means affording equal opportunities to everybody, whereas "fairness" of treatment in Japan requires affording preferential treatment to those with whom one has long-established personal relations, that is fellow nationals, family, and friends.

Japanese businessmen attached great worth to the process of negotiating, nearly as much as to the result. For Americans, the "bottom line" and the short-run advantage were all that mattered for profitability. In Japanese, the expression "I will make efforts" signified serious, businesslike intentions, where in an American setting it conveyed little more than a cheerful farewell. Language was a monumental obstacle. Far fewer Americans could conduct themselves in Japanese than Japanese could speak and write in English. If the interpreters were Japanese, the one-sidedness was accentuated. In 1989, speaking in Honolulu, Masami Atarashi, president of Johnson & Johnson's subsidiary in Japan, jokingly asked an East-West Center audience: What does one call someone who speaks two languages? *Bilingual.* How about someone who speaks three languages? *Trilingual.* How about someone who speaks several languages? *Multilingual.* What does one call a person who speaks only one language? *American!*

The shifting relationship between the United States and Japan depended on improving communicability. Unfortunately for Americans, most news stories only heightened their uneasiness, thus: "The East Village Becomes Japan West," "In the Realm of Technology, Japan Looms Ever Larger," and, worst of all, "Is Japan the Enemy?" "Is the United States Headed for Another War with Japan?"[2]

Toward China after the Korean War, the United States directed a "two China" policy, aimed against the Communists but supportive of the exiled Nationalist regime on Taiwan. Through SEATO, the Southeast Asia Treaty Organization organized by Eisenhower and Dulles, comprising the United States, Britain, France, the Philippines, Australia, New Zealand, Thailand, and Pakistan, the American government hoped to contain Communist uprisings from spreading, especially those backed by Russia and China in Vietnam, Laos, and Cambodia. The American air force and navy helped to guard Taiwan and the besieged offshore islands of Quemoy and Matsu from a Communist takeover, when both Mao Zedong and Chiang Kai-shek were claiming China's sovereignty overall. To retaliate for the Communists' shelling of Quemoy and Matsu, Taiwan's Nationalist aviators flying the latest American-made fighter bombers repeatedly pounded the mainland until foreign Minister Zhou En-Lai persuaded Chairman Mao to end the indecisive confrontation. Mao pledged the Beijing government to "strive for the liberation of Taiwan by peaceful means so far as it is possible." The bitter struggles for Vietnam, Laos, and Cambodia and the sporadically reheated standoff over Taiwan henceforth defined the volatile antagonism between Washington and Beijing.

Warily, the angry giants inched toward each other to reduce the tension between them. In Warsaw, the United States ambassador or his subordinates met routinely with Red China's emissaries to Poland mostly just to exchange defiant threats over Taiwan. The tension was broken, however, by President Nixon's withdrawal of American troops from Vietnam followed by Chairman Mao's positive response. Mao, in 1970, had to repair the devastation caused by the Cultural Revolution and deeply feared the Soviet troops massing against Chinese soldiers along their disputed frontier. His hard line softened. Mao invited Edgar Snow, the author of *Red Star over China* (1938) to stand beside him at the PRC's twenty-first anniversary celebration. Then, in April 1971, Mao's government unexpectedly invited the Asia-touring United States table tennis squad to China, opening the era of "ping-pong diplomacy." In July, Secretary of State Henry Kissinger secretly flew to Beijing to prepare for a summit meeting of the chiefs of state. In the United Nations, the United States dropped its boycott against Red China, forcing Taipei to relinquish China's Security Council seat to Beijing's ambassador. Washington lifted the anti-China trade and monetary restrictions in force since the Korean War. The president seemed, after his détente-making trip to Moscow, to be winning his campaign to thaw the Cold War.

On February 21, 1972, President Richard Milhous Nixon flew into Beijing for his historic meeting with Red China's Chairman Mao Zedong. Nixon's and Mao's promise to strive toward "the normalization of relations between the two countries," cautious though it was, afforded a sorely needed, fresh prospect for peaceful relations. The two former enemies accomplished all that was possible. Back home, however, Nixon's extraordinary defiance of the opposition to his Vietnam War policy twisted his thinking to countenance the bizarre burglaries of the Watergate affair. His coverup of the crimes would shatter a unique opportunity for lasting greatness, and historically tarnish his presidency.

The Watergate crisis, which caused President Nixon's resignation and the succession of Gerald R. Ford, unsettled American politics so much that, when coupled with Mao's death in 1976, their promising start toward normalizing relations between the United States and China stagnated. Chinese-Russian tensions remained acute meanwhile, further exacerbated by Beijing's unflagging support in Cambodia for Pol Pot's murderous Khmer Rouge government against the Moscow-backed Vietnamese effort to dislodge him. When President Jimmy Carter suggested establishing full diplomatic relations with China, his proposal met a warm response from the Chinese. To what extent, if any, the chronic Russophobia of Zbigniew Brzezinski, Carter's Polish-born national security advisor, encouraged the president to drive another wedge between the Communist superpowers was not clear. Carter's agreement to phase out American military support for Taiwan, as well as the resulting normalization agreements of 1979 and most-favored-nation trading status for mainland China, greatly alarmed the Nationalists' supporters in the United States. Outraged, Congress passed the Taiwan Relations Act for maintaining Taiwan's separate existence, affirming in no uncertain words that none other than "peaceful means" could alter Taiwan's status. Thereafter, American-Chinese relations, though perceptibly warming as shown by American sales of military hardware to China and the opening of cultural exchanges, remained, if no longer openly hostile, ambiguous.

In relaxing their post-1949 fears of Red China, Americans now saw the Chinese merely as Communists, not as dangerous revolutionaries. Scientists, students, and tourists, whether subsidized as guests or wealthy enough to travel on their own resources, flocked to explore China. Likewise, thousands and thousands of overseas Chinese, including Taiwanese, freed at last of exit or entry restrictions, rushed to visit long-unseen relatives and their ancestral burials. For Americans after 1972, a regard for China as once again a land of opportunity suggested that a renewing was taking place of the Open Door ideal of commercial penetrability combined with the once-lively hope for Western-style, nationalistic modernization. All of which, it romantically held, would redound to America's advantage. John K. Fairbank has suggested that this outlook was naively flawed and still interpreted China and the Chinese people in terms of American interests, aims, and achievements. That was what Confucius saw as "climbing a tree to catch a fish," or acting on a false assumption and relying on erroneous measures.

Suddenly, on June 3–4, 1989, Chinese government forces blasted such illusions by massacring hundreds of protesters in Beijing's Tiananmen Square. Most of them were students petitioning for democratic liberalization. The nauseating viciousness against China's idealistic youth, viewed worldwide on television, recalled the centuries of civil wars and the recent horrors of the Cultural Revolution. Although stunned, amid angry clamor, foreign governments chose not to sever their diplomatic ties. President George Bush managed to weather the uproar at home. Bush also resisted Beijing's demand to hand over Fang Lizhi, the prominent astrophysicist and dissident liberal, and his wife, who won sanctuary for over a year inside the United States embassy. Both Premier Deng Xiaoping, who chaired China's ruling gerontocracy, and China's legion of American friends hardly knew where next to turn. Once more, the open door closed itself against foreign devils.[3]

In Korea, four decades after the civil war between North and South had ended, the prospect of political change also far exceeded any accomplishment. Bitterly divided, Korea's condition represented not only the armistice demarcation that ended the fighting in 1953, but also an unforgiving debate over who and what started the Korean War in the first place. In North Korea in Kim Il Sung's time, who launched the war did not rest with history, but belonged entirely to the Pyongyang government's propaganda apparatus. North Korea's official position, though ridiculed by Westerners, held that American imperialists behind the scenes touched off the conflict that tragically separated the Korean people from each other. South Korea insisted that North Korea's thwarted attempt to reunify the country in 1950 demonstrated the necessity for American troops to remain for defense against another invasion. Either conviction, or its opposite, North or South, came to define the mentality of the Korean people themselves, not only about their past but the future as well. Equally for President Ronald Reagan, United States support for South Korea had to be unequivocal. In 1983, he addressed his country's troops facing North Korean soldiers across the peninsula's demilitarized zone: "You stand between the free world and the armed forces of a system hostile to everything we believe in as Americans. The Communist system to the north is based on hatred and oppression." In Reagan's verdict, there was no choice.

Ending the Cold War promised relaxation, if not an end, to such bipolarized militancy, but Korea, more than anywhere on earth, remained divided. With dramatic economic growth and new industrial prowess, South Korea on a small scale resembled Japan and, indeed, competed effectively in electronics and automotive markets against her longtime oppressor, as, on a smaller scale, notably in textiles and electronics, did Taiwan, Hong Kong, Malaysia, Singapore, and Thailand. Like their Japanese counterparts, South Korea's unruly students vented pent-up frustrations in antigovernment and anti-American rioting to protest, among other things, the military presence of the United States, which, they insisted, was preventing the reunification of Korea. In January 1990, Secretary of Defense Dick Cheyney announced the closing of three of the five United States air bases in South Korea and scheduled the withdrawal of about two thousand air force personnel. One month later, Seoul accepted Washington's intention to withdraw about five thousand noncombatant troops from the American force of more than forty-three thousand soldiers in South Korea. Not until 1991 did the North Korean government signify a willingness to search for nine thousand allied troops still listed as missing in action during the Korean War. Koreans wanted their country reunited. How reunification might be peacefully achieved was still problematic.[4]

Throughout the western Pacific, the mixed peoples of the United States' far-flung colonies, former and current alike, characteristically displayed the dependency and poverty of the Third World overlaid by the ephemeral features of American popular culture.

Toward the Philippines after 1946, the United States followed a vacillating path, a "spastic policy" in Stanley Karnow's term, by alternating, during its long vendetta against Asian communism, top priority and neglect.

Filipinos have been equally barometric. They expected American economic aid and military assistance as their birthright, but resented interference in their country's affairs. Relations between these "mortal friends" were dominated largely by negotiations over the United States bases and installations on Luzon, which acquired critical importance during the Vietnam War. Subic Bay Naval Station was the largest navy facility outside the United States, the main supply and repair center in the western Pacific. Clark Air Force Base, the headquarters of the Thirteenth Air Force, was the major supply and transit point for American air power in the Far East and Indian Ocean. Four other air defense, radar, communications, and electronic warfare installations underscored the island republic's military significance. In return, the United States extended rehabilitation grants and free trading rights, then, more recently, lease rentals and developmental loans. At the end of 1990, the United States government was contributing the second largest chunk of income to the Philippines' gross national product, second only to the national government's share. But in 1991, the gigantic volcanic eruptions of Mount Pinatubo sixty miles north of Manila caused the evacuation of thousands of Americans from Clark and Subic Bay, possibly settling the future of these bases by natural means if not otherwise.

Not surprisingly, in their turbulent democracy, sovereignty continues to be the crucial issue for Filipinos, while poverty characterizes the great majority of their lives. American bases constitute merely a part of the problem, albeit an inflammatory part, yet the rising nationalism usually expresses itself in anti-American outbursts. The long uprising of the Communist-led Hukbalahap guerillas for land reform and political power plagued the reconstructing of the war's devastation and the building of a self-sustaining economy. Ever since, the insurgent New People's Army and Muslim separatists on Mindanao and neighboring southern islands have violently aggravated the disorders while struggling to control entire regions of this predominantly Catholic Christian republic. The government in Manila seems powerless to overcome the divisions wrought during centuries of colonial subordination.

The overthrow of President Ferdinand E. Marcos and Imelda, his extravagant wife, February 25, 1986, to end two decades of autocratic and mismanaged rule, capped with his replacement by Corazon C. Aquino, his slain rival's wife, temporarily quelled the internal disharmony. Exiled, the Marcoses were flown to Guam in a U.S. Air Force plane, then on to Hawaii, where, in Honolulu, Marcos himself gradually sickened and died. Marcos left his widow to defend herself in federal court in New York City against charges of looting the Philippines Treasury and fraudulent conversion of their ill-gotten gains. Imelda Marcos won acquittal. Still, imperious Uncle Sam remained at the center of Filipino affairs.[5]

Elsewhere west of Hawaii, the Stars and Stripes flies over the islands of Micronesia. Many were World War II battlegrounds. Not all of them even support indigenous populations. Most important in size and population is the 209-square mile island of Guam, an unincorporated territory heading toward commonwealth status like Puerto Rico's. The Northern Mariana Islands already is a commonwealth. The American victory over Japan either restored these onetime colonies of Portugal, Spain, Germany, or Japan, to American control, as with Guam, Wake Island, and the Philippines, or took them away from Japan to be administered as United Nations trust territories under American supervision.

Guam, by far the most populous Micronesian island, with over ninety thousand inhabitants and a major naval base, is a tourist mecca. Saipan and Tinian in the Mariana Islands became, once captured, the bases for B-29 air raids against Japan. The nuclear bombs dropped on Hiroshima and Nagasaki came from Tinian. Except for Guam, most of the nearly one hundred and fifty thousand Micronesian natives inhabit volcanic islands or atolls sprinkled across three million square miles of ocean. Under agreements with Congress, in addition to the two nascent commonwealths, three heavily subsidized island nations—the Republic of the Marshall Islands, the Federated States of Micronesia, and the Republic of Palau—are emerging into a "free association" with the United States government, that is to say, unrestricted home rule save for defense.

Defense considerations prevail, but transformations take place anyway driven by foreign investments and pressures for self-government. From 1953 to 1962, war-battered Saipan based Chinese Nationalist guerrillas training to infiltrate their Communist-controlled mainland. Kwajelein, also battle-scarred, houses a guided missile monitoring complex to measure the accuracy of test firings from California's Vandenberg Air Force Base, while lonely Johnston Atoll stored chemical and nuclear weapons. The momentum lay with developers. Micronesia was coming to mean for Tokyo what the Caribbean playground signified for the Atlantic seaboard. By 1988, half a million Japanese tourists were thronging into Guam's resorts each year. Promoters were planning hotels, restaurants, and golf courses, even for remote Rota, an island paradise.

Change was everywhere evident. Dead in Tokyo at eighty-four was Minoru Genda, the aerial warfare genius, who planned the air attack on Pearl Harbor. In Hawaii, the upsurge of the Japanese yen struck like a tidal wave, bringing property inflation, economic speculation, booming prosperity, confusion and dismay. Japanese investors and tourists poured money into Kahala and Waikiki real estate and recreational facilities. Japanese spending or investing increased to constitute about one-quarter of the gross state product. Honolulu's stockbrokers had to open their doors on Wall

Street time. The "ice curtain" disappeared; after forty years, Siberians and Alaskans freely crossed the Bering Straits once more to reclaim long-lost relatives and friends. All five Pacific Ocean states—California, Oregon, Washington, Hawaii, and Alaska—anguished over pollution and its impartial threats to wildlife and human life. The gigantic 1989 oil spill by the *Exxon Valdez* in Alaska's Prince William Sound traumatized the nation into recognizing the fragility of life on earth. Congress voted funds at last to begin paying $1.2 billion in reparations to Japanese-Americans interned in World War II. Even the face of the nation was changing. The post-1965 influx of Asian immigrants and refugees represented, in the minds of many, Asia's second invasion of the Western Hemisphere, prompting a revised recognition of the nation's diversity. But one's livelihood was still the name of the game. "People on the West Coast are pretty good about remembering what time it is," observed Jay Itagaki, a Honolulu broker, "but not the East Coast. Easterners don't know how to look west. And it's not just the time zones. They don't seem to realize the money is all on this side of the world now. It's time for them to wake up."[6]

What an irony of history it is that the American republic, which in a passion for self-government won independence from a mighty empire, should have itself for a time after the Second World War imperially dominated the Pacific basin!

Since then, international prowess has turned economic in nature. Increasingly it becomes uncertain if the American economy, which at the close of the twentieth century still leads the world, could sufficiently mobilize its unequaled natural and human resources to turn back unprecedented levels of foreign competition, either from Japan or a unified Europe or, perhaps, from both together. Such a question, in truth, outweighed the available answers. Is the Pacific Ocean a new Mediterranean Sea already binding its peoples together instead of separating them? Do its restless currents forecast an enlightened, peaceful tomorrow, or renascent hostility ominous for the future of humankind? Will Americans continue to venture westward in the bold spirit of earlier generations? To do so, they shall have to reassert the courage, foresight, and sense of purpose of their forebearers. Otherwise, future historians may be compelled to record a waning of the American epoch.

Long ago, on September 17, 1787, while the last members of the convention were signing the Constitution in Philadelphia and America's China trade was barely begun, the venerable Benjamin Franklin, according to Madison's notes, gazed at the presiding officer's chair, where a decorative sun was painted, and observed, "I have . . . often and often, in the course of the session, and the vicissitudes of my hopes and fears as to its issue, looked at that behind the President without being able to tell whether it was rising or setting, but now at length, I have the happiness to know that it is a rising and not a setting sun."[7] Today, as the United States drifts ahead into its third century, the American people might well wonder if their own sun is still rising, like Dr. Franklin's, or this time setting somewhere in Asia far across the ever-restless Pacific, their ocean of destiny.

Bibliographical Notes

1. UNFURLING THE FLAG

1. Perry to the secretary of the navy, dated Madeira, December 14, 1852, originally published in *Senate Executive Documents*, No. 34 of 33d Cong., 2d Sess., Francis L. Hawks, comp., *Narrative of the Expedition of an American Squadron to the China Seas and Japan performed in the Years 1852, 1853, and 1854 under the Command of Commodore M. C. Perry* (Washington: A. O. P. Nicholson by order of Congress, 1856), vol. 2, p. 179.

2. For bibliography and guidance, I gratefully acknowledge my debt to Professor Emeritus Donald D. Johnson of the University of Hawaii at Manoa, who generously shared his work in progress, *The United States in the Pacific: Special Interests and Public Policies, 1784–1941* (Honolulu: University of Hawaii Bookstore, 1986); see Jonathan Goldstein, *Philadelphia and the China Trade, 1682–1846: Commercial, Cultural, and Attitudinal Effects* (University Park: Pennsylvania State University Press, 1978), 24–33 and passim. The history of the American Pacific belongs in a world setting. As John Cell put it, "Without the New World's treasure, it is hard to see how Europeans could have established themselves economically in Asia." Unpublished paper, "Europe and the World in an Expanding Economy, 1750–1850," November 13, 1987, East Asian Institute, Columbia University.

3. Jared Sparks, *The Life of John Ledyard, the American Traveller*, 2d ed. (Cambridge, MA: Hilliard and Brown, 1829) 70, 121–170.

4. Tyler Dennett, *Americans in Eastern Asia: A Critical Study of the Policy of the United States with Reference to China, Japan, and Korea in the 19th Century* (New York: Macmillan, 1922), 1–23; Foster Rhea Dulles, *China and America: The Story of Their Relations since 1784* (Princeton, NJ: Princeton University Press, 1946), 8; J. Wade Caruthers, *American Pacific Ocean Trade: Its Impact on Foreign Policy and Continental Expansion, 1784–1860* (New York: Exposition Press, 1973), 18–29. Caruthers states that Gray, on his departure, was ordered to return via Cape Horn, (22).

5. Alexander Starbuck, *History of the American Whale Fishery from Its Earliest Inception to the Year 1876* (Waltham, MA: the author, 1878), passim, also in *Report of the Commissioner of*

273

Fish and Fisheries for 1875–1876 (Washington: Bureau of Fisheries, 1878; reprinted in two volumes, New York: Argosy-Antiquarian, 1964); Elmo Paul Hohman, *The American Whaleman: A Study of Life and Labor in the Whaling Industry* (New York: Longmans, Green, 1929), 37–40; Edouard A. Stackpole; *The Sea-Hunters: New England Whalemen during the Two Centuries, 1635–1835* (New York: J. B. Lippincott, 1953), 145–163.

6. *The Works of John Adams . . . ,* edited by Charles Francis Adams (Boston: Little, Brown, 1853), vol. 8, pp. 343–344.

7. Immanuel C. Y. Hsu, *The Rise of Modern China,* 4th ed. (New York: Oxford University Press, 1990), 139–167; Donald D. Johnson, *The United States in the Pacific,* chapter 2, "The Old China Trade," 48–122. A neat sample of archaeological evidence is offered in Julia Blodgett Curtis, "Chinese Export Porcelain in Eighteenth-Century Tidewater Virginia," *Studies in Eighteenth-Century Culture,* vol. 27, edited by John Yolton and Leslie Ellen Brown (East Lansing, MI: Colleagues Press, 1987), 119–144.

8. Jonathan D. Spence, *The Search for Modern China* (New York: W. W. Norton, 1990), 128–132; Girard is quoted in Jonathan Goldstein, *Philadelphia and the China Trade,* 46; Jean Gordon Lee, *Philadelphia and the China Trade, 1784–1844* (Philadelphia: Museum of Art distributed by University of Pennsylvania Press, 1984), 14–15, 18, 104–5 footnotes.

9. Jonathan D. Spence, *The Search for Modern China,* 122, 145, 148–158; Tyler Dennett, *Americans in Eastern Asia,* 100; Immanuel C. Y. Hsu, *The Rise of Modern China,* 168–195; John K. Fairbank, Edwin O. Reischauer, Albert M. Craig, *East Asia: Tradition & Transformation* (Boston: Houghton, Mifflin, 1978), 454–460.

10. Tyler Dennett, *Americans in Eastern Asia,* 94–114; Paul H. Clyde, *United States Policy toward China: Diplomatic and Public Documents, 1839–1939* (Durham, NC: Duke University Press, 1940), 3–21; Hunter Miller, ed., *Treaties and Other International Acts of the United States of America* (Washington: Government Printing Office, 1934), vol. 4, pp. 559–669; John K. Fairbank, *Trade and Diplomacy on the China Coast* (Cambridge, MA: Harvard University Press, 1953), vol. 1, pp. 84–103.

11. Immanuel C. Y. Hsu, *The Rise of Modern China,* 196–220; John K. Fairbank et al., *East Asia,* 461; Warren I. Cohen, *America's Response to China: A History of Sino-American Relations,* 3d ed. (New York: Columbia University Press, 1990), 7–23.

12. Kenneth Scott Latourette, *A History of Christian Missions in China* (London: Society for Promoting Christian Knowledge, 1929), 209–281; John K. Fairbank, ed., *The Missionary Enterprise in China and America* (Cambridge, MA: Harvard University Press, 1974), 1–55; Suzanne Wilson Barnett and John K. Fairbank, eds., *Christianity in China: Early Protestant Missionary Writings* (Cambridge, MA: Harvard University Press, 1985), 1–18ff; Jonathan D. Spence, *The Search for Modern China,* 204–210.

13. Donald D. Johnson, *The United States in the Pacific,* 136–145, 149–159.

14. Ibid., 123–125, 181–184; J. Wade Caruthers, *American Pacific Ocean Trade,* 24–29; Foster Rhea Dulles, *The Old China Trade* (Boston: Houghton, Mifflin, 1930), 53–64; Thomas Hart Benton, *Thirty Years View . . . from 1820 to 1850* (New York: D. Appleton, 1856), vol. 1, pp. 13–14. For the fur trade of Russian Alaska, see Claus-M. Naske and Herman E. Slotnick, *Alaska: A History of the 49th State,* 2d ed. (Norman and London: University of Oklahoma Press, 1987), 28–44. Also see Kenneth J. Bertrand, *Americans in Antarctica, 1755–1948* (New York: American Geographical Society, 1971).

15. The literature on American whaling revolves around a single fiction by Herman Melville, *Moby-Dick, or the Whale* (New York: Harper, 1851), and the classic account by Alexander Starbuck, *History of the American Whale Fishery.* See Foster Rhea Dulles, *The Old China Trade,* 81–93; Elmo Paul Hohman, *The American Whaleman,* 289–308; Edouard A. Stackpole, *The Sea-Hunters,* 152–154, 254–395; Edouard A. Stackpole, *Whales and Destiny: The Rivalry between America, France, and Britain for Control of the Southern Whale Fishery, 1785–1828* (Amherst: University of Massachusetts Press, 1972), 299–383.

16. William H. Goetzmann, *New Lands, New Men: America and the Second Great Age of Discovery* (New York: Viking Penguin, 1986), 246–249; David F. Long, "David Porter: Pacific Ocean Gadfly," in *Command Under Sail: Makers of the American Naval Tradition, 1775–*

1850, edited by James C. Bradford (Annapolis: United States Naval Institute, 1985), 173–198.

17. The historic landing by Davis was unknown to scholars until 1956, when his logbook was discovered. William H. Goetzmann, *New Lands, New Men*, 253–256; Donald D. Johnson, *The United States in the Pacific*, 159–162; Thomas G. Patterson, J. Garry Clifford, Kenneth J. Hagan, *American Foreign Policy: A History to 1914*, 2d ed. (Lexington, MA: D. C. Heath, 1983), Vol. 1, p. 115.

18. William H. Goetzmann, *New Lands, New Men*, 265–297, 486–489; William Stanton, *The Great United States Exploring Expedition of 1838–1842* (Berkeley and Los Angeles: University of California Press, 1975), passim. Consult Charles Wilkes, *Narrative of the United States Exploring Expedition during the Years 1838 . . . 1842* (Philadelphia: Lee and Blanshard, 1835, a reprint of the 5-volume restricted edition); David C. Haskell, *The United States Exploring Expedition, 1838–1842 and Its Publications, 1844–1874* (New York: Greenwood Press Reprint, 1968).

19. William H. Goetzmann, *New Lands, New Men*, 332, 343–356; Charles E. Neu, *The Troubled Encounter: The United States and Japan* (New York: John Wiley, 1975), 3–12.

20. Francis L. Hawks, comp., *Narrative of the Expedition of an American Squadron*; William E. Griffis, *Matthew Calbraith Perry: A Typical American Naval Officer* (Boston: Cupples and Hurd, 1887); Arthur Walworth, *Black Ships off Japan: The Story of Commodore Perry's Expedition* (New York: Alfred A. Knopf, 1946); Samuel Elliot Morison, *"Old Bruin": Commodore Matthew C. Perry, 1794–1858* (Boston: Little, Brown, 1967), 310–399; Mario Emilio Cosenza, ed., *The Complete Journal of Townsend Harris, First American Consul General and Minister to Japan* (Garden City, NY: Doubleday, Doran for the Japan Society, 1930).

21. William H. Goetzmann, *New Lands, New Men*, 349–356; Allan B. Cole, ed., *Yankee Surveyors in the Shogun's Seas* (Princeton, NJ: Princeton University Press, 1947); Allan B. Cole, "The Ringgold-Rogers-Brooke Expedition to Japan and the North Pacific, 1853–1859," *Pacific Historical Review* 26, no. 1 (Feb. 1947):152–162.

22. Ernest N. Paolino, *The Foundations of the American Empire: William H. Seward and U.S. Foreign Policy* (Ithaca, NY: Cornell University Press, 1973), 106–118; Thomas G. Paterson et al., *American Foreign Policy*, vol. 1, pp. 166–170.

2. THE ALASKA BARGAIN

1. Robert W. Service, "The Spell of the Yukon," *The Spell of the Yukon and Other Verses* (New York: Barse & Hopkins, 1907), 11–14.

2. The best and most up-to-date general history of Alaska is by Claus-M. Naske and Herman E. Slotnick, *Alaska: A History of the 49th State*, 2d ed. (Norman and London: University of Oklahoma Press, 1987). For the pre-American era, see Barry M. Gough, *Distant Dominion, Britain and the Northwest Coast of North America, 1579–1809* (Vancouver: University of British Columbia Press, 1980); P. A. Tikhmenev, *A History of the Russian-American Company*, translated and edited by Richard A. Pierce and Alton S. Donnelly (Seattle: University of Washington Press, 1978); Glynn Barrett, *Russia in Pacific Waters* (Vancouver: University of British Columbia Press, 1981). Richard A. Pierce, *Builders of Alaska: The Russian Governors, 1818–1867* (Kingston, Ontario: Limestone Press, 1986), 44–53.

3. For the purchase and its aftermath, see David Hunter Miller, *The Alaska Treaty* (Vestal, NY: Limestone Press, 1981); Howard I. Kushner, *Conflict on the Northwest Coast: American-Russian Rivalry in the Pacific Northwest, 1790–1867* (Westport, CT: Greenwood Press, 1975); Ronald J. Jensen, *The Alaska Purchase and Russian-American Relations* (Seattle: University of Washington Press, 1975); Glyndon G. Van Deusen, *William Henry Seward* (New York: Oxford University Press, 1967), 535–549; for its assembled documentation, especially the press clippings and Sumner's oration of April 9, 1867, see Archie W. Shiels, *The Purchase of Alaska* (College, AK: University of Alaska Press, 1967); but for charges that

the purchase of Alaska was compromised by the issue of corruption in the appropriation, while further territorial expansion was thwarted as the result, see Paul S. Holbo, *Tarnished Expansion: The Alaska Scandal, The Press, and Congress* (Knoxville: University of Tennessee Press, 1983), 89 and passim. A satire close to the mark suggesting that Reconstruction politics of the baser sort convinced President Johnson of Alaska's desirability is by Petroleum Vesuvius Nasby [David Ross Locke], "The Russian Purchase," in *Ekkoes From Kentucky* (Boston: Lee and Shepard, 1868), 123–131. See also Melody Webb, *The Last Frontier* (Albuquerque: University of New Mexico Press, 1985), 46.

4. "Alaska's Native People," *Alaska Geographic* 6, no. 3 (1979):15–18, 285–298, and passim; "A Photographic Geography of Alaska," *Alaska Geographic* 7, no. 2 (1980):130–136 and passim. "Alaska's Great Interior," *Alaska Geographic* 7, no. 1 (1980):6–32, 37–49, 53–57. For the peoples and places of Alaska, the Yukon basin, and the Arctic Ocean, see Melody Webb, *The Last Frontier*, 2–5; "Close-up: U.S.A. Alaska" (June 1975), "Peoples of the Arctic," (February 1983), and "The Making of America: Alaska" (January 1984), maps with legends, *National Geographic Magazine*.

5. Claus-M. Naske and Herman E. Slotnick, *Alaska*, 23–62, 325–327, "Alaska's Native People," *Alaska Geographic* 6, no. 3 (1979):285–288.

6. Claus-M. Naske and Herman E. Slotnick, *Alaska*, 63–74, 276–278; "Alaska's Native People," *Alaska Geographic* 6, no. 3 (1979):288–291; Juneau, Alaska, *Capital City Weekly*, August 10–16, 1988, p. 1.

7. Claus-M. Naske and Herman E. Slotnick, *Alaska*, 68–71; Robert N. DeArmond, *The Founding of Juneau* (Juneau: Gastineau Channel Association, 1967), 74; Hubert Howe Bancroft, *History of Alaska, 1730–1885*, in *Works*, vol. 28 (San Francisco: A. L. Bancroft, 1886), 636–637; Jeannette Paddock Nichols, *Alaska: A History of Its Administration, Exploitation, and Industrial Development during Its First Half Century under the Rule of the United States* (Cleveland: Arthur H. Clark Co., 1924; republished New York: Russell & Russell, 1963), 18–21, 201–202. For the seal hunting grounds of Alaska, consult *Senate Executive Documents*, no. 32, 41 Cong., 2 Sess.; for Treasury agents in Alaska, *Report of the Joint Select Committee on Retrenchment* (*Senate Reports*, no. 47, 41 Cong., 2 Sess.), 228–230; for contemporary conditions in Alaska, *Congressional Globe*, 41 Cong., 2 Sess., VII (Appendix), 558–559, 675.

8. Alfred Hulse Brooks, *Blazing Alaska's Trails*, edited by Burton L. Fryxell (College, AK: University of Alaska Press and Arctic Institute of North America, Washington, 1953); Ernest Gruening, *The State of Alaska* (New York: Random House, 1954); Ernest Gruening, *The Battle for Alaska Statehood* (College, AK: University of Alaska Press, 1967); Melody Webb, *The Last Frontier*, 77–97, 123–141; William R. Hunt, *North of 53 Degrees: The Wild Days of the Alaska-Yukon Mining Frontier, 1870–1914* (New York: Macmillan, 1974); James Wickersham, *Old Yukon: Tales—Trails—and—Trials* (Washington: Washington Law Book Co., 1938); "Alaska's Oil/Gas & Minerals Industry," *Alaska Geographic* 9, no. 4 (1982):26–52.

9. Cf. Hawaii *v.* Mankichi (1903), Dorr *v.* United States (1904); Rasmussen *v.* United States (1905): Dowdell *v.* United States (1911). See Claus-M. Naske, *A History of Alaska Statehood* (Lanham, MD: University Press of America, 1985); Evangeline Atwood, *Frontier Politics: Alaska's James Wickersham* (Portland, OR: Binsford & Mort, 1979); George S. Ulibarri, comp., *Documenting Alaskan History: Guide to Federal Archives Relating to Alaska* (College, AK: University of Alaska Press, 1982); "Alaska's Oil/Gas & Minerals Industry," *Alaska Geographic* 9, no. 4 (1982):146–151.

10. For normalcy, Depression, and the New Deal in Alaska, see Claus-M. Naske and Herman E. Slotnick, *Alaska*, 100–117.

11. Brian Garfield, *The Thousand Mile War: World War II in Alaska and the Aleutians* (Garden City, NY: Doubleday, 1969); Samuel Eliot Morison, *History of United States Naval Operations in World War II: Coral Sea, Midway, and Submarine Actions* (Boston: Little Brown, 1962), vol. 4, pp. 163–65; and *The Aleutians, Gilberts, and Marshalls*, vol. 7, p. 17. Claus-M. Naske and Herman E. Slotnick, *Alaska*, 118–130; War Department, United States Army Signal Corps, *Report from the Aleutians* (Chicago: International Historic Films, 1984).

12. Claus-M. Naske and Herman E. Slotnick, *Alaska*, 131–139.

13. Ibid., for statehood, 140–185; for native land claims, native regional corporations, land claims, and land conservation, 140–240; and the oil boom, 241–274. For the inside story, see Claus-M. Naske, *Edward Lewis "Bob" Bartlett of Alaska: A Life in Politics* (Fairbanks: University of Alaska Press, 1979).

14. Walter LaFeber, *The New Empire: An Interpretation of American Expansion, 1860–1898* (Ithaca: Cornell University Press for the American Historical Association, 1963), 31–32; Tyler Dennett, "Seward's Far Eastern Policy," *American Historical Review* 28 (October 1922):45–62; Ronald J. Jensen, *The Alaska Purchase and Russian-American Relations*, 141–142.

3. THE HAWAIIAN ISLANDS

1. Ancient prayer reproduced on Hawaii Volcanoes National Park poster, Hawaii Natural History Association, 1974. For a neat evocation of the fire goddess Pele, see Scott C. S. Stone, *Volcano!!* (Norfolk Island, Australia: Island Heritage, 1977), 5–8. The major preannexation history is Ralph S. Kuykendall, *The Hawaiian Kingdom*, 3 vols. (Honolulu: University of Hawaii Press, 1938–1967).

2. *Mark Twain's Letters from Hawaii*, edited by A. Grove Day, as quoted in his introduction (Honolulu: University Press of Hawaii, reprinted from Appleton-Century Pacific Classics Edition, 1975), vi.

3. Gordon A. MacDonald and Douglass H. Hubbard, *Volcanoes of the National Parks in Hawaii* (Honolulu: Hawaii Natural History Association, 7th ed., 1975).

4. Gavan Daws, *The Illustrated Atlas of Hawaii with a History of Hawaii*, edited by O. A. Bushnell and illustrated by Joseph Feher (Norfolk Island, Australia: Island Heritage, 1970), 7–19; Joseph G. Mullins, *Hawaiian Journey* (Honolulu: Mutual Publishing Co., 1978), 1–13.

5. Gavan Daws, *The Illustrated Atlas of Hawaii*, 19–21; Joseph G. Mullins, *Hawaiian Journey*, 15–20; Louise E. Levathes, "Kamehameha: Hawaii's Warrior King," *National Geographic* 164 (November 1983): 559–599; Gwenfread E. Allen, "Kaahumanu," in *Notable Women of Hawaii*, edited by Barbara Bennett Peterson (Honolulu: University of Hawaii Press, 1984), 174–180.

6. Joseph G. Mullins, *Hawaiian Journey*, 34–37; Gavan Daws, *The Illustrated Atlas of Hawaii*, 21–23; Edward Joesting, *Hawaii: An Uncommon History* (New York: W. W. Norton, 1972), 68–77.

7. Donald D. Johnson, *The United States in the Pacific*, 170–185; Ralph S. Kuykendall, *The Hawaiian Kingdom, 1778–1854*, vol. 1, pp. 54–81, 133–268; Sylvester K. Stevens, *American Expansion in Hawaii, 1842–1898* (Harrisburg, PA: Archives Publishing Co., 1945), 1–7; Jon J. Chinen, *The Great Mahele: Hawaii's Land Division of 1848* (Honolulu: University of Hawaii Press, 1958), 8–9, 15, and passim; Thomas G. Paterson et al., *American Foreign Policy*, vol. 1, pp. 114–115; Gavan Daws, *The Illustrated Atlas of Hawaii*, 23; Harold W. Bradley, *The American Frontier in Hawaii: The Pioneers, 1789–1843* (London: Oxford University Press, 1942); 1–52; Jean I. Brookes, *International Rivalry in the Pacific Islands* (New York: Russell and Russell, 1941, 1972), 69–92.

8. Lawrence H. Fuchs, *Hawaii Pono: A Social History* (New York: Harcourt, Brace, Jovanovich, 1961), 251; William Graves, *Hawaii* (Washington, D.C.: National Geographic Society, 1970), 114; Joseph Brennan, *Paniolo* (Honolulu: Topgallant, 1978), 1–67; Donald D. Johnson, *The United States in the Pacific*, 187–191; Ralph S. Kuykendall, *The Hawaiian Kingdom*, vol. 1, pp. 388–424; James D. Richardson, ed., *A Compilation of the Messages and Papers of the Presidents* (New York: Bureau of National Literature by order of Congress, 1897), vol. 6, pp. 2555, 2657.

9. Walter LaFeber, *The New Empire*, 24–31, 55–56; Glyndon G. Van Deusen, *William Henry Seward*, 526–534; William Henry Seward, *Works*, edited by George E. Baker (New York: Redfield, 1853), vol. 3, p. 618.

10. Gavan Daws, *The Illustrated Atlas of Hawaii*, 23–26; Joseph G. Mullins, *Hawaiian Journey*, 58–65; Edward Joesting, *Hawaii*, 170–173; Gavan Daws, *Shoal of Time: A History of the Hawaiian Islands* (Honolulu: University of Hawaii Press, 1968), 173–182; Donald D. Johnson, *The United States in the Pacific*, 192–196; *Mark Twain's Letters from Hawaii*, 257.

11. Gavan Daws, *The Illustrated Atlas of Hawaii*, 24–25; Walter LaFeber, *The New Empire*, 35, 54; Thomas G. Paterson et al., *American Foreign Policy*, vol. 1, p. 174; Lawrence H. Fuchs, *Hawaii Pono*, 21, 27–28; Joseph G. Mullins, *Hawaiian Journey*, 61.

12. Ralph S. Kuykendall, *The Hawaiian Kingdom*, vol. 2, pp. 247–257; Sylvester K. Stevens, *American Expansion in Hawaii*, 112; Donald D. Johnson, *The United States in the Pacific*, 195–197; Walter LaFeber, *The New Empire*, 54, 138–140; Thomas G. Paterson et al., *American Foreign Policy*, vol. 1, pp. 173–176; Charles Callan Tansill, *The Foreign Policy of Thomas F. Bayard, 1885–1897* (New York: Fordham University Press, 1940), 359–409, particularly p. 400; Paul M. Kennedy, *The Samoan Tangle: A Study in Anglo-German Relations* (New York: Barnes and Noble for Harper & Row, 1974), 1–239; Robert Louis Stevenson, *A Footnote to History: Eight Years of Trouble in Samoa* (New York: Charles Scribner's Sons, 1892, 1901), 219–241; John Bassett Moore, *American Diplomacy: Its Spirit and Achievements* (New York: Harper & Bros., 1905), 239; John Bassett Moore, *Four Phases of American Development: Federalism, Democracy, Imperialism, Expansion* (Baltimore: Johns Hopkins University Press, 1912), 187–188.

13. Alfred Thayer Mahan, "The United States Looking Outward," *Atlantic Monthly* 66 (December 1890): 816–824; Gavan Daws, *The Illustrated Atlas of Hawaii*, 26–28; Joseph G. Mullins, *Hawaiian Journey*, 26–30; Lawrence H. Fuchs, *Hawaii Pono*, 29–39; Walter LaFeber, *The New Empire*, 203–209, 408–411; Gavan Daws, *Shoal of Time*, 251–291; Thomas G. Paterson et al., *American Foreign Policy*, vol. 1, pp. 166, 174–175, 188, 195, 204–206; *United States Statutes at Large*, vol. 30, pp. 750–751.

14. Donald D. Johnson, *The United States in the Pacific*, 201–202; Alfred H. Kelly et al., *The American Constitution: Its Origins and Development*, 6th ed. (New York: W. W. Norton, 1983), 393–396. Cf. Hawaii *v.* Mankichi (1903), Dorr *v.* United States (1904), Rasmussen *v.* United States (1905), Dowdell *v.* United States (1911).

15. Gavan Daws, *The Illustrated Atlas of Hawaii*, 28–31; Joseph G. Mullins, *Hawaiian Journey*, 64–73; Lawrence H. Fuchs, *Hawaii Pono*, 22–24, 86–149; United States Bureau of Immigration, *Annual Report of the Commissioner-General*, 1924, pp. 24ff; Dorothy Ochiai Hazama and Jane Okamoto Komeiji, *Okage Sama De: The Japanese in Hawaii, 1885–1985* (Honolulu: Bess Press, 1986); for a vivid, picaresque rendering of the *niseis'* plantation experience, an experience shared by much of Hawaii's population, read Milton Murayama, *All I Asking for Is My Body* (Honolulu of Hawaii Press, 1988), and the afterword by Franklin S. Odo, 105–110; Robert N. Anderson et al., *Filipinos in Rural Hawaii* (Honolulu: University of Hawaii Press, 1984); Antonio J. A. Pido, *The Filipinos in America* (New York: Center for Migration Studies, 1986).

16. Joseph G. Mullins, *Hawaiian Journey*, 62; Lawrence H. Fuchs, *Hawaii Pono*, 43–46, 63, 243–259; DeSoto Brown, *Hawaii Recalls: Selling Romance to America, Nostalgic Images of the Hawaiian Islands: 1910–1950* (Honolulu: Editions Limited, 1982), 34–35; Gavan Daws, *Shoal of Time*, 312–313.

17. Gavan Daws, *Shoal of Time*, 314–317; Gavan Daws, *The Illustrated Atlas of Hawaii*, 30–31; Joseph G. Mullins, *Hawaiian Journey*, 74–111; DeSoto Brown, *Hawaii Recalls*, 84–105; Lawrence H. Fuchs, *Hawaii Pono*, 263–307.

18. Gavan Daws, *The Illustrated Atlas of Hawaii*, 31–34; Gavan Daws, *Shoal of Time*, 339–391; Joseph G. Mullins, *Hawaiian Journey*, 100–107, 112–113; Lawrence H. Fuchs, *Hawaii Pono*, 308–449; Roger Bell, *Last Among Equals: Hawaiian Statehood and American Politics* (Honolulu: University of Hawaii Press, 1984), 76–296; George Cooper and Gavan Daws, *Land and Power in Hawaii: The Democratic Years* (Honolulu: Benchmark Books, 1985).

4. DESTINY IN THE PHILIPPINES

1. Rudyard Kipling, "The White Man's Burden," *A Choice of Kipling's Verse* made by T. S. Eliot (London: Faber and Faber, 1941), 136–137.

2. The best account with a most helpful bibliography is by Stanley Karnow, *In Our Image: America's Empire in the Philippines* (New York: Random House, 1989), 26–77, 455–458. See Edward Gaylord Bourne, *Discovery, Conquest, and Early History of the Philippine Islands*, being a separate issue (1907) of the historical introduction to the 55-volume documentary compilation by Emily Helen Blair and James Alexander Robertson, eds., *The Philippine Islands, 1493–1898* (Cleveland: Arthur H. Clark, 1903), 19–87; James C. Thomson, Jr., Peter W. Stanley, and John Curtis Perry, *Sentimental Imperialists: The American Experience in East Asia* (New York: Harper & Row, 1981), 31–60, 64–65, 106–111.

3. Stanley Karnow, *In Our Image*, 90–138, 458–460; Frank Freidel, *The Splendid Little War* (Boston: Little, Brown, 1958), 13–32, 279–294, 304–307; Charles S. Olcott, *The Life of William McKinley* (Boston and New York: Houghton, Mifflin, 1916), vol. 2, pp. 110–111, citing *The Christian Advocate*, January 22, 1903; Thomas G. Paterson et al., *American Foreign Policy*, vol. 1, pp. 203–207; Bonifacio S. Salamanca, *The Filipino Reaction to American Rule, 1901–1913* (Quezon City, P.I.: New Day, 1984), p. 174 n5; for Beveridge's speech, see Thomas G. Paterson, *Major Problems in American Foreign Policy*, 3d ed. (Lexington, MA: D. C. Heath, 1989), vol. 1, pp. 389–391; Finley Peter Dunne, "Young Oratory," *Mr. Dooley's Philosophy* (New York and London: Harper and Brothers, 1906), 129–133; Robert L. Breisner, *Twelve against Empire: the Anti-Imperialists, 1898–1900* (New York: McGraw-Hill, 1968).

4. Thomas G. Paterson et al., *American Foreign Policy*, vol. 1, pp. 201–207; Donald D. Johnson, *The United States in the Pacific*, 239–240; *Affairs in the Philippines, Hearings . . . , Senate Document* no. 331, 57 Cong., 1 Sess. (Washington: Government Printing Office, 1902), part III, p. 2969; Pratt is quoted in Teodoro A. Agoncillo, *Malalos: the Crisis of the Republic* (Quezon City: University of the Philippines Press, 1960), p. 125, from his despatch no. 212, April 28, 1898, *Senate Document* no. 62, part 2, 55 Cong., 3 Sess., p. 341; McKinley is quoted in H. H. Kohlsaat, *From McKinley to Harding: Personal Recollections of Our Presidents* (New York: Charles Scribner's Sons, 1923), 68. For an outstanding insider's efforts to shape his country's destiny, see *The Letters of Apolinario Mabini* (Manila, P.I.: National Heroes Commission and Vertex Press, 1965).

5. Stanley Karnow, *In Our Image*, 139–195; Thomas G. Paterson et al., *American Foreign Policy*, vol. 1, pp. 207–209; David Howard Bain, *Sitting in Darkness: Americans in the Philippines* (Boston: Houghton Mifflin, 1984), 389–390; Bonifacio S. Salamanca, *The Filipino Reaction to American Rule*, 24; John Morgan Gates, "The Philippines and Vietnam: Another False Analogy," *Asian Studies* 10 (April 1972):67 and passim; John Morgan Gates, *Schoolbooks and Krags: The United States Army in the Philippines, 1898–1902* (Westport, CT: Greenwood, 1973); Stuart Creighton Miller, *"Benevolent Assimilation": The American Conquest of the Philippines, 1899–1903* (New Haven: Yale University Press, 1982). There is no significant biography of Arthur MacArthur, but see Caroline Morris Cheston Shipley, "Arthur MacArthur, Jr., and the Filipinos" (Bryn Mawr College Master of Arts thesis, 1986). For the atrocities on Samar and the inevitable comparisons with Vietnam later on, see Stuart C. Miller, "Our Mylai of 1900: Americans in the Philippine Insurrection," *Transaction* 7, no. 11 (September 1970):19–28; Daniel B. Schirmer, "Mylai Was Not the First Time," *New Republic* 164 (April 24, 1971):18–21; Luzviminda Francisco, "The First Vietnam: The U.S.–Philippine War of 1899," *Bulletin of Concerned Asian Scholars* 5, no. 4 (December 1973):2–16, reprint of a broadside published by the Association for Radical East Asian Studies (London 1973); Dino J. Caterini, "Repeating Ourselves: The Philippine Insurrection and the Vietnam War," *Foreign Service Journal* 54 (December 1977):11–17, 31–32.

6. For William James and Charles Francis Adams, Jr., see Robert L. Breisner, *Twelve against Empire*, 35–52, 107–137; Thomas G. Paterson, *Major Problems in American Foreign*

Policy, 3d ed., vol. 1, p. 385; Mark Twain, "To the Person Sitting in Darkness," *North American Review* 172 (February 1901):161–176 (reprinted New York: Anti-Imperialist League, n.d.). The outcry against annexing the Philippine Islands can be found in Daniel B. Schirmer, *Republic or Empire: American Resistance to the Philippine War* (Cambridge, MA: Schenkman, 1972); Richard E. Welch, Jr., *Response to Imperialism: The United States and the Philippine War, 1899–1902* (Chapel Hill: University of North Carolina Press, 1979). A popularized history is Leon Wolff, *Little Brown Brother: How the United States Purchased and Pacified the Philippine Islands at the Century's Turn* (Garden City, NY: Doubleday, 1961).

7. Edward Gaylord Bourne, *Discovery, Conquest, and Early History of the Philippines*, 87; Stanley Karnow, *In Our Image*.

8. Guidebooks usefully introduce the fundamental geography and demography, thus: *Insight Guides: Philippines* (Singapore: APA, 1986); *Nagel's Encyclopedia Guides: Philippines* (Geneva: Nagel, 1982); Perry E. Gianakos, ed., *George Ade's "Stories of Benevolent Assimilation"* (Quezon City, P.I.: New Day, 1985), 1. For the Bates Memorandum Agreement, which adhered to the terms of Spain's compact with the Moros, see Jacob Gould Schurman, *Philippine Affairs: A Retrospect and Outlook* (New York: Charles Scribners's Sons, 1902), 16–17; W. Cameron Forbes, *The Philippine Islands* (Boston: Houghton, Mifflin, 1928), vol. 2, Appendix 19 (1899), pp. 470–471, also Appendix 20 (1915), pp. 472–473, and Appendix 21 (1921), pp. 475–486, which document the extraordinary relationship between the United States government and the Sultan of Sulu.

9. For the Taft epoch: Bonifacio S. Salamanca, *The Filipino Reaction to American Rule*, 24, 40–41, and his notes, 166–235; Michael P. Onorato, *Leonard Wood and the Philippine Cabinet Crisis of 1923*, rev. ed. (Manila, P.I.: J. E. Palabay, 1988), 1; William Manchester, *American Caesar: Douglas MacArthur, 1880–1964* (Boston: Little, Brown, 1978, and New York: Dell, 1979), 48–49; Perry E. Gianakos, ed., *George Ade's "Stories of Benevolent Assimilation,"* 42; Stanley Karnow, *In Our Image*, 196, 204–205; Finley Peter Dunne, "The Philippine Peace," *Observations by Mr. Dooley* (New York: R. H. Russell, 1906), 119; Henry Pringle, *The Life and Times of William Howard Taft* (New York: Farrar and Rinehart, 1939), vol. 1, p. 221; Theodore Friend, *Between Two Empires: The Ordeal of the Philippines, 1929–1946* (New Haven: Yale University Press, 1965), 3; Alfred McCoy and Alfredo Roces, *Philippine Cartoons: Political Caricature of the American Era, 1900–1941* (Quezon City, P.I.: Vera-Reyes, 1985), 14, 118; Lewis E. Gleeck, Jr., *The Manila Americans, 1901–1964* (Manila, P.I.: Carmelo & Bauerman, 1977), 41–43, Lewis E. Gleeck, Jr., *The American Governors-General and High Commissioners in the Philippines: Proconsuls, Nation-Builders, and Politicians* (Quezon City, P.I.: New Day, 1986), 5–133, 360–372; Romeo V. Cruz, *America's Colonial Desk and the Philippines, 1898–1934* (Quezon City, P.I.: University of the Philippines Press, 1974); Roger J. Bresnahan, "Philippine Perceptions of Colonial Rule: The Independence Campaign in the United States," *Festschriften: Leopold Y. Yabes*, edited by Elmer A. Ordoñez (Quezon City, P.I.: College of Arts and Letters, University of the Philippines, 1987), memorial vol. 2, p. 147.

10. Theodore Friend, "Philippine-American Tensions in History," *The Marcos Era and Beyond*, edited by John Bresnan (Princeton, NJ: Princeton University Press, 1986), 5–7; Theodore Friend, *Between Two Empires*, 3; Lewis E. Gleeck, Jr., *The American Governors-General and High Commissioners*, 134–161; Alfred McCoy and Alfredo Roces, *Philippine Cartoons*, 18. See Francis Burton Harrison, *The Corner-Stone of Philippine Independence: A Narrative of Seven Years* (New York: Century, 1922).

11. Theodore Friend, *Between Two Empires*, 3–11, 30–33, 45–92; Theodore Friend, "Philippine-American Tensions in History," *The Marcos Era*, 8; Michael P. Onorato, *Leonard Wood*, 4–5, 48–78; Lewis E. Gleeck, Jr., *The American Governors-General and High Commissioners*, 162–291; Stanley Karnow, *In Our Image*, 250–254; Hermann Hagedorn, *Leonard Wood: a Biography* (New York: Harper & Brothers, 1931), vol. 2, pp. 373–481; Elting E. Morison, *Turmoil and Tradition: A Study of the Life and Times of Henry L. Stimson* (Boston: Houghton, Mifflin, 1960), 271, 280–298.

12. Theodore Friend, *Between Two Empires*, 95–195; Stanley Karnow, *In Our Image*, 252–255; Lewis E. Gleeck, Jr., *The American Governors-General and High Commissioners*, 292–372; University of Michigan *Alumnus*, September–October 1989, p. 17. See Joseph Ralston Hayden, *The Philippines: A Study in National Development* (New York: Macmillan, 1942).

13. Theodore Friend, *Between Two Empires*, 164–167; Stanley Karnow, *In Our Image*, 270–286.

14. John H. Bradley et al., *The Second World War: Asia and the Pacific*, West Point Military History Series, edited by Thomas E. Greiss (Wayne, NJ: Avery, 1984), 65–94, 174–206; Theodore Friend, *Between Two Empires*, 211–263; Stanley Karnow, *In Our Image*, 304–305, 312–313, 320–324; Michael Schaller, *Douglas MacArthur, the Far Eastern General* (New York: Oxford University Press, 1989), 31–66. For the history of the Philippines during Japan's occupation: Teodoro A. Agoncillo, *The Fateful Years: Japan's Adventure in the Philippines, 1941–1945*, 2 vols. (Quezon City, P.I.: Garcia, 1965); Luis C. Dery, "Japan's New Order in Philippines: a Blueprint for Asia under Japan," *Philippines Social Sciences Review* 48, nos. 1–4 (January–December 1984), 291–361. After forty-five years, the Republic of the Philippines honored thousands of American veterans with its Philippine Liberation Medal. *Philadelphia Inquirer*, September 10, 1990, pp. B1–2. Recent legislation (PL 101–649: November 29, 1990) waived residency requirements in awarding American citizenship to former Filipino soldiers or recognized guerrillas who fought the Japanese. See *New York Times*, November 25, 1990, p. 24.

5. THE OPEN DOOR FOR CHINA

1. John Hay, Circular Letter to Austria-Hungary, France, Germany, Great Britain, Italy, Japan, and Russia, *Foreign Relations of the United States*, 1900, p. 299.

2. Thomas G. Paterson et al., *American Foreign Policy*, vol. 1, pp. 125–126, 193, 209–213; John K. Fairbank et al., *East Asia*, 454–479, 641–643; Immanuel C. Y. Hsu, *The Rise of Modern China*, 207; Jonathan D. Spence, *The Search for Modern China*, 158–164, 179–184, 230–235, 283; George F. Kennan, *American Diplomacy*, expanded edition (Chicago: University of Chicago Press, 1984), 21–37.

3. John K. Fairbank et al., *East Asia*, 469–475, 480–483, 560–561, 586–587, 600; Immanuel C. Y. Hsu, *The Rise of Modern China*, 221–258, 261–312; Jonathan D. Spence, *The Search for Modern China*, 170–178, 216–224.

4. John K. Fairbank et al., *East Asia*, 570–575, 593–596, 619–633; Immanuel C. Y. Hsu, *The Rise of Modern China*, 343, 358–359; Warren I. Cohen, *America's Response to China*, 26–38; Jonathan D. Spence, *The Search for Modern China*, 212–215; *Foreign Relations of the United States*, 1868, vol. 1, p. 494; Thomas G. Paterson et al., *American Foreign Policy*, vol. 1, pp. 209–212; Wei Peh Ti, *East Asian History, 1870–1952* (Hong Kong: Oxford University Press, 1981), 48–49; Ronald Takaki, *Strangers from a Distant Shore: A History of Asian-Americans* (Boston: Little, Brown, 1989), 76–131; Woman's Foreign Missionary Societies, *The United Study of Missions No. 4 Missionary Lesson Leaf* 21, no. 10 (May 1904):3. For an early summary of anti-Chinese agitation in California, see John R. Commons et al., *History of Labour in the United States* (New York: Macmillan, 1918), vol. 2, pp. 252–268.

5. John K, Fairbank et al., *East Asia*, 633–640; Wei Peh T'i, *East Asian History*, 49–50; John K. Fairbank, *The Great Chinese Revolution, 1800–1985* (New York: Harper & Row, 1986), 137–138; Jonathan D. Spence, *The Search for Modern China*, 140–141, 231–238; Thomas G. Paterson et al., *American Foreign Policy*, vol. 1, p. 211; Warren I. Cohen, *America's Response to China*, 45–48; Robert H. Felsing, ed., *China Journal, 1889–1900: An American Missionary Family during the Boxer Rebellion, with the Letters and Diaries of Eva Jane Price and Her Family* (New York: Charles Scribner's Sons, 1989).

6. Michael Hunt in Thomas G. Paterson, *Major Problems in American Foreign Policy*, vol. 1, p. 438; O. Edmund Clubb, *20th Century China*, 3d ed. (New York: Columbia University Press, 1978), 38–39; Thomas G. Paterson et al., *American Foreign Policy*, vol. 1, pp. 239–243;

Roosevelt to Taft, December 22, 1910, *The Letters of Theodore Roosevelt*, selected and edited by Elting E. Morison (Cambridge, MA: Harvard University Press, 1954), vol. 7, pp. 189–192; Warren I. Cohen, *America's Response to China*, 66–69; Willard Straight to Henry P. Davison, February 21, 1911, quoted in Herbert Croly, *Willard Straight* (New York: Macmillan, 1924), 392–393.

7. John K. Fairbank, *The Great Chinese Revolution*, 145–163; Jonathan D. Spence, *The Search for Modern China*, 262–268, 275–281.

8. Warren I. Cohen, *America's Response to China*, 71–74; Jonathan D. Spence, *The Search for Modern China*, 282–283; E. David Cronon, ed., *Cabinet Diaries of Josepheus Daniels, 1913–1921* (Lincoln, NE: University of Nebraska Press, 1963), 8; Immanuel C. Y. Hsu, *The Rise of Modern China*, 480; John K. Fairbank et al., *East Asia*, 753; John K. Fairbank, *The Great Chinese Revolution*, 167–174; Thomas G. Paterson et al., *American Foreign Policy*, vol. 1, pp. 242–243.

9. Warren I. Cohen, *America's Response to China*, 74–81; John K. Fairbank et al., *East Asia*, 769; Thomas G. Paterson et al., *American Foreign Policy*, vol. 1, 244; Wei Peh T'i, *East Asian History*, 104; Jonathan D. Spence, *The Search for Modern China*, 288–294.

10. John K. Fairbank et al., *East Asia*, 757–762, 767–770; John K. Fairbank, *The Great Chinese Revolution*, 176–203; Warren I. Cohen, *America's Response to China*, 79–81, 84–87; Jonathan D. Spence, *The Search for Modern China*, 310–319.

11. Warren I. Cohen, *America's Response to China*, 84–105; Thomas G. Paterson et al., *American Foreign Policy*, vol. 2, pp. 341–343; John Paton Davies, *Dragon by the Tail* (New York: W. W. Norton, 1972), 95; Wei Peh T'i, *East Asian History*, 109–110; John K. Fairbank, *The Great Chinese Revolution*, 204–216.

12. John K. Fairbank et al., *East Asia*, 777–797; Thomas G. Paterson et al., *American Foreign Policy*, vol. 2, pp. 335, 342–343; Warren I. Cohen, *America's Response to China*, 102–104; John K. Fairbank, *The Great Chinese Revolution*, 217–225. For the approximately four thousand Americans in Shanghai's foreign community, see James L. Huskey, "The Cosmopolitan Comparison: Americans and Chinese in Shanghai during the Interwar Years," *Diplomatic History* 11 (Summer 1987):227–242, and the accompanying "Commentary" by Charles R. Lilley and Michael H. Hunt, 243–249; see also Dorothy Borg, *American Policy and the Chinese Revolution, 1925–1928*, rev. ed. (New York: Octagon Books, 1968), 20–29, 205–226; 338–366, and for Nanking, see 290–317, 366–385.

13. Thomas G. Paterson et al., *American Foreign Policy*, vol. 2, pp. 335–339.

14. Ibid., pp. 344–348; Wei Peh T'i, *East Asian History*, 148–149; Barbara W. Tuchman, *Stilwell and the American Experience in China, 1911–1945* (New York: Macmillan, 1970, 1971), 178–179; John K. Fairbank, *The Great Chinese Revolution*, 225–239. For full details of American policy, see Dorothy Borg, *The United States and the Far Eastern Crisis of 1933–1938: From the Manchurian Incident through the Initial Stages of the Undeclared Sino-Japanese War* (Cambridge, MA: Harvard University Press, 1964).

6. JAPAN'S RISING SUN

1. *Meiji boshin*, pp. 81–82, Ryusaku Tsunoda, William Theodore de Bary, and Donald Keene, comps., *Sources of Japanese Tradition* (New York: Columbia University Press, 1958, 1964), vol. 2, pp. 136–137.

2. Edwin O. Reischauer, *Japan: The Story of a Nation*, rev. ed. (New York: Alfred A. Knopf, 1974), 3–144; Scott F. Runkle, *An Introduction to Japanese History* (Tokyo: International Society for Educational Information Press, 1976), 23–25; Roger Butterfield, *The American Past: A History of the United States from Concord to Hiroshima, 1775–1945* (New York: Simon and Schuster, 1947), 138–139; Russell F. Weigley, ed., *Philadelphia: A 300-Year History* (New York: W.W. Norton, 1982), 381–382.

3. Edwin O. Reischauer, *Japan*, 135; Scott F. Runkle, *Japanese History*, 25–27; Kido and Shinagawa are quoted in Ryusaku Tsunoda et al., *Sources*, vol. 2, pp. 145–146.

4. Thomas G. Paterson et al., *American Foreign Policy* vol. 1, pp. 176–177; for a highly colored account of these "armed attacks" by the United States, see "Outline of Korean History," *Korea Today*, Pyongyang, DPRK (1979, no. 5), pp. 68–69.

5. Dorothy Gondos Beers in Russell F. Weigley, *Philadelphia*, 382, 466–470; Marshall B. Davidson, *Life in America* (Boston: Houghton, Mifflin, 1951), vol. 1, pp. 538–541; Laurence Lafore and Sarah Lee Lippincott, *Philadelphia: The Unexpected City* (Garden City, NY: Doubleday, 1965), 20–21; Charles E. Neu, *The Troubled Encounter: The United States and Japan* (New York: John Wiley & Sons, 1975), 29–30.

6. Lafcadio Hearn, *Glimpses of Unfamiliar Japan*, two volumes in one, reprinted from the first edition published by Houghton, Mifflin, 1894 (Rutland, VT and Tokyo: Charles E. Tuttle, 1976), 166–167; George Chaplin, "Lafcadio Hearn: Adopted Son of Yesterday's Japan," Honolulu, *The Sunday Star-Bulletin & Advertiser*, March 29, 1987, p. B3; Elizabeth Bisland (Wetmore), *The Life and Letters of Lafcadio Hearn*, 2 vols. (Boston, Houghton, Mifflin, 1906); Elizabeth Stevenson, *Lafcadio Hearn* (New York: Macmillan, 1961); Jonathan Cott, *Wandering Ghost: The Odyssey of Lafcadio Hearn* (New York: Alfred A. Knopf, 1991). The Lafcadio Hearn Memorial Museum is in Matsue, Japan.

7. Charles E. Neu, *The Troubled Encounter*, 25–27; Edwin O. Reischauer, *Japan*, 116–118, 138, 140–141, 143–144.

8. Charles E. Neu, *The Troubled Encounter*, 33–34; Edwin O. Reischauer, *Japan*, 145–151; Wei Peh T'i, *East Asian History*, 29–30; Scott F. Runkle, *Japanese History*, 26.

9. Charles E. Neu, *The Troubled Encounter*, 34–36; Donald D. Johnson, *The United States in the Pacific*, 200–201; Thomas G. Paterson et al., *American Foreign Policy*, vol. 1, pp. 197–213; Finley Peter Dunne, "The Japanese Scare," *Mr. Dooley Says* (New York: Charles S. Scribner's Sons, 1910), 200.

10. Walter F. LaFeber, *The American Age: United States Foreign Policy at Home and Abroad since 1750* (New York: W.W. Norton, 1989), 235–238; Thomas G. Paterson et al., *American Foreign Policy*, vol. 1, pp. 239–240; Foster Rhea Dulles, *America's Rise to World Power, 1898–1954* (New York: Harper & Brothers, 1958), 70–71; Raymond A. Esthus in Ernest R. May and James C. Thomson, Jr., eds., *American-East Asian Relations: A Survey* (Cambridge, MA: Harvard University Press, 1972), 148–153; Charles E. Neu, *The Troubled Encounter*, 44–47; George E. Mowry, *The Era of Theodore Roosevelt, 1900–1912* (New York: Harper & Brothers, 1958), 186.

11. Charles E. Neu, *The Troubled Encounter*, 48–51; George E. Mowry, *Theodore Roosevelt*, 186–191; Walter F. LaFeber, *The American Age*, 239–240; Ronald Takaki, *Strangers from a Distant Shore*, 197–203; Akira Iriye, *Across the Pacific: An Inner History of American-East Asian Relations* (New York: Harcourt, Brace & World, 1967), 102–129.

12. Charles E. Neu, *The Troubled Encounter*, 55–65; Theodore Roosevelt to Kermit Roosevelt, April 19, 1908, *Letters* edited. by Elting E. Morison, vol. 6, p. 1013; Stanley Karnow, *In Our Image*, 264; Richard C. Ryder, "Yanks Down Under: Great White Fleet in Australia," *American History* 16 (August 1981): 8–17.

13. Charles E. Neu, *The Troubled Encounter*, 66–67, 75–77; Walter F. LaFeber, *The American Age*, 242–243; Foster Rhea Dulles, *America's Rise to World Power*, 79–81; Scott F. Runkle, *Japanese History*, 29; Charles E. Neu in Ernest R. May and James C. Thomson, Jr., eds., *American-East Asian Relations*, 157–172; Akira Iriye, *Across the Pacific*, 123–127.

14. Charles E. Neu, *The Troubled Encounter*, 80–85; Walter F. LaFeber, *The American Age*, 259; *Foreign Relations of the United States*, 1917, pp. 264–265, and *The Lansing Papers*, 1914–1920, vol. 2, pp. 450–451; Thomas G. Paterson et al., *American Foreign Policy*, vol. 1, p. 244; Roger Dingman in Ernest R. May and James C. Thomson, Jr., *American-East Asian Relations*, 199; Arthur S. Link, *Wilson: The New Freedom* (Princeton, NJ: Princeton University Press, 1956), 289–304; Arthur S. Link, *Wilson: The Struggle for Neutrality, 1914–1915* (Princeton, NJ: Princeton University Press, 1960), 267–309; Akira Iriye, *Across the Pacific*, 127–129.

15. Charles E. Neu, *The Troubled Encounter*, 94–96; Walter F. LaFeber, *The American Age*, 292–293; Roger Dingman in Ernest R. May and James C. Thomson, Jr., *American-East*

Asian Relations, 199–200; for the North Russian and Siberian interventions, see George F. Kennan, *Russia and the West under Lenin and Stalin* (Boston: Little, Brown, 1960), 64–79, 91–119.

16. Charles E. Neu, *The Troubled Encounter*, 96–101; Roger Dingman in Ernest R. May and James C. Thomson, Jr., *American-East Asian Relations*, 202–208; Edwin O. Reischauer, *Japan*, 168–175.

17. Charles E. Neu, *The Troubled Encounter*, 102–131; Roger Dingman and Akira Iriye in Ernest R. May and James C. Thomson, Jr., *American-East Asian Relations*, 208–218, 221–242; Edwin O. Reischauer, *Japan*, 175–178. The treaties as proclaimed in effect are in United States *Statutes at Large*, vol. 43, pp. 1646ff and 1655ff; vol. 44, pp. 2113ff; 46, p. 2343. The restrictive immigration acts of 1917 and 1921 are in the United States Bureau of Immigration, *Annual Report of the Commissioner-General*, 1923, pp. 2ff; the act of 1924 is in the *Annual Report*, 1924, pp. 24ff.

18. *Foreign Relations of the United States: Japan*, 1931–1941, vol. 1, pp. 1–309; Henry L. Stimson, *The Far Eastern Crisis: Recollections and Observations* (New York: Harper & Brothers for the Council on Foreign Relations, 1936), 3–84ff; Elting E. Morison, *Henry L. Stimson*, 368–402; Dorothy Borg, *The United States and the Far Eastern Crisis*, 1–99; Charles E. Neu, *The Troubled Encounter*, 132–159; Edwin O. Reischauer, *Japan*, 175–193; Gordon W. Prange, et al., *Pearl Harbor: The Verdict of History* (New York: McGraw-Hill, 1986), 6–8; John H. Bradley et al., *Asia and the Pacific*, 1–44.

19. *Foreign Relations of the United States: Japan*, 1931–1941, vol. 1, pp. 311–930; Waldo H. Heinrichs, Jr., and Louis Morton in Ernest R. May and James C. Thomson, Jr., *American-East Asian Relations*, 251–252, 258–259, 283; Edwin O. Reischauer, *Japan*, 193–210; John H. Bradley et al., *Asia and the Pacific*, 4–7, 208–210.

20. *Foreign Relations of the United States: Japan*, 1931–1941, vol. 1, pp. 901–930; Louis Morton in Ernest R. May and James C. Thomson, Jr., *American-East Asian Relations*, 272–273; Geoffrey Barraclough, ed., *The Times Concise Atlas of World History*, rev. ed. (Maplewood, NJ: Hammond, 1982, 1986), 134; Thomas G. Paterson et al., *American Foreign Policy*, vol. 2, pp. 383–388; Warren I. Cohen, *America's Response to China*, 122; Herbert Feis, *The Road to Pearl Harbor: The Coming of the War between the United States and Japan* (Princeton, NJ: Princeton University Press, 1950), 244 and passim; Akira Iriye, *Power and Culture: the Japanese-American War, 1941–1945* (Cambridge, MA: Harvard University Press, 1981), 1–35.

7. THE WAR IN THE PACIFIC

N.B. Wars breed fulsome privileged or official accounts, as is evident from the following citations to Samuel Eliot Morison for his fifteen-volume *History of United States Naval Operations in World War II* (Boston: Little, Brown, 1947–1962), to series editor Thomas E. Greiss and author John H. Bradley for their West Point Military Academy textbooks, and to the authors of the individual volumes within the categorical series of the enormous *History of the United States Army in World War II* (Washington: Government Printing Office, 1947–).

1. Gordon W. Prange et al., *At Dawn We Slept: The Untold Story of Pearl Harbor* (New York: McGraw-Hill, 1981), 504.

2. John H. Bradley et al., *Asia and the Pacific*, 5–7, 12–17; Geoffrey Barraclough, ed., *The Times Concise Atlas of World History*, 122–123, 126–129, 132–135; Charles E. Neu, *The Troubled Encounter*, 160–196.

3. John H. Bradley et al., *Asia and the Pacific*, 45–61; Gordon W. Prange et al., *At Dawn We Slept*, 499–504; Samuel Eliot Morison, *The Rising Sun in the Pacific, 1931–April 1942*, vol. 3 (1948).

4. John H. Bradley et al., *Asia and the Pacific*, 46–54, 58–60; Gordon W. Prange et al., *At Dawn We Slept*, 493–508, 839–850; See John Toland, *Infamy: Pearl Harbor and Its Aftermath* (New York: Doubleday, 1982, and Berkley Edition, 1983), 331–340, 341–351, and passim,

for the sensational charges that President Roosevelt and his inner circle of advisors knew in advance about Japan's intentions, but concealed their knowledge to force the United States in self-defense into the war against the Axis powers, then conspired to cover up the deception by blaming scapegoats; and for rebuttals against the revisionists in general and Toland in particular, see Gordon W. Prange et al., *Pearl Harbor: The Verdict of History*, 34–44, 52–65, 262–263.

5. *The Public Papers and Addresses of Franklin D. Rossevelt*, compiled and edited by Samuel I. Rosenman (New York: Harper & Brothers, 1938–1950), vol. 10, pp. 514–516, 532–533.

6. Dorothy Swaine Thomas, Richard S. Nishimoto, et al., *Japanese American Evacuation and Resettlement* (Berkeley and Los Angeles: University of California Press, 1946–1954), vol. 1 (*The Spoilage*), p. 27 and passim; Ronald Takaki, *Strangers from a Different Shore*, 379–405. See also Audrie Girdner and Anne Loftis, *The Great Betrayal: The Evacuation of the Japanese-Americans during World War II* (New York: Macmillan, 1969); Bill Hosokawa, *Nisei: The Quiet Americans* (New York: William Morrow, 1969); Roger Daniels, *Concentration Camps USA: Japanese Americans and World War II* (New York: Holt, Rinehart, and Winston, 1971). On Kay Sugahara, in addition to the author's memory of his friendship, see his profile as grand marshal in the *1983 Nisei Week Japanese Festival Booklet* (Los Angeles: Office of the Nisei Week Japanese Festival, 1983), 56; *Los Angeles Herald Examiner*, August 14, 1983, pp. B5 and 8; Arthur Zich, "Japanese Americans Home at Last," *National Geographic*, 169, no. 4 (April 1986):528; and his obituary in the *New York Times*, September 27, 1988, p. B1. For the official apology to the Japanese-American internees, *Wall Street Journal*, August 10, 1988, p. 1, and the commencing of payments, *Philadelphia Inquirer*, October 1, 1990, p. 2A.

7. John H. Bradley et al., *Asia and the Pacific*, 58–61, 65–94; Thomas E. Greiss, series editor, *Atlas of the Second World War: Asia and the Pacific*, West Point Military History Series (Wayne, NJ: Avery, 1985), maps 11–12; Louis Morton, *The Fall of the Philippines* (1953) in U.S. Army: *War in the Pacific*; Charles F. Romanus and Riley Sunderland, *Stilwell's Mission to China* (1953) in U.S. Army: *China-Burma-India Theater*; Barbara W. Tuchman, *Stilwell*, 300. For a vividly fictionalized account by a United States naval officer, himself captured on Guam, Lyle W. Eads, *Survival amidst the Ashes* (Winona, MN: Apollo, 1985).

8. John H. Bradley et al., *Asia and the Pacific*, 95; Thomas G. Paterson et al., *American Foreign Policy*, vol. 2, pp. 390–395; Thomas G. Paterson, *Major Problems in American Foreign Policy*, vol. 2, pp. 231–234; Louis Morton, *Strategy and Command: The First Two Years* (1962) in U.S. Army: *War in the Pacific*; Maurice Matlof and Edwin M. Small, *Strategic Planning for Coalition Warfare, 1941–1942* (1953) in U.S. Army: *War Department*.

9. John H. Bradley et al., *Asia and the Pacific*, 91–117, 247; Thomas E. Greiss, ed., *Atlas . . . of Asia and the Pacific*, maps 13–16; Samuel Eliot Morison, *Coral Sea, Midway and Submarine Actions, May 1942–August 1942*, vol. 4 (1949); Robert C. Mikesh, *Japan's World War II Balloon Bomb Attacks on North America*, originally published in *Annals of Flight*, No. 9 (Washington: Smithsonian Institution, 1972; republished Fallbrook, CA: Aero, 1982) 38, 82.

10. John H. Bradley et al., *Asia and the Pacific*, 121–139; Thomas E. Greiss, ed., *Atlas . . . of Asia and the Pacific*, maps 17–21; Samuel Eliot Morison, *The Struggles for Guadalcanal, August 1942–February 1943*, vol. 5 (1949); John Miller, Jr., *Cartwheel: The Reduction of Rabaul* (1959); Samuel Milner, *Victory in Papua* (1957), and Robert Ross Smith, *The Approach to the Philippines* (1953), all in U.S. Army: *War in the Pacific*. For the road ahead, according to Akira Iriye: "The year 1942 revealed to both Japan and America that it was extremely difficult to break with the past and plan for an alternative future," *Power and Culture*, 94.

11. John H. Bradley et al., *Asia and the Pacific*, 139–140; Thomas E. Greiss, ed., *Atlas . . . of Asia and the Pacific*, map 21; Maurice Matlof, *Strategic Planning for Coalition Warfare, 1943–1944* (1959) in U.S. Army: *War Department*, 1–42, 77–105, 135–143, 185–210, 230–240, 307–333, 335–338, 433–465, 475–489, 524–540; Thomas G. Paterson et al., *American Foreign Policy*, vol. 2, pp. 405–409.

12. John H. Bradley et al., *Asia and the Pacific*, 139–173; Thomas E. Greiss, ed., *Atlas . . . of Asia and the Pacific*, maps 23–28; Akira Iriye, *Power and Culture*, 173–176; Samuel Eliot Morison, *Breaking the Bismarcks Barrier, 22 July 1942–April 1944*, vol. 6 (1950), *Aleutians, Gilberts, and Marshalls, June 1942–April 1944*, vol. 7 (1951), and *New Guinea and the Marianas, March 1944–August 1944*, vol. 8 (1953); Philip A. Crowl and Edmund G. Love, *Seizure of the Gilberts and Marshalls* (1955), and Philip A. Crowl, *Campaign in the Marianas* (1960), both in U.S. Army: *War in the Pacific*; Representative Ben Blaz (D.–Guam) *Kuentos Kongressu*, newsletter (July 1989), p. 1.

13. John H. Bradley et al., *Asia and the Pacific*, 220–225; Thomas E. Greiss, ed., *Atlas . . . of Asia and the Pacific*, maps 39–46; Akira Iriye, *Power and Culture*, 197–201; Charles F. Romanus and Riley Sutherland, *Stilwell's Command Problems* (1956) in U.S. Army: *China-Burma-India Theater*; Barbara Tuchman, *Stilwell*, 301–509.

14. John H. Bradley et al., *Asia and the Pacific*, 170, 175–206; Thomas E. Greiss, ed., *Atlas . . . of Asia and the Pacific*, maps 29–34; M. Hamlin Cannon, *Leyte: The Return to the Philippines* (1954) in U.S. Army: *War in the Pacific*; Samuel Eliot Morison, *Leyte, June 1944–January, 1945*, vol. 12 (1958), and *The Liberation of the Philippines: Luzon, Mindanao, the Visayas*, vol. 13 (1959); Michael Schaller, *Douglas MacArthur*, 86–105; Stanley Karnow, *In Our Image*, 311–322.

15. John H. Bradley et al., *Asia and the Pacific*, 235–236; Thomas E. Greiss, ed., *Atlas . . . of Asia and the Pacific*, maps 46–49.

16. John H. Bradley et al., *Asia and the Pacific*, 236–238, 247–252; Thomas E. Greiss, ed., *Atlas . . . of Asia and the Pacific*, maps 51–52; Roy E. Appleman et al., *Okinawa: The Last Battle* (1948) in U.S. Army: *War in the Pacific*; Samuel Eliot Morison, *Victory in the Pacific, 1945*, vol. 14 (1960).

17. John H. Bradley et al., *Asia and the Pacific*, 252–256; Thomas G. Paterson et al., *American Foreign Policy*, vol. 2, pp. 417–418, 433–435; Robert J. Donovan, *Conflict and Crisis: The Presidency of Harry S Truman 1945–1948* (New York: W. W. Norton, 1977), 80–89; Akira Iriye, *Power and Culture*, 181–183, 252–264.

18. John H. Bradley et al., *Asia and the Pacific*, 231, 257–259; Robert J. Donovan, *Harry S Truman*, 90–100; John Hersey, *Hiroshima* (New York: Alfred A. Knopf, 1946; Bantam, 1948); The Pacific War Research Society, comp., *Japan's Longest Day* (Tokyo and New York: Kodansha International, 1968, 1989). For the Yalta agreement of February 4–11, 1945, on Soviet entry into the war against Japan, see Thomas G. Paterson, *Major Problems in American Foreign Policy*, vol. 2, pp. 244–245; Akira Iriye, *Power and Culture*, 230–238.

19. John H. Bradley et al., *Asia and the Pacific*, 259–260; William Manchester, *American Caesar*, 525–535; Michael Schaller, *Douglas MacArthur*, 120; Michael Schaller, *The American Occupation of Japan* (New York: Oxford University Press, 1985), 3–19ff.

8. THE COLD WAR SPREADS

1. "Carry the Revolution through to the End," December 30, 1948, *Selected Works*, vol. 4, p. 301, included in the little red book, *Quotations from Chairman Mao Tse-tung* (Peking: Foreign Language Press, 1966), 11.

2. Thomas G. Paterson et al., *American Foreign Policy*, vol. 2, pp. 435–444, 457–458; Walter LaFeber, *America, Russia and the Cold War, 1945–1984*, 6th ed. (New York: McGraw Hill, 1991), 8–28; Senator J. William Fulbright's viewpoint is embodied in Daniel Yergin, "Fulbright's Last Frustration," *New York Times Magazine* (November 24, 1974), 87.

3. Betty Peh-Ti Wei, *Shanghai: Crucible of Modern China* (Oxford University Press, 1987), 255–256; Thomas G. Paterson et al., *American Foreign Policy*, vol. 2, pp. 457–461; Roy K. Flint, Peter W. Kozumplik, Thomas J. Waraksa, *The Arab-Israeli Wars, The Chinese Civil War and the Korean War*, in West Point Military Series, edited by Thomas E. Greiss (Wayne, NJ: Avery, 1987), 33, 54–56; Barbara Tuchman, *Stilwell*, 522–527; John K. Fairbank, *The*

Great Chinese Revolution, 259–262; obituary of Albert C. Wedemeyer, *New York Times,* December 20, 1989, p. D23.

4. John K. Emmerson is quoted in Michael Schaller, *The American Occupation of Japan,* vii, and see 18–19, 24–27; William Manchester, *American Caesar,* 543–551.

5. William Manchester, *American Caesar,* 545–555; Michael Schaller, *The American Occupation of Japan,* 22–23; Michael Schaller, *Douglas MacArthur,* 77–84, 136–137; Faubian Bowers, "Hirohito Offered His Life for His Associates," Cleveland, OH, *Plain Dealer,* October 1, 1988; *Japan Economic Journal,* January 14, 1989, pp. 1, 4; obituary of Naruhiko Higashikuni, who lived to be 102, in *New York Times,* January 23, 1990, p. D22; J. H. M. Salmon, as related to the author, February 16, 1990; John Gunther, *The Riddle of MacArthur: Japan, Korea, and the Far East* (New York: Harper & Brothers, 1950, 1951), 92. For a singular outcome, see Helen Hardacre, *Shintō and the State, 1868–1988* (Princeton, NJ: Princeton University Press, 1989), 133–137ff.

6. Michael Schaller, *The American Occupation of Japan,* 20–51; Michael Schaller, *Douglas MacArthur,* 120–140; William Manchester, *American Caesar,* 536–605. Bin Akao, Japanese rightist, died at 91; *New York Times,* February 7, 1990, p. B8.

7. Letter to the editor by Toshiko Mori, associate representative in the United States of the Bank of Japan, *New York Times,* February 7, 1990, p. A24; Donna Raphael, "Japan Inc.'s U.S. Roots," *Wayne State,* the alumni magazine of Wayne State University, vol. 3 (Fall 1989):20–21.

8. Thomas McCormick in Thomas G. Paterson, ed., *Major Problems,* vol. 2, pp. 32–34; Michael Schaller, *The American Occupation of Japan,* 77ff; Walter LaFeber, *America, Russia and the Cold War,* 29–73; Thomas G. Paterson et al., *American Foreign Policy,* vol. 2, pp. 435–457; William H. Chafe, *The Unfinished Journey: America since World War II,* 2d ed. (New York: Oxford University Press, 1991), 31–78.

9. Roy K. Flint et al., *The Arab-Israeli Wars, the Chinese Civil War and the Korean War,* 57–61; Thomas E. Greiss, ed., *Atlas of the Arab-Israeli Wars, the Chinese Civil War and the Korean War* (Wayne, NJ: Avery, 1986), maps 21–25; Thomas G. Paterson et al., *American Foreign Policy,* vol. 2, pp. 461–463.

10. Thomas G. Paterson, ed., *Major Problems,* vol. 2, pp. 301–305, 361–367; Thomas G. Paterson et al., *American Foreign Policy,* vol. 2, pp. 461–465, 478; Michael Schaller, *The American Occupation of Japan,* vii–viii, 91–93; Michael Schaller, *Douglas MacArthur,* 135–137; Robert J. Donovan, *Harry S Truman,* 257–298; John Lie, "War, Absolution, and Amnesia: The Decline of War Responsibility in Postwar Japan," *Peace & Change,* vol. 16 (July 1991), 302–315.

11. Michael Schaller, *Douglas MacArthur,* 152–157; Robert J. Donovan, *Harry S Truman,* 388; Elmer L. Hann reported in *New York Times,* March 16, 1990, p. 37; Thomas E. Greiss, ed., *Atlas of . . . the Chinese Civil War and the Korean War,* map 26.

12. Thomas G. Paterson et al., *American Foreign Policy,* vol. 2, p. 458; John Gunther, *The Riddle of MacArthur,* 229.

9. CONTAINMENT IN KOREA

1. General of the Army Douglas MacArthur, Report to Congress, His Address before the Joint Meeting, April 19, 1951, RCA Victor Records, E1-LVB-3077.

2. Roy K. Flint et al., *The Arab-Israeli Wars, the Chinese Civil War and the Korean War,* pp. 71–72; William E. Henthorn, *A History of Korea* (New York: MacMillan, Free Press, 1971); *Facts about Korea,* 13th rev. ed. (Seoul: Korean Overseas Information Service, 1977), 8–35.

3. Official announcement by the Home Affairs Bureau, June 29, 1950, and report by Kim Il Sung, September 7, 1968, in *Immortal Juche Idea* (Pyongyang: Foreign Languages Publishing House, 1979), 169–170; Neil Sheehan, *A Bright Shining Lie: John Paul Vann and America in Vietnam* (New York: Random House Vintage Books, 1988, 1989), 443; Li San Cho's disclosure to the weekly *Moscow News* of Kim's duplicity is recounted in the *New*

York Times, July 6, 1990, p. A6; for the military details, see Roy K. Flint, et al., *The Arab-Israeli Wars, the Chinese Civil War and the Korean War*, 69–72.

4. Thomas G. Paterson et al., *American Foreign Policy*, vol. 2, pp. 470–474; Roy K. Flint et al., *The Arab-Israeli Wars, the Chinese Civil War and the Korean War*, 75–77; Merle Miller, *Plain Speaking, an Oral Biography of Harry S Truman* (New York: Berkley, 1973, 1974), 284–307; *Public Papers of the Presidents, Harry S Truman, 1952–1953* (Washington: Government Printing Office, 1966), 1200.

5. For useful overall accounts, see David Rees, *Korea: The Limited War* (New York: St. Martin's Press, 1964); Burton I. Kaufman, *The Korean War: Challenges in Crisis, Credibility, and Command* (New York: Alfred A. Knopf, 1986); Callum A. MacDonald, *Korea: The War Before Vietnam* (New York: Macmillan, Free Press, 1987); Clay Blair, *The Forgotten War: America in Korea, 1950–1953* (New York: Doubleday Anchor, 1989); Richard Whelan, *Drawing the Line: The Korean War, 1950–1953* (Boston: Little, Brown, 1990). The standard reference biography is D. Clayton James, *The Years of MacArthur*, 3 vols. (Boston: Houghton, Mifflin, 1970–1985).

6. Roy K. Flint et al., *The Arab-Israeli Wars, the Chinese Civil War and the Korean War*, 77–82; Thomas E. Greiss, ed., *Atlas . . . of the Chinese Civil War and the Korean War*, maps 26–29.

7. Roy K. Flint et al., *The Arab-Israeli Wars, the Chinese Civil War and the Korean War*, 82–86; Michael Schaller, *Douglas MacArthur*, 198–201.

8. Roy K. Flint et al., *The Arab-Israeli Wars, the Chinese Civil War and the Korean War*, 86–95; Thomas E. Greiss, ed., *Atlas . . . of the Chinese Civil War and the Korean War*, maps 30–31; MacArthur is quoted from Martin Lichterman, "To the Yalu and Back," in Harold Stein, ed., *American Civil-Military Decisions: A Book of Case Studies* (Birmingham: University of Alabama Press, 1963), 598. Merle Miller, *Plain Speaking*, 317–320, and Thomas G. Paterson, ed., *Major Problems*, vol. 2, p. 406; Michael Schaller, *Douglas MacArthur*, 200–206; James I. Matray, "Truman's Plan for Victory: National Self-Determination and the Thirty-Eighth Parallel Decision in Korea," *Journal of American History* 66 (September 1979): 314–333.

9. Thomas G. Paterson, ed., *Major Problems*, vol. 2, pp. 398, 406–407; Roy K. Flint et al., *The Arab-Israeli Wars, the Chinese Civil War and the Korean War*, 86–92, 95–109; Thomas E. Greiss, ed., *Atlas . . . of the Chinese Civil War and the Korean War*, maps 32–33.

10. Roy K. Flint et al., *The Arab-Israeli Wars, the Chinese Civil War and the Korean War*, 100–103; Thomas G. Paterson et al., *American Foreign Policy*, vol. 2, p. 476; Michael Schaller, *Douglas MacArthur*, 235–237.

11. Roy K. Flint et al., *The Arab-Israeli Wars, the Chinese Civil War and the Korean War*, 103–106; Thomas E. Greiss, ed., *Atlas . . . of the Chinese Civil War and the Korean War*, map 34; Matthew B. Ridgway, *The Korean War: How We Met the Challenge . . .* (Garden City, NY: Doubleday, 1967).

12. Roy K. Flint et al., *The Arab-Israeli Wars, the Chinese Civil War and the Korean War*, 106–109; Harry S Truman, *Off the Record, the Private Papers . . .* , edited by Robert H. Ferrell (New York: Harper & Row, 1980), diary entries for April 6, 9, and 10, 1951, pp. 210–211; Michael Schaller, *Douglas MacArthur*, 237–239; Merle Miller, *Plain Speaking*, 308–331; Thomas G. Paterson et al., *American Foreign Policy*, vol. 2, p. 477.

13. Michael Schaller, *Douglas MacArthur*, 239–242; Roy K. Flint et al., *The Arab-Israeli Wars, the Chinese Civil War and the Korean War*, 109–111; Thomas E. Greiss, ed., *Atlas . . . of the Chinese Civil War and the Korean War*, maps 35–37.

14. General of the Army Douglas MacArthur, Report to Congress, April 19, 1951; Michael Schaller, *Douglas MacArthur*, 243–250.

15. Michael Schaller, *Douglas MacArthur*, 246–250; Walter LaFeber, *The American Age*, 500–504; Eric F. Goldman, *The Crucial Decade—and After: America, 1945–1960* (New York: Random House Vintage, 1960), 202–203, 212–213; John W. Spanier, *The Truman-MacArthur Controversy and the Korean War* (New York: W. W. Norton, 1959, 1965), 157–164, 212–213, 268–273; Burton I. Kaufman, *The Korean War*, 202–203, 262–263. For Joe McCar-

thy's speech, see *Congressional Record—Senate*, 82 Cong., 1 Sess., vol. 97, part 5, pp. 6569–6603.

16. Roy K. Flint et al., *The Arab-Israeli Wars, the Chinese Civil War and the Korean War*, 111–120; Thomas G. Paterson et al., *American Foreign Policy*, vol. 2, pp. 477–481; review by Herbert Mitgang of Ahn Junghyo, *Silver Stallion: A Novel of Korea* (New York: Soho Press, 1989), *New York Times*, February 21, 1990, p. C17; Lee Suk Bok, *The Impact of U.S. Forces in Korea* (Washington: National Defense University Press, 1987), 77–86.

17. Michael Schaller, *Douglas MacArthur*, 251–252; *New York Times*, February 16, 1990, p. A7; Thomas E. Greiss, ed., *Atlas . . . of the Chinese Civil War and the Korean War*, map 38.

18. Roy K. Flint et al., *The Arab-Israeli Wars, the Chinese Civil War and the Korean War*, 120; John K. Fairbank et al., *East Asia*, 921–924.

10. THE VIETNAM WAR

1. Ho Chi Minh is quoted in Stanley Karnow, *Vietnam, a History: The First Complete Account of Vietnam at War* (New York: Viking Penguin, 1983, 1984), 16, 714–715.

2. Stanley Karnow, *Vietnam*, 98–160; George C. Herring, *America's Longest War: The United States and Vietnam*, 2d ed. (New York: Alfred A. Knopf, 1979, 1986), 3–9; Marvin E. Gettleman, Jane Franklin, Marilyn Young, H. Bruce Franklin, *Vietnam and America: A Documented History* (New York: Grove Press, 1985), 3–46; Steven Cohen, ed., *Vietnam Anthology and Guide to a Television History* (New York: Alfred A. Knopf, 1983), 9–26; for Ho's expectation of American support, see United States Senate Committee on Foreign Relations, Staff Study no. 2, *The United States and Vietnam, 1944–1947* (Washington: Government Printing Office, 1972), 3; Denis Warner, *The Last Confucian: Vietnam, Southeast Asia and the West* (New York: MacMillan, 1963, and Baltimore: Penguin Books, 1964), 36–53.

3. Thomas G. Paterson et al., *American Foreign Policy*, vol. 2, pp. 525–527; George C. Herring, *America's Longest War*, 9–42; Stanley Karnow, *Vietnam*, 148–205; Denis Warner, *The Last Confucian*, 54–83; Marvin E. Gettleman et al., *Vietnam and America*, 47–81.

4. Thomas G. Patterson et al., *American Foreign Policy*, vol. 2, pp. 528–529; Robert J. McMahon, "Eisenhower and Third World Nationalism: A Critique of the Revisionists," *Political Science Quarterly* 101, no. 3 (1986):457–461; Dulles is quoted in George C. Herring, *America's Longest War*, 42. While the French are grappling with the Viet Minh, a young and high-minded American, fictionalized from real life, begins to feed CIA assistance to a shadowy third force in Graham Greene, *The Quiet American* (London: William Heinemann, 1955, and New York: Viking, 1956).

5. Mao is quoted in Thomas G. Paterson et al., *American Foreign Policy*, vol. 2, pp. 499–501; Walter LaFeber, *The American Age*, 525.

6. Thomas G. Patterson et al., *American Foreign Policy*, vol. 2, pp. 546–548; Arthur M. Schlesinger, Jr., *A Thousand Days: John F. Kennedy in the White House* (Boston: Houghton, Mifflin, 1965), 329–334; Bernard B. Fall, *Anatomy of a Crisis: The Laotian Crisis of 1960–1961* (Garden City: Doubleday, 1969), 229; Walt W. Rostow, *The Diffusion of Power* (New York: Macmillan, 1972), 265; Roger Hilsman, *To Move a Nation: The Politics of Foreign Policy in the Administration of John F. Kennedy* (Garden City, NY: Doubleday, 1967), 142–155. For the tardily released official background, *Foreign Relations of the United States*, vol. 21, *East Asian Security; Cambodia; Laos* (Washington: Government Printing Office, 1990).

7. Thomas G. Paterson et al., *American Foreign Policy*, vol. 2, pp. 528–529, 546–552; James C. Thomson, Jr., "How Could Vietnam Happen? An Autopsy," *Atlantic Monthly* 221 (April 1968):47–53; George C. Herring, *America's Longest War*, 73–107.

8. George C. Herring, *America's Longest War*, 85–107; *New York Times*, November 2, 23, and 25, 1963, p. 1ff in each instance; Arthur M. Schlesinger, Jr., *A Thousand Days*, 995–1031; Neil Sheehan et al., *The Pentagon Papers* as first published by the *New York Times* (New York: Bantam, 1971), 232–233.

9. Paul K. Conkin, *Big Daddy from the Pedernales: Lyndon Baines Johnson* (Boston: Twayne, 1986), 171–177, 243, 364; James C. Thomson, Jr., "How Could Vietnam Happen?" 47–48; David Halberstam, *The Best and the Brightest* (New York: Random House, 1972, Fawcett, 1973). On the "credibility gap," see *New York Times*, October 1, 1988, p. 27; Stanley Karnow, *Vietnam*, 296–297; Neil Sheehan, *A Bright Shining Lie*, 345–351. For the 1965 debate between Secretary of Defense McNamara and Undersecretary of State George Ball over escalation, see Robert J. McMahon, ed., *Major Problems in the History of the Vietnam War* (Boston: D.C. Heath, 1990), 231–236.

10. Stanley Karnow, *Vietnam*, 338; Neil Sheehan et al., *The Pentagon Papers*, 234–242; Marvin E. Gettleman et al., *Vietnam and America*, 238–239, 250. For the home front, see Alexander Kendrick, *The Wound Within: America in the Vietnam Years, 1945–1974* (Boston: Little, Brown, 1974), 181.

11. Paul K. Conkin, *Lyndon Baines Johnson*, 189–190, 208–209; Marvin E. Gettleman et al., *Vietnam and America*, 239–266; Alexander Kendrick, *The Wound Within*, 182–186.

12. Robert J. McMahon, ed., *Vietnam War*, 224–239, 262–268; Alexander Kendrick, *The Wound Within*, 204–208; Neil Sheehan, *A Bright Shining Lie*, 579–580; George C. Herring, *America's Longest War*, 129–130, 146–147, 150–185. United States Senate, Committee on Foreign Relations, *The Vietnam Hearings*, with an introduction by J. William Fulbright (New York: Random House, 1966). On Senator Fulbright's disenchantment, Lee Riley Powell, *J. William Fulbright and America's Lost Crusade: Fulbright's Opposition to the Vietnam War* (Little Rock, AR: Rose, 1984); William C. Berman, *William Fulbright and the Vietnam War* (Kent State University Press: Kent, OH, 1988); J. William Fulbright with Seth P. Tillman, *The Price of Empire* (New York: Pantheon, 1989), 101–128.

13. Thomas G. Paterson et al., *American Foreign Policy*, vol. 2, pp. 560–562; Marvin E. Gettleman et al., *Vietnam and America*, 289–331; Alexander Kendrick, *The Wound Within*, 250; William H. Chafe, *The Unfinished Journey: America since World War II*, 344–345; Eric F. Goldman, *The Tragedy of Lyndon Johnson* (New York: Alfred A. Knopf, 1969), 511. For the antiwar movement in context, see Irwin Unger, *The Movement: A History of the American New Left, 1959–1972* (New York: Dodd Mead, 1974), 85–86, 92–93, 141–142, 191–196, 206–207. For the administration's ignoring of Hanoi's overture in December 1968, see Neil Sheehan, *A Bright Shining Lie*, 721.

14. George C. Herring, *America's Longest War*, 186–220; Stanley Karnow, *Vietnam*, 515–566; Neil Sheehan, *A Bright Shining Lie*, 711–722.

15. Stephen Ambrose, *Nixon*, vol. 2, *The Triumph of a Politician, 1962–1972* (New York: Simon and Schuster, 1989), 223–401; George C. Herring, *America's Longest War*, 221–225, 231–234; Stanley Karnow, *Vietnam*, 567–612; Richard Nixon, *RN: The Memoirs of Richard Nixon* (New York: Grossett & Dunlap, 1978), 403.

16. William Shawcross, *Sideshow: Kissinger, Nixon and the Destruction of Cambodia* (New York: Simon and Schuster, 1979); George C. Herring, *America's Longest War*, 238–256; Stephen Ambrose, *Nixon*, vol. 2, pp. 339–362, 446–466. For a chronology of the Cambodian ordeal, *New York Times*, July 19, 1990, p. A10; and an approving editiorial on Washington's long delayed about-face away from the Khmer Rouge, *Philadelphia Inquirer*, July 21, 1990, p. 6A.

17. George C. Herring, *America's Longest War*, 253–257. Kissinger and Tho were jointly awarded the Nobel Peace Prize for their work, but Tho, the first Asian selected for the honor, declined it, declaring that "peace has not yet been established," *New York Times*, October 14, 1990, p. 32.

For selected perspectives by participants and observers see Morley Safer, *Flashbacks: On Returning to Vietnam* (New York: Random House, 1990); William Colby with James McCarger, *Lost Victory: A Firsthand Account of America's Sixteen-Year Involvement in Vietnam* (Chicago: Contemporary Books, 1989); Dean Rusk as told to Richard Rusk, *As I Saw It*, edited by Daniel S. Papp (New York: W. W. Norton, 1990), 475–505; Larry Engelmann, *Tears before the Rain: An Oral History of the Fall of Vietnam* (New York: Oxford University Press, 1990). For a reflective point of view, Allan Goodman, "Scholars Must Give More

Serious Thought to How They Teach and Write about the War in Vietnam," *Chronicle of Higher Education*, July 25, 1990, p. A36. For an Anglo-French critique, Phil Melling, "Old History, New History, No History at All? The Vietnam War as Affirmation of American Values," *American Studies International* 28 (October 1990):93–105. For the Watergate scandal and the outcome, see Bob Woodward and Carl Bernstein, *All the President's Men* and *The Final Days* (New York: Simon and Schuster, 1974 and 1976); Theodore H. White, *Breach of Faith, the Fall of Richard Nixon* (New York: Atheneum, 1975).

11. THE NEW PACIFIC

N.B. Identically entitled, a different intention for this chapter's heading was advertised long ago on a book's jacket: "The world's problem of the near and distant future is the occupation and development by a superior civilization of the shores and islands of the Pacific Ocean." Hubert Howe Bancroft, *The New Pacific*, 3d rev. ed. (New York: Bancroft, 1915). For an insider's conclusion that Vietnam proved to be an "unwinnable" war, see Clark Clifford, *Counsel to the President: A Memoir*, with Richard Holbrook (New York: Random House, 1991). See also Richard Reeves, "Vietnam and Cambodia: Travels in the Forbidden Zone," *Travel & Leisure* 21 (June 1991):120–125, 174, 176–180.

1. *I Ching*, ed. by Raymond VanOver based on the translation by James Legge (New York: Mentor, 1971), 23.

2. "Frictions are Aired at U.S.–Japan Symposium," East-West Center *Centerviews*, September–October 1989, pp. 1, 4–5; and "U.S.–Japan Relations in a New Era," September–October, 1990, pp. 1, 4–5. *New York Times*, June 4, 1990, p. A2; June 8, 1990, p. A4; and April 4, 1991, p. A20, where Madigan is quoted; *Philadelphia Inquirer*, June 25, 1990, p. 8A; "Old and New Issues in the Pacific," Eighth Annual Symposium, University of Arkansas, Fulbright Institute *Forum*, no. 5 (1990–1991), pp. 4–6; for Japan's effort to enhance its image, *Honolulu Star-Bulletin & Advertiser*, January 6, 1991, p. A24. Books that have stirred great controversy are Karel van Wolferen, *The Enigma of Japanese Power* (New York: Alfred A. Knopf, 1989); Clyde V. Prestowitz, Jr., *Trading Places* (New York: Basic Books, 1990); and the original version, Morita Akio and Ishihara Shintaro, *"No" To Ieru Nihon* (Tokyo: Meibunsha, 1989). For the typical newsworthy alarms, see *New York Times*, May 28, pp. C1 and C8, and May 31, 1991, pp. C1 and C30; *The New York Review of Books*, May 30, 1991, pp. 31–37; *Philadelphia Inquirer*, June 7, 1991, p. 17-A.

3. Jonathan D. Spence, *The Search for Modern China*, 551–557, 628–633, 654, 670–671, 717, 732–733, 738–747. "The Open Door to China Revisited," *New York Times*, June 5, 1990, pp. A1, 8–9; June 26, 1990, pp. A1, 8–9. A plea for new intellectual leadership and ideas in America's confrontation with China rang out in John K. Fairbank's presidential address to the American Historical Association, December, 29, 1968, "Assignment for the '70s," *American Historical Review* 74 (February 1969):873–879.

4. *New York Times*, November 13, 1983, p.1; August 12, 1989, p. 4; February 16, 1990, p. A7; May 24, 1990, p. A15; *Philadelphia Inquirer*, June 25, 1991, p. 12-D. For the momentous changes of 1990 in the U.S.–Soviet relationship, Walter LaFeber, *America, Russia, and the Cold War*, pp. 284–335. See *New York Times*, October 6, 1991, p. 4.

5. Stanley Karnow, *In Our Image*, 324–325; *New York Times*, August 28, 1983, p. 4-1; September 29, 1989, p. B6; October 21, 1989, pp. 1 and 5; June 8, 1990, pp. B1 and 5; *Philadelphia Inquirer*, November 2, 1988, p. G1; April 14, 1990, p. 5A; May 14, 1990, pp. 1 and 4A; May 23, 1990, pp. 1 and 4A; Department of State, Press Release no. 237, November 30, 1989. For Mount Pinatubo's disruptiveness, *New York Times*, June 21, 1991, p. A3, and *Philadelphia Inquirer*, June 24, 1991, p. 3-A. See *New York Times*, October 4, 1991. p. A9.

6. For Micronesia, *Philadelphia Inquirer*, August 4, 1985, p. 2A; February 5, 1990, pp. 1 and 5A; February 6, 1990, p. 15A; February 16, 1990, p. 14A; for an unprecedented summit meeting on October 27, 1990, between President George Bush and leaders from eleven Pacific island nations, which included as a major topic of discussion the destruction of

chemical weapons on Johnston Atoll, East-West Center *Centerviews*, November–December 1990, pp. 1, 5. For the obituary of Minoru Genda, *New York Times*, August 17, 1989, p. B14; and Japan's impact, October 27, 1989, p. A14. For the Alaska–USSR frontier, Peter Iseman, "Lifting the Ice Curtain," *New York Times Magazine*, October, 23, 1988, pp. 48–51, 59–62; "Sausage Links Alaska/Soviet Joint Venture," *On the Rim* supplement to *Alaska Geographic* 17 (1990):95; and Hal Bernton, "Melting the Ice Curtain," *Alaska* (July, August, and September 1991). For immigration, James T. Fawcett and Benjamin F. Cariño, eds., *Pacific Bridges: The New Immigration from Asia and the Pacific Islands* (Staten Island, NY: Center for Migration Studies, 1987); *New York Times*, June 12, 1991, pp. A1 and D25. For the observation by Jay Itagaki, *Philadelphia Inquirer*, September 29, 1989, pp. 1C and 6C; and Japan's investments in Hawaii, *Far Eastern Economic Review*, August 3, 1989, pp. 48–49.

7. Benjamin Franklin was quoted by James Madison, *The Debates in the Federal Convention of 1787 . . .* , edited by Gaillard Hunt and James Brown Scott (New York: Oxford University Press, 1920), 583.

Index

Abeel, David, 8
Abrams, Creighton, 255, 257
Accelerated Pacification Campaign [Vietnam War], 256
Acheson, Dean, 206, 209–10, 211, 213, 216, 222, 227, 228, 229, 237, 254
Adams, Charles Francis, Jr., 90
Adams, John, 4
Adams, John Quincy, 12, 16
Ade, George, 94, 96–97
Admiralty Islands, 181
Aguinaldo, Emilio, 82, 83, 85, 86–87, 88, 91, 94, 95, 184
Ahn Junghyo, 230
Alaska: agriculture in, 38; and the Ballinger-Pinchot affair, 39, 41; boundaries of, 30–31, 37; and Canada, 24, 37; Chinese in, 36; and the Cold War, 43; economy of, 37–43, 45–46, 47–48; education in, 31, 34, 40; environmental issues in, 271; explorations in, 29, 32, 33, 37; fishing in, 13, 41–42, 43, 46, 48; and the fur trade, 12, 28, 29–30, 31, 35, 48; geography of, 24–27, 47; gold in, 33, 35–37, 39, 42; government in, 32–34, 37, 39, 40, 46; and Great Britain, 29, 30–31, 35, 37; homesteading in, 37, 43; and Japan, 35, 44; land in, 34, 43, 46, 47; legal system in, 34–35, 37, 39, 40, 69, 100; and manifest destiny, 24; minerals/natural resources in, 31–32, 37, 38–39, 40–41, 42, 43, 46, 47, 48; missionaries in, 29, 31, 34–35, 37; natives in, 27–28, 42, 43, 46, 47; Organic Acts for, 33, 34, 37, 40; population of, 35, 45; racism in, 40; and Russia/Soviet Union, 12, 22–24, 27–33, 35, 45, 46, 47; and Siberia, 27, 271; and Spain, 29; and statehood, 39, 43, 46–47, 48, 76–77, 263; strategic importance of, 43–45, 47–48; timber industry in, 35–36, 41, 48; transportation in, 38, 40, 41, 42; U.S. military in, 32, 33–34, 37, 44–45, 46, 47–48; U.S purchase of, 20, 22–24, 47; and World War II, 43–45, 46
Alaska-Canada Military Highway [ALCAN], 45
Alaska Commercial Company, 35
Alaska Native Claims Settlement Act [1971], 47
Alaska Peninsula Reserve, 41
Alaska Steamship Company, 38
Alaska Syndicate, 38, 39
Aleutian Islands, 13, 20, 26–27, 29, 31, 35, 44–45, 167, 178, 179, 227
Alexander & Baldwin, 71, 72

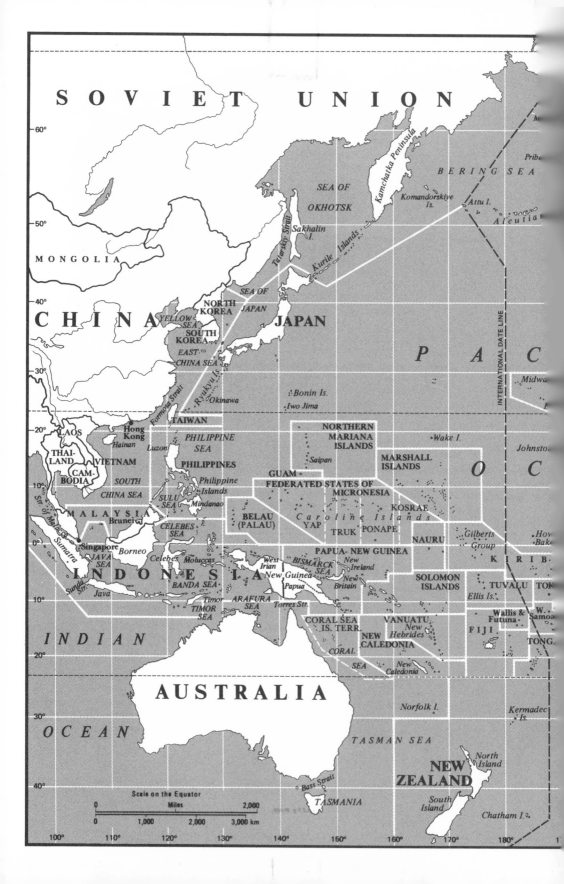